FIRST COURT-HOUSE, 1821.

HISTORY

OF

PIKE COUNTY

ILLINOIS;

TOGETHER WITH SKETCHES OF ITS CITIES, VILLAGES AND TOWNSHIPS, EDU-
CATIONAL, RELIGIOUS, CIVIL, MILITARY, AND POLITICAL HISTORY;
PORTRAITS OF PROMINENT PERSONS AND BIOGRAPHIES
OF REPRESENTATIVE CITIZENS.

HISTORY OF ILLINOIS,

EMBRACING ACCOUNTS OF THE PRE-HISTORIC RACES, ABORIGINES, FRENCH,
ENGLISH AND AMERICAN CONQUESTS, AND A GENERAL REVIEW
OF ITS CIVIL, POLITICAL AND MILITARY HISTORY.

DIGEST OF STATE LAWS.

ILLUSTRATED.

VOLUME 1

PELICAN PUBLISHING COMPANY
GRETNA 2006

*The word "Pelican" and the depiction of a pelican are trademarks
of Pelican Publishing Company, Inc., and are registered in the
U.S. Patent and Trademark Office.*

Printed in the United States of America
Published by Pelican Publishing Company, Inc.
1000 Burmaster Street, Gretna, Louisiana 70053

PREFACE.

The history of Pike county possesses features of unusual interest in comparison with those of other neighboring counties, especially those in the Military Tract. Here the sturdy pioneer located and began to exert his civilizing influence long before other sections contained a settler; and this is not only the oldest settled county of all north of its south line, but it was the first county organized in the Military Tract. Another fact worthy of note is, that it originally embraced all the country lying between the great Father of Waters and the placid Illinois, extending east to the Indiana line, and north to the Wisconsin line. Peoria, Rock Island, Galena and Chicago were originally little settlements of this then vast county.

In matters of general public interest and progress, Pike county has ever taken a leading and prominent position. Here have lived men who have taken no unimportant part in the affairs of the State,—in moulding the political sentiments and destiny of the country. Pike county has been the scene of conflict between some of the most giant intellects of the nation. Here the shrewd and enterprising Easterner, the courtly Southerner and the sturdy, practical Westerner, have met and mingled, have inherited the better traits possessed by each other, and thus have formed a society, a people superior in many particulars to that of most localities. The original settlers, the earliest pilgrims, have nearly all passed away. Here and there we see the bended form and whitened head of some of these veterans, but they are not numerous. Most of them have gone to that country which is always new, yet where the trials, struggles and hardships of pioneer life are never known.

Accurate and reliable history is most difficult to write. Those who have never experienced the difficulties incident to such labor cannot realize how nearly impossible it is, or can appreciate the earnest, honest and faithful labor of the historian. After the most careful and painstaking searches and inquiry upon any particular subject or about any event, he will even then find many doubts arising in his mind as to its accuracy and entire truthfulness. Each individual of whom inquiry is made will give you a different account of any event. One of them may be as honest as the other and try to relate his story correctly, yet they will be so widely different that the most searching and logical mind will be unable to harmonize them. This fact is forcibly illustrated in an incident related of Sir Walter Raleigh. While in prison in a tower of England he engaged himself in writing the history of the world. One day a brawl occurred in the yard of the tower, of which he desired to learn the particulars. Two of the principal actors came before him, and each related the account of the trouble, yet so widely different were they that he found it utterly impossible to tell what the facts were. He then remarked, "Here I am engaged in writing the history of events that occurred 3,000 years ago, and yet I am unable to learn the facts of what happens at my window." This has been the channel of our experience, and that of all others who have attempted national or local history. As an example in Pike county, we noticed in a Pittsfield cemetery "Orvillee" on the headstone as the name of the person buried in a certain grave, and "Orval E." on the footstone.

Aside from mistakes occurring from the above causes, doubtless there are many others to be found within these pages. To suppose that a volume of this magnitude, and containing so many thousands of names and dates and brief statements would be wholly accurate, is a supposition we presume no sane man will make. While we do not claim for this work critical accuracy or completeness, yet we are quite certain that it will be found measurably and practically so. Let it rest as the foundation for the future historian to build upon.

As one of the most interesting features of this work, we present the portraits of numerous representative citizens. It has been our aim to have the prominent men of to-day, as well as the pioneers, represented in this department, and we flatter ourselves on the uniform high character of the gentlemen whose portraits we present. They are in the strictest sense representative men, and are selected from all the callings and professions worthy to be represented. There are others, it is true, who claim equal prominence with those presented, but as a matter of course it was impossible for us to represent all the leading men of the county.

As we quit our long, tedious, yet nevertheless pleasant task of writing and compiling the History of Pike County, we wish to return the thanks of grateful hearts to those who have so freely aided us in collecting material, etc. To the county officials and editors of the various newspapers we are particularly grateful for the many kindnesses and courtesies shown us while laboring in the county. To James Gallaher, editor of *The Old Flag*, we especially acknowledge our indebtedness for the excellent historical sketch of Pittsfield presented in this volume. Last and most of all we wish to thank those who so liberally and materially aided the work by becoming subscribers to it. We feel we have discharged our duties fully, have fulfilled all our promises, have earned the laborer's pay. Thus feeling, we present the volume to the critical, yet we hope and believe justly charitable citizens of Pike county—or more especially, our subscribers.

CHAS. C. CHAPMAN & Co.

Chicago, May, 1880.

CONTENTS.

HISTORY OF ILLINOIS.

HISTORY OF PIKE COUNTY.

CONTENTS.

ILLUSTRATIONS.

PORTRAITS.

DIGEST OF STATE LAWS.

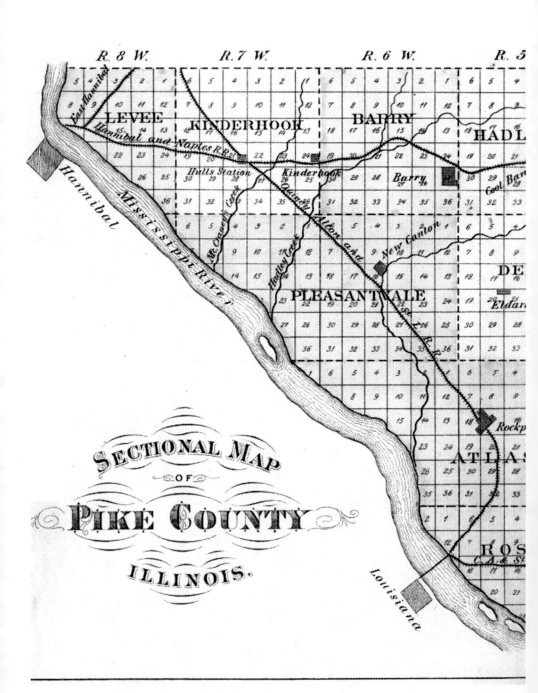

SECTIONAL MAP

OF

PIKE COUNTY

ILLINOIS.

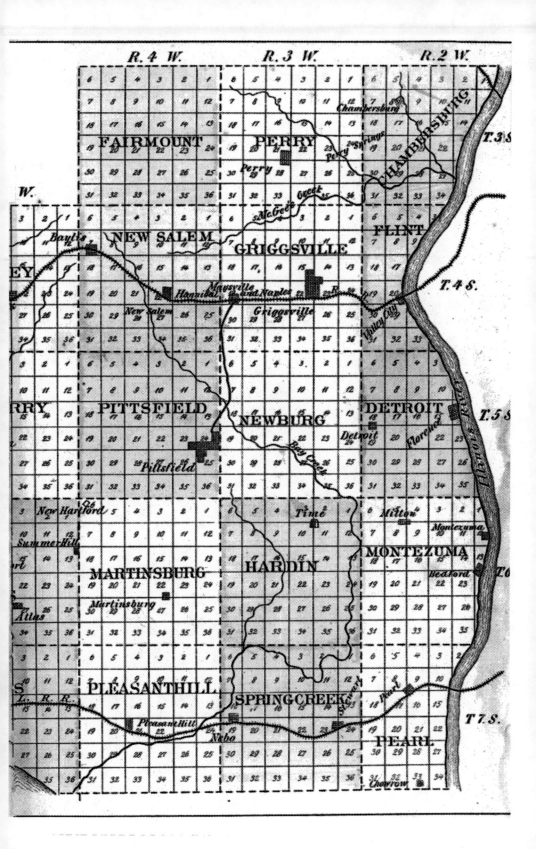

HISTORY OF ILLINOIS.

FORMER OCCUPANTS.

MOUND-BUILDERS.

The numerous and well-authenticated accounts of antiquities found in various parts of our country, clearly demonstrate that a people civilized, and even highly cultivated, occupied the broad surface of our continent before its possession by the present Indians; but the date of their rule of the Western World is so remote that all traces of their history, their progress and decay, lie buried in deepest obscurity. Nature, at the time the first Europeans came, had asserted her original dominion over the earth; the forests were all in their full luxuriance, the growth of many centuries; and naught existed to point out who and what they were who formerly lived, and loved, and labored, and died, on the continent of America. This pre-historic race is known as the Mound-Builders, from the numerous large mounds of earth-works left by them. The remains of the works of this people form the most interesting class of antiquities discovered in the United States. Their character can be but partially gleaned from the internal evidences and the peculiarities of the only remains left,—the mounds. They consist of remains of what were apparently villages, altars, temples, idols, cemeteries, monuments, camps, fortifications, pleasure grounds, etc., etc. Their habitations must have been tents, structures of wood, or other perishable material; otherwise their remains would be numerous. If the Mound-Builders were not the ancestors of the Indians, who were they? The oblivion which has closed over them is so complete that only conjecture can be given in answer to the question. Those who do not believe in the common parentage of mankind contend that they were an indigenous race of the Western hemisphere; others, with more plausibility, think they came from the East, and imagine they can see coincidences in the religion of the Hindoos and Southern Tartars and the supposed theology of the Mound-Builders. They were, no doubt, idolators, and it has been conjectured that the sun was the object of their adoration. The mounds were generally built in a situation affording a view of the rising sun: when enclosed in walls their gateways were toward the east; the caves in which their dead were occasionally buried always opened in the same direction; whenever a mound was partially enclosed by a semi-circular pavement, it was on the east side; when bodies were buried in graves, as was frequently the case, they were laid in a direction east and west; and, finally, medals have been found representing the sun and his rays of light.

At what period they came to this country, is likewise a matter of speculation. From the comparatively rude state of the arts among them, it has been inferred that the time was very remote. Their axes were of stone. Their raiment, judging from fragments which have been discovered, consisted of the bark of trees, interwoven with feathers; and their military works were such as a people would erect who had just passed to the pastoral state of society from that dependent alone upon hunting and fishing.

The mounds and other ancient earth-works constructed by this people are far more abundant than generally supposed, from the fact that while some are quite large, the greater part of them are small and inconspicuous. Along nearly all our water courses that are large enough to be navigated with a canoe, the mounds are almost invariably found, covering the base points and headlands of the bluffs which border the narrower valleys; so that when one finds himself in such positions as to command the grandest views for river scenery, he may almost always discover that he is standing upon, or in close proximity to, some one or more of these traces of the labors of an ancient people.

GALENA MOUNDS.

On the top of the high bluffs that skirt the west bank of the Mississippi, about two and a half miles from Galena, are a number of these silent monuments of a pre-historic age. The spot is one of surpassing beauty. From that point may be obtained a view of a portion of three States,—Illinois, Iowa and Wisconsin. A hundred feet below, at the foot of the perpendicular cliffs, the trains of the Illinois Central Railroad thunder around the curve, the portage is in full view, and the "Father of Waters," with its numerous bayous and islands, sketches a grand pamorama for miles above and below. Here, probably thousands of years ago, a race of men now extinct, and unknown even in the traditions of the Indians who inhabited that section for centuries before the discovery of America by Columbus, built these strangely wonderful and enigmatical mounds. At this point these mounds are circular and conical in form. The largest one is at least forty feet in diameter at the base, and not less than fifteen feet high, even yet, after it has been beaten by the storms of many centuries. On its top stands the large stump of an oak tree that was cut down about fifty years ago, and its annual rings indicate a growth of at least 200 years.

One of the most singular earth-works in the State was found on the top of a ridge near the east bank of the Sinsinawa creek in the lead region. It resembled some huge animal, the head, ears, nose, legs and tail, and general outline of which being as perfect as if made by men versed in modern art. The ridge on which it was situated stands on the prairie, 300 yards wide, 100 feet in height, and rounded on the top by a deep deposit of clay. Centrally, along the line of its summit, and thrown up in the form of an embankment three feet high, extended the outline of a quadruped measuring 250 feet from the tip of the nose to the end of the tail, and having a width of 18 feet at the center of the body. The head was 35 feet in length, the ears 10 feet, legs 60 and tail 75. The curvature in both the fore and hind legs was natural to an animal lying on its side. The general outline of the figure most nearly resembled the extinct animal known to geologists as the Megatherium. The question naturally arises, By whom and for what purpose was this earth figure raised? Some have conjectured that numbers of this now extinct animal lived and roamed over the prairies of Illinois when the Mound-Builders first made their appearance on the upper part of the Mississippi Valley, and that their wonder and admiration, excited by the colossal dimensions of these huge creatures, found some expression in the erection of this figure. The bones of some similar gigantic animals were exhumed on this stream about three miles from the same place.

LARGE CITIES.

Mr. Breckenridge, who examined the antiquities of the Western country in 1817, speaking of the mounds in the American Bottom, says: "The great number and extremely large size of some of them may be regarded as furnishing, with other circumstances, evidences of their antiquity. I have sometimes been induced to think that at the period when they were constructed there was a population here as numerous as that which once animated the borders of the Nile or Euphrates, or of Mexico. The most num-erous, as well as considerable, of these remains are found in pre-cisely those parts of the country where the traces of a numerous population might be looked for, namely, from the mouth of the Ohio on the east side of the Mississippi, to the Illinois river, and on the west from the St. Francis to the Missouri. I am perfectly satisfied that cities similar to those of ancient Mexico, of several hundred thousand souls, have existed in this country."

It must be admitted that whatever the uses of these mounds—whether as dwellings or burial places—these silent monuments were built, and the race who built them vanished from the face of the earth, ages before the Indians occupied the land, but their date must probably forever baffle human skill and ingenuity.

It is sometimes difficult to distinguish the places of sepulture raised by the Mound-Builders from the more modern graves of the Indians. The tombs of the former were in general larger than those of the latter, and were used as receptacles for a greater number of bodies, and contained relics of art, evincing a higher degree of civ-ilization than that attained by the Indians. The ancient earth-works of the Mound-Builders have occasionally been appropriated as burial places by the Indians, but the skeletons of the latter may be distinguished from the osteological remains of the former by their greater stature.

What finally became of the Mound-Builders is another query which has been extensively discussed. The fact that their works extend into Mexico and Peru has induced the belief that it was their posterity that dwelt in these countries when they were first visited by the Spaniards. The Mexican and Peruvian works, with the exception of their greater magnitude, are similar. Relics com-mon to all of them have been occasionally found, and it is believed that the religious uses which they subserved were the same. If, indeed, the Mexicans and Peruvians were the progeny of the more ancient Mound-Builders, Spanish rapacity for gold was the cause of their overthrow and final extermination.

A thousand other queries naturally arise respecting these nations which now repose under the ground, but the most searching investigation can give us only vague speculations for answers. No historian has preserved the names of their mighty chieftains, or given an account of their exploits, and even tradition is silent respecting them.

INDIANS.

Following the Mound-Builders as inhabitants of North America, were, as it is supposed, the people who reared the magnificent cities the ruins of which are found in Central America. This people was far more civilized and advanced in the arts than were the Mound-Builders. The cities built by them, judging from the ruins of broken columns, fallen arches and crumbling walls of temples, palaces and pyramids, which in some places for miles bestrew the ground, must have been of great extent, magnificent and very populous. When we consider the vast period of time necessary to erect such colossal structures, and, again, the time required to reduce them to their present ruined state, we can conceive something of their antiquity. These cities must have been old when many of the ancient cities of the Orient were being built.

The third race inhabiting North America, distinct from the former two in every particular, is the present Indians. They were, when visited by the early discoverers, without cultivation, refinement or literature, and far behind the Mound-Builders in the knowledge of the arts. The question of their origin has long interested archæologists, and is the most difficult they have been called upon to answer. Of their predecessors the Indian tribes knew nothing; they even had no traditions respecting them. It is quite certain that they were the successors of a race which had entirely passed away ages before the discovery of the New World. One hypothesis is that the American Indians are an original race indigenous to the Western hemisphere. Those who entertain this view think their peculiarities of physical structure preclude the possibility of a common parentage with the rest of mankind. Prominent among those distinctive traits is the hair, which in the red man is round, in the white man oval, and in the black man flat.

A more common supposition, however, is that they are a derivative race, and sprang from one or more of the ancient peoples of Asia. In the absence of all authentic history, and when even tradition is wanting, any attempt to point out the particular location of their origin must prove unsatisfactory. Though the exact place of origin may never be known, yet the striking coincidence of physical organization between the Oriental type of mankind and the Indians point unmistakably to some part of Asia as the place whence they emigrated, which was originally peopled to a great extent by the children of Shem. In this connection it has been claimed that the meeting of the Europeans, Indians and Africans on the continent of America, is the fulfillment of a prophecy as recorded in Genesis ix. 27: "God shall enlarge Japheth, and he shall dwell in the tents of Shem; and Canaan shall be his servant." Assuming the theory to be true that the Indian tribes are of Shemitic origin, they were met on this continent in the fifteenth century by the Japhetic race, after the two stocks had passed around the globe by directly different routes. A few years afterward the Hamitic branch of the human family were brought from the coast of Africa. During the occupancy of the continent by the three distinct races, the children of Japheth have grown and prospered, while the called and not voluntary sons of Ham have endured a servitude in the wider stretching valleys of the tents of Shem.

When Christopher Columbus had finally succeeded in demonstrating the truth of his theory that by sailing westward from Europe land would be discovered, landing on the Island of Bermuda he supposed he had reached the East Indies. This was an error, but it led to the adoption of the name of "Indians" for the inhabitants of the Island and the main land of America, by which name the red men of America have ever since been known.

Of the several great branches of North American Indians the only ones entitled to consideration in Illinois history are the Algonquins and Iroquois. At the time of the discovery of America the former occupied the Atlantic seaboard, while the home of the Iroquois was as an island in this vast area of Algonquin population. The latter great nation spread over a vast territory, and various tribes of Algonquin lineage sprung up over the country, adopting, in time, distinct tribal customs and laws. An almost continuous warfare was carried on between tribes; but later, on the entrance of the white man into their beloved homes, every foot of territory was fiercely disputed by the confederacy of many neighboring tribes. The Algonquins formed the most extensive alliance to resist the encroachment of the whites, especially the English. Such was the nature of King Philip's war. This King, with his Algonquin braves, spread terror and desolation throughout New England. With the Algonquins as the controlling spirit, a confederacy of continental proportions was the result, embracing in its alliance the tribes of every name and lineage from the Northern lakes to the gulf. Pontiac, having breathed into them his implacable hate of the English intruders, ordered the conflict to commence, and all the British colonies trembled before the desolating fury of Indian vengeance.

ILLINOIS CONFEDERACY.

The Illinois confederacy, the various tribes of which comprised most of the Indians of Illinois at one time, was composed of five tribes: the Tamaroas, Michigans, Kaskaskias, Cahokas, and Peorias. The Illinois, Miamis and Delawares were of the same stock. As early as 1670 the priest Father Marquette mentions frequent visits made by individuals of this confederacy to the missionary station at St. Esprit, near the western extremity of Lake Superior. At that time they lived west of the Mississippi, in eight villages, whither they had been driven from the shores of Lake Michigan by the Iroquois. Shortly afterward they began to return to their old hunting ground, and most of them finally settled in Illinois. Joliet and Marquette, in 1673, met with a band of them on their famous voyage of discovery down the Mississippi. They were treated with the greatest hospitality by the principal chief. On their return voyage up the Illinois river they stopped at the principal town of the confederacy, situated on the banks of the river seven miles below the present town of Ottawa. It was then called Kaskaskia. Marquette returned to the village in 1675 and established the mission of the Immaculate Conception, the oldest in Illinois. When, in 1679, LaSalle visited the town, it had greatly increased numbering 460 lodges, and at the annual assembly of the different tribes, from 6,000 to 8,000 souls. In common with other western tribes, they became involved in the conspiracy of Pontiac, although displaying no very great warlike spirit. Pontiac lost his life by the hands of one of the braves of the Illinois tribe, which so enraged the nations that had followed him as their leader that they fell upon the Illinois to avenge his death, and almost annihilated them.

STARVED ROCK.

Tradition states that a band of this tribe, in order to escape the general slaughter, took refuge upon the high rock on the Illinois

river since known as Starved Rock.   Nature has made this one of
the most formidable military fortresses in the world.   From the
waters which wash its base it rises to an altitude of 125 feet.   Three
of its sides it is impossible to scale, while the one next to the land
may be climbed with difficulty.   From its summit, almost as inaccessible as an eagle's nest, the valley of the Illinois is seen as
a landscape of exquisite beauty.   The river near by struggles
between a number of wooded islands, while further below it quietly
meanders through vast meadows till it disappears like a thread of
light in the dim distance.   On the summit of this rock the Illinois
were besieged by a superior force of the Pottawatomies whom the
great strength of their natural fortress enabled them to keep at bay.
Hunger and thirst, however, soon accomplished what the enemy
was unable to effect.   Surrounded by a relentless foe, without food
or water, they took a last look at their beautiful hunting grounds,
and with true Indian fortitude lay down and died from starvation.
Years afterward their bones were seen whitening in that place.

At the beginning of the present century the remnants of this
once powerful confederacy were forced into a small compass around
Kaskaskia.   A few years later they emigrated to the Southwest,
and in 1850 they were in Indian Territory, and numbered but 84
persons.

SACS AND FOXES.

The Sacs and Foxes, who figured most conspicuously in the later
history of Illinois, inhabited the northwestern portion of the State.
By long residence together and intermarriage they had substantially become one people.   Drake, in his "Life of Black Hawk,"
speaks of these tribes as follows: "The Sacs and Foxes fought their
way from the waters of the St. Lawrence to Green Bay, and after
reaching that place, not only sustained themselves against hostile
tribes, but were the most active and courageous in the subjugation,
or rather the extermination, of the numerous and powerful Illinois
confederacy.   They had many wars, offensive and defensive, with
the Sioux, the Pawnees, the Osages, and other tribes, some of which
are ranked among the most fierce and ferocious warriors of the
whole continent; and it does not appear that in these conflicts, running through a long period of years, they were found wanting in
this, the greatest of all savage virtues.   In the late war with Great
Britain, a party of the Sacs and Foxes fought under the British

standard as a matter of choice; and in the recent contest between a fragment of these tribes and the United States, although defeated and literally cut to pieces by an overwhelming force, it is very questionable whether their reputation as braves would suffer by a comparison with that of their victors. It is believed that a careful review of their history, from the period when they first established themselves on the waters of the Mississippi down to the present time, will lead the inquirer to the conclusion that the Sacs and Foxes were truly a courageous people, shrewd, politic, and enterprising, with no more ferocity and treachery of character than is common among the tribes by whom they were surrounded." These tribes at the time of the Black Hawk War were divided into twenty families, twelve of which were Sacs and eight Foxes. The following were other prominent tribes occupying Illinois: the Kickapoos, Shawnees, Mascoulins, Piaukishaws, Pottawatomies, Chippewas, and Ottawas.

MANNERS AND CUSTOMS.

The art of hunting not only supplied the Indian with food, but, like that of war, was a means of gratifying his love of distinction. The male children, as soon as they acquired sufficient age and strength, were furnished with a bow and arrow and taught to shoot birds and other small game. Success in killing large quadrupeds required years of careful study and practice, and the art was as sedulously inculcated in the minds of the rising generation as are the elements of reading, writing and arithmetic in the common schools of civilized communities. The mazes of the forest and the dense, tall grass of the prairies were the best fields for the exercise of the hunter's skill. No feet could be impressed in the yielding soil but that the tracks were the objects of the most searching scrutiny, and revealed at a glance the animal that made them, the direction it was pursuing, and the time that had elapsed since it had passed. In a forest country he selected the valleys, because they were most frequently the resort of game. The most easily taken, perhaps, of all the animals of the chase was the deer. It is endowed with a curiosity which prompts it to stop in its flight and look back at the approaching hunter, who always avails himself of this opportunity to let fly the fatal arrow.

Their general councils were composed of the chiefs and old men. When in council, they usually sat in concentric circles around the

speaker, and each individual, notwithstanding the fiery passions
that rankled within, preserved an exterior as immovable as if cast
in bronze. Before commencing business a person appeared with
the sacred pipe, and another with fire to kindle it. After being
lighted, it was first presented to heaven, secondly to the earth,
thirdly to the presiding spirit, and lastly the several councilors,
each of whom took a whiff. These formalities were observed with
as close exactness as state etiquette in civilized courts.

The dwellings of the Indians were of the simplest and rudest
character. On some pleasant spot by the bank of a river, or near
an ever-running spring, they raised their groups of wigwams, constructed of the bark of trees, and easily taken down and removed
to another spot. The dwelling-places of the chiefs were sometimes
more spacious, and constructed with greater care, but of the same
materials. Skins taken in the chase served them for repose.
Though principally dependent upon hunting and fishing, the
uncertain supply from those sources led them to cultivate small
patches of corn. Every family did everything necessary within
itself, commerce, or an interchange of articles, being almost unknown
to them. In cases of dispute and dissension, each Indian relied
upon himself for retaliation. Blood for blood was the rule, and
the relatives of the slain man were bound to obtain bloody revenge
for his death. This principle gave rise, as a matter of course, to
innumerable and bitter feuds, and wars of extermination where such
were possible. War, indeed, rather than peace, was the Indian's
glory and delight,—war, not conducted as civilization, but war
where individual skill, endurance, gallantry and cruelty were prime
requisites. For such a purpose as revenge the Indian would make
great sacrifices, and display a patience and perseverance truly heroic;
but when the excitement was over, he sank back into a listless, un-
occupied, well-nigh useless savage. During the intervals of his
more exciting pursuits, the Indian employed his time in decorating
his person with all the refinement of paint and feathers, and in the
manufacture of his arms and of canoes. These were constructed of
bark, and so light that they could easily be carried on the shoulder
from stream to stream. His amusements were the war-dance, ath-
letic games, the narration of his exploits, and listening to the oratory of the chiefs; but during long periods of such existence he
remained in a state of torpor, gazing listlessly upon the trees of
the forests and the clouds that sailed above them; and this vacancy

imprinted an habitual gravity, and even melancholy, upon his general deportment.

The main labor and drudgery of Indian communities fell upon the women. The planting, tending and gathering of the crops, making mats and baskets, carrying burdens,—in fact, all things of the kind were performed by them, thus making their condition but little better than that of slaves. Marriage was merely a matter of bargain and sale, the husband giving presents to the father of the bride. In general they had but few children. They were subjected to many and severe attacks of sickness, and at times famine and pestilence swept away whole tribes.

SINGLE-HANDED COMBAT WITH INDIANS.

The most desperate single-handed combat with Indians ever fought on the soil of Illinois was that of Tom Higgins, August 21, 1814. Higgins was 25 years old, of a muscular and compact build, not tall, but strong and active. In danger he possessed a quick and discerning judgment, and was without fear. He was a member of Journey's rangers, consisting of eleven men, stationed at Hill's Fort, eight miles southwest of the present Greenville, Putnam county. Discovering Indian signs near the fort, the company, early the following morning, started on the trail. They had not gone far before they were in an ambuscade of a larger party. At the first fire their commander, Journey, and three men fell, and six retreated to the fort; but Higgins stopped to "have another pull at the red-skins," and, taking deliberate aim at a straggling savage, shot him down. Higgins' horse had been wounded at the first fire, as he supposed, mortally. Coming to, he was about to effect his escape, when the familiar voice of Burgess hailed him from the long grass, "Tom, don't leave me." Higgins told him to come along, but Burgess replied that his leg was smashed. Higgins attempted to raise him on his horse, but the animal took fright and ran away. Higgins then directed Burgess to limp off as well as he could; and by crawling through the grass he reached the fort, while the former loaded his gun and remained behind to protect him against the pursuing enemy. When Burgess was well out of the way, Higgins took another route, which led by a small thicket, to throw any wandering enemy off the trail. Here he was confronted by three savages approaching. He ran to a little ravine near for shelter, but in the effort discovered for the first time that he was badly wounded in the leg. He was closely pressed by the largest, a powerful Indian, who lodged a ball in his thigh. He fell, but instantly rose again, only, however, to draw the fire of the other two, and again fell wounded. The Indians now advanced upon him with their tomahawks and scalping knives; but as he presented his gun first at one, then at another, from his place in the ravine, each wavered in his purpose. Neither party had time to load, and the large Indian, supposing finally that Higgins' gun was empty, rushed forward with uplifted tomahawk and a yell; but as he came near enough, was shot down. At this the others raised the war-whoop, and rushed upon the wounded Higgins, and now a hand-to-hand conflict ensued. They darted at him with their knives time and again, inflicting many ghastly flesh-wounds, which bled profusely. One of the assailants threw his tomahawk at him with such precision as to sever his ear and lay bare his skull, knocking him down. They now rushed in on him, but he kicked them off, and grasping one of their spears thrust at him, was raised up by it. He quickly seized his gun, and by a powerful blow crushed in the skull of one, but broke his rifle. His remaining antagonist still kept up the contest, making thrusts with his knife at the bleeding and exhausted Higgins, which he parried with his broken gun as well as he could. Most of this desperate engagement was in plain view of the fort; but the rangers, having been in one ambuscade, saw in this fight only a ruse to draw out the balance of the garrison. But a Mrs. Pursely, residing at the fort, no longer able to see so brave a man contend for his life unaided, seized a gun, mounted a horse, and started to his rescue. At this the men took courage and hastened along. The Indian, seeing aid coming, fled. Higgins, being nearly hacked to pieces, fainted from loss of blood. He was carried to the fort. There being no surgeon, his comrades cut two balls from his flesh; others remained in. For days his life was despaired of; but by tender nursing he ultimately regained his health, although badly crippled. He resided in Fayette county for many years after, and died in 1829.

EARLY DISCOVERIES

NICHOLAS PERROT.

The first white man who ever set foot on the soil embraced within the boundary of the present populous State of Illinois was Nicholas Perrot, a Frenchman. He was sent to Chicago in the year 1671 by M. Talon, Intendant of Canada, for the purpose of inviting the Western Indians to a great peace convention to be held at Green Bay. This convention had for its chief object the promulgation of a plan for the discovery of the Mississippi river. This great river had been discovered by De Soto, the Spanish explorer, nearly one hundred and fifty years previously, but his nation left the country a wilderness, without further exploration or settlement within its borders, in which condition it remained until the river was discovered by Joliet and Marquette in 1673. It was deemed a wise policy to secure, as far as possible, the friendship and co-operation of the Indians, far and near, before venturing upon an enterprise which their hostility might render disastrous. Thus the great convention was called.

JOLIET AND MARQUETTE.

Although Perrot was the first European to visit Illinois, he was not the first to make any important discoveries. This was left for Joliet and Marquette, which they accomplished two years thereafter. The former, Louis Joliet, was born at Quebec in 1645. He was educated for the clerical profession, but he abandoned it to engage in the fur trade. His companion, Father Jacques Marquette, was a native of France, born in 1637. He was a Jesuit priest by education, and a man of simple faith and great zeal and devotion in extending the Roman Catholic religion among the Indians. He was sent to America in 1666 as a missionary. To convert the Indians he penetrated the wilderness a thousand miles in advance of civilization, and by his kind attention in their afflictions he won their affections and made them his lasting friends. There were others, however, who visited Illinois even prior to the famous exploration of Joliet and Marquette. In 1672 the Jesuit missionaries, Fathers Claude Allouez and Claude Dablon, bore the standard of the Cross from their mission at Green Bay through western Wisconsin and northern Illinois.

According to the pre-arranged plan referred to above, at the Jesuit mission on the Strait of Mackinaw, Joliet joined Marquette, and with five other Frenchmen and a simple outfit the daring explorers on the 17th of May, 1673, set out on their perilous voyage to discover the Mississippi. Coasting along the northern shore of Lake Michigan, they entered Green Bay, and passed thence up Fox river and Lake Winnebago to a village of the Muscatines and Miamis, where great interest was taken in the expedition by the natives. With guides they proceeded down the river. Arriving at the portage, they soon carried their light canoes and scanty baggage to the Wisconsin, about three miles distant. Their guides now refused to accompany them further, and endeavored, by reciting the dangers incident to the voyage, to induce them to return. They stated that huge demons dwelt in the great river, whose voices could be heard a long distance, and who engulfed in the raging waters all who came within their reach. They also represented that if any of them should escape the dangers of the river, fierce tribes of Indians dwelt upon its banks ready to complete the work of destruction. They proceeded on their journey, however, and on the 17th of June pushed their frail barks on the bosom of the stately Mississippi, down which they smoothly glided for nearly a hundred miles. Here Joliet and Marquette, leaving their canoes in charge of their men, went on the western shore, where they discovered an Indian village, and were kindly treated. They journeyed on down the unknown river, passing the mouth of the Illinois, then running into the current of the muddy Missouri, and afterward the waters of the Ohio joined with them on their journey southward. Near the mouth of the Arkansas they discovered Indians who showed signs of hostility; but when Marquette's mission of peace was made known to them, they were kindly received. After proceeding up the Arkansas a short distance, at the advice of the natives they turned their faces northward to retrace their steps. After several weeks of hard toil they reached the Illinois, up which stream they proceeded to Lake Michigan. Following the western shore of the lake, they entered Green Bay the latter part of September, having traveled a distance of 2,500 miles.

On his way up the Illinois, Marquette visited the Kaskaskias, near what is now Utica, in LaSalle county. The following year he returned and established among them the mission of the Immaculate Virgin Mary. This was the last act of his life. He died in Michigan, May 18, 1675.

LASALLE'S EXPLORATIONS.

The first French occupation of Illinois was effected by LaSalle, in 1680. Having constructed a vessel, the "Griffin," above the falls of Niagara, he sailed to Green Bay, and passed thence in canoe to the mouth of the St. Joseph river, by which and the Kankakee he reached the Illinois in January, 1680; and on the 3d he entered the expansion of the river now called Peoria lake. Here, at the lower end of the lake, on its eastern bank, now in Tazewell county, he erected Fort Crevecœur. The place where this ancient fort stood may still be seen just below the outlet of Peoria lake. It had, however, but a temporary existence. From this point LaSalle determined, at that time, to descend the Mississippi to its mouth. This he did not do, however, until two years later. Returning to Fort Frontenac for the purpose of getting material with which to rig his vessel, he left the fort at Peoria in charge of his lieutenant, Henri Tonti, an Italian, who had lost one of his hands by the explosion of a grenade in the Sicilian wars. Tonti had with him fifteen men, most of whom disliked LaSalle, and were ripe for a revolt the first opportunity. Two men who had, previous to LaSalle's departure, been sent to look for the "Griffin" now returned and reported that the vessel was lost and that Fort Frontenac was in the hands of LaSalle's creditors. This disheartening intelligence had the effect to enkindle a spirit of mutiny among the garrison. Tonti had no sooner left the fort, with a few men, to fortify what was afterward known as Starved Rock, than the garrison at the fort refused longer to submit to authority. They destroyed the fort, seized the ammunition, provisions, and other portables of value, and fled. Only two of their number remained true. These hastened to apprise Tonti of what had occurred. He thereupon sent four of the men with him to inform LaSalle. Thus was Tonti in the midst of treacherous savages, with only five men, two of whom were the friars Ribourde and Membre. With these he immediately returned to the fort, collected what tools had not been destroyed, and conveyed them to the great town of the Illinois Indians.

By this voluntary display of confidence he hoped to remove the jealousy created in the minds of the Illinois by the enemies of La-Salle. Here he awaited, unmolested, the return of LaSalle.

GREAT BATTLE OF THE ILLINOIS.

Neither Tonti nor his wild associates suspected that hordes of Iroquois were gathering preparatory to rushing down upon their country and reducing it to an uninhabited waste. Already these hell-hounds of the wilderness had destroyed the Hurons, Eries, and other natives on the lakes, and were now directing their attention to the Illinois for new victims. Five hundred Iroquois warriors set out for the home of the Illinois. All was fancied security and idle repose in the great town of this tribe, as the enemy stealthily approached. Suddenly as a clap of thunder from a cloudless sky the listless inhabitants were awakened from their lethargy. A Shawnee' Indian, on his return home after a visit to the Illinois, first discovered the invaders. To save his friends from the impending danger, he hurriedly returned and apprised them of the coming enemy. This intelligence spread with lightning rapidity over the town, and each wigwam disgorged its boisterous and astounded inmates. Women snatched their children, and in a delirium of f.ight wandered aimlessly about, rending the air with their screams. The men, more self-possessed, seized their arms ready for the coming fray. Tonti, long an object of suspicion, was soon surrounded by an angry crowd of warriors, who accused him of being an emissary of the enemy. His inability to defend himself properly, in consequence of not fully understanding their language left them still inclined to believe him guilty, and they seized his effects from the fort and threw them into the river. The women and children were sent down the river for safety, and the warriors, not exceeding four hundred, as most of their young men were off hunting, returned to the village. Along the shores of the river they kindled huge bonfires, and spent the entire night in greasing their bodies, painting their faces, and performing the war-dance, to prepare for the approaching enemy. At early dawn the scouts who had been sent out returned, closely followed by the Iroquois. The scouts had seen a chief arrayed in French costume, and reported their suspicions that LaSalle was in the camp of the enemy, and Tonti again became an object of jealousy. A concourse of wildly gesticulating savages immediately gathered about him, demanding his life, and nothing saved him from their uplifted weapons but a promise that he and his men would go with them to meet the enemy. With their suspicions partly lulled, they hurriedly crossed the river and met the foe, when both commenced firing. Tonti, seeing that the Illinois were outnumbered and likely to be defeated, determined, at the imminent risk of his life, to stay the fight by an attempt at mediation. Presuming on the treaty of peace then existing between the French and Iroquois, he exchanged his gun for a belt of wampum and advanced to meet the savage multitude, attended by three companions, who, being unnecessarily exposed to danger, were dismissed, and he proceeded alone. A short walk brought him in the midst of a pack of yelping devils, writhing and distorted with fiendish rage, and impatient to shed his blood. As the result of his swarthy Italian complexion and half-savage costume, he was at first taken for an Indian, and before the mistake was discovered a young warrior approached and stabbed at his heart. Fortunately the blade was turned aside by coming in contact with a rib, yet a large flesh wound was inflicted, which bled profusely. At this juncture a chief discovered his true character, and he was led to the rear and efforts were made to staunch his wound. When sufficiently recovered, he declared the Illinois were under the protection of the French, and demanded, in consideration of the treaty between the latter and the Iroquois, that they should be suffered to remain without further molestation. During this conference a young warrior snatched Tonti's hat, and, fleeing with it to the front, held it aloft on the end of his gun in view of the Illinois. The latter, judging that Tonti had been killed, renewed the fight with great vigor. Simultaneously, intelligence was brought to the Iroquois that Frenchmen were assisting their enemies in the fight, when the contest over Tonti was renewed with redoubled fury. Some declared that he should be immediately put to death, while others, friendly to LaSalle, with equal earnestness demanded that he should be set at liberty. During their clamorous debate, his hair was several times lifted by a huge savage who stood at his back with a scalping knife ready for execution.

Tonti at length turned the current of the angry controversy in his favor, by stating that the Illinois were 1,200 strong, and that there were 60 Frenchmen at the village ready to assist them. This statement obtained at least a partial credence, and his tormentors now determined to use him as an instrument to delude the Illinois with a pretended truce. The old warriors, therefore, advanced to the front and ordered the firing to cease, while Tonti, dizzy from the loss of blood, was furnished with an emblem of peace and sent staggering across the plain to rejoin the Illinois. The two friars who had just returned from a distant hut, whither they had repaired for prayer and meditation, were the first to meet him and bless God for what they regarded as a miraculous deliverance. With the assurance brought by Tonti, the Illinois re-crossed the river to their lodges, followed by the enemy as far as the opposite bank. Not long after, large numbers of the latter, under the pretext of hunting, also crossed the river and hung in threatening groups about the town. These hostile indications, and the well-known disregard which the Iroquois had always evinced for their pledges, soon convinced the Illinois that their only safety was in flight. With this conviction they set fire to their village, and while the vast volume of flames and smoke diverted the attention of the enemy, they quietly dropped down the river to join their women and children. As soon as the flames would permit, the Iroquois entrenched themselves on the site of the village. Tonti and his men were ordered by the suspicious savages to leave their hut and take up their abode in the fort.

At first the Iroquois were much elated at the discomfiture of the Illinois, but when two days afterward they discovered them reconnoitering their intrenchments, their courage greatly subsided. With fear they recalled the exaggerations of Tonti respecting their numbers, and concluded to send him with a hostage to make overtures of peace. He and his hostage were received with delight by the Illinois, who readily assented to the proposal which he brought, and in turn sent back with him a hostage to the Iroquois. On his return to the fort his life was again placed in jeopardy, and the treaty was with great difficulty ratified. The young and inexperienced Illinois hostage betrayed to his crafty interviewers the numerical weakness of his tribe, and the savages immediately rushed upon Tonti, and charged him with having deprived them of the spoils and honors of victory. It now required all the tact of which he was master to escape. After much difficulty however, the treaty was concluded, but the savages, to show their contempt for it, immediately commenced constructing canoes in which to descend the river and attack the Illinois.

AN IROQUOIS CHIEF.

FRENCHMEN DRIVEN AWAY.

Tonti managed to apprise the latter of their designs, and he and Membre were soon after summoned to attend a council of the Iroquois, who still labored under a wholesome fear of Count Frontenac, and disliking to attack the Illinois in the presence of the French, they thought to try to induce them to leave the country. At the assembling of the council, six packages of beaver skins were introduced, and the savage orator, presenting them separately to Tonti, explained the nature of each. "The first two," said he, " were to declare that the children of Count Frontenac, that is, the Illinois, should not be eaten; the next was a plaster to heal the wounds of Tonti; the next was oil wherewith to anoint him and Membre, that they might not be fatigued in traveling; the next proclaimed that the sun was bright; and the sixth and last required them to decamp and go home."

At the mention of going home, Tonti demanded of them when they intended to set the example by leaving the Illinois in the peaceable possession of their country, which they had so unjustly invaded. The council grew boisterous and angry at the idea that they should be demanded to do what they required of the French, and some of its members, forgetting their previous pledge, declared that they would "eat Illinois flesh before they departed." Tonti, in imitation of the Indians' manner of expressing scorn, indignantly kicked away the presents of fur, saying, since they intended to devour the children of Frontenac with cannibal ferocity, he would not accept their gifts. This stern rebuke resulted in the expulsion of Tonti and his companion from the council, and the next day the chiefs ordered them to leave the country.

Tonti had now, at the great peril of his life, tried every expedient to prevent the slaughter of the Illinois. There was little to be accomplished by longer remaining in the country, and as longer delay might imperil the lives of his own men, he determined to depart, not knowing where or when he would be able to rejoin LaSalle. With this object in view, the party, consisting of six persons, embarked in canoes, which soon proved leaky, and they were compelled to land for the purpose of making repairs. While thus employed, Father Ribourde, attracted by the beauty of the surrounding landscape, wandered forth among the groves for meditation and prayer. Not returning in due time, Tonti became alarmed, and started with a companion to ascertain the cause of the long delay. They soon discovered tracks of Indians, by whom it was supposed he had been seized, and guns were fired to direct his return, in case he was alive. Seeing nothing of him during the day, at night they built fires along the bank of the river and retired to the opposite side, to see who might approach them. Near midnight a number of Indians were seen flitting about the light, by whom, no doubt, had been made the tracks seen the previous day. It was afterward learned that they were a band of Kickapoos, who had for several days been hovering about the camp of the Iroquois in quest of scalps. They had fell in with the inoffensive old friar and scalped him. Thus, in the 65th year of his age, the only heir to a wealthy Burgundian house perished under the war-club of the savages for whose salvation he had renounced ease and affluence.

INHUMAN BUTCHERY.

During this tragedy a far more revolting one was being enacted in the great town of Illinois. The Iroquois were tearing open the graves of the dead, and wreaking their vengeance upon the bodies made hideous by putrefaction. At this desecration, it is said, they even ate portions of the dead bodies, while subjecting them to every indignity that brutal hate could inflict. Still unsated by their hellish brutalities, and now unrestrained by the presence of the French, they started in pursuit of the retreating Illinois. Day after day they and the opposing forces moved in compact array down the river, neither being able to gain any advantage over the other. At length the Iroquois obtained by falsehood that which number and prowess denied them. They gave out that their object was to possess the country, not by destroying, but by driving out its present inhabitants. Deceived by this false statement, the Illinois separated, some descending the Mississippi and others crossing to the western shore. The Tamaroas, more credulous than the rest, remained near the mouth of the Illinois, and were suddenly attacked by an overwhelming force of the enemy. The men fled in dismay, and the women and children, to the number of 700, fell into the hands of the ferocious enemy. Then followed the tortures, butcheries and burnings which only the infuriated and imbruted Iroquois could perpetrate. LaSalle on his return discovered the half-charred bodies of women and children still bound to the stakes where they had suffered all the torments hellish hate could devise. In addition to those who had been burnt, the mangled bodies of women and children thickly covered the ground, many of which bore marks of brutality too horrid for record.

After the ravenous horde had sufficiently glutted their greed for carnage, they retired from the country. The Illinois returned and rebuilt their town.

TONTI SAFE AT GREEN BAY.

After the death of Ribourde, Tonti and his men again resumed their journey. Soon again their craft became disabled, when they abandoned it and started on foot for Lake Michigan. Their supply of provisions soon became exhausted, and they were compelled to subsist in a great measure on roots and herbs. One of their companions wandered off in search of game, and lost his way, and several days elapsed before he rejoined them. In his absence he was without flints and bullets, yet contrived to shoot some turkeys by using slugs cut from a pewter porringer and a fire-brand to discharge his gun. Tonti fell sick of a fever and greatly retarded the progress of the march. Nearing Green Bay, the cold increased and the means of subsistence decreased and the party would have perished had they not found a few ears of corn and some frozen squashes in the fields of a deserted village. Near the close of November they had reached the Pottawatomies, who warmly greeted them. Their chief was an ardent admirer of the French, and was accustomed to say: "There were but three great captains in the world,—himself, Tonti and LaSalle." For the above account of Tonti's encounter with the Iroquois, we are indebted to Davidson and Stuvé's History of Illinois.

LASALLE'S RETURN.

LaSalle returned to Peoria only to meet the hideous picture of devastation. Tonti had escaped, but LaSalle knew not whither. Passing down the lake in search of him and his men, LaSalle discovered that the fort had been destroyed; but the vessel which he had partly constructed was still on the stocks, and but slightly injured. After further fruitless search he fastened to a tree a painting representing himself and party sitting in a canoe and bearing a pipe of peace, and to the painting attached a letter addressed to Tonti.

LaSalle was born in France in 1643, of wealthy parentage, and educated in a college of the Jesuits, from which he separated and came to Canada, a poor man, in 1666. He was a man of daring genius, and outstripped all his competitors in exploits of travel and commerce with the Indians. He was granted a large tract of land at LaChine, where he established himself in the fur trade. In 1669 he visited the headquarters of the great Iroquois confederacy, at Onondaga, New York, and, obtaining guides, explored the Ohio river to the falls at Louisville. For many years previous, it must be remembered, missionaries and traders were obliged to make their way to the Northwest through Canada on account of the fierce hostility of the Iroquois along the lower lakes and Niagara river, which entirely closed this latter route to the upper lakes. They carried on their commerce chiefly by canoes, paddling them through Ottawa river to Lake Nipissing, carrying them across the portage to French river, and descending that to Lake Huron. This being the route by which they reached the Northwest, we have an explanation of the fact that all the earliest Jesuit missions were established in the neighborhood of the upper lakes. LaSalle conceived the grand idea of opening the route by Niagara river and the lower lakes to Canada commerce by sail vessels, connecting it with the navigation of the Mississippi, and thus opening a magnificent water communication from the Gulf of St. Lawrence to the Gulf of Mexico. This truly grand and comprehensive purpose seems to have animated him in his wonderful achievements, and the matchless difficulties and hardships he surmounted. As the first step in the accomplishment of this object he established himself on Lake Ontario, and built and garrisoned Fort Frontenac, the site of the present city of Kingston, Canada. Here he obtained a grant of land from the French crown, and a body of troops, by which he repulsed the Iroquois and opened passage to Niagara Falls. Having by this masterly stroke made it safe to attempt a hitherto untried expedition, his next step, as we have seen, was to build a ship with which to sail the lakes. He was successful in this undertaking, though his ultimate purpose was defeated by a strange combination of untoward circumstances. The Jesuits evidently hated LaSalle and plotted against him, because he had abandoned them and united with a rival order. The fur traders were also jealous of his success in opening new channels of commerce. While they were plodding with their bark canoes through the Ottawa, he was constructing sailing vessels to command the trade of the lakes and the Mississippi. These great plans excited the jealousy and envy of small traders, introduced treason and revolt into the ranks of his men, and finally led to the foul assassination by which his great achievements were permanently ended.

LASALLE'S ASSASSINATION.

Again visiting the Illinois in the year 1682, LaSalle descended the Mississippi to the Gulf of Mexico. He erected a standard upon which he inscribed the arms of France, and took formal possession of the whole valley of this mighty river in the name of Louis XIV., then reigning, and in honor of whom he named the country Louisiana. LaSalle then returned to France, was appointed Governor, and returned with a fleet of immigrants for the purpose of planting a colony in Illinois. They arrived in due time in the Gulf of Mexico, but failing to find the mouth of the Mississippi, up which they intended to sail, his supply ship, with the immigrants, was driven ashore and wrecked on Matagorda Bay. With the fragments of the vessel he constructed rude huts and stockades on the shore for the protection of his followers, calling the post Fort St. Louis. He then made a trip into New Mexico in search of silver mines, but, meeting with disappointment, returned to find his colony reduced to forty souls. He then resolved to travel on foot to Illinois. With some twenty of his men they filed out of their fort on the 12th of January, 1687, and after the parting,—which was one of sighs, of tears, and of embraces, all seeming intuitively to know that they should see each other no more,—they started on their disastrous journey. Two of the party, Du Haut and Leotot, when on a hunting expedition in company with a nephew of LaSalle, assassinated him while asleep. The long absence of his nephew caused LaSalle to go in search of him. On approaching the murderers of his nephew, they fired upon him, killing him instantly. They then despoiled the body of its clothing, and left it to be devoured by the wild beasts of the forest. Thus, at the age of 43, perished one whose exploits have so greatly enriched the history of the New World. To estimate aright the marvels of his patient fortitude, one must follow on his track through the vast scene of his interminable journeyings, those thousands of weary miles of forest, marsh and river, where, again and again, in the bitterness of baffled striving, the untiring pilgrim pushed onward toward the goal he never was to attain. America owes him an enduring memory; for in this masculine figure, cast in iron, she sees the heroic pioneer who guided her to the possession of her richest heritage.

Tonti, who had been stationed at the fort on the Illinois, learning of LaSalle's unsuccessful voyage, immediately started down the Mississippi to his relief. Reaching the Gulf, he found no traces of the colony. He then returned, leaving some of his men at the mouth of the Arkansas. These were discovered by the remnant of LaSalle's followers, who guided them to the fort on the Illinois, where they reported that LaSalle was in Mexico. The little band left at Fort St. Louis were finally destroyed by the Indians, and the murderers of LaSalle were shot. Thus ends the sad chapter of Robert Cavalier de LaSalle's exploration.

FRENCH OCCUPATION.

FIRST SETTLEMENTS.

The first mission in Illinois, as we have already seen, was commenced by Marquette in April, 1675. He called the religious society which he established the "Mission of the Immaculate Conception," and the town Kaskaskia. The first military occupation of the country was at Fort Crevecœur, erected in 1680; but there is no evidence that a settlement was commenced there, or at Peoria, on the lake above, at that early date. The first settlement of which there is any authentic account was commenced with the building of Fort St. Louis on the Illinois river in 1682; but this was soon abandoned. The oldest permanent settlement, not only in Illinois, but in the valley of the Mississippi, is at Kaskaskia, situated six miles above the mouth of the Kaskaskia river. This was settled in 1690 by the removal of the mission from old Kaskaskia, or Ft. St. Louis, on the Illinois river. Cahokia was settled about the same time. The reason for the removal of the old Kaskaskia settlement and mission, was probably because the dangerous and difficult route by Lake Michigan and the Chicago portage had been almost abandoned, and travelers and traders traveled down and up the Mississippi by the Fox and Wisconsin rivers. It was removed to the vicinity of the Mississippi in order to be in the line of travel from Canada to Louisiana, that is, the lower part of it, for it was all Louisiana then south of the lakes. Illinois came into possession of the French in 1682, and was a dependency of Canada and a part of Louisiana. During the period of French rule in Louisiana, the population probably never exceeded ten thousand. To the year 1730 the following five distinct settlements were made in the territory of Illinois, numbering, in population, 140 French families, about 600 "converted" Indians, and many traders; Cahokia, near the mouth of Cahokia creek and about five miles below the present city of St. Louis; St. Philip, about forty-five miles below Cahokia; Fort Chartres, twelve miles above Kaskaskia; Kaskaskia, situated on the Kaskaskia river six miles above its confluence with the Mississippi, and Prairie du Rocher, near Fort Chartres. Fort Chartres was built under the direction of the Mississippi Company in 1718, and was for a time the headquarters of the military commandants of the district of Illinois, and the most impregnable fortress in North America. It was also the center of wealth and fashion in the West. For about eighty years the French retained peaceable possession of Illinois. Their amiable disposition and tact of ingratiating themselves with the Indians enabled them to escape almost entirely the broils which weakened and destroyed other colonies. Whether exploring remote rivers or traversing hunting grounds in pursuit of game, in the social circle or as participants in the religious exercises of the church, the red men became their associates and were treated with the kindness and consideration of brothers. For more than a hundred years peace between the white man and the red was unbroken, and when at last this reign of harmony terminated it was not caused by the conciliatory Frenchman, but by the blunt and sturdy Anglo-Saxon. During this century, or until the country was occupied by the English, no regular court was ever held. When, in 1765, the country passed into the hands of the English, many of the French, rather than submit to a change in their institutions, preferred to leave their homes and seek a new abode. There are, however, at the present time a few remnants of the old French stock in the State, who still retain to a great extent the ancient habits and customs of their fathers.

THE MISSISSIPPI COMPANY.

During the earliest period of French occupation of this country, M. Tonti, LaSalle's attendant, was commander-in-chief of all the territory embraced between Canada and the Gulf of Mexico, and extending east and west of the Mississippi as far as his ambition or imagination pleased to allow. He spent twenty-one years in establishing forts and organizing the first settlements of Illinois. September 14, 1712, the French government granted a monopoly of all the trade and commerce of the country to M. Crozat, a wealthy merchant of Paris, who established a trading company in Illinois, and it was by this means that the early settlements became permanent and others established. Crozat surrendered his charter in 1717, and the Company of the West, better known as the Mississippi Company, was organized, to aid and assist the banking system of John Law, the most famous speculator of modern times, and perhaps at one time the wealthiest private individual the world has ever known; but his treasure was transitory. Under the Company of the West a branch was organized called the Company of St. Philip's, for the purpose of working the rich silver mines supposed to be in Illinois, and Philip Renault was appointed as its agent. In 1719 he sailed from France with two hundred miners, laborers and mechanics. During 1719 the Company of the West was by royal order united with the Royal Company of the Indies, and had the influence and support of the crown, who was deluded by the belief that immense wealth would flow into the empty treasury of France. This gigantic scheme, one of the most extensive and wonderful bubbles ever blown up to astonish, deceive and ruin thousands of people, was set in operation by the fertile brain of John Law. Law was born in Scotland in 1671, and so rapid had been his career that at the age of twenty-three he was a " bankrupt, an adulterer, a murderer and an exiled outlaw." But he possessed great financial ability, and by his agreeable and attractive manners, and his enthusiastic advocacy of his schemes, he succeeded in inflaming the imagination of the mercurial Frenchmen, whose greed for gain led them to adopt any plans for obtaining wealth.

Law arrived in Paris with two and a half millions of francs, which he had gained at the gambling table, just at the right time. Louis XIV. had just died and left as a legacy empty coffers and an immense public debt. Every thing and everybody was taxed to the last penny to pay even the interest. All the sources of industry were dried up; the very wind which wafted the barks of commerce seemed to have died away under the pressure of the time; trade stood still; the merchant, the trader, the artificer, once flourishing in affluence, were transformed into clamorous beggars. The life-blood that animated the kingdom was stagnated in all its arteries, and the danger of an awful crisis became such that the nation was on the verge of bankruptcy. At this critical juncture John Law arrived and proposed his grand scheme of the Mississippi Company; 200,000 shares of stock at 500 livres each were at first issued. This sold readily and great profits were realized. More stock was issued, speculation became rife, the fever seized everybody, and the wildest speculating frenzy pervaded the whole nation. Illinois was thought to contain vast and rich mines of minerals. Kaskaskia, then scarcely more than the settlement of a few savages, was spoken of as an emporium of the most extensive traffic, and as rivaling some of the cities of Europe in refinement, fashion and religious culture. Law was in the zenith of his glory, and the people in the zenith of their infatuation. The high and the low, the rich and the poor, were at once filled with visions of untold wealth, and every age, set, rank and condition were buying and selling stocks. Law issued stock again and again, and readily sold until 2,235,000,000 livres were in circulation, equaling about $450,000,000. While confidence lasted an impetus was given to trade never before known. An illusory policy everywhere prevailed, and so dazzled the eye that none could see in the horizon the dark cloud announcing the approaching storm. Law at the time was the most influential man in Europe. His house was beset from morning till night with eager applicants for stock. Dukes, marquises and counts, with their wives and daughters, waited for hours in the street below his door. Finding his residence too small, he changed it for the Place Vendome, whither the crowd followed him, and the spacious square had the appearance of a public market. The boulevards and public gardens were forsaken, and the Place Vendome became the most fashionable place in Paris; and he was unable to wait upon even one-tenth part of his applicants. The bubble burst after a few years, scattering ruin and distress in every direction. Law, a short time previous the most popular man in Europe, fled to Brussels, and in 1729 died in Venice, in obscurity and poverty.

ENGLISH RULE.

As early as 1750 there could be perceived the first throes of the revolution, which gave a new master and new institutions to Illinois. France claimed the whole valley of the Mississippi, and England the right to extend her possessions westward as far as she might desire. Through colonial controversies the two mother countries were precipitated into a bloody war within the North-western Territory, George Washington firing the first gun of the military struggle which resulted in the overthrow of the French not only in Illinois but in North America. The French evinced a determination to retain control of the territory bordering the Ohio and Mississippi from Canada to the Gulf, and so long as the English colonies were confined to the sea-coast there was little reason for controversy. As the English, however, became acquainted with this beautiful and fertile portion of our country, they not only learned the value of the vast territory, but also resolved to set up a counter claim to the soil. The French established numerous military and trading posts from the frontiers of Canada to New Orleans, and in order to establish also their claims to jurisdiction over the country they carved the lilies of France on the forest trees, or sunk plates of metal in the ground. These measures did not, however, deter the English from going on with their explorations; and though neither party resorted to arms, yet the conflict was gathering, and it was only a question of time when the storm should burst upon the frontier settlement. The French based their claims upon discoveries, the English on grants of territory extending from ocean to ocean, but neither party paid the least attention to the prior claims of the Indians. From this position of affairs, it was evident that actual collision between the contending parties would not much longer be deferred. The English Government, in anticipation of a war, urged the Governor of Virginia to lose no time in building two forts, which were equipped by arms from England. The French anticipated the English and gathered a considerable force to defend their possessions. The Governor determined to send a messenger to the nearest French post and demand an explanation. This resolution of the Governor brought into the history of our country for the first time the man of all others whom America most loves to honor, namely, George Washington. He was chosen, although not yet twenty-one years of age, as the one to perform this delicate and difficult mission. With five companions he set out on Nov. 10, 1753, and after a perilous journey returned Jan. 6, 1754. The struggle commenced and continued long, and was bloody and fierce; but on the 10th of October, 1765, the ensign of France was replaced on the ramparts of Fort Chartres by the flag of Great Britain. This fort was the

GEN. GEORGE ROGERS CLARK.

depot of supplies and the place of rendezvous for the united forces of the French. At this time the colonies of the Atlantic seaboard were assembled in preliminary congress at New York, dreaming of liberty and independence for the continent; and Washington, who led the expedition against the French for the English king, in less than ten years was commanding the forces opposed to the English tyrant. Illinois, besides being constructively a part of Florida for over one hundred years, during which time no Spaniard set foot upon her soil or rested his eyes upon her beautiful plains, for nearly ninety years had been in the actual occupation of the French, their puny settlements slumbering quietly in colonial dependence on the distant waters of the Kaskaskia, Illinois and Wabash.

GEN. CLARK'S EXPLOITS.

The Northwest Territory was now entirely under English rule, and on the breaking out of the Revolutionary war the British held every post of importance in the West. While the colonists of the East were maintaining a fierce struggle with the armies of England, their western frontiers were ravaged by merciless butcheries of Indian warfare. The jealousy of the savage was aroused to action by the rapid extension of American settlement westward and the improper influence exerted by a number of military posts garrisoned by British troops. To prevent indiscriminate slaughters arising from these causes, Illinois became the theater of some of the most daring exploits connected with American history. The hero of the achievements by which this beautiful land was snatched as a gem from the British Crown, was George Rogers Clark, of Virginia. He had closely watched the movements of the British throughout the Northwest, and understood their whole plan; he also knew the Indians were not unanimously in accord with the English, and therefore was convinced that if the British could be defeated and expelled from the Northwest, the natives might be easily awed into neutrality. Having convinced himself that the enterprise against the Illinois settlement might easily succeed, he repaired to the capital of Virginia, arriving Nov. 5, 1777. While he was on his way, fortunately, Burgoyne was defeated (Oct. 17), and the spirits of the colonists were thereby greatly encouraged. Patrick Henry was Governor of Virginia, and at once entered heartily into Clark's plans. After satisfying the Virginia leaders of the feasibility of his project, he received two sets of instructions,—one secret, the other open. The latter authorized him to enlist seven companies to go to Kentucky, and serve three months after their arrival in the West. The secret order authorized him to arm these troops, to procure his powder and lead of General Hand at Pittsburg, and to proceed at once to subjugate the country.

HE TAKES KASKASKIA.

With these instructions Col. Clark repaired to Pittsburg, choosing rather to raise his men west of the mountains, as he well knew all were needed in the colonies in the conflict there. He sent Col. W. B. Smith to Holstein and Captains Helm and Bowman to other localities to enlist men; but none of them succeeded in raising the required number. The settlers in these parts were afraid to leave their own firesides exposed to a vigilant foe, and but few could be induced to join the expedition. With these companies and several private volunteers Clark commenced his descent of the Ohio, which he navigated as far as the falls, where he took possession of and fortified Corn Island, a small island between the present cities of Louisville, Ky., and New Albany, Ind. Here, after having completed his arrangements and announced to the men their real destination, he left a small garrison; and on the 24th of June, during a total eclipse of the sun, which to them augured no good, they floated down the river. His plan was to go by water as far as Fort Massac, and thence march direct to Kaskaskia. Here he intended to surprise the garrison, and after its capture go to Cahokia, then to Vincennes, and lastly to Detroit. Should he fail, he intended to march directly to the Mississippi river and cross it into the Spanish country. Before his start he received good items of information: one that an alliance had been formed between France and the United States, and the other that the Indians throughout the Illinois country and the inhabitants at the various frontier posts had been led by the British to believe that the " Long Knives," or Virginians, were the most fierce, bloodthirsty and cruel savages that ever scalped a foe. With this impression on their minds, Clark saw that proper management would cause them to submit at once from fear, if surprised, and then from gratitude would become friendly, if treated with unexpected lenity. The march to Kaskaskia was made through a hot July sun, they arriving on the evening of the 4th of July, 1778. They captured the fort near the village and soon after the village itself, by surprise, and without the loss of

a single man and without killing any of the enemy. After sufficiently working on the fears of the natives, Clark told them they
were at perfect liberty to worship as they pleased, and to take
whichever side of the great conflict they would; also he would protect them against any barbarity from British or Indian foe. This
had the desired effect; and the inhabitants, so unexpectedly and so
gratefully surprised by the unlooked-for turn of affairs, at once
swore allegiance to the American arms; and when Clark desired
to go to Cahokia on the 6th of July, they accompanied him, and
through their influence the inhabitants of the place surrendered
and gladly placed themselves under his protection.

In the person of M. Gibault, priest of Kaskaskia, Clark found a
powerful ally and generous friend. Clark saw that, to retain possession of the Northwest and treat successfully with the Indians, he
must establish a government for the colonies he had taken. St. Vincent, the post next in importance to Detroit, remained yet to be
taken before the Mississippi valley was conquered. M. Gibault
told him that he would alone, by persuasion, lead Vincennes to
throw off its connection with England. Clark gladly accepted this
offer, and July 14th, in company with a fellow-townsman, Gibault
started on his mission of peace. On the 1st of August he returned
with the cheerful intelligence that everything was peaceably adjusted at Vincennes in favor of the Americans. During the interval, Col. Clark established his courts, placed garrisons at Kaskaskia
and Cahokia, successfully re-enlisted his men, and sent word to
have a fort (which proved the germ of Louisville) erected at the
falls of the Ohio.

While the American commander was thus negotiating with the
Indians, Hamilton, the British Governor of Detroit, heard of Clark's
invasion, and was greatly incensed because the country which he
had in charge should be wrested from him by a few ragged militia.
He therefore hurriedly collected a force, marched by way of the
Wabash, and appeared before the fort at Vincennes. The inhabitants made an effort to defend the town, and when Hamilton's
forces arrived, Captain Helm and a man named Henry were the
only Americans in the fort. These men had been sent by Clark.
The latter charged a cannon and placed it in the open gateway, and
the Captain stood by it with a lighted match and cried out, as Hamilton came in hailing distance, "Halt!" The British officer, not

knowing the strength of the garrison, stopped, and demanded the surrender of the fort. Helm exclaimed, " No man shall enter here till I know the terms." Hamilton responded, " You shall have the honors of war." The entire garrison consisted of one officer and one private.

VINCENNES CAPTURED.

On taking Kaskaskia, Clark made a prisoner of Rocheblave, commander of the place, and got possession of all his written instructions for the conduct of the war. From these papers he received important information respecting the plans of Col. Hamilton, Governor at Detroit, who was intending to make a vigorous and concerted attack upon the frontier. After arriving at Vincennes, however, he gave up his intended campaign for the winter, and trusting to his distance from danger and to the difficulty of approaching him, sent off his Indian warriors to prevent troops from coming down the Ohio, and to annoy the Americans in all ways. Thus he sat quietly down to pass the winter with only about eighty soldiers, but secure, as he thought, from molestation. But he evidently did not realize the character of the men with whom he was contending. Clark, although he could muster only one hundred and thirty men, determined to take advantage of Hamilton's weakness and security, and attack him as the only means of saving himself; for unless he captured Hamilton, Hamilton would capture him. Accordingly, about the beginning of February, 1779, he dispatched a small galley which he had fitted out, mounted with two four-pounders and four swivels and manned with a company of soldiers, and carrying stores for his men, with orders to force her way up the Wabash, to take her station a few miles below Vincennes, and to allow no person to pass her. He himself marched with his little band, and spent sixteen days in traversing the country from Kaskaskia to Vincennes, passing with incredible fatigue through woods and marshes. He was five days in crossing the bottom lands of the Wabash; and for five miles was frequently up to the breast in water. After overcoming difficulties which had been thought insurmountable, he appeared before the place and completely surprised it. The inhabitants readily submitted, but Hamilton at first defended himself in the fort. Next day, however, he surrendered himself and his garrison prisoners-of-war. By his activity in encouraging the hostilities of the Indians and by the revolting enormities perpetrated by those savages, Hamilton had rendered himself so obnoxious that he was thrown in prison and put in irons. During his command of the British frontier posts he offered prizes to the Indians for all the scalps of the Americans they would bring him, and earned in consequence thereof the title, "Hair-Buyer General," by which he was ever afterward known.

The services of Clark proved of essential advantage to his countrymen. They disconcerted the plans of Hamilton, and not only saved the western frontier from depredations by the savages, but also greatly cooled the ardor of the Indians for carrying on a contest in which they were not likely to be the gainers. Had it not been for this small army, a union of all the tribes from Maine to Georgia against the colonies might have been effected, and the whole current of our history changed.

ILLINOIS.

COUNTY OF ILLINOIS.

In October, 1778, after the successful campaign of Col. Clark, the assembly of Virginia erected the conquered country, embracing all the territory northwest of the Ohio river, into the County of Illinois, which was doubtless the largest county in the world, exceeding in its dimensions the whole of Great Britian and Ireland. To speak more definitely, it contained the territory now embraced in the great States of Ohio, Indiana, Illinois, Wisconsin and Michigan. On the 12th of December, 1778, John Todd was appointed Lieutenant-Commandant of this county by Patrick Henry, then Governor of Virginia, and accordingly, also, the first of Illinois County.

NORTHWESTERN TERRITORY.

Illinois continued to form a part of Virginia until March 1, 1784, when that State ceded all the territory north of the Ohio to the United States. Immediately the general Government proceeded to establish a form of government for the settlers in the territories thus ceded. This form continued until the passage of the ordinance of 1787, for the government of the Northwestern Territory. No man can study the secret history of this ordinance and not feel that Providence was guiding with sleepless eye the destinies of these unborn States. American legislation has never achieved anything more admirable, as an internal government, than this comprehensive ordinance. Its provisions concerning the distribution of property, the principles of civil and religious liberty which it laid at the foundation of the communities since established, and the efficient and simple organization by which it created the first machinery of civil society, are worthy of all the praise that has ever been given them.

ORDINANCE OF 1787.

This ordinance has a marvelous and interesting history. Considerable controversy has been indulged in as to who is entitled to the credit for framing it. This belongs, undoubtedly, to Nathan Dane; and to Rufus King and Timothy Pickering belong the credit for suggesting the proviso contained in it against slavery, and also for aids to religion and knowledge, and for assuring forever the common use, without charge, of the great national highways of the Mississippi, the St. Lawrence and their tributaries to all the citizens of the United States. To Thomas Jefferson is also due much credit, as some features of this ordinance were embraced in his ordinance of 1784. But the part taken by each in the long, laborious and eventful struggle which had so glorious a consummation in the ordinance, consecrating forever, by one imprescriptible and unchangeable monument, the very heart of our country to Freedom, Knowledge, and Union, will forever honor the names of those illustrious statesmen.

Mr. Jefferson had vainly tried to secure a system of government for the Northwestern Territory. He was an emancipationist and favored the exclusion of slavery from the territory, but the South voted him down every time he proposed a measure of this nature. In 1787, as late as July 10, an organizing act without the anti-slavery clause was pending. This concession to the South was expected to carry it. Congress was in session in New York. On July 5, Rev. Manasseh Cutler, of Massachusetts, came into New York to lobby on the Northwestern Territory. Everything seemed to fall into his hands. Events were ripe. The state of the public credit, the growing of Southern prejudice, the basis of his mission, his personal character, all combined to complete one of those sudden and marvelous revolutions of public sentiment that once in five or ten centuries are seen to sweep over a country like the breath of the Almighty.

Cutler was a graduate of Yale. He had studied and taken degrees in the three learned professions, medicine, law, and divinity. He had published a scientific examination of the plants of New England. As a scientist in America his name stood second only to that of Franklin He was a courtly gentleman of the old style, a man of commanding presence and of inviting face. The Southern members said they had never seen such a gentleman in the North. He came representing a Massachusetts company that desired to purchase a tract of land, now included in Ohio, for the purpose of planting a colony. It was a speculation. Government money was worth eighteen cents on the dollar. This company had collected enough to purchase 1,500,000 acres of land. Other speculators in New York made Dr. Cutler their agent, which enabled him to represent a demand for 5,500,000 acres. As this would reduce the national debt, and Jefferson's policy was to provide for the public credit, it presented a good opportunity to do something.

Massachusetts then owned the territory of Maine, which she was crowding on the market. She was opposed to opening the North-western region. This fired the zeal of Virginia. The South caught the inspiration, and all exalted Dr. Cutler. The entire South rallied around him. Massachusetts could not vote against him, because many of the constituents of her members were interested personally in the Western speculation. Thus Cutler, making friends in the South, and doubtless using all the arts of the lobby, was enabled to command the situation. True to deeper convictions, he dictated one of the most compact and finished documents of wise statesmanship that has ever adorned any human law book. He borrowed from Jefferson the term "Articles of Compact," which, preceding the federal constitution, rose into the most sacred character. He then followed very closely the constitution of Massachusetts, adopted three years before. Its most prominent points were:

1. The exclusion of slavery from the territory forever.

2. Provision for public schools, giving one township for a seminary and every section numbered 16 in each township; that is, one thirty-sixth of all the land for public schools.

3. A provision prohibiting the adoption of any constitution or

the enactment of any law that should nullify pre-existing contracts.

Be it forever remembered that this compact declared that "religion, morality, and knowledge being necessary to good government and the happiness of mankind, schools and the means of education shall always be encouraged." Dr. Cutler planted himself on this platform and would not yield. Giving his unqualified declaration that it was that or nothing,—that unless they could make the land desirable they did not want it,—he took his horse and buggy and started for the constitutional convention at Philadelphia. On July 13, 1787, the bill was put upon its passage, and was unanimously adopted. Thus the great States of Ohio, Indiana, Illinois, Michigan, and Wisconsin, a vast empire, were consecrated to freedom, intelligence, and morality. Thus the great heart of the nation was prepared to save the union of States, for it was this act that was the salvation of the republic and the destruction of slavery. Soon the South saw their great blunder and tried to have the compact repealed. In 1803 Congress referred it to a committee, of which John Randolph was chairman. He reported that this ordinance was a compact and opposed repeal. Thus it stood, a rock in the way of the on-rushing sea of slavery.

SYMPATHY WITH SLAVERY.

With all this timely aid it was, however, a most desperate and protracted struggle to keep the soil of Illinois sacred to freedom. It was the natural battle-field for the irrepressible conflict. In the southern end of the State slavery preceded the compact. It existed among the old French settlers, and was hard to eradicate. That portion was also settled from the slave States, and this population brought their laws, customs, and institutions with them. A stream of population from the North poured into the northern part of the State. These sections misunderstood and hated each other perfectly. The Southerners regarded the Yankees as a skinning, tricky, penurious race of peddlers, filling the country with tinware, brass clocks, and wooden nutmegs. The Northerner thought of the Southerner as a lean, lank, lazy creature, burrowing in a hut, and rioting in whisky, dirt, and ignorance. These causes aided in making the struggle long and bitter. So strong was the sympathy with slavery that, in spite of the ordinance of 1787, and in spite of the deed of cession, it was determined to allow the old French settlers to retain their slaves. Planters from the slave States might

GEN. ARTHUR ST. CLAIR.

bring their slaves if they would give them an opportunity to choose freedom or years of service and bondage for their children till they should become thirty years of age. If they chose freedom they must leave the State within sixty days, or be sold as fugitives. Servants were whipped for offenses for which white men were fined. Each lash paid forty cents of the fine. A negro ten miles from home without a pass was whipped. These famous laws were imported from the slave States, just as the laws for the inspection of flax and wool were imported when there was neither in the State.

ST. CLAIR, GOVERNOR OF NORTHWESTERN TERRITORY.

On October 5, 1787, Maj. Gen. Arthur St. Clair was, by Congress, elected Governor of this vast territory. St. Clair was born in Scotland and emigrated to America in 1755. He served in the French and English war, and was major general in the Revolution. In 1786 he was elected to Congress and chosen President of that body.

ILLINOIS TERRITORY.

After the division of the Northwestern Territory Illinois became one of the counties of the Territory of Indiana, from which it was separated by an act of Congress Feb. 3, 1809, forming the Territory of Illinois, with a population estimated at 9,000, and then included the present State of Wisconsin. It was divided, at the time, into two counties,—St. Clair and Randolph. John Boyle, of Kentucky, was appointed Governor, by the President, James Madison, but declining, Ninian Edwards, of the same State, was then appointed and served with distinction; and after the organization of Illinois as a State he served in the same capacity, being its third Governor.

WAR OF 1812. THE OUTBREAK.

For some years previous to the war between the United States and England in 1812, considerable trouble was experienced with the Indians. Marauding bands of savages would attack small settlements and inhumanly butcher all the inhabitants, and mutilate their dead bodies. To protect themselves, the settlers organized companies of rangers, and erected block houses and stockades in every settlement. The largest, strongest and best one of these was Fort Russell, near the present village of Edwardsville. This stockade was made the main rendezvous for troops and military stores, and Gov. Edwards, who during the perilous times of 1812, when Indian hostilities threatened on every hand, assumed command of the Illinois forces, established his headquarters at this place. The Indians were incited to many of these depredations by English emissaries, who for years continued their dastardly work of "setting the red men, like dogs, upon the whites."

In the summer of 1811 a peace convention was held with the Pottawatomies at Peoria, when they promised that peace should prevail; but their promises were soon broken. Tecumseh, the great warrior, and fit successor of Pontiac, started in the spring of 1811, to arouse the Southern Indians to war against the whites. The purpose of this chieftain was well known to Gov. Harrison, of Indiana Territory, who determined during Tecumseh's absence to strike and disperse the hostile forces collected at Tippecanoe. This he successfully did on Nov. 7, winning the sobriquet of "Tippecanoe," by which he was afterwards commonly known. Several peace councils were held, at which the Indians promised good behavior, but only to deceive the whites. Almost all the savages of the Northwest were thoroughly stirred up and did not desire peace. The British agents at various points, in anticipation of a war with the United States, sought to enlist the favor of the savages by distributing to them large supplies of arms, ammunition and other goods.

The English continued their insults to our flag upon the high seas, and their government refusing to relinquish its offensive course, all hopes of peace and safe commercial relations were abandoned, and Congress, on the 19th of June, 1812, formally declared war against Great Britain. In Illinois the threatened Indian troubles had already caused a more thorough organization of the militia and greater protection by the erection of forts. As intimated, the Indians took the war-path long before the declaration of hostilities between the two civilized nations, committing great depredations, the most atrocious of which was the

MASSACRE AT FORT DEARBORN.

During the war of 1812 between the United States and England, the greatest, as well as the most revolting, massacre of whites that ever occurred in Illinois, was perpetrated by the Pottawatomie Indians, at Fort Dearborn. This fort was built by the Government, in 1804, on the south side of the Chicago river, and was garrisoned by 54 men under command of Capt. Nathan Heald, assisted by Lieutenant Helm and Ensign Ronan; Dr. Voorhees, surgeon. The residents at the post at that time were the wives of officers Heald and Helm and a few of the soldiers, Mr. Kinzie and his family, and a few Canadians. The soldiers and Mr. Kinzie were on the most friendly terms with the Pottawatomies and Winnebagoes, the principal tribes around them.

On the 7th of August, 1812, arrived the order from Gen. Hull, at Detroit, to evacuate Fort Dearborn, and distribute all United States property to the Indians. Chicago was so deep in the wilderness

OLD FORT DEARBORN.

that this was the first intimation the garrison received of the declaration of war made on the 19th of June. The Indian chief who brought the dispatch advised Capt. Heald not to evacuate, and that if he should decide to do so, it be done immediately, and by forced marches elude the concentration of the savages before the news could be circulated among them. To this most excellent advice the Captain gave no heed, but on the 12th held a council with the Indians, apprising them of the orders received, and offering a liberal reward for an escort of Pottawatomies to Fort Wayne. The Indians, with many professions of friendship, assented to all he proposed, and promised all he required. The remaining officers refused to join in the council, for they had been informed that treachery was designed,—that the Indians intended to murder those in the council, and then destroy those in the fort. The port holes were open, displaying cannons pointing directly upon the council. This action, it is supposed, prevented a massacre at that time.

Mr. Kinzie, who knew the Indians well, begged Capt. Heald not to confide in their promises, or distribute the arms and ammunitions among them, for it would only put power in their hands to destroy the whites. This argument, true and excellent in itself, was now certainly inopportune, and would only incense the treacherous foe. But the Captain resolved to follow it, and accordingly on the night of the 13th, after the distribution of the other property, the arms were broken, and the barrels of whisky, of which there was a large quantity, were rolled quietly through the sally-port, their heads knocked in and their contents emptied into the river. On that night the lurking red-skins crept near the fort and discovered the destruction of the promised booty going on within. The next morning the powder was seen floating on the surface of the river, and the Indians asserted that such an abundance of "fire-water" had been emptied into the river as to make it taste "groggy." Many of them drank of it freely.

On the 14th the desponding garrison was somewhat cheered by the arrival of Capt. Wells, with 15 friendly Miamis. Capt. Wells heard at Fort Wayne of the order to evacuate Fort Dearborn, and knowing the hostile intentions of the Indians, made a rapid march through the wilderness to protect, if possible, his niece, Mrs. Heald, and the officers and the garrison from certain destruction. But he came too late. Every means for its defense had been destroyed the night before, and arrangements were made for leaving the fort on the following morning.

The fatal morning of the 16th at length dawned brightly on the world. The sun shone in unclouded splendor upon the glassy waters of Lake Michigan. At 9 A. M., the party moved out of the southern gate of the fort, in military array. The band, feeling the solemnity of the occasion, struck up the Dead March in Saul. Capt.

Wells, with his face blackened after the manner of the Indians, led the advance guard at the head of his friendly Miamis, the garrison with loaded arms, the baggage wagons with the sick, and the women and children following, while the Pottawatomie Indians, about 500 in number, who had pledged their honor to escort the whites in safety to Fort Wayne, brought up the rear. The party took the road along the lake shore. On reaching the range of sand-hills separating the beach from the prairie, about one mile and a half-from the fort, the Indians defiled to the right into the prairie, bring ing the sand-hills between them and the whites. This divergence was scarcely effected when Capt. Wells, who had kept in advance with his Indians, rode furiously back and exclaimed, "They are about to attack us. Form instantly and charge upon them!" These words were scarcely uttered before a volley of balls from Indian muskets was poured in upon them. The troops were hastily formed into line, and charged up the bank. One veteran of 70 fell as they ascended. The Indians were driven back to the prairie, and then the battle was waged by 54 soldiers, 12 civilians, and three or four women—the cowardly Miamis having fled at the outset—against 500 Indian warriors. The whites behaved gallantly, and sold their lives dearly. They fought desperately until two-thirds of their number were slain; the remaining 27 surrendered. And now the most sickening and heart-rending butchery of this calamitous day was committed by a young savage, who assailed one of the baggage wagons containing 12 children, every one of which fell beneath his murderous tomahawk. When Capt. Wells, who with the others had become prisoner, beheld this scene at a distance, he exclaimed in a tone loud enough to be heard by the savages, " If this be your game, I can kill too;" and turning his horse, started for the place where the Indians had left their squaws and children. The Indians hotly pursued, but he avoided their deadly bullets for a time. Soon his horse was killed and he severely wounded. With a yell the young braves rushed to make him their prisoner and reserve him for torture. But an enraged warrior stabbed him in the back, and he fell dead. His heart was afterwards taken out, cut in pieces and distributed among the tribes. Billy Caldwell, a half-breed Wyandot, well-known in Chicago long afterward, buried his remains the next day. Wells street in Chicago, perpetuates his memory.

In this fearful combat women bore a conspicuous part. A wife of one of the soldiers, who had frequently heard that the Indians subjected their prisoners to tortures worse than death, resolved not to be taken alive, and continued fighting until she was literally cut to pieces. Mrs. Heald was an excellent equestrian, and an expert in the use of the rifle. She fought bravely, receiving several wounds. Though faint from loss of blood, she managed to keep in her saddle. A savage raised his tomahawk to kill her, when she looked him full in the face, and with a sweet smile and gentle voice said, in his own language, " Surely you will not kill a squaw." The arm of of the savage fell, and the life of this heroic woman was saved. Mrs. Helm had an encounter with a stalwart Indian, who attempted to tomahawk her. Springing to one side, she received the glancing blow on her shoulder, and at the same time she seized the savage round the neck and endeavored to get his scalping-knife which hung in a sheath at his breast. While she was thus struggling, she was dragged from his grasp by another and an older Indian. The latter bore her, struggling and resisting, to the lake and plunged her in. She soon perceived it was not his intention to drown her, because he held her in such a position as to keep her head out of the water. She recognized him to be a celebrated chief called Black Partridge. When the firing ceased she was conducted up the sand-bank.

SLAUGHTER OF PRISONERS.

The prisoners were taken back to the Indian camp, when a new scene of horror was enacted. The wounded not being included in the terms of the surrender, as it was interpreted by the Indians, and the British general, Proctor, having offered a liberal bounty for American scalps, nearly all the wounded were killed and scalped, and the price of the trophies was afterwards paid by the British general. In the stipulation of surrender, Capt. Heald had not particularly mentioned the wounded. These helpless sufferers, on reaching the Indian camp, were therefore regarded by the brutal savages as fit subjects upon which to display their cruelty and satisfy their desire for blood. Referring to the terrible butchery of the prisoners, in an account given by Mrs. Helm, she says: "An old squaw, infuriated by the loss of friends or excited by the sanguinary scenes around her, seemed possessed of demoniac fury. She seized a stable-fork and assaulted one miserable victim, who lay groaning and writhing in the agonies of his wounds, aggravated by the scorching beams of the sun. With a delicacy of feeling, scarcely to have been expected under such circumstances, Wan-bee-nee-wan stretched a mat across two poles, between me and this dreadful scene. I was thus spared, in some degree, a view of its horrors, although I could not entirely close my ears to the cries of the sufferer. The following night five more of the wounded prisoners were tomahawked."

KINZIE FAMILY SAVED.

That evening, about sundown, a council of chiefs was held to decide the fate of the prisoners, and it was agreed to deliver them

. OLD KINZIE HOUSE.

to the British commander at Detroit. After dark, many warriors from a distance came into camp, who were thirsting for blood, and were determined to murder the prisoners regardless of the terms of surrender. Black Partridge, with a few of his friends, surrounded Kinzie's house to protect the inmates from the tomahawks of the bloodthirsty savages. Soon a band of hostile warriors rushed by them into the house, and stood with tomahawks and scalping-knives, awaiting the signal from their chief to commence the work of death.

Black Partridge said to Mrs. Kinzie: "We are doing everything in our power to save you, but all is now lost; you and your friends, together with all the prisoners of the camp, will now be slain." At that moment a canoe was heard approaching the shore, when Black Partridge ran down to the river, trying in the darkness to make out the new comers, and at the same time shouted, ".Who are you?" In the bow of the approaching canoe stood a tall, manly personage, with a rifle in his hand. He jumped ashore exclaiming, "I am Sau-ga-nash." "Then make all speed to the house; our friends are in danger, and you only can save them." It was Billy Caldwell, the half-breed Wyandot. He hurried forward, entered the house with a resolute step, deliberately removed his accouterments, placed his rifle behind the door, and saluted the Indians: "How now, my friends! a good day to you. I was told there were enemies here, but am glad to find only friends." Diverted by the coolness of his manner, they were ashamed to avow their murderous purpose, and simply asked for some cotton goods to wrap their dead, for burial. And thus, by his presence of mind, Caldwell averted the murder of the Kinzie family and the prisoners. The latter, with their wives and children, were dispersed among the Pottawatomie tribes along the Illinois, Rock and Wabash rivers, and some to Milwaukee. The most of them were ransomed at Detroit the following spring. A part of them, however, remained in captivity another year.

EXPEDITION AGAINST THE INDIANS.

By the middle of August, through the disgraceful surrender of Gen. Hull, at Detroit, and the evacuation of Fort Dearborn and massacre of its garrison, the British and Indians were in possession of the whole Northwest. The savages, emboldened by their successes, penetrated deeper into the settlements, committing great depredations. The activity and success of the enemy aroused the people to a realization of the great danger their homes and families were in. Gov. Edwards collected a force of 350 men at Camp Russell, and Capt. Russell came from Vincennes with about 50 more. Being officered and equipped, they proceeded about the middle of October on horseback, carrying with them 20 days' rations, to Peoria. Capt. Craig was sent with two boats up the Illinois, with provisions and tools to build a fort. The little army proceeded to Peoria Lake, where was located a Pottawatomie village. They arrived late at night, within a few miles of the village, without their presence being known to the Indians. Four men were sent out that night to reconnoiter the position of the village. The four brave men who volunteered for this perilous service were Thomas Carlin (afterward Governor), and Robert, Stephen and Davis Whiteside. They proceeded to the village, and explored it and the approaches to it thoroughly, without starting an Indian or provoking the bark of a dog. .The low lands between the Indian village and the troops were covered with a rank growth of tall grass, so high and dense as to readily conceal an Indian on horseback, until within a few feet of him. The ground had become still more yielding by recent rains, rendering it almost impassable by mounted men. To prevent detection, the soldiers had camped without lighting the usual campfires. The men lay down in their cold and cheerless camp, with many misgivings. They well remembered how the skulking savages fell upon Harrison's men at Tippecanoe during the night. To add to their fears, a gun in the hands of a soldier was carelessly discharged, raising great consternation in the camp.

AN INDIAN KILLED.

Through a dense fog which prevailed the following morning, the army took up its line of march for the Indian town, Capt. Judy with his corps of spies in advance. In the tall grass they came up with an Indian and his squaw, both mounted. The Indian wanted to surrender, but Judy observed that he "did not leave home to take prisoners," and instantly shot one of them. With the blood streaming from his mouth and nose, and in his agony "singing the death song," the dying Indian raised his gun, shot and mortally wounded a Mr. Wright, and in a few minutes expired. Many guns were immediately discharged at the other Indian, not then known to be a squaw, all of which missed her. Badly scared, and her husband killed by her side, the agonizing wails of the squaw were heart-rending. She was taken prisoner, and afterwards restored to her nation.

TOWN BURNED.

On nearing the town a general charge was made, the Indians fleeing to the interior wilderness. Some of their warriors made a stand, when a sharp engagement occurred, but the Indians were routed. In their flight they left behind all their winter's store of provisions, which was taken, and their town burned. Some Indian children were found who had been left in the hurried flight, also some disabled adults, one of whom was in a starving condition and with a voracious appetite partook of the bread given him. He is said to have been killed by a cowardly trooper straggling behind, after the main army had resumed its retrograde march, who wanted to be able to boast that he had killed an Indian.

About the time Gov. Edwards started with his little band against the Indians, Gen. Hopkins, with 2,000 Kentucky riflemen, left Vincennes to cross the prairies of Illinois and destroy the Indian villages along the Illinois river. Edwards, with his rangers, expected to act in concert with Gen. Hopkins' riflemen. After marching 80 or 90 miles into the enemy's country, Gen. Hopkins' men became dissatisfied, and on Oct. 20 the entire army turned and retreated homeward before even a foe had been met. After the victory of the Illinois rangers they heard nothing of Gen. Hopkins and his 2,000 mounted Kentucky riflemen; and apprehensive that a large force of warriors would be speedily collected, it was deemed prudent not to protract their stay, and accordingly the retrograde march was commenced the very day of the attack.

PEORIA BURNED.

The force of Capt. Craig, in charge of the provision boats, was not idle during this time. They proceeded to Peoria, where they were fired on by ten Indians during the night, who immediately fled. Capt. Craig discovered, at daylight, their tracks leading up into the French town. He inquired of the French their whereabouts, who denied all knowledge of them, and said they "had heard or seen nothing;" but he took the entire number prisoners, burned and destroyed Peoria, and bore the captured inhabitants away on his boats to a point below the present city of Alton, where he landed and left them in the woods,—men, women, and children,— in the inclement month of November, without shelter, and without food other than the slender stores they had themselves gathered up before their departure. They found their way to St. Louis in an almost starving condition. The burning of Peoria and taking its inhabitants prisoners, on the mere suspicion that they sympathized with the Indians, was generally regarded as a needless, if not wanton, act of military power.

PONTIAC, THE OTTAWA CHIEF.

SECOND EXPEDITION AGAINST THE INDIANS.

In the early part of 1813, the country was put in as good defense as the sparse population admitted. In spite of the precaution taken, numerous depredations and murders were committed by the Indians, which again aroused the whites, and another expedition was sent against the foe, who had collected in large numbers in and around Peoria. This army was composed of about 900 men, collected from both Illinois and Missouri, and under command of Gen. Howard. They marched across the broad prairies of Illinois to Peoria, where there was a small stockade in charge of United States troops. Two days previously the Indians made an attack on the fort, but were repulsed. Being in the enemy's country, knowing their stealthy habits, and the troops at no time observing a high degree of discipline, many unnecessary night alarms occurred, yet the enemy were far away. The army marched up the lake to Chilicothe, burning on its way two deserted villages. At the present site of Peoria the troops remained in camp several weeks. While there they built a fort, which they named in honor of Gen. George Rogers Clark, who with his brave Virginians wrested Illinois from the English during the Revolutionary struggle. This fort was destroyed by fire in 1818. It gave a name to Peoria which it wore for several years. After the building of Fort Crevecœur, in 1680, Peoria lake was very familiar to Western travel and history; but there is no authentic account of a permanent European settlement there until 1778, when Laville de Meillet, named after its founder, was started. Owing to the quality of the water and its greater salubrity, the location was changed to the present site of Peoria, and by 1796 the old had been entirely abandoned for the new village. After its destruction in 1812 it was not settled again until 1819, and then by American pioneers, though in 1813 Fort Clark was built there.

EXPEDITION UP THE MISSISSIPPI.

The second campaign against the Indians at Peoria closed without an engagement, or even a sight of the enemy, yet great was the benefit derived from it. It showed to the Indians the power and resources of his white foe. Still the calendar of the horrible deeds of butchery of the following year is long and bloody. A joint expedition again moved against the Indians in 1814, under Gov.

Clark of Missouri. This time they went up the Mississippi in barges, Prairie du Chien being the point of destination. There they found a small garrison of British troops, which, however, soon fled, as did the inhabitants, leaving Clark in full possession. He immediately set to work and erected Fort Shelby. The Governor returned to St. Louis, leaving his men in peaceable possession of the place, but a large force of British and Indians came down upon them, and the entire garrison surrendered. In the mean time Gen. Howard sent 108 men to strengthen the garrison. Of this number 66 were Illinois rangers, under Capts. Rector and Riggs, who occupied two boats. The remainder were with Lieut. Campbell.

A DESPERATE FIGHT.

At Rock Island Campbell was warned to turn back, as an attack was contemplated. The other boats passed on up the river and were some two miles ahead when Campbell's barge was struck by a strong gale which forced it against a small island near the Illinois shore. Thinking it best to lie to till the wind abated, sentinels were stationed while the men went ashore to cook breakfast. At this time a large number of Indians on the main shore under Black Hawk commenced an attack. The savages in canoes passed rapidly to the island, and with a war-whoop rushed upon the men, who retreated and sought refuge in the barge. A battle of brisk musketry now ensued between the few regulars aboard the stranded barge and the hordes of Indians under cover of trees on the island, with severe loss to the former. Meanwhile Capt. Rector and Riggs, ahead with their barges, seeing the smoke of battle, attempted to return; but in the strong gale Riggs' boat became unmanageable and was stranded on the rapids. Rector, to avoid a similar disaster, let go his anchor. The rangers, however, opened with good aim and telling effect upon the savages. The unequal combat having raged for some time and about closing, the commander's barge, with many wounded and several dead on board,—among the former of whom, very badly, was Campbell himself,—was discovered to be on fire. Now Rector and his brave Illinois rangers, comprehending the horrid situation, performed, without delay, as cool and heroic a deed—and did it well—as ever imperiled the life of mortal man. In the howling gale, in full view of hundreds of infuriated savages, and within range of their rifles, they deliberately raised anchor, lightened their barge by casting overboard quantities of provisions, and guided it with the utmost labor down the swift current, to the windward of the burning barge, and under the galling fire of the enemy rescued all the survivors, and removed the wounded and dying to their vessel. This was a deed of noble daring and as heroic as any performed during the war in the West. Rector hurried with his over-crowded vessel to St. Louis.

It was now feared that Riggs and his company were captured and sacrificed by the savages. His vessel, which was strong and well armed, was for a time surrounded by the Indians, but the whites on the inside were well sheltered. The wind becoming allayed in the evening, the boat, under cover of the night, glided safely down the river without the loss of a single man.

STILL ANOTHER EXPEDITION.

Notwithstanding the disastrous termination of the two expeditions already sent out, during the year 1814, still another was projected. It was under Maj. Zachary Taylor, afterward President. Rector and Whiteside, with the Illinoisan, were in command of boats. The expedition passed Rock Island unmolested, when it was learned the country was not only swarming with Indians, but that the English were there in command with a detachment of regulars and artillery. The advanced boats in command of Rector, Whiteside and Hempstead, turned about and began to descend the rapids, fighting with great gallantry the hordes of the enemy, who were pouring their fire into them from the shore at every step.

Near the mouth of Rock river Maj. Taylor anchored his fleet out in the Mississippi. During the night the English planted a battery of six pieces down at the water's edge, to sink or disable the boats, and filled the islands with red-skins to butcher the whites, who might, unarmed, seek refuge there. But in this scheme they were frustrated. In the morning Taylor ordered all the force, except 20 boatmen on each vessel, to the upper island to dislodge the enemy. The order was executed with great gallantry, the island scoured, many of the savages killed, and the rest driven to the lower island. In the meantime the British cannon told with effect upon the fleet. The men rushed back and the boats were dropped down the stream out of range of the cannon. Capt. Rector was now ordered with his company to make a sortie on the lower island, which he did, driving the Indians back among the willows; but they being re-in-forced, in turn hurled Rector back upon the sand-beach.

A council of officers called by Taylor had by this time decided that their force was too small to contend with the enemy, who outnumbered them three to one, and the boats were in full retreat down the river. As Rector attempted to get under way his boat grounded, and the savages, with demoniac yells, surrounded it, when a most desperate hand-to-hand conflict ensued. The gallant ranger, Samuel Whiteside, observing the imminent peril of his brave Illinois comrade, went immediately to his rescue, who but for his timely aid would undoubtedly have been overpowered, with all his force, and murdered.

Thus ended the last, like the two previous expeditions up the Mississippi during the war of 1812, in defeat and disaster. The enemy was in undisputed posession of all the country north of the Illinois river, and the prospects respecting those territories boded nothing but gloom. With the approach of winter, however, Indian depredations ceased to be committed, and the peace of Ghent, Dec. 24, 1814, closed the war.

ILLINOIS AS A STATE.

ORGANIZATION.

In January of 1818 the Territorial Legislature forwarded to Nathaniel Pope, delegate in Congress from Illinois, a petition pray-ing for admission into the national Union as a State. On April 18th of the same year Congress passed the enabling act, and Dec. 3, after the State government had been organized and Gov. Bond had signed the Constitution, Congress by a resolution declared Illi-nois to be "one of the United States of America, and admitted into the Union on an equal footing with the original States in all respects."

The ordinance of 1787 declared that there should be at least three States carved out of the Northwestern Territory. The boundaries of the three, Ohio, Indiana and Illinois, were fixed by this law. Congress reserved the power, however, of forming two other States out of the territory which lies north of an east and west line drawn through the southern boundary of Lake Michigan. It was generally conceded that this line would be the northern boundary of Illinois ;

but as this would give the State no coast on Lake Michigan; and rob her of the port of Chicago and the northern terminus of the Illinois & Michigan canal which was then contemplated, Judge Pope had the northern boundary moved fifty miles further north.

BOUNDARY CHANGED.

Not only is Illinois indebted to Nathaniel Pope for the port where now enter and depart more vessels during the year than in any other port in the world, for the northern terminus of the Illinois & Michigan canal, and for the lead mines at Galena, but the nation, the undivided Union, is largely indebted to him for its perpetuity. It was he,—his foresight, statesmanship and energy,—that bound our confederated Union with bands of iron that can never be broken. The geographical position of Illinois, with her hundreds of miles of water-courses, is such as to make her the key to the grand arch of Northern and Southern States. Extending from the great chain of lakes on the north, with snow and ice of the arctic region, to the cotton-fields of Tennessee ; peopled, as it is, by almost all races, classes and conditions of the human family ; guided by the various and diversified political, agricultural, religious and educational teachings common to both North and South,—Illinois can control, and has controlled, the destinies of our united and beloved republic. Pope seemingly foresaw that a struggle to dissolve the Union would be made. With a prophetic eye he looked down the stream of time for a half century and saw the great conflict between the South and North, caused by a determination to dissolve the confederation of States; and to preserve the Union, he gave to Illinois a lake coast.

Gov. Ford, in his History of Illinois, written in 1847, while speaking of this change of boundary and its influence upon our nation, says:

"What, then, was the duty of the national Government? Illinois was certain to be a great State, with any boundaries which that Government could give. Its great extent of territory, its unrivaled fertility of soil and capacity for sustaining a dense population, together with its commanding position, would in course of time give the new State a very controlling influence with her sister States situated upon the Western rivers, either in sustaining the federal Union as it is, or in dissolving it and establishing new governments. If left entirely upon the waters of these great rivers, it was plain that, in case of threatened disruption, the interest of the new State would be to join a Southern and Western confederacy; but if a large portion of it could be made dependent upon the commerce and navigation of the great northern lakes, connected as they are with the Eastern States, a rival interest would be created to check the wish for a Western and Southern confederacy.

"It therefore became the duty of the national Government not only to make Illinois strong, but to raise an interest inclining and binding her to the Eastern and Northern portions of the Union. This could be done only through an interest in the lakes. At that time the commerce on the lakes was small, but its increase was confidently expected, and, indeed, it has exceeded all anticipations, and is yet only in its infancy. To accomplish this object effectually, it was not only necessary to give to Illinois the port of Chicago and a route for the canal, but a considerable coast on Lake Michigan, with a country back of it sufficiently extensive to contain a population capable of exerting a decided influence upon the councils of the State.

"There would, therefore, be a large commerce of the north, western and central portion of the State afloat on the lakes, for it was then foreseen that the canal would be made; and this alone would be like turning one of the many mouths of the Mississippi into Lake Michigan at Chicago. A very large commerce of the center and south would be found both upon the lakes and rivers. Associations in business, in interest, and of friendship would be formed, both with the North and the South. A State thus situated, having such a decided interest in the commerce, and in the preservation of the whole confederacy, can never consent to disunion; for the Union cannot be dissolved without a division and disruption of the State itself. These views, urged by Judge Pope, obtained the unqualified assent of the statesmen of 1818.

"These facts and views are worthy to be recorded in history as a standing and perpetual call upon Illinoisans of every age to remember the great trust which has been reposed in them, as the peculiar champions and guardians of the Union by the great men and patriot sages who adorned and governed this country in the earlier and better days of the Republic."

During the dark and trying days of the Rebellion, well did she remember this sacred trust, to protect which two hundred thousand of her sons went to the bloody field of battle, crowning their arms with the laurels of war, and keeping inviolate the solemn obligations bequeathed to them by their fathers.

FIRST CONSTITUTION.

In July and August of 1818 a convention was held at Kaskaskia for the purpose of drafting a constitution. This constitution was not submitted to a vote of the people for their approval or rejection, it being well known that they would approve it. It was about the first organic law of any State in the Union to abolish imprisonment for debt. The first election under the constitution was held on the third Thursday and the two succeeding days in September, 1818. Shadrach Bond was elected Governor, and Pierre Menard Lieutenant Governor. Their term of office extended four years. At this time the State was divided into fifteen counties, the population being about 40,000. Of this number by far the larger portion were from the Southern States. The salary of the Governor was $1,000, while that of the Treasurer was $500. The Legislature re-enacted, verbatim, the Territorial Code, the penalties of which were unnecessarily severe. Whipping, stocks and pillory were used for minor offenses, and for arson, rape, horse-stealing, etc., death by hanging was the penalty. These laws, however, were modified in 1821.

The Legislature first convened at Kaskaskia, the ancient seat of empire for more than one hundred and fifty years, both for the French and Americans. Provisions were made, however, for the removal of the seat of government by this Legislature. A place in the wilderness on the Kaskaskia river was selected and named Vandalia. From Vandalia it was removed to Springfield in the year 1837.

DERIVATION OF THE NAME ILLINOIS.

The name of this beautiful "Prairie State" is derived from *Illini*, an Indian word signifying superior men. It has a French termination, and is a symbol of the manner in which the two races, the French and Indians, were intermixed during the early history of the country. The appellation was no doubt well applied to the primitive inhabitants of the soil, whose prowess in savage warfare long withstood the combined attacks of the fierce Iroquois on the one side, and the no less savage and relentless Sacs and Foxes on the other. The Illinois were once a powerful confederacy, occupying the most beautiful and fertile region in the great valley of the

Mississippi, which their enemies coveted and struggled long and hard to wrest from them. By the fortunes of war they were diminished in number and finally destroyed. "Starved Rock," on the Illinois river, according to tradition, commemorates their last tragedy, where, it is said, the entire tribe starved rather than surrender.

The low cognomen of "Sucker," as applied to Illinoisans, is said to have had its origin at the Galena lead mines. In an early day, when these extensive mines were being worked, men would run up the Mississippi river in steamboats in the spring, work the lead mines, and in the fall return, thus establishing, as was supposed, a similitude between their migratory habits and those of the fishy tribe called "Suckers." For this reason the Illinoisans have ever since been distinguished by the epithet "Suckers." Those who stayed at the mines over winter were mostly from Wisconsin, and were called "Badgers." One spring the Missourians poured into the mines in such numbers that the State was said to have taken a puke, and the offensive appellation of "Pukes" was afterward applied to all Missourians.

The southern part of the State, known as "Egypt," received this appellation because, being older, better settled and cultivated, grain was had in greater abundance than in the central and northern portion, and the immigrants of this region, after the manner of the children of Israel, went "thither to buy and to bring from thence that they might live and not die."

STATE BANK.

The Legislature, during the latter years of territorial existence, granted charters to several banks. The result was that paper money became very abundant, times flush, and credit unlimited; and everybody invested to the utmost limit of his credit, with confident expectation of realizing a handsome advance before the expiration of his credit, from the throng of immigrants then pouring into the country. By 1819 it became apparent that a day of reckoning would approach before their dreams of fortune could be realized. Banks everywhere began to waver, paper money became depreciated, and gold and silver driven out of the country. The Legislature sought to bolster up the times by incorporating the "Bank of Illinois," which, with several branches, was created by the session of 1821. This bank, being wholly supported by the credit of the State, was to issue one, two, three, five, ten and twenty-dollar notes. It was the duty of the bank to advance, upon personal property, money to the amount of $100, and a larger amount upon real estate. All taxes and public salaries could be paid in such bills; and if a creditor refused to take them, he had to wait three years longer before he could collect his debt. The people imagined that simply because the government had issued the notes, they would remain at par; and although this evidently could not be the case, they were yet so infatuated with their project as actually to request the United States government to receive them in payment for their public lands! Although there were not wanting men who, like John McLean, the Speaker of the House of Representatives, foresaw the dangers and evils likely to arise from the creation of such a bank, by far the greater part of the people were in favor of it. The new bank was therefore started. The new issue of bills by the bank of course only aggravated the evil, heretofore so grievously felt, of the absence of specie, so that the people were soon compelled to cut their bills in halves and quarters, in order to make small change in trade. Finally the paper currency so rapidly depreciated that three dollars in these bills were considered worth only one in specie, and the State not only did not increase its revenue, but lost full two-thirds of it, and expended three times the amount required to pay the expenses of the State government.

LAFAYETTE'S VISIT.

In the spring of 1825 the brave and generous LaFayette visited Illinois, accepting the earnest invitation of the General Assembly, and an affectionately written letter of Gov. Cole's, who had formed his personal acquaintance in France in 1817. The General in reply said: "It has been my eager desire, and it is now my earnest intention, to visit the Western States, and particularly the State of Illinois. The feelings which your distant welcome could not fail to excite have increased that patriotic eagerness to admire on that blessed spot the happy and rapid results of republican institutions, public and domestic virtues. I shall, after the 22d of February (anniversary day), leave here for a journey to the Southern States, and from New Orleans to the Western States, so as to return to Boston on the 14th of June, when the corner-stone of the Bunker Hill monument is to be laid,—a ceremony sacred to the whole Union and in which I have been engaged to act a peculiar and honorable part."

General LaFayette and suite, attended by a large delegation of prominent citizens of Missouri, made a visit by the steamer Natchez to the ancient town of Kaskaskia. No military parade was attempted, but a multitude of patriotic citizens made him welcome. A reception was held, Gov. Cole delivering a glowing address of welcome. During the progress of a grand ball held that night, a very interesting interview took place between the honored General and an Indian squaw whose father had served under him in the Revolutionary war. The squaw, learning that the great white chief was to be at Kaskaskia on that night, had ridden all day, from early dawn till sometime in the night, from her distant home, to see the man whose name had been so often on her father's tongue, and with which she was so familiar. In identification of her claim to his distinguished acquaintance, she brought with her an old, worn letter which the General had written to her father, and which the Indian chief had preserved with great care, and finally bequeathed on his death-bed to his daughter as the most precious legacy he had to leave her.

By 12 o'clock at night Gen. LaFayette returned to his boat and started South. The boat was chartered by the State.

EARLY GOVERNORS.

In the year 1822 the term of office of the first Governor, Shadrach Bond, expired. Two parties sprung up at this time,—one favorable, the other hostile, to the introduction of slavery, each proposing a candidate of its own for Governor. Both parties worked hard to secure the election of their respective candidates; but the people at large decided, as they ever have been at heart, in favor of a free State. Edward Coles, an anti-slavery man, was elected, although a majority of the Legislature were opposed to him. The subject of principal interest during his administration was to make Illinois a slave State. The greatest effort was made in 1824, and the proposition was defeated at the polls by a majority of 1,800. The aggregate vote polled was 11,612, being about 6,000 larger than at the previous State election. African slaves were first introduced into Illinois in 1720 by Renault, a Frenchman.

Senator Duncan, afterward Governor, presented to the Legislature of 1824-5 a bill for the support of schools by a public tax; and William S. Hamilton presented another bill requiring a tax to be used for the purpose of constructing and repairing the roads,—both of which bills passed and became laws. But although these laws conferred an incalculable benefit upon the public, the very name of a tax was so odious to the people that, rather than pay a tax of the smallest possible amount, they preferred working as they formerly did, five days during the year on the roads, and would allow their children to grow up without any instruction at all. Consequently both laws were abolished in 1826.

In the year 1826 the office of Governor became again vacant. Ninian Edwards, Adolphus F. Hubbard and Thomas C. Sloe were candidates. Edwards, though the successful candidate, had made himself many enemies by urging strict inquiries to be made into the corruption of the State bank, so that had it not been for his talents and noble personal appearance, he would most probably not have been elected. Hubbard was a man of but little personal merit. Of him tradition has preserved, among other curious sayings, a speech on a bill granting a bounty on wolf-scalps. This speech, delivered before the Legislature, is as follows: " Mr. Speaker, I rise before the question is put on this bill, to say a word for my constituents. Mr. Speaker, I have never seen a wolf. I cannot say that I am very well acquainted with the nature and habits of wolves. Mr. Speaker, I have said that I had never seen a wolf; but now I remember that once on a time, as Judge Brown and I were riding across the Bonpas prairie, we looked over the prairie about three miles, and Judge Brown said, ' Hubbard, look! there goes a wolf; ' and I looked, and I looked, and I looked, and I said, ' Judge, where?' and he said, 'There!' And I looked again, and this time in the edge of a hazel thicket, about three miles across the prairie, I think I saw the wolf's tail. Mr. Speaker, if I did not see a wolf that time, I think I never saw one; but I have heard much, and read more, about this animal. I have studied his natural history.

" By the bye, history is divided into two parts. There is first the history of the fabulous; and secondly, of the non-fabulous, or unknown age. Mr. Speaker, from all these sources of information I learn that the wolf is a very noxious animal; that he goes prowling about, seeking something to devour; that he rises up in the dead and secret hours of night, when all nature reposes in silent oblivion, and then commits the most terrible devastation upon the rising generation of hogs and sheep.

" Mr. Speaker, I have done; and I return my thanks to the house for their kind attention to my remarks."

Gov. Edwards was a large and well-made man, with a noble, princely appearance. Of him Gov. Ford says: " He never condescended to the common low art of electioneering. Whenever he went out among the people he arrayed himself in the style of a gentleman of the olden time, dressed in fine broadcloth, with short breeches, long stockings, and high, fair-topped boots; was drawn in a fine carriage driven by a negro; and for success he relied upon his speeches, which were delivered in great pomp and in style of diffuse and florid eloquence. When he was inaugurated in 1826, he appeared before the General Assembly wearing a golden-laced cloak, and with great pomp pronounced his first message to the houses of the Legislature."

GRAMMAR AND COOK CONTRASTED.

Demagogism had an early development.   One John Grammar, who was elected to the Territorial Legislature in 1816, and held the position for about twenty years, invented the policy of opposing every new thing, saying, " If it succeeds, no one will ask who voted against it: if it proves a failure, he could quote its record." When first honored with a seat in the Assembly, it is said that he lacked the apparel necessary for a member of the Legislature, and in order to procure them he and his sons gathered a large quantity of hazel-nuts, which were taken to the Ohio Saline and sold for cloth to make a coat and pantaloons.   The cloth was the blue strouding commonly used by the Indians.

The neighboring women assembled to make up the garments; the cloth was measured every way,—across, lengthwise, and from corner to corner,—and still was found to be scant. It was at last concluded to make a very short, bob-tailed coat and a long pair of leggins, which being finished, Mr. Grammar started for the State capital. In sharp contrast with Grammar was the character of D. P. Cook, in honor of whom Cook county was named.   Such was his transparent integrity and remarkable ability that his will was almost the law of the State.   In Congress, a young man and from a poor State, he was made Chairman of the Ways and Means Committee. He was pre-eminent for standing by his committee, regardless of consequences. It was his integrity that elected John Quincy

Adams to the Presidency. There were four candidates in 1824, Jackson, Clay, Crawford and Adams. There being no choice by the people, the election was thrown into the House. It was so balanced that it turned on his vote, and that he cast for Adams, electing him. He then came home to face the wrath of the Jackson party in Illinois.

The first mail route in the State was established in 1805. This was from Vincennes to Cahokia. In 1824 there was a direct mail route from Vandalia to Springfield. The first route from the central part of the State to Chicago was established in 1832, from Shelbyville. The difficulties and dangers encountered by the early mail carriers, in time of Indian troubles, were very serious. The bravery and ingenious devices of Harry Milton are mentioned with special commendation. When a boy, in 1812, he conveyed the mail on a wild French pony from Shawneetown to St. Louis, over swollen streams and through the enemy's country. So infrequent and irregular were the communications by mail a great part of the time, that to-day, even the remotest part of the United States is unable to appreciate it by example.

The first newspaper published in Illinois was the *Illinois Herald*, established at Kaskaskia by Mathew Duncan. There is some variance as to the exact time of its establishment. Gov. Reynolds claimed it was started in 1809. Wm. H. Brown, afterwards its editor, gives the date as 1814.

In 1831 the criminal code was first adapted to penitentiary punishment, ever since which time the old system of whipping and pillory for the punishment of criminals has been disused.

There was no legal rate of interest till 1830. Previously the rate often reached as high as 150 per cent., but was usually 50 per cent. Then it was reduced to 12, then to 10, and lastly to 8 per cent.

INDIAN TROUBLES.

WINNEBAGO WAR.

The Indians, who for some years were on peaceful terms with the whites, became troublesome in 1827. The Winnebagoes, Sacs and Foxes and other tribes had been at war for more than a hundred years. In the summer of 1827 a war party of the Winnebagoes surprised a party of Chippewas and killed eight of them. Four of the murderers were arrested and delivered to the Chippewas, by whom they were immediately shot. This was the first irritation of the Winnebagoes. Red Bird, a chief of this tribe, in order to avenge the execution of the four warriors of his own people, attacked the Chippewas, but was defeated; and being determined to satisfy his thirst for revenge by some means, surprised and killed several white men. Upon receiving intelligence of these murders, the whites who were working the lead mines in the vicinity of Galena formed a body of volunteers, and, re-inforced by a company of United States troops, marched into the country of the Winnebagoes. To save their nation from the miseries of war, Red Bird and six other men of his nation voluntarily surrendered themselves. Some of the number were executed, some of them imprisoned and destined, like Red Bird, ingloriously to pine away within the narrow confines of a jail, when formerly the vast forests had proven too limited for them.

JOHN REYNOLDS ELECTED GOVERNOR.

In August, 1830, another gubernatorial election was held. The candidates were William Kinney, then Lieutenant Governor, and John Reynolds, formerly an Associate Justice of the Supreme Court, both Jackson Democrats. The opposition brought forward no candidate, as they were in a helpless minority. Reynolds was the successful candidate, and under his administration was the famous

BLACK HAWK WAR.

In the year of 1804 a treaty was concluded between the United States and the chiefs of the Sac and Fox nations. One old chief of the Sacs, however, called Black Hawk, who had fought with great bravery in the service of Great Britain during the war of 1812, had always taken exceptions to this treaty, pronouncing it void. In 1831 he established himself, with a chosen band of warriors, upon the disputed territory, ordering the whites to leave the country at once. The settlers complaining, Gov. Reynolds dispatched Gen. Gaines, with a company of regulars and 1,500 volunteers, to the scene of action. Taking the Indians by surprise, the troops burnt their villages and forced them to conclude a treaty, by which they ceded all lands east of the Mississippi, and agreed to remain on the western side of the river. Necessity forced the proud spirit of Black Hawk into submission, which made him more than ever determined to be

BLACK HAWK, THE SAC CHIEF.

avenged upon his enemies. Having rallied around him the warlike braves of the Sac and Fox nations, he crossed the Mississippi in the spring of 1832. Upon hearing of the invasion, Gov. Reynolds hastily collected a body of 1,800 volunteers, placing them under the command of Brig-Gen. Samuel Whiteside.

STILLMAN'S RUN.

The army marched to the Mississippi, and having reduced to ashes the Indian village known as "Prophet's Town," proceeded for several miles up the river to Dixon, to join the regular forces under Gen. Atkinson. They found at Dixon two companies of volunteers, who, sighing for glory, were dispatched to reconnoiter the enemy. They advanced under command of Maj. Stillman, to a creek afterwards called "Stillman's run;" and while encamping there saw a party of mounted Indians at the distance of a mile. Several of Stillman's party mounted their horses and charged the Indians, killing three of them; but, attacked by the main body under Black Hawk, they were routed, and by their precipitate flight spread such a panic through the camp that the whole company ran off to Dixon as fast as their legs could carry them. On their arrival it was found that there had been eleven killed. The party came straggling into camp all night long, four or five at a time, each squad positive that all who were left behind were massacred.

It is said that a big, tall Kentuckian, with a loud voice, who was a colonel of the militia but a private with Stillman, upon his arrival in camp gave to Gen. Whiteside and the wondering multitude the following glowing and bombastic account of the battle: "Sirs," said he, "our detachment was encamped among some scattering timber on the north side of Old Man's creek, with the prairie from the north gently sloping down to our encampment. It was just after twilight, in the gloaming of the evening, when we discovered Black Hawk's army coming down upon us in solid column; they displayed in the form of a crescent upon the brow of the prairie, and such accuracy and precision of military movements were never witnessed by man; they were equal to the best troops of Wellington in Spain. I have said that the Indians came down in solid columns, and displayed in the form of a crescent; and what was most wonderful, there were large squares of cavalry resting upon the points of the curve, which squares were supported again by other columns fifteen deep, extending back through the woods and over a swamp three-quarters of a mile, which again rested on the main body of Black Hawk's army bivouacked upon the banks of the Kishwakee. It was a terrible and a glorious sight to see the tawny warriors as they rode along our flanks attempting to outflank us, with the glittering moonbeams glistening from their polished blades and burnished spears. It was a sight well calculated to strike consternation in the stoutest and boldest heart; and accordingly our men soon began to break in small squads, for tall timber. In a very little time the rout became general, the Indians were soon upon our flanks and threatened the destruction of our entire detachment. About this time Maj. Stillman, Col. Stephenson, Maj. Perkins, Capt. Adams, Mr. Hackelton, and myself, with some others, threw ourselves into the rear to rally the fugitives and protect the retreat. But in a short time all my companions fell bravely fighting hand-to-hand with the savage enemy, and I alone was left upon the field of battle. About this time I discovered not far to the left a corps of horsemen which seemed to be in tolerable order. I immediately deployed to the left, when, leaning down and placing my body in a recumbent posture upon the mane of my horse so as to bring the heads of the horsemen between my eye and the horizon, I discovered by the light of the moon that they were gentlemen who did not wear hats, by which token I knew they were no friends of mine. I therefore made a retrogade movement and recovered my position, where I remained some time meditating what further I could do in the service of my country, when a random ball came whistling by my ear and plainly whispered to me, 'Stranger, you have no further business here.' Upon hearing this I followed the example of my companions in arms, and broke for tall timber, and the way I ran was not a little."

For a long time afterward Maj. Stillnan and his men were subjects of ridicule and merriment, which was as undeserving as their expedition was disastrous. Stillman's defeat spread consternation throughout the State and nation. The number of Indians was greatly exaggerated, and the name of Black Hawk carried with it associations of great military talent, savage cunning and cruelty.

ASSAULT ON APPLE RIVER FORT.

A regiment sent to spy out the country between Galena and Rock Island was surprised by a party of seventy Indians, and was on the point of being thrown into disorder when Gen. Whiteside, then serving as a private, shouted out that he would shoot the first man who should turn his back to the enemy. Order being restored, the battle began. At its very outset Gen. Whiteside shot the leader of the Indians, who thereupon commenced a hasty retreat.

In June, 1832, Black Hawk, with a band of 150 warriors, attacked the Apple River Fort, near Galena, defended by 25 men. This fort, a mere palisade of logs, was erected to afford protection to the miners. For fifteen consecutive hours the garrison had to sustain the assault of the savage enemy; but knowing very well that no quarter would be given them, they fought with such fury and desperation that the Indians, after losing many of their best warriors, were compelled to retreat.

Another party of eleven Indians murdered two men near Fort Hamilton. They were afterwards overtaken by a company of twenty men and every one of them was killed.

ROCK RIVER EXPEDITION.

A new regiment, under the command of Gen. Atkinson, assembled on the banks of the Illinois in the latter part of June. Maj. Dement, with a small party, was sent out to reconnoiter the movements of a large body of Indians, whose endeavors to surround him made it advisable for him to retire. Upon hearing of this engagement, Gen. Atkinson sent a detachment to intercept the Indians, while he with the main body of his army, moved north to meet the Indians under Black Hawk. They moved slowly and cautiously through the country, passed through Turtle village, and marched up along Rock river. On their arrival news was brought of the discovery of the main trail of the Indians. Considerable search was made, but they were unable to discover any vestige of Indians save two who had shot two soldiers the day previous.

Hearing that Black Hawk was encamped on Rock river, at the Manitou village, they resolved at once to advance upon the enemy; but in the execution of their design they met with opposition from their officers and men. The officers of Gen. Henry handed to him a written protest; but he, a man equal to any emergency, ordered the officers to be arrested and escorted to Gen. Atkinson. Within a few minutes after the stern order was given, the officers all collected around the General's quarters, many of them with tears in their eyes, pledging themselves that if forgiven they would return to duty and never do the like again. The General rescinded the order, and they at once resumed duty.

THE BATTLE OF BAD-AXE.

Gen. Henry marched on the 15th of July in pursuit of the Indians, reaching Rock river after three days' journey, where he learned Black Hawk was encamped further up the river. On July 19th the troops were ordered to 'commence their march. After having made fifty miles, they were overtaken by a terrible thunder-storm which lasted all night. Nothing cooled, however, in their courage and zeal, they marched again fifty miles the next day, encamping near the place where the Indians had encamped the night before. Hurrying along as fast as they could, the infantry keeping up an equal pace with the mounted force, the troops on the morning of the 21st crossed the river connecting two of the four lakes, by which the Indians had been endeavoring to escape. They found, on their way, the ground strewn with kettles and articles of baggage, which the haste of their retreat had obliged the Indians to throw away. The troops, inspired with new ardor, advanced so rapidly that at noon they fell in with the rear guard of the Indians. Those who closely pursued them were saluted with a sudden fire of musketry by a body of Indians who had concealed them-selves in the high grass of the prairie. A most desperate charge was made upon the Indians, who, unable to resist, retreated obliquely, in order to out-flank the volunteers on the right; but the latter charged the Indians in their ambush, and expelled them from their thickets at the point of the bayonet, and dispersed them. Night set in and the battle ended, having cost the Indians 68 of their bravest men, while the loss of the Illinoisans amounted to but one killed and 8 wounded.

Soon after this battle Gens. Atkinson and Henry joined their forces and pursued the Indians. Gen. Henry struck the main trail, left his horses behind, formed an advance guard of eight men, and marched forward upon their trail. When these eight men came within sight of the river, they were suddenly fired upon and five of them killed, the remaining three maintaining their ground till Gen. Henry came up. Then the Indians, charged upon with the bayonet, fell back upon their main force. The battle now became general; the Indians fought with desperate valor, but were furiously assailed by the volunteers with their bayonets, cutting many of the Indians to pieces and driving the rest into the river. Those who escaped from being drowned took refuge on an island. On hearing the frequent discharge of musketry, indicating a general engagement, Gen. Atkinson abandoned the pursuit of the twenty Indians under Black Hawk himself, and hurried to the scene of action, where he arrived too late to take part in the battle. He immediately forded the river with his troops, the water reaching up to their necks, and landed on the island where the Indians had secreted themselves. The soldiers rushed upon the Indians, killed several of them, took others prisoner, and chased the rest into the river, where they were either drowned or shot before reaching the opposite shore. Thus ended the battle, the Indians losing 300, besides 50 prisoners; the whites but 17 killed and 12 wounded.

INCIDENTS OF THE BATTLE.

Many painful incidents occurred during this battle. A Sac woman, the sister of a warrior of some notoriety, found herself in the thickest of the fight, but at length succeeded in reaching the river, when, keeping her infant child safe in its blankets by means of her teeth, she plunged into the water, seized the tail of a horse with her hands whose rider was swimming the stream, and was drawn safely across. A young squaw during the battle was standing in the grass a short distance from the American line, holding her child—a little girl of four years—in her arms. In this position a ball struck the right arm of the child, shattering the bone, and passed into the breast of the young mother, instantly killing her. She fell upon the child and confined it to the ground till the Indians were driven from that part of the field. Gen. Anderson, of the United States army, hearing its cries, went to the spot, took it from under the dead body and carried it to the surgeon to have its wound dressed. The arm was amputated, and during the operation the half-starved child did not cry, but sat quietly eating a hard piece of biscuit. It was sent to Prairie du Chien, where it entirely recovered.

BLACK HAWK CAPTURED.

Black Hawk, with his twenty braves, retreated up the Wisconsin. river. The Winnebagoes, desirous of securing the friendship of

the whites, went in pursuit and captured and delivered them to
Gen. Street, the United States Indian agent. Among the prisoners
were the son of Black Hawk and the prophet of the tribe. These
with Black Hawk were taken to Washington, D. C., and soon consigned as prisoners at Fortress Monroe.

At the interview Black Hawk had with the President, he closed
his speech delivered on the occasion in the following words: " We
did not expect to conquer the whites. They have too many houses,
too many men. I took up the hatchet, for my part, to revenge
injuries which my people could no longer endure. Had I borne
them longer without striking, my people would have said, ' Black
Hawk is a woman; he is too old to be a chief; he is no Sac.' These
reflections caused me to raise the war-whoop. I say no more. It
is known to you. Keokuk once was here; you took him by the
hand, and when he wished to return to his home, you were willing.
Black Hawk expects, like Keokuk, he shall be permitted to return
too."

BIOGRAPHICAL SKETCH OF BLACK HAWK.

Black Hawk, or Ma-ka-tai-me-she-kia-kiah, was born in the principal Sac village, near the junction of Rock river with the Mississippi, in the year 1767. His father's name was Py-e-sa. Black
Hawk early distinguished himself as a warrior, and at the age of
fifteen was permitted to paint, and was ranked among the braves.
About the year 1783 he went on an expedition against the enemies
of his nation, the Osages, one of whom he killed and scalped; and
for this deed of Indian bravery he was permitted to join in the
scalp dance. Three or four years afterward he, at the head of two
hundred braves, went on another expedition against the Osages, to
avenge the murder of some women and children belonging to his
own tribe. Meeting an equal number of Osage warriors, a fierce
battle ensued in which the latter tribe lost one-half their number.
The Sacs lost only about nineteen warriors. He next attacked the
Cherokees for a similar cause. In a severe battle with them near
the present city of St. Louis his father was slain, and Black Hawk,
taking possession of the " Medicine Bag," at once announced himself chief of the Sac nation. He had now conquered the Cherokees,
and about the year 1800, at the head of five hundred Sacs and
Foxes and a hundred Iowas, he waged war against the Osage

nation, and subdued it. For two years he battled successfully with other Indian tribes, all of which he conquered.

The year following the treaty at St. Louis, in 1804, the United States Government erected a fort near the head of Des Moines Rapids, called Fort Edwards. This seemed to enrage Black Hawk, who at once determined to capture Fort Madison, standing on the west side of the Mississippi, above the mouth of the Des Moines. The fort was garrisoned by about fifty men. Here he was defeated. The difficulties with the British Government arose about this time, and the war of 1812 followed. That government, extending aid to the Western Indians, induced them to remain hostile to the Americans. In August, 1812, Black Hawk, at the head of about five hundred braves, started to join the British forces at Detroit, passing on his way the site of Chicago, where the famous Fort Dearborn massacre had a few days before been perpetrated. Of his connection with the British but little is known.

In the early part of 1815, the Indians west of the Mississippi were notified that peace had been declared between the United States and England, and nearly all hostilities had ceased. Black Hawk did not sign any treaty, however, until May of the following year. From the time of signing this treaty, in 1816, until the breaking out of the Black Hawk war, he and his band passed their time in the common pursuits of Indian life.

Ten years before the commencement of this war, the Sac and Fox Indians were urged to move to the west of the Mississippi. All were agreed, save the band known as the British Band, of which Black Hawk was leader. He strongly objected to the removal, and was induced to comply only after being threatened by the Government. This action, and various others on the part of the white settlers, provoked Black Hawk and his band to attempt the capture of his native village, now occupied by the whites. The war followed. He and his actions were undoubtedly misunderstood, and had his wishes been complied with at the beginning of the struggle, much bloodshed would have been prevented.

BLACK HAWK SET AT LIBERTY.

By order of the President, Black Hawk and his companions, who were in confinement at Fortress Monroe, were set free on the 4th day of June, 1833. Before leaving the fort Black Hawk made the following farewell speech to the commander, which is not only eloquent but shows that within his chest of steel there beat a heart keenly alive to the emotions of gratitude:

"Brother, I have come on my own part, and in behalf of my companions, to bid you farewell. Our great father has at length been pleased to permit us to return to our hunting grounds. We have buried the tomahawk, and the sound of the rifle hereafter will only bring death to the deer and the buffalo. Brothers, you have treated the red man very kindly. Your squaws have made them presents, and you have given them plenty to eat and drink. The memory of your friendship will remain till the Great Spirit says it is time for Black Hawk to sing his death song. Brother, your houses are as numerous as the leaves on the trees, and your young warriors like the sands upon the shore of the big lake that rolls before us. The red man has but few houses and few warriors, but the red man has a heart which throbs as warmly as the heart of his white brother. The Great Spirit has given us our hunting grounds, and the skin of the deer which we kill there is his favorite, for its color is white, and this is the emblem of peace. This hunting dress and these feathers of the eagle are white. Accept them, my brother. I have given one like this to the White Otter. Accept it as a memorial of Black Hawk. When he is far away this will serve to remind you of him. May the Great Spirit bless you and your children. Farewell."

After their release from prison they were conducted, in charge of Major Garland, through some of the principal cities, that they might witness the power of the United States and learn their own inability to cope with them in war. Great multitudes flocked to see them wherever they were taken, and the attention paid them rendered their progress through the country a triumphal procession, instead of the transportation of prisoners by an officer. At Rock Island the prisoners were given their liberty, amid great and impressive ceremony. In 1838 Black Hawk built him a dwelling near Des Moines, Iowa, and furnished it after the manner of the whites, and engaged in agricultural pursuits and hunting and fishing. Here, with his wife, to whom he was greatly attached, he passed the few remaining days of his life. To his credit, it may be said, that Black Hawk remained true to his wife, and served her

with a devotion uncommon among Indians, living with her upward of forty years.

BLACK HAWK'S DEATH AND BURIAL.

At all times when Black Hawk visited the whites he was
received with marked attention. He was an honored guest at the
old settlers' re-union in Lee county, Illinois, at some of their
meetings and received many tokens of esteem. In September,
1838, while on his way to Rock Island to receive his annuity from
the Government, he contracted a severe cold which resulted in a
fatal attack of bilious fever, and terminated his life October 3.
After his death, he was dressed in the uniform presented to him by
the President while in Washington. He was buried in a grave six
feet in depth, situated upon a beautiful eminence. The body was
placed in the middle of the grave, in a sitting posture upon a seat
constructed for the purpose. On his left side the cane given him
by Henry Clay was placed upright, with his right hand resting
upon it. Thus, after a long, adventurous and shifting life, Black
Hawk was gathered to his fathers.

FROM 1834 TO 1842.

INTERNAL IMPROVEMENTS.

No sooner was the Black Hawk war concluded than settlers
began rapidly to pour into the northern part of Illinois, now free
from Indian depredations. Chicago, from a trading post, had
grown into a commercial center, and was rapidly coming into
prominence.

At the general election in 1834 Joseph Duncan was chosen
Governor, by a handsome majority. His principal opponent was
ex-Lieutenant Governor Kinney. A reckless and uncontrollable
desire for internal public improvements seized the minds of the
people. In his message to the Legislature, in 1835, Gov. Duncan
said: " When we look abroad and see the extensive lines of inter-
·communication penetrating almost every section of our sister States;
when we see the canal boat and the locomotive bearing with seeming triumph the rich productions of the interior to the rivers, lakes
and ocean, almost annihilating time, burthen and space, what
patriot bosom does not beat high with a laudable ambition to give
Illinois her full share of those advantages which are adorning her

sister States, and which a magnificent Providence seems to invite by a wonderful adaptation of our whole country to such improvements?"

STUPENDOUS SYSTEM OF IMPROVEMENTS INAUGURATED.

The Legislature responded to the ardent words of the Governor, and enacted a system of internal improvements without a parallel in the grandeur of its conception. They ordered the construction of 1,300 miles of railroad, crossing the State in all directions. This was surpassed by the river and canal improvements. There were a few counties not touched by railroad, or river or canal, and they were to be comforted and compensated by the free distribution of $200,000 among them. To inflate this balloon beyond credence, it was ordered that work should commence on both ends of each of these railroads and rivers, and at each river-crossing, all at the same time. This provision, which has been called the crowning folly of the entire system, was the result of those jealous combinations emanating from the fear that advantages might accrue to one section over another in the commencement and completion of the works. We can appreciate better, perhaps, the magnitude of this grand system by reviewing a few figures. The debt authorized for these improvements in the first instance was $10,230,000. But this, as it was soon found, was based upon estimates at least too low by half. This, as we readily see, committed the State to a liability of over $20,000,000, equivalent to $200,000,000, at the present time, with over ten times the population and more than ten times the wealth.

Such stupendous undertakings by the State naturally engendered the fever of speculation among individuals. That particular form known as the town-lot fever assumed the malignant type at first in Chicago, from whence it spead over the entire State and adjoining States. It was an epidemic. It cut up men's farms without regard to locality, and cut up the purses of the purchasers without regard to consequences. It was estimated that building lots enough were sold in Indiana alone to accommodate every citizen then in the United States.

Chicago, which in 1830 was a small trading-post, had within a few years grown into a city. This was the starting point of the wonderful and marvelous career of that city. Improvements, unsurpassed by individual efforts in the annals of the world, were then begun and have been maintained to this day. Though visited by the terrible fire fiend and the accumulations of years swept away in a night, yet she has arisen, and to-day is the best built city in the world. Reports of the rapid advance of property in Chicago spread to the East, and thousands poured into her borders, bringing money, enterprise and industry. Every ship that left her port carried with it maps of splendidly situated towns and additions, and every vessel that returned was laden with immigrants. It was said at the time that the staple articles of Illinois export were town plots, and that there was danger of crowding the State with towns to the exclusion of land for agriculture.

ILLINOIS AND MICHIGAN CANAL.

The Illinois and Michigan canal again received attention. This enterprise is one of the most important in the early development of Illinois, on account of its magnitude and cost, and forming as it does the connecting link between the great chain of lakes and the Illinois and Mississippi rivers. Gov. Bond, the first Governor, recommended in his first message the building of the canal. In 1821 the Legislature appropriated $10,000 for surveying the route. This work was performed by two young men, who estimated the cost at $600,000 or $700,000. It cost, however, when completed, $8,000,000. In 1825 a law was passed to incorporate the Canal Company, but no stock was sold. In 1826, upon the solicitation of Daniel P. Cook, Congressman from this State, Congress gave 800,000 acres of land on the line of the work. In 1828 commissioners were appointed, and work commenced with a new survey and new estimates. In 1834–5 the work was again pushed forward, and continued until 1848, when it was completed.

PANIC—REPUDIATION ADVOCATED.

Bonds of the State were recklessly disposed of both in the East and in Europe. Work was commenced on various lines of railroad, but none were ever completed. On the Northern Cross Railroad, from Meredosia east eight miles, the first locomotive that ever turned a wheel in the great valley of the Mississippi, was run. The date of this remarkable event was Nov. 8, 1838. Large sums of money were being expended with no assurance of a revenue,

and consequently, in 1840, the Legislature repealed the improvement laws passed three years previously, not, however, until the
State had accumulated a debt of nearly $15,000,000. Thus fell,
after a short but eventful life, by the hands of its creator, the most
stupendous, extravagant and almost ruinous folly of a grand system of internal improvements that any civil community, perhaps,
ever engaged in. The State banks failed, specie was scarce, an
enormous debt was accumulated, the interest of which could not
be paid, people were disappointed in the accumulation of wealth,
and real estate was worthless. All this had a tendency to create a
desire to throw off the heavy burden of State debt by repudiation.
This was boldly advocated by some leading men. The fair fame
and name, however, of the State was not tarnished by repudiation.
Men, true, honest, and able, were placed at the head of affairs; and
though the hours were dark and gloomy, and the times most trying, yet our grand old State was brought through and prospered,
until to-day, after the expenditure of millions for public improvements and for carrying on the late war, she has, at present, a debt
of only about $300,000.

MARTYR FOR LIBERTY.

The year 1837 is memorable for the death of the first martyr for
liberty, and the abolishment of American slavery, in the State.
Elijah P. Lovejoy was shot by a mob in Alton, on the night of the
7th of November of that year. He was at the time editor of the
Alton *Observer*, and advocated anti-slavery principles in its
columns. For this practice three of his presses had been destroyed.
On the arrival of the fourth the tragedy occurred which cost him
his life. In anticipation of its arrival a series of meetings were
held in which the friends of freedom and of slavery were represented.
The object was to effect a compromise, but it was one in which
liberty was to make concessions to oppression. In a speech made
at one of these meetings, Lovejoy said: "Mr. Chairman, what
have I to compromise? If freely to forgive those who have so greatly
injured me; if to pray for their temporal and eternal happiness; if
still to wish for the prosperity of your city and State, notwithstanding the indignities I have suffered in them,—if this be the
compromise intended, then do I willingly make it. I do not admit
that it is the business of any body of men to say whether I shall

PASSENGER DEPOT OF THE CHICAGO, ROCK ISLAND & PACIFIC RAILWAY CO., AT CHICAGO.

or shall not publish a paper in this city. That right was given to me by my Creator, and is solemnly guaranteed by the Constitution of the United States and of this State. But if by compromise is meant that I shall cease from that which duty requires of me, I cannot make it, and the reason is, that I fear God more than man. It is also a very different question, whether I shall, voluntarily or at the request of my friends, yield up my position, or whether I shall forsake it at the hands of a mob. The former I am ready at all times to do when circumstances require it, as I will never put my personal wishes or interests in competition with the cause of that Master whose minister I am. But the latter, be assured I never will do. You have, as lawyers say, made a false issue. There are no two parties between whom there can be a compromise. I plant myself down on my unquestionable rights, and the question to be decided is, whether I shall be protected in those rights. You may hang me, as the mob hung the individuals at Vicksburg; you may burn me at the stake, as they did old McIntosh at St. Louis; or, you may tar and feather me, or throw me into the Mississippi as you have threatened to do; but you cannot disgrace me. I, and I alone, can disgrace myself, and the deepest of all disgrace would be at a time like this to deny my Maker by forsaking his cause. He died for me, and I were most unworthy to bear his name should I refuse, if need be, *to die for him.*" Not long afterward Mr. Lovejoy was shot. His brother Owen, being present on the occasion, kneeled down on the spot beside the corpse, and sent up to God, in the hearing of that very mob, one of the most eloquent prayers ever listened to by mortal ear. He was bold enough to pray to God to take signal vengeance on the infernal institution of slavery, and he then and there dedicated his life to the work of overthrowing it, and hoped to see the day when slavery existed no more in this nation. He died, March 24, 1864, nearly three months after the Emancipation Proclamation of President Lincoln took effect. Thus he lived to see his most earnest and devout prayer answered. But few men in the nation rendered better service in overthrowing the institution of slavery than Elijah P. and Owen Lovejoy.

CARLIN ELECTED GOVERNOR.

Thomas Carlin, Democrat, was elected Governor in 1838, over Cyrus Edwards, Whig. In 1842 Adam W. Snyder was nominated

for Governor on the Democratic ticket, but died before election.
Thomas Ford was placed in nomination, and was elected, ex-Governor Duncan being his opponent.

PRAIRIE PIRATES.

The northern part of the State also had its mob experiences, but
of an entirely different nature from the one just recounted. There
has always hovered around the frontier of civilization bold, desperate men, who prey upon the unprotected settlers rather than gain
a livelihood by honest toil. Theft, robbery and murder were carried on by regularly organized bands in Ogle, Lee, Winnebago and
DeKalb counties. The leaders of these gangs of cut-throats were
among the first settlers of that portion of the State, and consequently had the choice of location. Among the most prominent of
the leaders were John Driscoll, William and David, his sons; John
Brodie and three of his sons; Samuel Aikens and three of his sons;
William K. Bridge and Norton B. Boyce.

These were the representative characters, those who planned
and controlled the movements of the combination, concealed them
when danger threatened, nursed them when sick, rested them when
worn by fatigue and forced marches, furnished hiding places for
their stolen booty, shared in the spoils, and, under cover of darkness
and intricate and devious ways of travel, known only to themselves
and subordinates, transferred stolen horses from station to station;
for it came to be known as a well-established fact that they had
stations, and agents, and watchmen scattered throughout the country at convenient distances, and signals and pass-words to assist
and govern them in all their nefarious transactions.

Ogle county, particularly, seemed to be a favorite and chosen
field for the operations of these outlaws, who could not be convicted
for their crimes. By getting some of their number on the juries,
by producing hosts of witnesses to sustain their defense by perjured evidence, and by changing the venue from one county to
another, and by continuances from term to term, they nearly always
managed to be acquitted. At last these depredations became too
common for longer endurance; patience ceased to be a virtue, and
determined desperation seized the minds of honest men, and they
resolved that if there were no statute laws that could protect them

against the ravages of thieves, robbers and counterfeiters, they would protect themselves. It was a desperate resolve, and desperately and bloodily executed.

BURNING OF OGLE COUNTY COURT-HOUSE.

At the Spring term of court, 1841, seven of the "Pirates of the Prairie," as they were called, were confined in the Ogle county jail to await trial. Preparatory to holding court, the judge and lawyers assembled at Oregon in their new court-house, which had just been completed. Near it stood the county jail in which were the prisoners. The "Pirates" assembled Sunday night and set the court-house on fire, in the hope that as the prisoners would have to be removed from the jail, they might, in the hurry and confusion of the people in attending to the fire, make their escape. The whole population were awakened that dark and stormy night, to see their new court edifice enwrapped in flames. Although the building was entirely consumed, none of the prisoners escaped. Three of them were tried, convicted and sent to the penitentiary for a year. They had, however, contrived to get one of their number on the jury, who would not agree to a verdict until threatened to be lynched. The others obtained a change of venue and were not convicted, and finally they all broke jail and escaped.

Thus it was that the law was inadequate to the protection of the people. The best citizens held a meeting and entered into a solemn compact with each other to rid the country of the desperadoes that infested it. They were regularly organized and known as "Regulators." They resolved to notify all suspected parties to leave the country within a given time; if they did not comply, they would be severely dealt with. Their first victim was a man named Hurl, who was suspected of having stolen his neighbor's horse. He was ordered to strip, his hands were tied, when thirty-six lashes of a raw-hide were applied to his bare back. The next was a man named Daggett, formerly a Baptist preacher. He was sentenced to receive five hundred lashes on his bare back. He was stripped, and all was ready, when his beautiful daughter rushed into the midst of the men, begging for mercy for her father. Her appeals, with Daggett's promise to leave the country immediately, secured his release. That night, new crimes having been discovered, he was taken out and whipped, after which he left the country, never again to be heard from.

The friends and comrades of the men who had been whipped were fearfully enraged, and swore eternal and bloody vengeance Eighty of them assembled one night soon after, and laid plans to visit White Rock and murder every man, woman and child in that hamlet. They started on this bloody mission, but were prevailed upon by one of their number to disband. Their coming, however, had been anticipated, and every man and boy in the town was armed to protect himself and his family.

CAMPBELL KILLED—THE MURDERERS SHOT.

John Campbell, Captain of the "Regulators," received a letter from William Driscoll, filled with most direful threats,—not only threatening Campbell's life, but the life of any one who should oppose their murderous, thieving operations. Soon after the receipt of this letter, two hundred of the "Regulators" marched to Driscoll's and ordered him to leave the county within twenty days, but he refused to comply with the order. One Sunday evening, just after this, Campbell was shot down in his own door-yard by David Driscoll. He fell in the arms of his wife, at which time Taylor Driscoll raised his rifle and pointed it toward her, but lowered it without firing.

News of this terrible crime spread like wild-fire. The very air was filled with threats and vengeance, and nothing but the lives of the murderous gang would pay the penalty. Old John Driscoll was arrested, was told to bid his family good-bye, and then with his son went out to his death. The "Regulators," numbering 111, formed a large circle, and gave the Driscolls a fair hearing. They were found guilty, and the "Regulators" divided into two "death divisions,"—one, consisting of fifty-six, with rifles dispatched the father, the other fifty-five riddled and shattered the body of the son with balls from as many guns. The measures thus inaugurated to free the country from the dominion of outlaws was a last desperate resort, and proved effectual.

MORMON WAR.

In April, 1840, the "Latter-Day Saints," or Mormons, came in large numbers to Illinois and purchased a tract of land on the east side of the Mississippi river, about ten miles above Keokuk. Here they commenced building the city of Nauvoo. A more picturesque or eligible site for a city could not have been selected.

The origin, rapid development and prosperity of this religious sect are the most remarkable and instructive historical events of the present century. That an obscure individual, without money, education, or respectability, should persuade hundreds of thousands of people to believe him inspired of God, and cause a book, contemptible as a literary production, to be received as a continuation of the sacred revelation, appears almost incredible; yet in less than half a century, the disciples of this obscure individual have increased to hundreds of thousands; have founded a State in the distant wilderness, and compelled the Government of the United States to practically recognize them as an independent people.

THE FOUNDER OF MORMONISM.

The founder of Mormonism was Joseph Smith, a native of Vermont, who emigrated while quite young with his father's family to western New York. Here his youth was spent in idle, vagabond life, roaming the woods, dreaming of buried treasures, and in endeavoring to learn the art of finding them by the twisting of a forked stick in his hands, or by looking through enchanted stones. Both he and his father became famous as " water wizards," always ready to point out the spot where wells might be dug and water found. Such was the character of the young profligate when he made the acquaintance of Sidney Rigdon, a person of considerable talent and information, who had conceived the design of founding a new religion. A religious romance, written by Mr. Spaulding, a Presbyterian preacher of Ohio, then dead, suggested the idea, and finding in Smith the requisite duplicity and cunning to reduce it to practice, it was agreed that he should act as prophet; and the two devised a story that gold plates had been found buried in the earth containing a record inscribed on them in unknown characters, which, when deciphered by the power of inspiration, gave the history of the ten lost tribes of Israel.

ATTEMPT TO ARREST JOE SMITH.

After their settlement in and about Nauvoo, in Hancock county, great depredations were committed by them on the "Gentiles." The Mormons had been received from Missouri with great kindness by the people of this State, and every possible aid granted them. The depredations committed, however, soon made them odious, when the question of getting rid of them was agitated. In the fall of 1841, the Governor of Missouri made a demand on Gov. Carlin for the arrest and delivery of Joe Smith as a fugitive from justice. An executive warrant issued for that purpose was placed in the hands of an agent to be executed, but was returned without being complied with. Soon afterward the Governor handed the same writ to his agent, who this time succeeded in arresting Joe Smith. He was, however, discharged by Judge Douglas, upon the grounds that the writ upon which he had been arrested had been once returned before it was executed, and was *functus officio*. In 1842 Gov. Carlin again issued his writ, Joe Smith was arrested again, and again escaped. Thus it will be seen it was impossible to reach and punish the leader of this people, who had been driven from Missouri because of their stealing, murdering and unjust dealing, and came to Illinois but to continue their depredations. Emboldened by success, the Mormons became more arrogant and overbearing. Many people began to believe that they were about to set up a separate government for themselves in defiance of the laws of the State. Owners of property stolen in other counties made pursuit into Nauvoo, and were fined by the Mormon courts for daring to seek their property in the holy city. But that which made it more certain than anything else that the Mormons contemplated a separate government, was that about this time they petitioned Congress to establish a territorial government for them in Nauvoo.

ORIGIN OF POLYGAMY.

To crown the whole folly of the Mormons, in the Spring of 1844 Joe Smith announced himself as a candidate for President of the United States, and many of his followers were confident he would be elected. He next caused himself to be anointed king and priest, and to give character to his pretensions, he declared his lineage in an unbroken line from Joseph, the son of Jacob, and that of his wife from some other important personage of the ancient Hebrews. To strengthen his political power he also instituted a body of police styled the "Danite band," who were sworn to protect his person and obey his orders as the commands of God. A female order previously existing in the church, called "Spiritual wives," was modified so as to suit the licentiousness of the prophet. A doctrine was revealed that it was impossible for a woman to get to heaven except as the wife of a Mormon elder; that each elder might marry as many women as he could maintain, and that any female might be sealed to eternal life by becoming their concubine. This licentiousness, the origin of polygamy in that church, they endeavored to justify by an appeal to Abraham, Jacob and other favorites of God in former ages of the world.

JOE SMITH AS A TYRANT.

Smith soon began to play the tyrant over his people. Among the first acts of this sort was an attempt to take the wife of William Law, one of his most talented disciples, and make her his spiritual wife. He established, without authority, a recorder's office, and an office to issue marriage licenses. He proclaimed that none could deal in real estate or sell liquor but himself. He ordered a printing office demolished, and in many ways controlled the freedom and business of the Mormons. Not only did he stir up some of the Mormons, but by his reckless disregard for the laws of the land raised up opposition on every hand. It was believed that he instructed the Danite band, which he had chosen as the ministers of his vengeance, that no blood, except that of the church, was to be regarded as sacred, if it contravened the accomplishment of his object. It was asserted that he inculcated the legality of perjury and other crimes, if committed to advance the cause of true believers; that God had given the world and all it contained to his saints, and since they were kept out of their rightful inheritance by force, it was no moral offense to get possession of it by stealing. It was reported that an establishment existed in Nauvoo for the manufacture of counterfeit money, and that a set of outlaws was maintained for the purpose of putting it in circulation. Statements were circulated to the effect that a reward was offered for the destruction of the Warsaw *Signal*, an anti-Mormon paper, and that Mormons dispersed over the country threatened all persons who offered to assist the constable in the execution of the law, with the destruction of their property and the murder of their families. There were rumors also afloat that an alliance had been formed with the Western Indians, and in case of war they would be used in murdering their enemies. In short, if only one-half of these reports were true the Mormons must have been the most infamous people that ever existed.

MILITARY FORCES ASSEMBLING.

William Law, one of the proprietors of the printing-press destroyed by Smith, went to Carthage, the county-seat, and obtained warrants for the arrest of Smith and the members of the City Council, and others connected with the destruction of the press. Some of the parties having been arrested, but discharged by the authorities in Nauvoo, a convention of citizens assembled at Carthage and appointed a committee to wait upon the Governor for the purpose of procuring military assistance to enforce the law. The Governor visited Carthage in person. Previous to his arrival the militia had been called out and armed forces commenced assembling in Carthage and Warsaw to enforce the service of civil process. All of them, however, signified a willingness to co-operate with the Governor in preserving order. A constable and ten men were then sent to make the arrest. In the meantime, Smith declared martial law; his followers residing in the country were summoned to his assistance; the Legion was assembled and under arms, and the entire city was one great military encampment.

THE SMITHS ARRESTED.

The prophet, his brother Hiram, the members of the City Council and others, surrendered themselves at Carthage June 24, 1845, on the charge of riot. All entered into recognizance before a Justice of the Peace to appear at court, and were discharged. A new writ, however, was immediately issued and served on the two Smiths, and both were arrested and thrown into prison. The citizens had assembled from Hancock, Schuyler and McDonough counties, armed and ready to avenge the outrages that had been committed by the Mormons. Great excitement prevailed at Carthage. The force assembled at that place amounted to 1,200 men, and about 500 assembled at Warsaw. Nearly all were anxious to march into Nauvoo. This measure was supposed to be necessary to search for counterfeit money and the apparatus to make it, and also to strike a salutary terror into the Mormon people by an exhibition of the force of the State, and thereby prevent future outrages, murders, robberies, burnings, and the like. The 27th of June was appointed for the march; but Gov. Ford, who at the time was in Carthage, apprehended trouble if the militia should attempt to invade Nauvoo, disbanded the troops, retaining only a guard to the jail.

JOE SMITH AND HIS BROTHER KILLED.

Gov. Ford went to Nauvoo on the 27th. The same morning about 200 men from Warsaw, many being disguised, hastened to Carthage. On learning that one of the companies left as a guard had disbanded, and the other stationed 150 yards from the jail while eight men were left to guard the prisoners, a communication was soon established between the Warsaw troops and the guard; and it was arranged that the guard should have their guns charged with blank cartridges and fire at the assailants when they attempted to enter the jail. The conspirators came up, jumped the fence around the jail, were fired upon by the guard, which, according to arrangement, was overpowered, and the assailants entered the prison, to the door of the room where the two prisoners were confined. An attempt was made to break open the door; but Joe Smith, being armed with a pistol, fired several times as the door was bursted open, and three of the assailants were wounded. At the same time several shots were fired into the room, by some of which John Taylor, a friend of the Smiths, received four wounds, and Hiram Smith was instantly killed. Joe Smith, severely wounded, attempted to escape by jumping out of a second-story window, but was so stunned by the fall that he was unable to rise. In this position he was dispatched by balls shot through his body. Thus fell Joe Smith, the most successful imposter of modern times. Totally ignorant of almost every fact in science, as well as in law, he made up in constructiveness and natural cunning whatever in him was wanting of instruction.

CONSTERNATION AT QUINCY.

Great consternation prevailed among the anti-Mormons at Carthage, after the killing of the Smiths. They expected the Mormons would be so enraged on hearing of the death of their leaders that they would come down in a body, armed and equipped, to seek revenge upon the populace at Carthage. Messengers were dispatched to various places for help in case of an attack. The women and children were moved across the river for safety. A committee was sent to Quincy and early the following morning, at the ringing of the bells, a large concourse of people assembled to devise means of defense. At this meeting, it was reported that the Mormons attempted to rescue the Smiths; that a party of Missourians and others had killed them to prevent their escape; that

the Governor and his party were at Nauvoo at the time when intelligence of the fact was brought there; that they had been attacked
by the Nauvoo Legion, and had retreated to a house where they
were closely besieged; that the Governor had sent out word that
he could maintain his position for two days, and would be certain
to be massacred if assistance did not arrive by that time. It is
unnecessary to say that this entire story was fabricated. It was
put in circulation, as were many other stories, by the anti-Mormons,
to influence the public mind and create a hatred for the Mormons.
The effect of it, however, was that by 10 o'clock on the 28th,
between two and three hundred men from Quincy, under command
of Maj. Flood, went on board a steamboat for Nauvoo, to assist in
raising the siege, as they honestly believed.

VARIOUS DEPREDATIONS.

It was thought by many, and indeed the circumstances seem to warrant the conclusion, that the assassins of Smith had arranged that the
murder should occur while the Governor was in Nauvoo; that the
Mormons would naturally suppose he planned it, and in the first out-
pouring of their indignation put him to death, as a means of retaliation. They thought that if they could have the Governor of the State
assassinated by Mormons, the public excitement would be greatly
increased against that people, and would cause their extermination,
or at least their expulsion from the State. That it was a brutal and
premeditated murder cannot be and is not denied at this day; but
the desired effect of the murder was not attained, as the Mormons
did not evacuate Nauvoo for two years afterward. In the meantime,
the excitement and prejudice against this people were not allowed
to die out. Horse-stealing was quite common, and every case that
occurred was charged to the Mormons. That they were guilty of
such thefts cannot be denied, but a great deal of this work done at
that time was by organized bands of thieves, who knew they could
carry on their nefarious business with more safety, as long as suspicion could be placed upon the Mormons. In the summer and
fall of 1845 were several occurrences of a nature to increase the
irritation existing between the Mormons and their neighbors. A
suit was instituted in the United States Circuit Court against one
of the apostles, to recover a note, and a marshal sent to summons

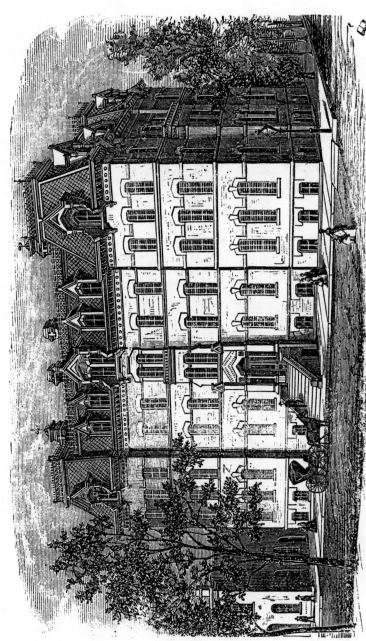

ILLINOIS CHARITABLE EYE AND EAR INFIRMARY, CHICAGO—FOUNDED 1858—DESTROYED 1871—REBUILT 1874.

the defendant, who refused to be served with the process. Indignation meetings were held by the saints, and the marshal threatened for attempting to serve the writ. About this time, General
Denning, sheriff, was assaulted by an anti-Mormon, whom he killed.
Denning was friendly to the Mormons, and a great outburst of
passion was occasioned among the friends of the dead man.

INCENDIARISM.

It was also discovered, in trying the rights of property at Lima,
Adams county, that the Mormons had an institution connected
with their church to secure their effects from execution. Incensed
at this and other actions, the anti-Mormons of Lima and Green
Plains, held a meeting to devise means for the expulsion of the
Mormons from that part of the country. It was arranged that a
number of their own party should fire on the building in which
they were assembled, in such a manner as not to injure anyone,
and then report that the Mormons had commenced the work of
plunder and death. This plot was duly executed, and the startling
intelligence soon called together a mob, which threatened the Mormons with fire and sword if they did not immediately leave. The
Mormons refusing to depart, the mob at once executed their threats
by burning 125 houses and forcing the inmates to flee for their
lives. The sheriff of Hancock county, a prominent Mormon
armed several hundred Mormons and scoured the country, in search
of the incendiaries, but they had fled to neighboring counties, and
he was unable either to bring them to battle or make any arrests.
One man, however, was killed without provocation; another
attempting to escape was shot and afterwards hacked and muti-
lated; and Franklin A. Worrell, who had charge of the jail when
the Smiths were killed, was shot by some unknown person concealed in a thicket. The anti-Mormons committed one murder.
A party of them set fire to a pile of straw, near the barn of an old
Mormon, nearly ninety years of age, and when he appeared to ex-
tinguish the flames, he was shot and killed.

The anti-Mormons left their property exposed in their hurried
retreat, after having burned the houses of the Mormons. Those
who had been burned out sallied forth from Nauvoo and plundered
the whole country, taking whatever they could carry or drive
away. By order of the Governor, Gen. Hardin raised a force of
350 men, checked the Mormon ravages, and recalled the fugitive
anti-Mormons home.

MAKING PREPARATION TO LEAVE.

At this time a convention, consisting of delegates from eight of the adjoining counties, assembled to concert measures for the expulsion of the Mormons from the State. The Mormons seriously contemplated emmigration westward, believing the times forboded evil for them. Accordingly, during the winter of 1845–'46, the most stupendous preparations were made by the Mormons for removal. All the principal dwellings, and even the temple, were converted into work-shops, and before spring, 12,000 wagons were in readiness; and by the middle of February the leaders, with 2,000 of their followers, had crossed the Mississippi on the ice.

Before the spring of 1846 the majority of the Mormons had left Nauvoo, but still a large number remained.

THE BATTLE OF NAUVOO.

In September a writ was issued against several prominent Mormons, and placed in the hands of John Carlin, of Carthage, for execution. Carlin called out a posse to help make the arrest, which brought together quite a large force in the neighborhood of Nauvoo. Carlin, not being a military man, placed in command of the posse, first, Gen. Singleton, and afterward Col. Brockman, who proceeded to invest the city, erecting breastworks, and taking other means for defensive as well as offensive operations. What was then termed a battle next took place, resulting in the death of one Mormon and the wounding of several others, and loss to the anti-Mormons of three killed and four wounded. At last, through the intervention of an anti-Mormon committee of one hundred, from Quincy, the Mormons and their allies were induced to submit to such terms as the posse chose to dictate, which were that the Mormons should immediately give up their arms to the Quincy committee, and remove from the State. The trustees of the church and five of their clerks were permitted to remain for the sale of Mormon property, and the posse were to march in unmolested, and leave a sufficient force to guarantee the performance of their stipulations. Accordingly, the constable's posse marched in with Brockman at their head. It consisted of about 800 armed men and 600 or 700 unarmed, who had assembled from all the country around, through motives of curiosity, to see the once proud city of Nauvoo humbled and delivered up to its enemies. They proceeded into the

ILLINOIS INSTITUTE FOR DEAF AND DUMB, AT JACKSONVILLE.

city slowly and carefully, examining the way for fear of the explosion of a mine, many of which had been made by the Mormons, by burying kegs of powder in the ground, with a man stationed at a distance to pull a string communicating with the trigger of a percussion lock affixed to the keg. This kind of a contrivance was called by the Mormons " hell's half-acre." When the posse arrived in the city, the leaders of it erected themselves into a tribunal to decide who should be forced away and who remain. Parties were dispatched to hunt for fire-arms, and for Mormons, and to bring them to judgment. When brought, they received their doom from the mouth of Brockman, who sat a grim and unawed tyrant for the time. As a general rule, the Mormons were ordered to leave within an hour or two; and by rare grace some of them were allowed until next day, and in a few cases longer time was granted.

MALTREATMENT OF NEW CITIZENS.

Nothing was said in the treaty in regard to the new citizens, who had with the Mormons defended the city; but the posse no sooner had obtained possession than they commenced expelling them. Some of them were ducked in the river, and were in one or two instances actually baptized in the name of some of the leaders of the mob; others were forcibly driven into the ferry-boats to be taken over the river before the bayonets of armed ruffians. Many of these new settlers were strangers in the country from various parts of the United States, who were attracted there by the low price of property; and they knew but little of previous difficulties or the merits of the quarrel. They saw with their own eyes that the Mormons were industriously preparing to go away, and they knew " of their own knowledge " that any effort to expel them by force was gratuitous and unnecessary cruelty. They had been trained, by the States whence they came, to abhor mobs and to obey the law, and they volunteered their services under executive authority to defend their town and their property against mob violence, and, as they honestly believed, from destruction; but in this they were partly mistaken; for although the mob leaders in the exercise of unbridled power were guilty of many injuries to the persons of individuals, although much personal property was stolen, yet they abstained from materially injuring houses and buildings.

THE MORMONS REACH SALT LAKE.

The fugitives proceeded westward, taking the road through Missouri, but were forcibly ejected from that State and compelled to move indirectly through Iowa. After innumerable hardships the advance guard reached the Missouri river at Council Bluffs, when a United States officer presented a requisition for 500 men to serve in the war with Mexico. Compliance with this order so diminished their number of effective men, that the expedition was again delayed and the remainder, consisting mostly of old men, women and children, hastily prepared habitations for winter. Their rudely constructed tents were hardly completed before winter set in with great severity, the bleak prairies being incessantly swept by piercing winds. While here cholera, fever and other diseases, aggravated by the previous hardships, the want of comfortable quarters and medical treatment, hurried many of them to premature graves, yet, under the influence of religious fervor and fanaticism, they looked death in the face with resignation and cheerfulness, and even exhibited a gayety which manifested itself in music and dancing during the saddest hours of this sad winter.

At length welcome spring made its appearance, and by April they were again organized for the journey; a pioneer party, consisting of Brigham Young and 140 others, was sent in advance to locate a home for the colonists. On the 21 of July, 1847, a day memorable in Mormon annals, the vanguard reached the valley of the Great Salt Lake, having been directed thither, according to their accounts, by the hand of the Almighty. Here in a distant wilderness, midway between the settlements of the East and the Pacific, and at that time a thousand miles from the utmost verge of civilization, they commenced preparations for founding a colony, which has since grown into a mighty empire.

MEXICAN WAR.

During the month of May, 1846, the President called for four regiments of volunteers from Illinois for the Mexican war. This was no sooner known in the State than nine regiments, numbering 8,370 men, answered the call, though only four of them, amounting to 3,720 men, could be taken. These regiments, as well as their officers, were everywhere foremost in the American ranks, and distinguished themselves by their matchless valor in the bloodiest battles of the war. Veterans never fought more nobly and effectively than did the volunteers from Illinois. At the bloody battle of Buena Vista they crowned their lives—many their death—with the laurels of war. Never did armies contend more bravely, determinedly and stubbornly than the American and Mexican forces at this famous battle; and as Illinois troops were ever in the van and on the bloodiest portions of the field, we believe a short sketch of the part they took in the fierce contest is due them, and will be read with no little interest.

BATTLE OF BUENA VISTA.

General Santa Anna, with his army of 20,000, poured into the valley of Aqua Nueva early on the morning of the 22d of February, hoping to surprise our army, consisting of about 5,000 men, under Gen. Taylor and which had retreated to the "Narrows." They were hotly pursued by the Mexicans who, before attacking, sent Gen. Taylor a flag of truce demanding a surrender, and assuring him that if he refused he would be cut to pieces; but the demand was promptly refused. At this the enemy opened fire, and the conflict began. In honor of the day the watchword with our soldiers was, "The memory of Washington." An irregular fire was kept up all day, and at night both armies bivouacked on the field, resting on their arms. Santa Anna that night made a spirited address to his men, and the stirring strains of his own band till late in the night were distinctly heard by our troops; but at last silence fell over the hosts that were to contend unto death in that narrow pass on the morrow.

Early on the following morning the battle was resumed, and continued without intermission until nightfall. The solid columns of the enemy were hurled against our forces all day long, but were met and held in check by the unerring fire of our musketry and artillery. A portion of Gen. Lane's division was driven back by the enemy under Gen. Lombardini, who, joined by Gen. Pacheco's division, poured upon the main plateau in so formidable numbers as to appear irresistible.

BRAVERY OF THE SECOND ILLINOIS.

At this time the 2d Illinois, under Col. Bissell, with a squadron of cavalry and a few pieces of artillery came handsomely into action and gallantly received the concentrated fire of the enemy, which they returned with deliberate aim and terrible effect; every discharge of the artillery seemed to tear a bloody path through the heavy columns of enemy.   Says a writer: "The rapid musketry of the gallant troops from Illinois poured a storm of lead into their serried ranks, which literally strewed the ground with the dead and dying."   But, notwithstanding his losses, the enemy steadily advanced until our gallant regiment received fire from three sides.   Still they maintained their position for a time with unflinching firmness against that immense host.   At length, perceiving the danger of being entirely surrounded, it was determined to fall back to a ravine.   Col. Bissel, with the coolness of ordinary drill, ordered the signal " cease firing " to be made; he then with the same deliberation gave the command, " Face to the rear, Battalion, about face; forward march," which was executed with the regularity of veterans to a point beyond the peril of being outflanked.   Again, in obedience to command these brave men halted, faced about, and under a murderous tempest of bullets from the foe, resumed their well-directed fire.   The conduct of no troops could have been more admirable; and, too, until that day they had never been under fire, when, within less than half an hour eighty of their comrades dropped by their sides.   How different from the Arkansas regiment, which were ordered to the plateau, but after delivering their first volley gave way and dispersed.

SADDEST EVENT OF THE BATTLE.

But now we have to relate the saddest, and, for Illinois, the most mournful, event of that battle-worn day.   We take the account from Colton's History of the battle of Buena Vista. "As the enemy on our left was moving in retreat along the head of the Plateau, our artillery was advanced until within range, and opened a heavy fire upon him, while Cols. Hardin, Bissell and McKee, with their Illinois and Kentucky troops, dashed gallantly forward in hot pursuit.   A powerful reserve of the Mexican army was then just emerging from the ravine, where it had been organized, and advanced on the plateau, opposite the head of the southernmost gorge.   Those who were giving way rallied quickly upon it; when the whole force, thus increased to over 12,000 men, came forward in a perfect blaze of fire.   It was a single column, composed of the best soldiers of the republic, having for its advanced battalions the

SCENE ON FOX RIVER.

veteran regiments. The Kentucky and Illinois troops were soon
obliged to give ground before it and seek the shelter of the second
gorge. The enemy pressed on, arriving opposite the head of the
second gorge. One-half of the column suddenly enveloped it, while
the other half pressed on across the plateau, having for the moment
nothing to resist them but the three guns in their front. The portion that was immediately opposed to the Kentucky and Illinois
troops, ran down along each side of the gorge, in which they had
sought shelter, and also circled around its head, leaving no possible
way of escape for them except by its mouth, which opened
upon the road. Its sides, which were steep,—at least an angle of
45 degrees,—were covered with loose pebbles and stones, and con-
verged to a point at the bottom. Down there were our poor fellows, nearly three regiments of them (1st and 2d Illinois and 2d
Kentucky), with but little opportunity to load or fire a gun, being
hardly able to keep their feet. Above the whole edge of the
gorge, all the way around, was darkened by the serried masses of
the enemy, and was bristling with muskets directed on the crowd
beneath. It.was no time to pause. Those who were not immediately shot down rushed on toward the road, their number growing
less and less as they went, Kentuckians and Illinoisans, officers and
men, all mixed up in confusion, and all pressing on over the loose
pebbles and rolling stones of those shelving, precipitous banks,
and having lines and lines of the enemy firing down from each
side and rear as they went. Just then the enemy's cavalry, which
had gone to the left of the reserve, had come over the spur that
divides the mouth of the second gorge from that of the third, and
were now closing up the only door through which there was the
least shadow of a chance for their lives. Many of those ahead
endeavored to force their way out, but few succeeded. The lancers
were fully six to one, and their long, weapons were already reeking
with blood. It was at this time that those who were still back in
that dreadful gorge heard, above the din of the musketry and the
shouts of the enemy around them, the roar of Washington's Battery. No music could have been more grateful to their ears. A
moment only, and the whole opening, where the lancers were busy,
rang with the repeated explosions of spherical-case shot. They
gave way. The gate, as it were, was clear, and out upon the road
a stream of our poor fellows issued. They ran panting down

toward the battery, and directly under the flight of iron then passing over their heads, into the retreating cavalry. Hardin, McKee, Clay, Willis, Zabriskie, Houghton—but why go on? It would be a sad task indeed to name over all who fell during this twenty minutes' slaughter. The whole gorge, from the plateau to its mouth, was strewed with our dead. All dead! No wounded there —not a man; for the infantry had rushed down the sides and completed the work with the bayonet."

VICTORY FOR OUR ARMY.

The artillery on the plateau stubbornly maintained its position, The remnants of the 1st and 2d Illinois regiments, after issuing from the fated gorge, were formed and again brought into action, the former, after the fall of the noble Hardin, under Lieut. Col. Weatherford, the latter under Bissell. The enemy brought forth reinforcements and a brisk artillery duel was kept up; but gradually, as the shades of night began to cover the earth, the rattle of musketry slackened, and when the pall of night was thrown over that bloody field it ceased altogether. Each army, after the fierce and long struggle, occupied much the same position as it did in the morning. However, early on the following morning, the glad tidings were heralded amidst our army that the enemy had retreated, thus again crowning the American banners with victory.

OTHER HONORED NAMES OF THIS WAR.

Other bright names from Illinois that shine as stars in this war are those of Shields, Baker, Harris and Coffee, which are indissolubly connected with the glorious capture of Vera Cruz and the not less famous storming of Cerro Gordo. In this latter action, when, after the valiant Gen. Shields had been placed *hors de combat*, the command of his force, consisting of three regiments, devoled upon Col. Baker. This officer, with his men, stormed with unheard-of prowess the last stronghold of the Mexicans, sweeping everything before them. Such indeed were the intrepid valor and daring courage exhibited by Illinois volunteers during the Mexican war that their deeds should live in the memory of their countrymen until those latest times when the very name of America shall have been forgotten.

THE WAR FOR THE UNION.

On the fourth day of March, 1861, after the most exciting and momentous political campaign known in the history of this country, Abraham Lincoln—America's martyred President—was inaugurated Chief Magistrate of the United States. This fierce contest was principally sectional, and as the announcement was flashed over the telegraph wires that the Republican Presidential candidate had been elected, it was hailed by the South as a justifiable pretext for dissolving the Union. Said Jefferson Davis in a speech at Jackson, Miss., prior to the election, "If an abolitionist be chosen President of the United States you will have presented to you the question whether you will permit the government to pass into the hands of your avowed and implacable enemies. Without pausing for an answer, I will state my own position to be that such a result would be a species of revolution by which the purpose of the Government would be destroyed, and the observances of its mere forms entitled to no respect. In that event, in such manner as should be most expedient, I should deem it your duty to provide for your safety outside of the Union." Said another Southern politician, when speaking on the same subject, "We shall fire the Southern heart, instruct the Southern mind, give courage to each, and at the proper moment, by one organized, concerted action, we can precipitate the Cotton States into a revolution." To disrupt the Union and form a government which recognized the absolute supremacy of the white population and the perpetual bondage of the black was what they deemed freedom from the galling yoke of a Republican administration.

ABRAHAM LINCOLN DID NOT SEEK THE PRESIDENCY.

Hon. R. W. Miles, of Knox county, sat on the floor by the side of Abraham Lincoln in the Library room of the Capitol, in Springfield, at the secret caucus meeting, held in January, 1859, when Mr. Lincoln's name was first spoken of in caucus as candidate for President. When a gentleman, in making a short speech, said, "We are going to bring Abraham Lincoln out as a candidate for President," Mr. Lincoln at once arose to his feet, and exclaimed, "For God's sake, let me alone! I have suffered enough!" This was soon after he had been defeated in the Legislature for United States Senate by Stephen A. Douglas, and only those who are intimate with that important and unparalleled contest can appreciate the full force and meaning of these expressive words of the martyred President. They were spontaneous, and prove beyond a shadow of doubt that Abraham Lincoln did not seek the high position of President. Nor did he use any trickery or chicanery to obtain it. But his expressed wish was not to be complied with; our beloved country needed a savior and a martyr, and Fate had decreed that he should be the victim. After Mr. Lincoln was elected President, Mr. Miles sent him an eagle's quill, with which the chief magistrate wrote his first inaugural address. The letter written by Mr. Miles to the President, and sent with the quill, which was two feet in length, is such a jewel of eloquence and prophecy that it should be given a place in history:

PERSIFER, December 21, 1860.

HON. A. LINCOLN :

Dear Sir :—Please accept the eagle quill I promised you, by the hand of our Representative, A. A. Smith. The bird from whose wing the quill was taken, was shot by John F. Dillon, in Persifer township, Knox Co., Ills., in Feb., 1857 Having heard that James Buchanan was furnished with an eagle quill to write his Inaugural with, and believing that in 1860, a Republican would be elected to take his place, I determined to save this quill and present it to the fortunate man, whoever he might be. Reports tell us that the bird which furnished Buchanan's quill was a captured bird,—fit emblem of the man that used it ; but the bird from which this quill was taken, yielded the quill only with his life,—fit emblem of the man who is expected to use it, for true Republicans believe that you would not think life worth the keeping after the surrender of principle. Great difficulties surround you ; traitors to their country have threatened your life ; and should you be called upon to surrender it at the post of duty, your memory will live forever in the heart of every freeman ; and that is a grander monument than can be built of brick or marble.

"For if hearts may not our memories keep,
Oblivion haste each vestige sweep,
And let our memories end."

Yours Truly,

R. W. MILES.

STATES SECEDING.

At the time of President Lincoln's accession to power, several members of the Union claimed they had withdrawn from it, and styling themselves the "Confederate States of America," organized a separate government. The house was indeed divided against itself, but it should not fall, nor should it long continue divided, was the hearty, determined response of every loyal heart in the nation. The accursed institution of human slavery was the primary cause for this dissolution of the American Union. Doubtless other agencies served to intensify the hostile feelings which existed between the Northern and Southern portions of our country, but their remote origin could be traced to this great national evil. Had Lincoln's predecessor put forth a timely, energetic effort, he might have prevented the bloody war our nation was called to pass through. On the other hand every aid was given the rebels; every advantage and all the power of the Government was placed at their disposal, and when Illinois' honest son took the reins of the Republic he found Buchanan had been a traitor to his trust, and given over to the South all available means of war.

THE FALL OF SUMTER.

On the 12th day of April, 1861, the rebels, who for weeks had been erecting their batteries upon the shore, after demanding of Major Anderson a surrender, opened fire upon Fort Sumter. For thirty-four hours an incessant cannonading was continued; the fort was being seriously injured; provisions were almost gone, and Major Anderson was compelled to haul down the stars and stripes. That dear old flag which had seldom been lowered to a foreign foe by rebel hands was now trailed in the dust. The first blow of the terrible conflict which summoned vast armies into the field, and moistened the soil of a nation in fraternal blood and tears, had been struck. The gauntlet thus thrown down by the attack on Sumter by the traitors of the South was accepted—not, however, in the spirit with which insolence meets insolence—but with a firm, determined spirit of patriotism and love of country. The duty of the President was plain under the constitution and the laws, and above and beyond all, the people from whom all political power is derived, demanded the suppression of the Rebellion, and stood ready to sustain the authority of their representative and executive officers. Promptly did the new President issue a proclamation calling for his countrymen to join with him to defend their homes and their country, and vindicate her honor. This call was made April 14, two days after Sumter was first fired upon, and was for 75,000 men. On the 15th, the same day he was notified, Gov. Yates issued his proclamation convening the Legislature. He also ordered the organization of six regiments. Troops were in abundance, and the call was no sooner made than filled. Patriotism thrilled and vibrated and pulsated through every heart. The farm, the workshop, the office, the pulpit, the bar, the bench, the college, the school-house,—every calling offered its best men, their lives and their fortunes, in defense of the Government's honor and unity.

Bitter words spoken in moments of political heat were forgotten and forgiven, and joining hands in a common cause, they repeated the oath of America's soldier-statesman: "*By the Great Eternal, the Union must and shall be preserved.*" The honor, the very life and glory of the nation was committed to the stern arbitrament of the sword, and soon the tramp of armed men, the clash of musketry and the heavy boom of artillery reverberated throughout the continent; rivers of blood saddened by tears of mothers, wives, sisters, daughters and sweethearts flowed from the lakes to the gulf, but a nation was saved. The sacrifice was great, but the Union was preserved.

CALL FOR TROOPS PROMPTLY ANSWERED.

Simultaneously with the call for troops by the President, enlistments commenced in this State, and within ten days 10,000 volunteers offered service, and the sum of $1,000,000 was tendered by patriotic citizens. Of the volunteers who offered their services, only six regiments could be accepted under the quota of the State. But the time soon came when there was a place and a musket for every man. The six regiments raised were designated by numbers commencing with seven, as a mark of respect for the six regiments which had served in the Mexican war. Another call was anticipated, and the Legislature authorized ten additional regiments to be organized. Over two hundred companies were immediately raised from which were selected the required number. No sooner was this done than the President made another call for troops, six regiments were again our proportion, although by earnest solicitation the remaining four were accepted. There were a large number of men with a patriotic desire to enter the service who were denied this privilege. Many of them wept, while others joined regiments from other States. In May, June and July seventeen regiments of infantry and five of cavalry were raised, and in the latter month, when the President issued his first call for 500,000 volunteers, Illinois tendered thirteen regiments of infantry and three of cavalry, and so anxious were her sons to have the Rebellion crushed that the number could have been increased by thousands. At the close of 1861 Illinois had sent to the field nearly 50,000 men, and had 17,000 in camp awaiting marching orders, thus exceeding her full quota by 15,000.

A VAST ARMY RAISED IN ELEVEN DAYS.

In July and August of 1862 the President called for 600,000 men—our quota of which was 52,296—and gave until August 18 as the limits in which the number might be raised by volunteering, after which a draft would be ordered. The State had already furnished 17,000 in excess of her quota, and it was first thought this number would be deducted from the present requisition, but that could not be done. But thirteen days were granted to enlist this vast army, which had to come from the farmers and mechanics. The former were in the midst of harvest, but, inspired by love of country, over 50,000 of them left their harvests ungathered, their tools and their benches, the plows in their furrows, turning their backs on their homes, and before eleven days had expired the demands of the Government were met and both quotas filled.

The war went on, and call followed call, until it began to look as if there would not be men enough in all the Free States to crush out and subdue the monstrous war traitors had inaugurated. But to every call for either men or money there was a willing and ready response. And it is a boast of the people that, had the supply of men fallen short, there were women brave enough, daring enough, patriotic enough, to have offered themselves as sacrifices on their country's altar. On the 21st of December, 1864, the last call for troops was made. It was for 300,000. In consequence of an im- perfect enrollment of the men subject to military duty, it became evident, ere this call was made, that Illinois was furnishing thous- ands of men more than what her quota would have been, had it been correct. So glaring had this disproportion become, that under this call the quota of some districts exceeded the number of able-bodied men in them.

A GENERAL SUMMARY.

Following this sketch we give a schedule of all the volunteer troops organized from this State, from the commencement to the close of the war. It is taken from the Adjutant General's report. The number of the regiment, name of original Colonel, call under which recruited, date of organization and muster into the United States' service, place of muster, and aggregate strength of each organization, from which we find that Illinois put into her one hun- dred and eighty regiments 256,000 men, and into the United States army, through other States, enough to swell the number to 290,000. This far exceeds all the soldiers of the Federal Government in all the war of the Revolution. Her total years of service were over 600,000. She enrolled men from eighteen to forty-five years of age, when the law of Congress in 1864—the test time—only asked for those from twenty to forty-five. Her enrollments were otherwise excessive. Her people wanted to go, and did not take the pains to correct the enrollment; thus the basis of fixing the quota was too great, and the quota itself, at least in the trying time, was far above any other State. The demand on some counties, as Monroe, for example, took every able-bodied man in the county, and then did not have enough to fill the quota. Moreover, Illinois sent 20,844 men for one hundred days, for whom no credit was asked. She gave to the country 73,000 years of service above all calls. With one-thirteenth of the population of the loyal States, she sent regularly one-tenth of all the soldiers, and in the perils of the closing calls, when patriots were few and weary, she sent one-eighth of all that were called for by her loved and honored son in the White House. Of the brave boys Illinois sent to the front, there were killed in action, 5,888; died of wounds, 3,032; of disease, 19,496; in prison, 967; lost at sea, 205; aggregate, 29,588. As upon every field and upon every page of the history of this war, Illinois bore her part of the suffering in the prison-pens of the South. More than 800 names make up the awful column of Illinois' brave sons who died in the rebel prison of Andersonville, Ga. Who can measure or imagine the atrocities which would be laid before the world were the panorama of sufferings and terrible trials of these gallant men but half unfolded to view? But this can never be done until new words of horror are invented, and new arts discovered by which demoniacal fiendishness can be portrayed, and the intensest anguish of the human soul in ten thousand forms be painted.

No troops ever fought more heroically, stubbornly, and with better effect, than did the boys from the "Prairie State." At Pea Ridge, Donelson, Pittsburg Landing, Iuka, Corinth, Stone River, Holly Springs, Jackson, Vicksburg, Chicamauga, Lookout Mountain, Murfreesboro, Atlanta, Franklin, Nashville, Chattanooga, and on every other field where the clash of arms was heard, her sons were foremost.

CAPTURE OF THE ST. LOUIS ARSENAL.

Illinois was almost destitute of firearms at the beginning of the conflict, and none could be procured in the East. The traitorous Floyd had turned over to the South 300,000 arms, leaving most arsenals in the North empty. Gov. Yates, however, received an order on the St. Louis arsenal for 10,000 muskets, which he put in the hands of Captain Stokes, of Chicago. Several unsuccessful attempts were made by the Captain to pass through the large crowd of rebels which had gathered around the arsenal, suspecting an attempt to move the arms would be made. He at last succeeded in gaining admission to the arsenal, but was informed by the commander that the slightest attempt to move the arms would be discovered and bring an infuriated mob upon the garrison. This fear was well founded, for the following day Gov. Jackson ordered 2,000 armed men from Jefferson City down to capture the arsenal. Capt. Stokes telegraphed to Alton for a steamer to descend the river, and about midnight land opposite the arsenal, and proceeding to the same place with 700 men of the 7th Illinois, commenced loading the vessel. To divert attention from his real purpose, he had 500 guns placed upon a different boat. As designed, this movement was discovered by the rabble, and the shouts and excitement upon their seizure drew most of the crowd from the arsenal. Capt. Stokes not only took all the guns his requisition called for, but emptied the arsenal. When all was ready, and the signal given to start, it was found that the immense weight had bound the bow of the boat to a rock, but after a few moments' delay the boat fell away from the shore and floated into deep water.

"Which way?" said Capt. Mitchell, of the steamer. "Straight in the regular channel to Alton," replied Capt. Stokes. "What if we are attacked?" said Capt. Mitchell. "Then we will fight," was the reply of Capt. Stokes. "What if we are overpowered?" said Mitchell. "Run the boat to the deepest part of the river and sink her," replied Stokes. "I'll do it," was the heroic answer of Mitchell, and away they went past the secession battery, past the St. Louis levee, and in the regular channel on to Alton. When they touched the landing, Capt. Stokes, fearing pursuit, ran to the market house and rang the fire bell. The citizens came flocking pell-mell to the river, and soon men, women and children were tugging away at that vessel load of arms, which they soon had deposited in freight cars and off to Springfield.

LIBERALITY AS WELL AS PATRIOTISM.

The people were liberal as well as patriotic; and while the men were busy enlisting, organizing and equipping companies, the ladies were no less active, and the noble, generous work performed by their tender, loving hands deserves mention along with the bravery, devotion and patriotism of their brothers upon the Southern fields of carnage.

The continued need of money to obtain the comforts and necessaries for the sick and wounded of our army suggested to the loyal women of the North many and various devices for the raising of funds. Every city, town and village had its fair, festival, picnic, excursion, concert, which netted more or less to the cause of hospital relief, according to the population of the place and the amount of energy and patriotism displayed on such occasions. Especially was this characteristic of our own fair State, and scarcely a hamlet within its borders which did not send something from its stores to hospital or battlefield, and in the larger towns and cities were well-organized soldiers' aid societies, working systematically and continuously from the beginning of the war till its close. The great State Fair held in Chicago in May, 1865, netted $250,000. Homes for traveling soldiers were established all over the State, in which were furnished lodging for 600,000 men, and meals valued at $2,500,000. Food, clothing, medicine, hospital delicacies, reading matter, and thousands of other articles, were sent to the boys at the front.

MESSAGES OF LOVE AND ENCOURAGEMENT.

Letters, messages of love and encouragement, were sent by noble women from many counties of the State to encourage the brave sons and brothers in the South. Below we give a copy of a printed letter sent from Knox county to the "boys in blue," as showing the feelings of the women of the North. It was headed, "FROM THE WOMEN OF KNOX COUNTY TO THEIR BROTHERS IN THE FIELD." It was a noble, soul-inspiring message, and kindled anew the intensest love for home, country, and a determination to crown the stars and stripes with victory:

"You have gone out from our homes, but not from our hearts. Never for one moment are you forgotten. Through weary march and deadly conflict our prayers have ever followed you; your sufferings are our sufferings, your victories our great joy.

" If there be one of you who knows not the dear home ties, for whom no mother prays, no sister watches, to him especially we speak. Let him feel that though he may not have *one* mother he has *many;* he is the adopted child and brother of all our hearts. Not one of you is beyond the reach of our sympathies; no picket-station so lonely that it is not enveloped in the halo of our prayers.

" During all the long, dark months since our country called you from us, your courage, your patient endurance, your fidelity, have awakened our keenest interest, and we have longed to give you an expression of that interest.

" By the alacrity with which you sprang to arms, by the valor with which those arms have been wielded, you have placed our State in the front ranks; you have made her worthy to be the home of our noble President. For thus sustaining the honor of our State, dear to us as life, we thank you.

" Of your courage we need not speak. Fort Donelson, Pea Ridge, Shiloh, Stone River, Vicksburg, speak with blood-bathed lips of your heroism. The Army of the Southwest fights beneath no defeat-shadowed banner; to it, under God, the nation looks for deliverance.

" But we, as women, have other cause for thanks. We will not speak of the debt we owe the defenders of our Government; that blood-sealed bond no words can cancel. But we are your debtors in a way not often recognized. You have aroused us from the aimlessness into which too many of our lives had drifted, and have infused into those lives a noble pathos. We could not dream our time away while our brothers were dying for us. Even your sufferings have worked together for our good, by inciting us to labor for their alleviation, thus giving us a work worthy of our womanhood. Everything that we have been permitted to do for your comfort has filled our lives so much the fuller of all that makes life valuable. You have thus been the means of developing in us a nobler type of womanhood than without the example of your heroism we could ever have attained. For this our whole lives, made purer and nobler by the discipline, will thank you.

" This war will leave none of us as it found us. We cannot buffet the raging wave and escape all trace of the salt sea's foam. Toward better or toward worse we are hurried with fearful haste. If we at home feel this, what must it be to you! Our hearts throb with agony when we think of you wounded, suffering, dying; but the thought of no physical pain touches us half so deeply as the thought of the temptations which surround you. We could better give you up to die on the battle-field, true to your God and to your country, than to have you return to us with blasted, blackened souls. When temptations assail fiercely, you must let the thought that your mothers are praying for strength enable you to overcome them. But fighting for a worthy cause worthily ennobles one; herein is our confidence that you will return better men than you went away.

" By all that is noble in your manhood; by all that is true in our womanhood; by all that is grand in patriotism; by all that is sacred in religion, we adjure you to be faithful to yourselves, to us, to your country, and to your God. Never were men permitted to fight in a cause more worthy of their blood. Were you fighting for mere conquest, or glory, we could not give you up; but to sustain a *principle*, the greatest to which human lips have ever given utterance, even your dear lives are not too costly a sacrifice. Let that principle, the corner-stone of our independence, be crushed, and we are *all slaves*. Like the Suliote mothers, we might well clasp our children in our arms and leap down to death.

"To the stern arbitrament of the sword is now committed the honor, the very life of this nation. You fight not for yourselves alone; the eyes of the whole world are on you; and if you fail our Nation's death-wail will echo through all coming ages, moaning a requiem over the lost hopes of oppressed humanity. But you will not fail, so sure as there is a God in Heaven. He never meant this richest argosy of the nations, freighted with the fears of all the world's tyrants, with the hopes of all its oppressed ones, to flounder in darkness and death. Disasters may come, as they have come, but they will only be, as they have been, ministers of good. Each one has led the nation upward to a higher plane, from whence it has seen with a clearer eye. Success could not attend us at the West so long as we scorned the help of the black hand, which alone had power to open the gate of redemption; the God of battles would not vouchsafe a victory at the East till the very footprints of a McClellan were washed out in blood.

"But now all things seem ready; we have accepted the aid of

that hand; those footsteps are obliterated. In his own good time we feel that God will give us the victory. Till that hour comes we bid you fight on. Though we have not attained that heroism, or decision, which enables us to give you up without a struggle, which can prevent our giving *tears* for your *blood*, though many of us must own our hearts desolate till you return, still we bid you stay and fight for our country, till from this fierce baptism of blood she shall be raised *complete;* the dust shaken from her garments purified, a new Memnon singing in the great Godlight."

SHERMAN'S MARCH TO THE SEA.

On the 15th of November, 1864, after the destruction of Atlanta, and the railroads behind him, Sherman, with his army, began his march to the sea-coast. The almost breathless anxiety with which his progress was watched by the loyal hearts of the nation, and the trembling apprehension with which it was regarded by all who hoped for rebel success, indicated this as one of the most remarkable events of the war; and so it proved. Of Sherman's army, 45 regiments of infantry, three companies of artillery, and one of cavalry were from this State. Lincoln answered all rumors of Sherman's defeat with, "It is impossible; there is a mighty sight of fight in 100,000 Western men." Illinois soldiers brought home 300 battle flags. The first United States flag that floated over Richmond was an Illinois flag. She sent messengers and nurses to every field and hospital to care for her sick and wounded sons.

Illinois gave the country the great general of the war, U. S. Grant.

CHARACTER OF ABRAHAM LINCOLN.

One other name from Illinois comes up in all minds, embalmed in all hearts, that must have the supreme place in this sketch of our glory and of our nation's honor: that name is Abraham Lincoln. The analysis of Mr. Lincoln's character is difficult on account of its symmetry. In this age we look with admiration at his uncompromising honesty; and well we may, for this saved us. Thousands throughout the length and breadth of our country, who knew him only as "Honest Old Abe," voted for him on that account; and wisely did they choose, for no other man could have carried us through the fearful night of war. When his plans were too vast for our comprehension, and his faith in the cause too sub-

time for our participation; when it was all night about us, and all
dread before us, and all sad and desolate behind us; when not one
ray shone upon our cause; when traitors were haughty and exultant at the South, and fierce and blasphemous at the North; when
the loyal men seemed almost in the minority; when the stoutest
heart quailed, the bravest cheek paled; when generals were defeating each other for place, and contractors were leeching out the very
heart's blood of the republic; when everything else had failed us,
we looked at this calm, patient man standing like a rock in the
storm, and said, " Mr. Lincoln is honest, and we can trust him still."
Holding to this single point with the energy of faith and despair,
we held together, and under God he brought us through to victory.
His practical wisdom made him the wonder of all lands.   With
such certainty did Mr. Lincoln follow causes to their ultimate
effects, that his foresight of contingencies seemed almost prophetic.
He is radiant with all the great virtues, and his memory will shed
a glory upon this age that will fill the eyes of men as they look
into history.   Other men have excelled him in some points; but,
taken at all points, he stands head and shoulders above every other
man of 6,000 years.   An administrator, he saved the nation in the
perils of unparalleled civil war;   a statesman, he justified his
measures by their success; a philanthropist, he gave liberty to one
race and salvation to another; a moralist, he bowed from the summit of human power to the foot of the cross; a mediator, he exercised mercy under the most absolute obedience to law; a leader,
he was no partisan; a commander, he was untainted with blood; a
ruler in desperate times, he was unsullied with crime; a man, he
has left no word of passion, no thought of malice, no trick of craft,
no act of jealousy, no purpose of selfish ambition.   Thus perfected,
without a model and without a peer, he was dropped into these
troubled years to adorn and embellish all that is good and all that
is great in our humanity, and to present to all coming time the
representative of the divine idea of free government.   It is not
too much to say that away down in the future, when the republic
has fallen from its niche in the wall of time; when the great war
itself shall have faded out in the distance like a mist on the
horizon; when the Anglo-Saxon shall be spoken only by the tongue
of the stranger, then the generations looking this way shall see
the great President as the supreme figure in this vortex of history.

THE WAR ENDED—THE UNION RESTORED.

The rebellion was ended with the surrender of Lee and his army, and Johnson and his command in April, 1865. Our armies at the time were up to their maximum strength, never so formidable, never so invincible; and, until recruiting ceased by order of Secretary Stanton, were daily strengthening. The necessity, however,

LINCOLN MONUMENT AT SPRINGFIELD.

for so vast and formidable numbers ceased with the disbanding of the rebel forces, which had for more than four years disputed the supremacy of the Government over its domain. And now the joyful and welcome news was to be borne to the victorious legions that their work was ended in triumph, and they were to be permitted "to see homes and friends once more."

Schedule—Showing statement of volunteer troops organized within the State, and sent to the field, commencing April, 1861, and ending December 31, 1865, with number of regiment. name of original commanding officer, date of organization and muster into United States' service, place of muster, and the aggregate strength of each organization.

INFANTRY.

No.	Commanding officer at organization.	Date of organization and muster into the United States service.	Place where mustered into the United States service.	Aggr. strength since organization.
7	Col. John Cook........	July 25, 1861....	Cairo, Illinois......	1747
8	" Richard J. Oglesby........	"	"	1853
9	" Eleazer A. Paine..........	"	"	1265
10	" Jas. D. Morgan....	"	"	1759
11	" W. H. L. Wallace...	"	"	1384
12	" John McArthur............	"		1675
13	" John B. Wyman..........	May 24, 1861....	Dixon......	1112
14	" John M. Palmer..........	May 25, 1861............	Jacksonville....	2015
15	" Thos. J. Turner..........	May 24, 1861............	Freeport.............	2028
16	" Robert F. Smith....	"	Quincy..........	1833
17	" Leonard F. Ross............	"	Peoria..........	1259
18	" Michael K. Lawler........	May 28, 1861............	Anna...	2043
19	" John B. Turchin........		....	1095
20	" Chas. C. Marsh..........	June 13, 1861............	Joliet	1817
21	" Ulysses S. Grant..........	June 15, 1861............	Mattoon............	1266
22	" Henry Dougherty..........	June 25, 1861............	Belleville............	1164
23	" Jas. A. Mulligan..........	June 18, 1861............	Chicago...... ...	1983
24	" Frederick Hecker..........	July 8, 1861............	Chicago............	989
25	" Wm. N. Coler............			1082
26	" John M. Loomis............	Oct. 31, 1861............ ...	Camp Butler...	1602
27	" Nap. B. Buford............			1193
28	" A. K. Johnson....	Aug. 3, 1861............	Camp Butler..........	1939
29	" Jas. S. Rearden..........	July 27, 1861............	Camp Butler........	1547
30	" Philip B. Fouke..........	Sept. 30, 1861............	Camp Butler....	1878
31	" John A. Logan....	Sept. 8, 1861.	Camp Butler...... ..	1973
32	" John Logan............	Dec. 31, 1861............	Camp Butler..........	1711
33	" Chas. E. Hovey............	Aug. 15, 1861............	Camp Butler.	1660
34	" Edward N. Kirk..........	Sept. 7, 1861....	Camp Butler.......... ..	1558
35	" Gus. A. Smith............		Aurora............	1012
36	" Nich. Greusel........	Sept. 23, 1861............	Aurora............	1593
37	" Julius White............	Sept. 18, 1361............	Chicago..........	1157
38	" Wm. P. Carlin............	Aug. 15, 1861.	Camp Butler..........	1388
39	" Austin Light............	December, 1861....	Chicago.....	1807
40	" Steph. G. Hicks............	Aug. 10, 1861............	Salem............	1277
41	" Isaac C. Pugh............	Aug. 9, 1861............	Decatur............	1211
42	" Wm. A. Webb............	Sept. 17, 1861............	Chicago............	1824
43	" Julius Raith.	Dec. 16, 1861............	Camp Butler..........	1902
44	" Chas. Noblesdorff..........	Sept. 13, 1861............	Chicago............	1512
45	" John E. Smith..	Dec. 24, 1861............	Galena............	1716
46	" John A. Davis..	Dec. 28, 1861............	Camp Butler.......... ..	2015
47	" John Bryner....ʼ....	Oct. 1, 1861 .	Peoria............	2051
48	" Isham N. Haynie....	Nov. 18, 1861....	Camp Butler..........	1874
49	" Wm. R. Morrison..........	Dec. 31, 1861............	Camp Butler.	1482
50	" Moses M. Bane...........	Sept. 12, 1861	Quincy............	1761
51	" G. W. Cumming..........	Dec. '61, Feb. '62.......	Camp Douglas.	1550
52	" Isaac G. Wilson....	Nov. 19, 1861............	Geneva............	1519
53	" W. H. W. Cushman........	March. 1862............	Ottawa............	1424
54	" Thos. W. Harris..........	Feb. 18, 1862....	Anna	1720
55	" David Stuart............	Oct. 31, 1861............	Camp Douglas	1287
56	" Robert Kirkham....	Feb. 27, 1862............	Shawneetown..........	1180
57	" Silas D. Baldwin..........	Dec. 26, 1861............	Camp Douglas.	1754
58	" Wm. F. Lynch............	Dec. 24, 1861............	Camp Douglas ....•....	2202
59	" P. Sidney Post............	August. 1861............	St. Louis, Mo..........	1762
60	" Silas C. Toler.............	Feb. 17, 1862............	Anna............	1647
61	" Jacob Fry............	March 7, 1862....	Carrollton.......... ..	1385
62	" James M. True..........	April 10, 1862............	Anna....	1730
63	" Francis Mora...... ...	"	Anna............	1228
64	Lt. Col. D. D. Williams	Dec. 31, 1862............	Camp Butler............	1624
65	Col. Daniel Cameron	May 15, 1862............	Camp Douglas........	1684
66	" Patrick E. Burke..........	April. 1862............	St. Louis, Mo....	1694
67	" Rosell M. Hough..........	June 13, 1862............	Camp Douglas..........	979
68	" Elias Stuart....	June 20, 1862............	Camp Butler.....	889
69	" Jos. H. Tucker............	June 14, 1862............	Camp Douglas..........	912
70	" O. T. Reeves....	July 4, 1862............	Camp Butler..........	1006
71	" Othniel Gilbert......	July 26, 1862............	Camp Douglas............	940

SCHEDULE—Showing statement of volunteer troops organized within the State, and sent to the field, commencing April, 1861, and ending December 31, 1865, with number of regiment, name of original commanding officer, date of organization and muster into United States' service, place of muster, and the aggregate strength of each organization.

INFANTRY.

No.	Commanding officer at organization.	Date of organization and muster into the United States service.	Place where mustered into the United States service.	Aggr. strength since organization.
72	Col. Frederick A. Starring	Aug. 21, 1862	Camp Douglas	1471
73	" Jas. F. Jaquess	"	Camp Butler	968
74	" Jason Marsh	Sept. 4, 1862	Rockford	989
75	" George Ryan	Sept. 2. 1862	Dixon	987
76	" Alonzo W. Mack	Aug. 22, 1862	Kankakee	1110
77	" David P. Grier	*Sept. 3, 1862	Peoria	1051
78	" W. H. Bennison	Sept. 1, 1862	Quincy	1028
79	" Lyman Guinnip	Aug. 28, 1862	Danville	974
80	" Thos. G. Allen	Aug. 25, 1862	Centralia	928
81	" Jas. J. Dollins	Aug. 26, 1862	Anna	1187
82	" Frederick Hecker	"	Camp Butler	961
83	" Abner C. Harding	Aug. 21, 1862	Monmouth	1286
84	" Louis H. Waters	Sept. 1, 1862	Quincy	956
85	" Robert S. Moore	Aug. 27, 1862	Peoria	959
86	" David D. Irons	"	Peoria	993
87	" John E. Whiting	Sept. 22, 1862	Shawneetown	994
88	" F. T. Sherman	Aug. 27, 1862	Camp Douglas	907
89	" John Christopher	*Aug 25, 1862	Camp Douglas	1.85
90	" Timothy O'Mera	Nov. 22, 1862	Camp Douglas	958
91	" Henry M. Day	Sept. 8, 1862	Camp Butler	1041
92	" Smith D. Atkins	Sept. 4, 1862	Rockford	1265
93	" Holden Putnam	Oct. 13, 1862	Princeton and Chicago	1036
94	" Wm. W. Orme	Aug. 20, 1862	Bloomington,	1091
95	" Lawr'n S. Church	Sept. 4, 1862	Rockford	1427
96	" Thos. E. Champion	Sept. 6, 1862	Rockford	1206
97	" F. S. Rutherford	Sept. 8, 1862	Camp Butler	1082
98	" J. J. Funkhouser	Sept. 3, 1862	Centralia	1078
99	" G. W. K. Bailey	Aug. 26, 1862	Florence, Pike Co.,	936
100	" Fred. A. Bartleson	Aug. 30, 1862	Joliet	921
101	" Chas. H. Fox	Sept. 2, 1862	Jacksonville	911
102	" Wm. McMurtry	"	Knoxville	998
103	" Amos C. Babcock	Oct. 2, 1862	Peoria	917
104	" Absalom B. Moore	Aug. 27, 1862	Ottawa	977
105	" Daniel Dustin	Sept. 2, 1862	Chicago	1001
106	" Robert B. Latham	Sept. 17, 1862	Lincoln	1097
107	" Thomas Snell	Sept. 4, 1862	Camp Butler	944
108	" John Warner	Aug. 28, 1862	Peoria	927
109	" Alex. J. Nimmo	Sept. 11, 1861	Anna	967
110	" Thos. S. Casey		Anna	873
111	" James S. Martin	Sept. 18, 1862	Salem	994
112	" T. J. Henderson	Sept. 12, 1862	Peoria	1095
113	" Geo. B. Hoge	Oct. 1, 1862	Camp Douglas	1258
114	" James W. Judy	Sept. 18, 1862	Camp Butler	990
115	" Jesse H. Moore	Sept. 13, 1862	Camp Butler	960
116	" Nathan H. Tupper	Sept. 30 1862	Decatur	952
117	" Risden M. Moore	Sept. 19, 1862	Camp Butler	995
118	" John G. Fonda	Nov. 29, 1862	Camp Butler	1101
119	" Thos. J. Kenney	Oct. 7, 1862	Quincy	952
120	" George W. McKeaig	Oct. 29, 1862	Camp Butler	844
121	Never organized			....
122	Col. John I. Rinaker	Sept. 4, 1862	Carlinville	934
123	" James Moore	Sept. 6 1862	Mattoon	1050
124	" Thomas J. Sloan	Sept. 10 1862	Camp Butler	1130
125	" Oscar F. Harmon	Sept. 4, 1862	Danville	933
126	" Jonathan Richmond	"	Chicago	998
127	" John VanArman	*Sept. 5, 1862	Camp Douglas	957
128	" Robert M. Hudley	Dec. 18, 1862	Camp Butler	866
129	" George P. Smith	Sept. 8, 1862	Pontiac	1011
130	" Nathaniel Niles	Oct. 25, 1865	Camp Butler	932
131	" George W. Neeley	Nov. 13, 1862	Camp Massac	880
132	" Thomas C. Pickett	June 1, 1864	Camp Fry	853
133	" Thad. Phillips	May 31, 1864	Camp Butler	851
134	" W. W McChesney	"	Camp Fry	878
135	" John S. Wolfe	June 6, 1864	Mattoon	852

SCHEDULE—Showing statement of volunteer troops organized within the State, and sent to the field, commencing April, 1861, and ending December 31, 1865, with number of regiment, name of original commanding officer, date of organization and muster into United States' service, place of muster, and the aggregate strength of each organization.

INFANTRY.

No.	Commanding officer at organization.	Date of organization and muster into the United States service.	Place where mustered into the United States service.	Aggr. strength since organization.
136	Col. Fred. A. Johns..	June 1, 1864	Centralia	842
137	" John Wood	June 5, 1864	Quincy	849
138	" J. W. Goodwin	June 21, 1864	Quincy	835
139	" Peter Davidson	June 1, 1864	Peoria	878
140	" L. H. Whitney	June 18, 1864	Camp Butler	871
41	" Stephen Bronson	June 16, 1864	Elgin	842
142	" Rollin V. Ankney	June 18, 1864	Camp Butler	851
143	" Dudley C. Smith	June 11, 1864	Mattoon	865
144	" Cyrus Hall	Oct. 21, 1864	Alton, Ills	1159
145	" George W. Lackey	June 9, 1864	Camp Butler	880
146	" Henry H. Dean	Sept. 20, 1864	Camp Butler	1056
147	" Hiram F. Sickles	Feb. 18, 1865	Chicago	1047
148	" Horace H. Wilsie	"	Quincy	917
149	" Wm. C. Kueffner	Feb. 11, 1865	Camp Butler	983
150	" George W. Keener	Feb. 14, 1865	Camp Butler	933
151	" French B. Woodall	Feb. 25, 1865	Quincy	970
152	" F. D. Stephenson	Feb. 18, 1865	Camp Butler	845
153	" Stephen Bronson	Feb. 27, 1865	Chicago	1076
154	" McLean F. Wood	Feb. 22, 1865	Camp Butler	994
155	" Gustavus A. Smith	Feb. 28, 1865	Camp Butler	929
156	" Alfred F. Smith	March 9, 1865	Chicago	975
...	" J. W. Wilson	Dec. 1, 1861	Chicago	985
...	" John A. Bross		Quincy	903
...	Capt. John Curtis	June 21, 1864	Camp Butler	91
...	" Simon J. Stookey	"	Camp Butler	90
...	" James Steele	June 15, 1864	Chicago	86

CAVALRY.

No.	Commanding officer at organization.	Date of organization.	Place where mustered.	Aggr. strength
1	Col. Thomas A. Marshall	June, 1861	Bloomington	1206
2	" Silas Noble	Aug. 24, "	Camp Butler	1861
3	" Eugene A. Carr	Sept. 21, "	Camp Butler	2183
4	" T. Lyle Dickey	Sept. 30, "	Ottawa	1656
5	" John J. Updegraff	December "	Camp Butler	1669
6	" Thomas H. Cavanaugh	Nov., '61, Jan., '62	Camp Butler	2248
7	" Wm. Pitt Kellogg	August, '61	Camp Butler	2282
8	" John F. Farnsworth	Sept. 18, '61	St. Charles	2412
9	" Albert G. Brackett	Oct. 26, '61	Camp Douglas	2619
10	" James A. Barrett	Nov. 25, '61	Camp Butler	1934
11	" Robert G. Ingersoll	Dec. 20, '61	Peoria	2362
12	" Arno Voss	Dec., '61, Feb., '62	Camp Butler	2174
13	" Joseph W. Bell	" "	Camp Douglas	1759
14	" Horace Capron	Jan. 7, '63	Peoria	1565
15	" Warren Stewart	Organized Dec. 25, '63	Camp Butler	1473
16	" Christian Thielman	Jan. and April, '63	Camp Butler	1462
17	" John L. Beveridge	Jan. 28, '64	St. Charles	1247

FIRST REGIMENT—ILLINOIS LIGHT ARTILLERY.

Co	Commanding officer	Date	Place	Aggr. strength
	Field and Staff			7
A	Capt. C. M. Willard		Chicago	168
B	" Ezra Taylor		Chicago	204
C	" C. Haughtaling	Oct. 31, 1861	Ottawa	175
D	" Edward McAllister	Jan. 14, '62	Plainfield	141
E	" A. C. Waterhouse	Dec. 19, '61	Chicago	148
F	" John T. Cheney	Feb. 25, '62	Camp Butler	159
G	" Arthur O'Leary	Feb. 28, '62	Cairo	113
H	" Axel Silversparr	Feb. 20, '62	Chicago	147
I	" Edward Bouton	Feb. 15, '62	Chicago	169
K	" A. Franklin	Jan. 9, '62	Shawneetown	96
L	" John Rourke	Feb. 22, '62	Chicago	153
M	" John B. Miller	Aug 12, '62	Chicago	154
	Recruits			883

SCHEDULE—Showing statement of volunteer troops organized within the State, and sent to the field commencing April, 1861, and ending December 31, 1865, with number of regiment, name of original commanding officer, date of organization and muster into United States service, place of muster, and the aggregate strength of each organization.

LIGHT ARTILLERY.

Co.	Commanding officer at organization.	Date of organization and muster into the United States service.	Place where mustered into the United States service.	Aggr. strength since organization.

SECOND REGIMENT—ILLINOIS LIGHT ARTILLERY.

Co.	Commanding officer	Date	Place	Aggr.
A	Capt. Peter Davidson	Aug. 17, 1861	Peoria	116
B	" Riley Madison	June 20, '61	Springfield	127
C	" Caleb Hopkins	Aug. 5, '61	Cairo	154
D	" Jasper M. Dresser	Dec. 17, '61	Cairo	117
E	" Adolph Schwartz	Feb. 1, '62	Cairo	136
F	" John W. Powell	Dec. 11, '61	Cape Girardeau, Mo.	190
G	" Charles J. Stolbrand	Dec. 31, '61	Camp Butler.	108
H	" Andrew Steinbeck	"	Camp Butler.	115
I	" Charles W. Keith.	"	Camp Butler.	107
K	" Benjamin F. Rogers	"	Camp Butler.	108
L	" William H. Bolton	Feb. 28, '62	Chicago	145
M	" John C. Phillips	June 6, '62	Chicago	100
	Field and Staff			10
	Recruits			1171

INDEPENDENT BATTERIES.

Name	Commanding officer	Date	Place	Aggr.
Board of Trade	Capt. James S. Stokes	July 31, 1862	Chicago	258
Springfield	" Thomas F. Vaughn	Aug. 21, '62	Camp Butler.	199
Mercantile	" Charles G. Cooley	Aug. 29, '62	Chicago	270
Elgin	" George W. Renwick	Nov. 15, '62	Elgin	242
Coggswell's	" William Coggswell	Sept 23, '61	Camp Douglas	221
Henshaw's	" Ed. C. Henshaw	Oct. 15, '62	Ottawa	196
Bridges'	" Lyman Bridges	Jan. 1, '62	Chicago	232
Colvin's	" John H. Colvin	Oct. 10, '63	Chicago	91
Busteed's			Chicago	127

RECAPITULATION.

Infantry	185,941
Cavalry	32 082
Artillery	7,277

DUELS.

The code of chivalry so common among Southern gentlemen and so frequently brought into use in settling personal differences has also been called to settle the " affairs of honor " in our own State, however, but few times, and those in the earlier days. Several attempts at duels have occurred; before the disputants met in mortal combat the differences were amicably and satisfactorily settled; honor was maintained without the sacrifice of life. In 1810 a law was adopted to suppress the practice of dueling. This law held the fatal result of dueling to be murder, and, as it was intended, had the effect of making it odious and dishonorable. Prior to the constitution of 1848, parties would evade the law by going beyond the jurisdiction of the State to engage in their contests of honor. At that time they incorporated in the Constitution an oath of office, which was so broad as to cover the whole world. Any person who had ever fought a duel, ever sent or accepted a challenge or acted the part of second was disfranchised from holding office, even of minor importance. After this went into effect, no other duel or attempt at a duel has been engaged in within the State of Illinois, save those fought by parties living outside of the State, who came here to settle their personal differences.

THE FIRST DUEL.

The first duel fought within the boundaries of this great State was between two young military officers, one of the French and the other of the English army, in the year 1765. It was at the time the British troops came to take possession of Fort Chartres, and a woman was the cause of it. The affair occurred early Sunday morning, near the old fort. They fought with swords, and in the combat one sacrificed his life.

BOND AND JONES.

In 1809 the next duel occurred and was bloodless of itself, but out of it grew a quarrel which resulted in the assassination of one of the contestants. The principals were Shadrach Bond, the first Governor, and Rice Jones, a bright young lawyer, who became quite a politician and the leader of his party. A personal difference arose between the two, which to settle, the parties met for mortal combat on an island in the Mississippi. The weapons selected were hair-trigger pistols. After taking their position Jones' weapon was prematurely discharged. Bond's second, Dunlap, now claimed that according to the code Bond had the right to the next fire. But Bond would not take so great advantage of his opponent, and said it was an accident and would not fire. Such noble conduct touched the generous nature of Jones, and the difficulty was at once amicably settled. Dunlap, however, bore a deadly hatred for Jones, and one day while he was standing in the street in Kaskaskia, conversing with a lady, he crept up behind him and shot him dead in his tracks. Dunlap successfully escaped to Texas.

RECTOR AND BARTON.

In 1812 the bloody code again brought two young men to the field of honor. They were Thomas Rector, a son of Capt. Stephen

ILLINOIS ASYLUM FOR FEEBLE MINDED CHILDREN, AT LINCOLN.

Rector who bore such a noble part in the war of 1812, and Joshua Barton. They had espoused the quarrel of older brothers. The affair occurred on Bloody Island, in the Mississippi, but in the limits of Illinois. This place was frequented so often by Missourians to settle personal difficulties, that it received the name of Bloody Island. Barton fell in this conflict.

STEWART AND BENNETT.

In 1819 occurred the first duel fought after the admission of the State into the Union. This took place in St. Clair county between Alphonso Stewart and William Bennett. It was intended to be a sham duel, to turn ridicule against Bennett, the challenging party. Stewart was in the secret but Bennett was left to believe it a reality. Their guns were loaded with blank cartridges. Bennett, suspecting a trick, put a ball into his gun without the knowledge of his seconds. The word "fire" was given, and Stewart fell mortally wounded. Bennett made his escape but was subsequently captured, convicted of murder and suffered the penalty of the law by hanging.

PEARSON AND BAKER.

In 1840 a personal difference arose between two State Senators, Judge Pearson and E. D. Baker. The latter, smarting under the epithet of "falsehood," threatened to chastise Pearson in the public streets, by a "fist fight." Pearson declined making a "blackguard" of himself but intimated a readiness to fight as gentlemen, according to the code of honor. The affair, however. was carried no further.

HARDIN AND DODGE.

The exciting debates in the Legislature in 1840–'41 were often bitter in personal "slings," and threats of combats were not infrequent. During these debates, in one of the speeches by the Hon. J. J. Hardin, Hon. A. R. Dodge thought he discovered a personal insult, took exceptions, and an "affair" seemed imminent. The controversy was referred to friends, however, and amicably settled.

M'CLERNAND AND SMITH.

Hon. John A. McClernand, a member of the House, in a speech delivered during the same session made charges against the Whig Judges of the Supreme Court. This brought a note from Judge

T. W. Smith, by the hands of his "friend" Dr. Merriman, to
McClernand. This was construed as a challenge, and promptly
accepted, naming the place of meeting to be Missouri; time, early;
the weapons, rifles; and distance, 40 paces. At this critical juncture, the Attorney General had a warrant issued against the Judge,
whereupon he was arrested and placed under bonds to keep the
peace. Thus ended this attempt to vindicate injured honor.

LINCOLN AND SHIELDS.

During the hard times subsequent to the failure of the State and
other banks, in 1842, specie became scarce while State money was
plentiful, but worthless. The State officers thereupon demanded
specie payment for taxes. This was bitterly opposed, and so fiercely
contested that the collection of taxes was suspended.

During the period of the greatest indignation toward the State
officials, under the *nom de plume* of "Rebecca," Abraham Lincoln
had an article published in the *Sangamo Journal*, entitled "Lost
Township." In this article, written in the form of a dialogue, the
officers of the State were roughly handled, and especially Auditor
Shields. The name of the author was demaded from the editor by
Mr. Shields, who was very indignant over the manner in which he
was treated. The name of Abraham Lincoln was given as the
author. It is claimed by some of his biographers, however, that
the article was prepared by a lady, and that when the name of the
author was demanded, in a spirit of gallantry, Mr. Lincoln gave
his name. In company with Gen. Whiteside, Gen. Shields pursued Lincoln to Tremont, Tazewell county, where he was in attendance upon the court, and immediately sent him a note "requiring
a full, positive and absolute retraction of all offensive allusions"
made to him in relation to his "private character and standing as
a man, or an apology for the insult conveyed." Lincoln had been
forewarned, however, for William Butler and Dr. Merriman, of
Springfield, had become acquainted with Shields' intentions and by
riding all night arrived at Tremont ahead of Shields and informed
Lincoln what he might expect. Lincoln answered Shields' note,
refusing to offer any explanation, on the grounds that Shields' note
assumed the fact of his (Lincoln's) authorship of the article, and
not pointing out what the offensive part was, and accompanying the
same with threats as to consequences. Mr. Shields answered this,
disavowing all intention to menace; inquired if he was the author,

asked a retraction of that portion relating to his private character. Mr. Lincoln, still technical, returned this note with the verbal statement "that there could be no further negotiations until the first note was withdrawn." At this Shields named Gen. White-side as his " friend," when Lincoln reported Dr. Merriman as his "friend." These gentlemen secretly pledged themselves to agree upon some amicable terms, and compel their principals to accept them. The four went to Springfield, when Lincoln left for Jacksonville, leaving the following instructions to guide his friend, Dr. Merriman:

" In case Whiteside shall signify a wish to adjust this affair without further difficulty, let him know that if the present papers be withdrawn and a note from Mr. Shields, asking to know if I am the author of the articles of which he complains, and asking that I shall make him gentlemanly satisfaction, if I am the author, and this without menace or dictation as to what that satisfaction shall be, a pledge is made that the following answer shall be given:

I did write the "Lost Township" letter which appeared in the *Journal* of the 2d inst., but had no participation, in any form, in any other article alluding to you. I wrote that wholly for political effect. I had no intention of injuring your personal or private character or standing, as a man or gentleman; and I did not then think, and do not now think, that that article could produce or has produced that effect against you; and, had I anticipated such an effect, would have foreborne to write it. And I will add that your conduct toward me, so far as I know, had always been gentlemanly, and that I had no personal pique against you, and no cause for any.

" If this should be done, I leave it to you to manage what shall and what shall not be published. If nothing like this is done, the preliminaries of the fight are to be:

" 1st. *Weapons*.—Cavalry broad swords of the largest size, precisely equal in all respects, and such as are now used by the cavalry company at Jacksonville.

" 2d. *Position*.—A plank ten feet long and from nine to twelve inches broad, to be firmly fixed on edge, on the ground, as a line between us which neither is to pass his foot over on forfeit of his life. Next a line drawn on the ground on either side of said plank, and parallel with it, each at the distance of the whole length of the sword, and three feet additional from the plank; and the passing of his own such line by either party during the fight, shall be deemed a surrender of the contest.

"3d. *Time.*—On Thursday evening at 5 o'clock, if you can get it so; but in no case to be at a greater distance of time than Friday evening at 5 o'clock.

"4th. *Place.*—Within three miles of Alton, on the opposite side of the river, the particular spot to be agreed on by you.

" Any preliminary details coming within the above rules, you are at liberty to make at your discretion, but you are in no case to swerve from these rules, or pass beyond their limits."

The position of the contestants, as prescribed by Lincoln, seems to have been such as both would have been free from coming in contact with the sword of the other, and the first impression is that it is nothing more than one of Lincoln's jokes. He possessed very long arms, however, and could reach his adversary at the stipulated distance.

Not being amicably arranged, all parties repaired to the field of combat in Missouri. Gen. Hardin and Dr. English, as mutual friends of both Lincoln and Shields, arrived in the meantime, and after much correspondence at their earnest solicitation the affair was satisfactorily arranged, Lincoln making a statement similar to the one above referred to.

SHIELDS AND BUTLER.

William Butler, one of Lincoln's seconds, was dissatisfied with the bloodless termination of the Lincoln–Shields affair, and wrote an account of it for the *Sangamo Journal.* This article reflected dis-creditably upon both the principals engaged in that controversy. Shields replied by the hands of his friend Gen. Whiteside, in a curt, menacing note, which was promptly accepted as a challenge by Butler, and the inevitable Dr. Merriman named as his friend, who submitted the following as preliminaries of the fight:

Time.—Sunrise on the following morning.

Place.—Col. Allen's farm (about one mile north of State House.)

Weapons.—Rifles.

Distance.—One hundred yards.

The parties to stand with their right sides toward each other— the rifles to be held in both hands horizontally and cocked, arms extended downwards. Neither party to move his person or his rifle after being placed, before the word fire. The signal to be: " Are you ready? Fire! one—two—three!" about a second of time intervening between each word. Neither party to fire before the word "fire," nor after the word "three."

Gen. Whiteside, in language curt and abrupt, addressed a note to Dr. Merriman declining to accept the terms. Gen. Shields, however, addressed another note to Butler, explaining the feelings of his second, and offering to go out to a lonely place on the prairie to fight, where there would be no danger of being interrupted; or, if that did not suit, he would meet him on his own conditions, when and where he pleased. Butler claimed the affair was closed and declined the proposition.

WHITESIDE AND MERRIMAN.

Now Gen. Whiteside and Dr. Merriman, who several times had acted in the capacity of friends or seconds, were to handle the deadly weapons as principals. While second in the Shields–Butler *fiasco*, Whiteside declined the terms proposed by Butler, in curt and abrupt language, stating that the place of combat could not be dictated to him, for it was as much his right as Merriman's, who, if he was a gentleman, would recognize and concede it. To this Merriman replied by the hands of Capt. Lincoln. It will be remembered that Merriman had acted in the same capacity for Lincoln. Whiteside then wrote to Merriman, asking to meet him at St. Louis, when he would hear from him further. To this Merriman replied, denying his right to name place, but offered to meet in Louisiana, Mo. This Whiteside would not agree to, but later signified his desire to meet him there, but the affair being closed, the doctor declined to re-open it.

PRATT AND CAMPBELL.

These two gentlemen were members of the Constitutional Convention of 1847, and both from Jo Davies county. A dispute arose which ended in a challenge to meet on the field of honor. They both repaired to St. Louis, but the authorities gaining knowledge of their bloody intentions, had both parties arrested, which ended this "affair."

DRESS AND MANNERS.

The dress, habits, etc., of a people throw so much light upon their conditions and limitations that in order better to show the circumstances surrounding the people of the State, we will give a short exposition of the manner of life of our Illinois people at different epochs. The Indians themselves are credited by Charlevoix with being "very laborious,"—raising poultry, spinning the wool of the buffalo and manufacturing garments therefrom. These must have been, however, more than usually favorable representatives of their race.

"The working and voyaging dress of the French masses," says Reynolds, "was simple and primitive. The French were like the lilies of the valley (the Old Ranger was not always exact in his quotations),—they neither spun nor wove any of their clothing, but purchased it from the merchants. The white blanket coat, known as the *capot*, was the universal and eternal coat for the winter with the masses. A cape was made of it that could be raised over the head in cold weather.

"In the house, and in good weather, it hung behind, a cape to the blanket coat. The reason that I know these coats so well is, that I have worn many in my youth, and a working man never wore a better garment. Dressed deer-skins and blue cloth were worn commonly in the winter for pantaloons. The blue handkerchief and the deer-skin moccasins covered the head and feet generally of the French Creoles. In 1800, scarcely a man thought himself clothed unless he had a belt tied around his blanket coat, and on one side was hung the dressed skin of a pole-cat, filled with tobacco, pipe, flint and steel. On the other side was fastened, under the belt, the the butcher-knife. A Creole in this dress felt like Tam O'Shanter filled with usquebaugh; he could face the devil. Checked calico shirts were then common, but in winter flannel was frequently worn. In the summer the laboring men and the voyagers often took their shirts off in hard work and hot weather, and turned out the naked back to the air and sun."

"Among the Americans," he adds, "home-made wool hats were the common wear. Fur hats were not common, and scarcely a boot was seen. The covering of the feet in winter was chiefly moccasins made of deer-skins, and shoe packs of tanned leather. Some wore shoes, but not common in very early times. In the summer the greater portion of the young people, male and female, and many of the old, went barefoot. The substantial and universal outside wear was the blue linsey hunting-shirt. This is an excellent garment, and I have never felt so happy and healthy since I laid it off. It is

SOUTHERN ILLINOIS NORMAL UNIVERSITY, AT CARBONDALE.

made of wide sleeves, open before, with ample size so as to envelop the body almost twice around. Sometimes it had a large cape, which answers well to save the shoulders from the rain. A belt is mostly used to keep the garment close around the person, and, nevertheless, there is nothing tight about it to hamper the body. It is often fringed, and at times the fringe is composed of red, and other gay colors. The belt, frequently, is sewed to the hunting-shirt. The vest was mostly made of striped linsey. The colors were made often with alum, copperas and madder, boiled with the bark of trees, in such a manner and proportions as the old ladies prescribed. The pantaloons of the masses were generally made of deer-skin and linsey. Course blue cloth was sometimes made into pantaloons.

" Linsey, neat and fine, manufactured at home, composed generally the outside garments of the females as well as the males. The ladies had linsey colored and woven to suit their fancy. A bonnet, composed of calico, or some gay goods, was worn on the head when they were in the open air. Jewelry on the pioneer ladies was uncommon; a gold ring was an ornament not often seen."

In 1820 a change of dress began to take place, and before 1830, according to Ford, most of the pioneer costume had disappeared. "The blue linsey hunting-shirt, with red or white fringe, had given place to the cloth coat. [Jeans would be more like the fact.] The raccoon cap, with the tail of the animal dangling down behind, had been thrown aside for hats of wool or fur. Boots and shoes had supplied the deer-skin moccasins; and the leather breeches, strapped tight around the ankle, had disappeared before unmentionables of a more modern material. The female sex had made still greater pro_gress in dress. The old sort of cotton or woolen frocks, spun, woven and made with their own fair hands, and striped and cross-barred with blue dye and turkey red, had given place to gowns of silk and calico. The feet, before in a state of nudity, now charmed in shoes of calf-skin or slippers of kid; and the head, formerly unbonneted, but covered with a cotton handkerchief, now displayed the charms of the female face under many forms of bonnets of straw, silk and leghorn. The young ladies, instead of walking a mile or two to church on Sunday, carrying their shoes and stockings in their hands until within a hundred yards of the place of worship, as formerly, now came forth arrayed complete in all the pride of dress, mounted on fine horses and attended by their male admirers."

The last half century has doubtless witnessed changes quite as great as those set forth by our Illinois historian. The chronicler of to day, looking back to the golden days of 1830 to 1840, and comparing them with the present, must be struck with the tendency of an almost monotonous uniformity in dress and manners that comes from the easy inter communication afforded by steamer, railway, telegraph and newspaper. Home manufacturers have been driven from the household by the lower-priced fabrics of distant mills. The Kentucky jeans, and the copperas-colored clothing of home manufacture, so familiar a few years ago, have given place to the cassimeres and cloths of noted factories. The ready-made-clothing stores, like a touch of nature, made the whole world kin and may drape the charcoal man in a dress-coat and a stove-pipe hat. The prints and silks of England and France give a variety of choice, and an assortment of colors and shades such as the pioneer women could hardly have dreamed of. Godey, and Demorest, and Harper's Bazar are found in our modern farm-houses, and the latest fashions of Paris are not uncommon.

PHYSICAL FEATURES OF ILLINOIS.

In area the State has 55,410 square miles of territory. It is about 150 miles wide and 400 miles long, stretching in latitude from Maine to North Carolina. The climate varies from Portland to Richmond. It favors every product of the continent, including the tropics, with less than half a dozen exceptions. It produces every great food of the world except bananas and rice. It is hardly too much to say that it is the most productive spot known to civilization. With the soil full of bread and the earth full of minerals; with an upper surface of food and an under layer of fuel; with perfect natural drainage, and abundant springs, and streams, and navigable rivers; half way between the forests of the North and the fruits of the South; within a day's ride of the great deposits of iron, coal, copper, lead and zinc; and containing and controlling the great grain, cattle, pork and lumber markets of the world, it is not strange that Illinois has the advantage of position.

There are no mountains in Illinois; in the southern as well as in the northern part of the State there are a few hills; near the banks of the Illinois, Mississippi, and several other rivers, the ground is elevated, forming the so-called bluffs, on which at the present day may be found, uneffaced by the hand of Time, the marks and traces left by the water which was formerly much higher; whence it may be safe to conclude that, where now the fertile prairies of Illinois extend, and the rich soil of the country yields its golden harvests, must have been a vast sheet of water, the mud deposited by which formed the soil, thus accounting for the present great fertility of the country.

Illinois is a garden 400 miles long and 150 miles wide. Its soil is chiefly a black, sandy loam, from 6 inches to 60 feet thick. About the old French towns it has yielded corn for a century and a half without rest or help. She leads all other States in the number of acres actually under plow. Her mineral wealth is scarcely second to her agricultural power. She has coal, iron, lead, zinc, copper, many varieties of building stone, marble, fire clay, cuma clay, common brick clay, sand of all kinds, gravel, mineral paint,—in fact, everything needed for a high civilization.

AGRICULTURE.

If any State of the Union is adapted for agriculture, and the other branches of rural economy relating thereto, such as the raising of cattle and the culture of fruit trees, it is pre-eminently Illinois. Her extremely fertile prairies recompense the farmer at less trouble and expense than he would be obliged to incur elsewhere, in order to obtain the same results. Her rich soil, adapted by nature for immediate culture, only awaits the plow and the seed in order to mature, within a few months, a most bountiful harvest. A review of statistics will be quite interesting to the reader, as well as valuable, as showing the enormous quantities of the various cereals produced in our prairie State:

In 1876 there was raised in the State 130,000,000 of bushels of corn,—twice as much as any other State, and one-sixth of all the corn raised in the United States. It would take 375,000 cars to transport this vast amount of corn to market, which would make 15,000 trains of 25 cars each. . She harvested 2,747,000 tons of hay, nearly one-tenth of all the hay in the Republic. It is not generally appreciated, but it is true, that the hay crop of the country is worth more than the cotton crop. The hay of Illinois equals the cotton of Louisiana-

Go to Charleston, S. C., and see them peddling handfuls of hay or grass, almost as a curiosity, as we regard Chinese gods or the cryolite of Greenland; drink your coffee and condensed milk; and walk back from the coast for many a league through the sand and burs till you get up into the better atmosphere of the mountains, without seeing a waving meadow or a grazing herd; then you will begin to appreciate the meadows of the Prairie State.

The value of her farm implements was, in 1876, $211,000,000, and the value of live stock was only second to New York. The same year she had 25,000,000 hogs, and packed 2,113,845, about one-half of all that were packed in the United States. She marketed $57,000,000 worth of slaughtered animals,—more than any other State, and a seventh of all the States.

Illinois excels all other States in miles of railroads and in miles of postal service, and in money orders sold per annum, and in the amount of lumber sold.

Illinois was only second in many important matters, taking the reports of 1876. This sample list comprises a few of the more important: Permanent school fund; total income for educational purposes; number of publishers of books, maps, papers, etc.; value of farm products and implements, and of live stock; in tons of coal mined.

The shipping of Illinois was only second to New York. Out of one port during the business hours of the season of navigation she sent forth a vessel every nine minutes. This did not include canalboats, which went one every five minutes.

No wonder she was only second in number of bankers or in physicians and surgeons.

She was third in colleges, teachers and schools; also in cattle, lead, hay, flax, sorghum and beeswax.

She was fourth in population, in children enrolled in public schools, in law schools, in butter, potatoes and carriages.

She was fifth in value of real and personal property, in theological seminaries, and colleges exclusively for women, in milk sold, and in boots and shoes manufactured, and in book-binding.

She was only seventh in the production of wood, while she was the twelfth in area. Surely that was well done for the Prairie State. She then had, in 1876, much more wood and growing timber than she had thirty years before.

A few leading industries will justify emphasis. She manufactured $205,000,000 worth of goods, which placed her well up toward New York and Pennsylvania. The number of her manufacturing establishments increased from 1860 to 1870, 300 per cent.; capital employed increased 350 per cent.; and the amount of product increased 400 per cent. ' She issued 5,500,000 copies of commercial and financial newspapers, being only second to New York. She had 6,759 miles of railroad, then leading all other States, worth $636,-458,000, using 3,245 engines, and 67,712 cars; making a train long enough to cover one-tenth of the entire roads of the State. Her stations were only five miles apart. She carried, in 1876, 15,795,-000 passengers an average of $36\frac{1}{2}$ miles, or equal to taking her entire population twice across the State. More than two-thirds of her land was within five miles of a railroad, and less than two per cent. was more than fifteen miles away.

The State has a large financial interest in the Illinois Central railroad. The road was incorporated in 1850, and the State gave each alternate section for six miles on each side, and doubled the price of the remaining land, so keeping herself good. The road received 2,595,000 acres of land, and paid to the State one-seventh of the gross receipts. The State received in 1877, $350,000, and had received up to that year in all about $7,000,000. It was practically the people's road, and it had a most able and gentlemanly management. Add to the above amount the annual receipts from the canal, $111,000, and a large per cent. of the State tax was provided for.

GOVERNORS OF ILLINOIS.

Shadrach Bond—Was the first Governor of Illinois. He was a native of Maryland and born in 1773; was raised on a farm; received a common English education, and came to Illinois in 1794. He served as a delegate in Congress from 1811 to 1815, where he procured the right of pre-emption of public land. He was elected Governor in 1818; was beaten for Congress in 1824 by Daniel P. Cook. He died at Kaskaskia, April 11, 1830.

Edward Coles—Was born Dec. 15, 1786, in Virginia. His father was a slave-holder; gave his son a collegiate education, and left to him a large number of slaves. These he liberated, giving each head of a family 160 acres of land and a considerable sum of money.

He was President Madison's private secretary.   He came to Illinois in 1819, was elected Governor in 1822, on the anti-slavery ticket; moved to Philadelphia in 1833, and died in 1868.

Ninian Edwards.—In 1809, on the formation of the Territory of Illinois, Mr. Edwards was appointed Governor, which position he retained until the organization of the State, when he was sent to the United States Senate.   He was elected Governor in 1826.   He was a native of Maryland and born in 1775; received a collegiate education; was Chief Justice of Kentucky, and a Republican in politics.

John Reynolds—Was born in Pennsylvania in 1788, and came with his parents to Illinois in 1800, and in 1830 was elected Governor on the Democratic ticket, and afterwards served three terms in Congress.   He received a classical education, yet was not polished. He was an ultra Democrat; attended the Charleston Convention in 1860, and urged the seizure of United States arsenals by the South.   He died in 1865 at Belleville, childless.

Joseph Duncan.—In 1834 Joseph Duncan was elected Governor by the Whigs, although formerly a Democrat.   He had previously served four terms in Congress.   He was born in Kentucky in 1794; had but a limited education; served with distinction in the war of 1812; conducted the campaign of 1832 against Black Hawk.   He came to Illinois when quite young.

Thomas Carlin—Was elected as a Democrat in 1838.   He had but a meager education; held many minor offices, and was active both in the war of 1812 and the Black Hawk war.   He was born in Kentucky in 1789; came to Illinois in 1812, and died at Carrollton, Feb. 14, 1852.

Thomas Ford—Was born in Pennsylvania in the year 1800; was brought by his widowed mother to Missouri in 1804, and shortly afterwards to Illinois.   He received a good education, studied law; was elected four times Judge, twice as Circuit Judge, Judge of Chicago and Judge of Supreme Court.   He was elected Governor by the Democratic party in 1842; wrote his history of Illinois in 1847 and died in 1850.

Augustus C. French—Was born in New Hampshire in 1808; was admitted to the bar in 1831, and shortly afterwards moved to Illinois when in 1846 he was elected Governor.   On the adoption of the Constitution of 1848 he was again chosen, serving until 1853. He was a Democrat in politics.

Joel A. Matteson—Was born in Jefferson county, N. Y., in 1808. His father was a farmer, and gave his son only a common school education. He first entered upon active life as a small tradesman, but subsequently became a large contractor and manufacturer. He was a heavy contractor in building the Canal. He was elected Governor in 1852 upon the Democratic ticket.

William H. Bissell—Was elected by the Republican party in 1856. He had previously served two terms in Congress; was colonel in the Mexican war and has held minor official positions. He was born in New York State in 1811; received a common education; came to Illinois early in life and engaged in the medical profession. This he changed for the law and became a noted orator, and the standard bearer of the Republican party in Illinois. He died in 1860 while Governor.

Richard Yates—"The war Governor of Illinois," was born in Warsaw, Ky., in 1818; came to Illinois in 1831: served two terms in Congress; in 1860 was elected Governor, and in 1865 United States Senator. He was a college graduate, and read law under J. J. Hardin. He rapidly rose in his chosen profession and charmed the people with oratory. He filled the gubernatorial chair during the trying days of the Rebellion, and by his energy and devotion won the title of " War Governor." He became addicted to strong drink, and died a drunkard.

Richard J. Oglesby—Was born in 1824, in Kentucky; an orphan at the age of eight, came to Illinois when only 12 years old. He was apprenticed to learn the carpenter's trade; worked some at farming and read law occasionally. He enlisted in the Mexican War and was chosen First Lieutenant. After his return he again took up the law, but during the gold fever of 1849 went to California; soon returned, and, in 1852, entered upon his illustrious political career. He raised the second regiment in the State, to suppress the Rebellion, and for gallantry was promoted to Major General. In 1864 he was elected Governor, and re-elected in 1872, and resigned for a seat in the United States Senate. He is a staunch Republican and resides at Decatur.

Shelby M. Cullom—Was born in Kentucky in 1828; studied law, was admitted to the bar, and commenced the practice of his profession in 1848; was elected to the State Legislature in 1856, and again in 1860. Served on the war commission at Cairo, 1862.

and was a member of the 39th, 40th and 41st Congress, in all of which he served with credit to his State. He was again elected to the State Legislature in 1872, and re-elected in 1874, and was elected Governor of Illinois in 1876, which office he still holds, and has administered with marked ability.

LIEUTENANT GOVERNORS.

Pierre Menard—Was the first Lieut. Gov. of Illinois. He was born in Quebec, Canada, in 1767. He came to Illinois in 1790 where he engaged in the Indian trade and became wealthy. He died in 1844. Menard county was named in his honor.

Adolphus F. Hubbard—Was elected Lieut. Gov. in 1822. Four years later he ran for Governor against Edwards, but was beaten.

William Kinney—Was elected in 1826. He was a Baptist clergyman; was born in Kentucky in 1781 and came to Illinois in 1793.

Zadock Casey—Although on the opposition ticket to Governor Reynolds, the successful Gubernatorial candidate, yet Casey was elected Lieut. Gov. in 1830. He subsequently served several terms in Congress.

Alexander M. Jenkins—Was elected on ticket with Gov. Duncan in 1834 by a handsome majority.

S. H. Anderson—Lieut. Gov. under Gov. Carlin, was chosen in 1838. He was a native of Tennessee.

John Moore—Was born in England in 1793; came to Illinois in 1830; was elected Lieut. Gov. in 1842. He won the name of " Honest John Moore."

Joseph B. Wells—Was chosen with Gov. French at his first election in 1846.

William McMurtry.—In 1848 when Gov. French was again chosen Governor, William McMurtry of Knox county, was elected Lieut. Governor.

Gustavus P. Koerner—Was elected in 1852. He was born in Germany in 1809. At the age of 22 came to Illinois. In 1872 he was a candidate for Governor on Liberal ticket, but was defeated.

John Wood—Was elected in 1856, and on the death of Gov. Bissell became Governor.

Francis A. Hoffman—Was chosen with Gov. Yates in 1860. He was born in Prussia in 1822, and came to Illinois in 1840.

William Bross—Was born in New Jersey, came to Illinois in 1848, was elected to office in 1864.

John Dougherty—Was elected in 1868.

John L. Beveredge—Was chosen Lieut. Gov. in 1872. In 1873 Oglesby was elected to the U. S. Senate when Beveridge became Governor.

Andrew Shuman—Was elected Nov. 7, 1876, and is the present incumbent.

SUPERINTENDENT OF PUBLIC INSTRUCTION.

Ninian W. Edwards..........1854–56	Newton Bateman..............1859–75
W. H. Powell...............1857–58	Samuel M. Etter..........1876

ATTORNEY GENERALS.

Daniel P. Cook...............1819	Geo. W. Olney...............1838
William Mears...............1820'	Wickliffe Kitchell...........1839
Samuel D. Lockwood.........1821–22	Josiah Lamborn...........1841–42
James Turney................1823–28	James A. McDougall........1843–46
George Forquer.............1829–32	David B. Campbell...........1846
James Semple...............1833–34	[Office abolished and re-created in 1867]
Ninian E. Edwards..........1834–35	Robert G. Ingersoll..........1867–68
Jesse B. Thomas, Jr..........1835	Washington Bushnell.........1869–72
Walter B. Scates............1836	James K. Edsall..............1873–79
Asher F. Linder.............1837	

TREASURERS.

John Thomas................1818–19	James Miller.................1857–60
R. K. McLaughlin...........1819–22	William Butler...............1861–62
Ebner Field.................1823–26	Alexander Starne............1863–64
James Hall.................1827–30	James H. Beveridge..........1865–66
John Dement................1831–36	George W. Smith.............1867–68
Charles Gregory............1836	Erastus N. Bates............869–72
John D. Whiteside..........1837–40	Edward Rutz 1873–75
M. Carpenter...............1841–48	Thomas S. Ridgeway.........1876–77
John Moore.................1848–56	Edward Rutz................1878–79

SECRETARIES OF STATE.

Elias K. Kane...............1818–22	Thompson Campbell.........1843–46
Samuel D. Lockwood.........1822–23	Horace S. Cooley............1846–49
David Blackwell 1823–24	David L. Gregg..............1850–52
Morris Birkbeck.............1824	Alexander Starne............1853–56
George Forquer.............1825–28	Ozias M. Hatch.............1857–60
Alexander P. Field..........1829–40	Sharon Tyndale.............1865–68
Stephen A. Douglas.........1840	Edward Rummel.............1869–72
Lyman Trumbull........1841–42	George H. Harlow.........1873–79

AUDITORS.

Elijah C. Berry	1818–31	Thompson Campbell	1846
I. T. B. Stapp	1831–35	Jesse K. Dubois	1857–64
Levi Davis	1835–40	Orlin H. Miner	1865–68
James Shields	1841–42	Charles E. Lippencott	1869–76
W. L. D. Ewing	1843–45	Thompson B. Needles	1877–79

UNITED STATES SENATORS.

Ninian Edwards.—On the organization of the State in 1818, Edwards, the popular Territorial Governor, was chosen Senator for the short term, and in 1819 re-elected for full term.

Jesse B. Thomas—One of the federal judges during the entire Territorial existence was chosen Senator on organization of the State, and re-elected in 1823, and served till 1829.

John McLean—In 1824 Edwards resigned, and McLean was elected to fill his unexpired term. He was born in North Carolina in 1791, and came to Illinois in 1815; served one term in Congress, and in 1829 was elected to the U. S. Senate, but the following year died. He is said to have been the most gifted man of his period in Illinois.

Elias Kent Kane—Was elected Nov. 30, 1824, for the term beginning March 4, 1825. In 1830 he was re-elected, but died before the expiration of his term. He was a native of New York, and in 1814 came to Illinois. He was first Secretary of State, and afterwards State Senator.

David Jewett Baker—Was appointed to fill the unexpired term of John McLean, in 1830, Nov. 12, but the Legislature refused to endorse the choice. Baker was a native of Connecticut, born in 1792, and died in Alton in 1869.

John M. Robinson.—Instead of Baker, the Governor's appointee, the Legislature chose Robinson, and in 1834 he was re-elected. In 1843 was elected Supreme Judge of the State, but within two months died. He was a native of Kentucky, and came to Illinois while quite young.

William L. D. Ewing—Was elected in 1835, to fill the vacancy occasioned by the death of Kane. He was a Kentuckian.

Richard M. Young—Was elected in 1836, and held his seat from March 4, 1837, to March 4, 1843, a full term. He was a native of Kentucky; was Circuit Judge before his election to the Senate, and Supreme Judge in 1842. He died in an insane asylum at Washington.

Samuel McRoberts—The first native Illinoisian ever elevated to the high office of U. S. Senator from this State, was born in 1799, and died in 1843 on his return home from Washington. He was elected Circuit Judge in 1824, and March 4, 1841, took his seat in the U. S. Senate.

Sidney Breese—Was elected to the U. S. Senate, Dec. 17, 1842, and served a full term. He was born in Oneida county, N. Y. He was Major in the Black Hawk war; Circuit Judge, and in 1841 was elected Supreme Judge. He served a full term in the U. S. Senate, beginning March 4, 1843, after which he was elected to the Legislature, again Circuit Judge, and, in 1857, to the Supreme Court, which position he held until his death in 1878.

James Semple—Was the successor of Samuel McRoberts, and was appointed by Gov. Ford in 1843. He was afterwards elected Judge of the Supreme Court.

Stephen A. Douglas—Was elected Dec. 14, 1846. He had previously served three terms as Congressman. He became his own successor in 1853 and again in 1859. From his first entrance in the Senate he was acknowledged the peer of Clay, Webster and Calhoun, with whom he served his first term. His famous contest with Abraham Lincoln for the Senate in 1858 is the most memorable in the annals of our country. It was called the battle of the giants, and resulted in Douglas' election to the Senate, and Lincoln to the Presidency. He was born in Brandon, Vermont, April 23, 1813, and came to Illinois in 1833, and died in 1861. He was appointed Secretary of State by Gov. Carlin in 1840, and shortly afterward to the Supreme Bench.

James Shields—Was elected and assumed his seat in the U. S. Senate in 1849, March 4. He was born in Ireland in 1810, came to the United States in 1827. He served in the Mexican army, was elected Senator from Wisconsin, and in 1879 from Missouri for a short term.

Lyman Trumbull—Took his seat in the U. S. Senate March 4, 1855, and became his own successor in 1861. He had previously served one term in the Lower House of Congress, and served on the Supreme Bench. He was born in Connecticut; studied law and came to Illinois early in life, where for years he was actively engaged in politics. He resides in Chicago.

Orvill H. Browning—Was appointed U. S. Senator in 1861, to fill the seat made vacant by the death of Stephen A. Douglas, until a Senator could be regularly elected. Mr. Browning was born in Harrison county, Kentucky; was admitted to the bar in 1831, and settled in Quincy, Illinois, where he engaged in the practice of law, and was instrumental, with his friend, Abraham Lincoln, in forming the Republican party of Illinois at the Bloomington Convention. He entered Johnson's cabinet as Secretary of the Interior, and in March, 1868, was designated by the President to perform the duties of Attorney General, in addition to his own, as Secretary of the Interior Department.

William A. Richardson—Was elected to the U. S. Senate in 1863, to fill the unexpired term of his friend, Stephen A Douglas. He was born in Fayette county, Ky., about 1810, studied law, and settled in Illinois; served as captain in the Mexican War, and, on the battle-field of Buena Vista, was promoted for bravery, by a unanimous vote of his regiment. He served in the Lower House of Congress from 1847 to 1856, continually.

Richard Yates—Was elected to the U. S. Senate in 1865, serving a full term of six years. He died in St. Louis, Mo., Nov. 27, 1873.

John A. Logan—Was elected to the U. S. Senate in 1871. He was born in Jackson county, Ill., Feb. 9, 1826, received a common school education, and enlisted as a private in the Mexican War, where he rose to the rank of Regimental Quartermaster. On returning home he studied law, and came to the bar in 1852; was elected in 1858 a Representative to the 36th Congress and re-elected to the 37th Congress, resigning in 1861 to take part in the suppression of the Rebellion; served as Colonel and subsequently as a Major General, and commanded, with distinction, the armies of the Tennessee. He was again elected to the U. S. Senate in 1879 for six years.

David Davis—Was elected to the U. S. Senate in 1877 for a term of six years. He was born in Cecil county, Md., March 9, 1815, graduated at Kenyon College, Ohio, studied law, and removed to Illinois in 1835; was admitted to the bar and settled in Bloomington, where he has since resided and amassed a large fortune. He was for many years the intimate friend and associate of Abraham Lincoln, rode the circuit with him each year, and after Lincoln's election to the Presidency, was appointed by him to fill the position of Judge of the Supreme Court of the United States.

REPRESENTATIVES IN CONGRESS.

FIFTEENTH CONGRESS.
John McLean....................1818

SIXTEENTH CONGRESS.
Daniel P. Cook..............1819-20

SEVENTEENTH CONGRESS.
Daniel P. Cook..............1821-22

EIGHTEENTH CONGRESS.
Daniel P. Cook..............1823-24

NINETEENTH CONGRESS.
Daniel P. Cook....... 1825-26

TWENTIETH CONGRESS.
Joseph Duncan........... ...1827-28

TWENTY-FIRST CONGRESS.
Joseph Duncan.... 1829-30

TWENTY-SECOND CONGRESS.
Joseph Duncan 1831-32

TWENTY-THIRD CONGRESS.

Joseph Duncan....... 1833-34
Zadock Casey................1833-34

TWENTY-FOURTH CONGRESS.

Zadock Casey................1835-36
John Reynolds...............1835-36
William L. May..............1835-36

TWENTY-FIFTH CONGRESS.

Zadock Casey................1837-38
John Reynolds...............1837-38
William L. May..............1837-38

TWENTY-SIXTH CONGRESS.

Zadock Casey... 1839-40
John Reynolds....... ,.......1839-40
John T. Stuart.......... 1839-40

TWENTY-SEVENTH CONGRESS.

Zadock Casey................1841-42
John Reynolds...............1841-42
John T. Stuart 1841-42

TWENTY-EIGHTH CONGRESS.

Robert Smith......... 1843-44
Orlando B. Finklin...........1843-44
Stephen A. Douglas..........1843-44
John A. McClernand.........1843-44
Joseph P. Hoge....... 1843-44
John J. Hardin..............1843-44
John Wentworth.............1843-44

TWENTY-NINTH CONGRESS.

Robert Smith................1845-46
Stephen A. Douglas..........1845-46
Orlando B. Finklin...........1845-46
John J. Hardin..............1845
Joseph P. Hoge.... 1845-46
John A. McClernand.........1845-46
John Wentworth.............1845-46

THIRTIETH CONGRESS.

John Wentworth.............1847-48
Thomas J. Turner............ 1847
Abraham Lincoln............1847-48
John A. McClernand.........1847-48
Orlando B. Finklin...........1847-48
Robert Smith................1847-48
William A. Richardson.......1847-48

THIRTY-FIRST CONGRESS.

John A. McClernand.........1849–50
John Wentworth.............1849–50
Timothy R. Young...........1849–50
William A. Richardson.......1849–50

Edward D. Baker.............1849–50
William H. Bissell...........1849–50
Thomas L. Harris............1849

THIRTY-SECOND CONGRESS.

William A. Richardson........1851–52
Thompson Campbell....... ..1851–52
Orlando B. Finklin. 1851–52
John Wentworth.............1851–52

Richard Yates 1851–52
Richard S. Maloney..........1851–52
——————— Willis..........1851–52
William H. Bissell...........1851–52

THIRTY-THIRD CONGRESS.

William H. Bissell...........1853–54
John C. Allen................1853–54
—— —— Willis..........1853–54
Elihu B. Washburne.........1853–54
Richard Yates...............1853–54

Thompson Campbell..........1853–54
James Knox..................1853–54
Jesse O. Norton..............1853–54
William A. Richardson.......1863–54

THIRTY-FOURTH CONGRESS.

Elihu B. Washburne.........1855–56
Lyman Trumbull............1855–56
James H. Woodworth........1855–56
James Knox..... 1855–56
Thompson Campbell.........1855–56

Samuel S. Marshall..........1855–56
J. L. D. Morrison............1855–56
John C. Allen................1855–56
Jesse O. Norton..............1855–56
William A. Richardson.......1855–56

THIRTY-FIFTH CONGRESS.

Elihu B. Washburne.........1857–58
Charles D. Hodges...........1857–58
William Kellogg.............1857–58
Thompson Campbell.. 1857–58
John F. Farnsworth..........1857–58
Owen Lovejoy...............1857–58

Samuel S. Marshall..........1857–58
Isaac N. Morris..............1857–58
Aaron Shaw..................1857–58
Robert Smith......... 1857–58
Thomas L. Harris..... 1857–58

THIRTY-SIXTH CONGRESS.

Elihu B. Washburne..........1859–60
John A. Logan.... 1859–60
Owen Lovejoy...............1859–60
John A. McClernand.........1859–60
Isaac N Morris.............1859–60

John F. Farnsworth...........1859–60
Philip B. Fouke.............1859–60
Thomas L. Harris..... 1859–60
William Kellogg.............1859–60
James C. Robinson..........1859–60

THIRTY-SEVENTH CONGRESS.

Elihu B. Washburne.........1861–62
James C. Robinson...........1861–62
John A. Logan..............1861–62
Owen Lovejoy...............1861–62
John A. McClernand. 1861–62

Isaac N. Arnold..............1861–62
Philip B. Fouke..............1861–62
William Kellogg.............1861–62
Anthony L. Knapp...........1861–62
William A. Richardson.......1861–62

THIRTY-EIGHTH CONGRESS.

Elihu B. Washburne.........1863–64
Jesse O. Norton.............1863–64
James C. Robinson...........1863–64

William J. Allen..............1863–64
Isaac N. Arnold..............1863–64
John R. Eden................1863–64

CENTRAL HOSPITAL FOR THE INSANE, JACKSONVILLE.

MECHANIC AND MILITARY HALL.

DORMITORY BUILDING.

ILLINOIS INDUSTRIAL UNIVERSITY, CHAMPAIGN—FOUNDED BY THE STATE
ENDOWED BY CONGRESS.

Lewis W. Ross..............1863-64
John T. Stuart..............1863-64
Owen Lovejoy..............1863-64
William R. Morrison..........1863-64
John C. Allen..............1863-64

John F. Farnsworth...........1863-64
Charles W. Morris...........1863-64
Eben C. Ingersoll............1863-64
Antnony L. Knapp...........1863-64

THIRTY-NINTH CONGRESS.

Elihu B. Washburne..........1865-66
Anthony B. Thornton.........1865-66
John Wentworth.............1865-66
Abner C. Hardin............1865-66
Eben C. Ingersoll............1865-66
Barton C. Cook.............1865-66
Shelby M. Cullom...........1865-66

Jonn F. Farnsworth..........1865-66
Jehu Baker.................1865-66
Henry P. H. Bromwell......1865-66
Andrew Z. Kuykandall.......1865-66
Samuel S. Marshall..........1865-66
Samuel W. Moulton.........1865-66
Lewis W. Ross.............1865-66

FORTIETH CONGRESS.

Elihu B. Washburne..........1867-68
Abner C. Hardin............1867-68
Eben C. Ingersoll............1867-68
Norman B. Judd.............1867-68
Albert G. Burr..............1867-68
Burton C. Cook 1867-68
Shelby M. Cullom...........1867-68

John F. Farnsworth..........1867-68
Jehu Baker.................1867-68
Henry P. H. Bromwell.......1867-68
John A Logan..............1867-68
Samuel S. Marshall..........1867-68
Green B. Raum..............1867-68
Lewis W. Ross.............1867-68

FORTY-FIRST CONGRESS.

Norman B. Judd.............1869-70
John F. Farnsworth..........1869-70
H. C. Burchard.............1869-70
John B. Hawley............1869-70
Eben C. Ingersoll...........1869-70
Burton C. Cook............1869-70
Jesse H. Moore.............1869-70

Shelby M. Cullom...........1869-70
Thomas W. McNeely........1869-70
Albert G. Burr.............1869-70
Samuel S. Marshall..........1869-70
John B. Hay................1869-70
John M. Crebs.............1869-70
John A. Logan..............1869-70

FORTY-SECOND CONGRESS.

Charles B. Farwell...........1871-72
John F. Farnsworth..........1871-72
Horatio C. Burchard..........1871-72
John B. Hawley.............1871-72
Bradford N. Stevens..........1871-72
Henry Snapp...............1871-72
Jesse H. Moore.............1871-72

James C. Robinson...........1871-72
Thomas W. McNeely.........1871-72
Edward Y. Rice.............1871-72
Samuel S. Marshall..........1871-72
John B. Hay................1871-72
John M. Crebs..............1871-72
John S. Beveredge..........1871-72

FORTY-THIRD CONGRESS.

John B. Rice................1873-74
Jasper D. Ward.............1873-74
Charles B. Farwell 1873-74
Stephen A. Hurlbut..........1873-74
Horatio C. Burchard..........1873-74
John B. Hawley.............1873-74
Franklin Corwin............1873-74

Robert M. Knapp............1873-74
James C. Robinson...........1873-74
John B. McNulta............1873-74
Joseph G. Cannon...........1873-74
John R. Eden...............1873-74
James S. Martin.............1873-74
William R. Morrison.........1873-74

Greenbury L. Fort............1873–74   Isaac Clements................1873–74
Granville Barrere............1873–74   Samuel S. Marshall........ 1873–74
William H. Ray..............1873–74

FORTY-FOURTH CONGRESS.

Bernard G. Caulfield..........1875–76   Scott Wike... 1875–76
Carter H. Harrison...........1875–76   William M. Springer........ .1875–76
Charles B. Farwell...........1875–76   Adlai E. Stevenson...........1875–76
Stephen A. Hurlbut..........1875–76   Joseph G. Cannon...........1875–76
Horatio C. Burchard.........1875–76   John R. Eden..............1875–76
Thomas J. Henderson........1875–76   W. A. J. Sparks..............1875–76
Alexander Campbell..........1875–76   William R. Morrison.........1875–76
Greenbury L. Fort........ 1875–76   William Hartzell............1875–76
Richard H. Whiting.........1875–76   William B. Anderson........1875–76
John C. Bagby..............1875–76

FORTY-FIFTH CONGRESS.

William Aldrich.............1877–78   Robert M. Knapp.............1877–78
Carter H. Harrison..........1877–78   William M. Springer........ 1877–78
Lorenzo Brentano...........1877–78   Thomas F. Tipton...........1877–78
William Lathrop............1877–78   Joseph G. Cannon...........1877–78
Horatio C. Burchard.........1877–78   John R. Eden...............1877–78
Thomas J. Henderson........1877–78   W. A. J. Sparks..............1877–78
Philip C. Hayes..... 1877–78   William R. Morrison.........1877–78
Greenbury L. Fort...........1877–78   William Hartzell............1877–78
Thomas A. Boyd.............1877–78   Richard W. Townshend.......1877–78
Benjamin F. Marsh..........1877–78

FORTY-SIXTH CONGRESS.

William Aldrich.............1879–80   James W. Singleton..........1879–80
George R. Davis............1879–80   William M. Springer.........1879–80
Hiram Barber..............1879–80   A. E. Stevenson..............1879–80
John C. Sherwin............1879–80   Joseph G. Cannon...........1879–80
R. M. A. Hawk..............1879–80   Albert P. Forsythe...........1879–80
Thomas J. Henderson........1879–80   W. A. J. Sparks......... 1879–80
Philip C. Hayes.............1879–80   William R. Morrison.........1879–80
Greenbury L. Fort...........1879–80   John R. Thomas.............1879–80
Thomas A. Boyd.............1879–80   R. W. Townshend............1879–80
Benjamin F. Marsh...........1879–80

CHICAGO.

While we cannot, in the brief space we have, give more than a meager sketch of such a city as Chicago, yet we feel the history of the State would be incomplete without speaking of its metropolis, the most wonderful city on the globe.

In comparing Chicago as it was a few years since with Chicago of to-day, we behold a change whose veritable existence we should be inclined to doubt were it not a stern, indisputable fact. Rapid as is the customary development of places and things in the United States, the growth of Chicago and her trade stands without a parallel. The city is situated on the west shore of Lake Michigan at the mouth of the Chicago river. It lies 14 feet above the lake, having been raised to that grade entirely by the energy of its citizens, its site having originally been on a dead level with the water of the lake.

The city extends north and south along the lake about ten miles, and westward on the prairie from the lake five or six miles, embracing an area of over 40 square miles. It is divided by the river into three distinct parts, known as the North, West and South Divisions, or "Sides," by which they are popularly and commonly known. These are connected by 33 bridges and two tunnels.

The first settlement of Chicago was made in 1804, during which year Fort Dearborn was built. At the close of 1830 Chicago contained 12 houses, with a population of about 100. The town was organized in 1833, and incorporated as a city in 1837. The first frame building was erected in 1832, and the first brick house in 1833. The first vessel entered the harbor June 11, 1834; and at the first official census, taken July 1, 1837, the entire population was found to be 4,170. In 1850 the population had increased to 29,963; in 1860, to 112,172; in 1870, 298,977; and, according to the customary mode of reckoning from the number of names in the City Directory, the population of 1879 is over 500,000.

Nicholas Perrot, a Frenchman, was the first white man to visit the site of Chicago. This he did in 1671, at the instigation of M. Toulon, Governor of Canada. He was sent to invite the Western Indians to a convention at Green Bay. It has been often remarked that the first white man who became a resident of Chicago was a negro. His name was Jean Baptiste Pointe au Sable, a mulatto from the West Indies. He settled there in 1796 and built a rude cabin on the north bank of the main river, and laid claim to a tract of land surrounding it. He disappeared from the scene, and his claim was "jumped" by a Frenchman named Le Mai, who commenced trading with the Indians. A few years later he sold out to John Kinzie, who was then an Indian trader in the country about St. Joseph, Mich., and agent for the American Fur Company, which had traded at Chicago with the Indians for some time; and this fact had, probably more than any other, to do with the determination of the Government to establish a fort there. The Indians were growing numerous in that region, being attracted by the facilities for selling their wares, as well as being pressed northward by the tide of emigration setting in from the south. It was judged necessary to have some force near that point to keep them in check, as well as to protect the trading interests. Mr. Kinzie moved his family there the same year Fort Dearborn was built, and converted the Jean Baptiste cabin into a tasteful dwelling.

For about eight years things moved along smoothly. The garrison was quiet, and the traders prosperous. Then the United States became involved in trouble with Great Britain. The Indians took the war-path long before the declaration of hostilities between the civilized nations, committing great depredations, the most atrocious of which was the massacre of Fort Dearborn, an account of which may be found in this volume under the heading of "The War of 1812."

THE GREAT FIRE.

From the year 1840 the onward march of the city of Chicago to the date of the great fire is well known. To recount its marvelous growth in population, wealth, internal resources and improvements and everything else that goes to make up a mighty city, would consume more space than we could devote, however interesting it might be. Its progress astonished the world, and its citizens stood almost appalled at the work of their own hands. She was happy, prosperous and great when time brought that terrible October night (Oct. 9, 1871) and with it the great fire, memorable as the greatest fire ever occurring on earth. The sensation conveyed to the spectator of this unparalleled event, either through the eye, the ear, or other senses or sympathies, cannot be adequately described, and any attempt to do it but shows the poverty of language. As a spectacle it was beyond doubt the grandest as well as the most appalling ever offered to mortal eyes. From any elevated standpoint the appearance was that of a vast ocean of flame, sweeping in mile-long billows and breakers over the doomed city.

Added to the spectacular elements of the conflagration—the intense and lurid light, the sea of red and black, and the spires and pyramids of flame shooting into the heavens—was its constant and terrible roar, drowning even the voices of the shrieking multitude; and ever and anon—for a while as often as every half-minute—resounded far and wide the rapid detonations of explosions, or falling walls. In short, all sights and sounds which terrify the weak and unnerve the strong abounded. But they were only the accompaniment which the orchestra of nature were furnishing to the terrible tragedy there being enacted.

The total area burned over, including streets, was three and a third square miles. The number of buildings destroyed was 17,450; persons rendered homeless, 98,500; persons killed, about 200. Not including depreciation of real estate, or loss of business, it is estimated that the total loss occasioned by the fire was $190,000,000, of which but $44,000,000 was recovered on insurance. The business of the city was interrupted but a short time; and in a year after the fire a large part of the burned district was rebuilt, and at present there is scarcely a trace of the terrible disaster, save in the improved character of the new buildings over those destroyed, and the general better appearance of the city—now the finest, in an architectural sense, in the world.

One of the features of this great city worthy of mention is the Exposition, held annually. The smouldering ruins were yet smoking when the Exposition Building was erected, only ninety days being consumed in its construction. The accompanying engraving of the building, the main part of which is 1,000 feet long, will give an idea of its magnitude.

COMMERCE OF CHICAGO.

The trade of Chicago is co-extensive with the world. Everywhere, in every country and in every port, the trade-marks of her merchants are seen. Everywhere, Chicago stands prominently identified with the commerce of the continent. A few years ago, grain was carted to the place in wagons; now more than 10,000 miles of railroad, with thousands of trains heavily ladened with the products of the land center there. The cash value of the produce handled during the year 1878 was $220,000,000, and its aggregate weight was 7,000,000 tons, or would make 700,000 car loads. Divided into trains, it would make 28,000 long, heavily ladened freight trains, wending their way from all parts of the United States toward our great metropolis. These trains, arranged in one continuous line, would stretch from London across the broad Atlantic to New York and on across our continent to San Francisco.

In regard to the grain, lumber and stock trade, Chicago has surpassed all rivals, and, indeed, not only is without a peer but excels any three or four cities in the world in these branches. Of grain, the vast quantity of 134,851,193 bushels was received during the year 1878. This was about two-fifths more than ever received before in one year. It took 13,000 long freight trains to carry it from the fields of the Northwest to Chicago. This would make a continuous train that would reach across the continent from New York to San Francisco. Speaking more in detail, we have of the various cereals received during the year, 62,783,577 bushels of corn, 29,901,220 bushels of wheat, 18,251,529 bushels of oats, 133,981,104 pounds of seed. The last item alone would fill about 7,000 freight cars.

The lumber received during the year 1878 was, 1,171,364,000 feet, exceeded only in 1872, the year after the great fire. This vast amount of lumber would require 195,000 freight cars to transport it. It would build a fence, four boards high, four and one-half times around the globe.

In the stock trade for the year 1878, the figures assume proportions almost incredible. They are, however, from reliable and trustworthy sources, and must be accepted as authentic. There were received during the year, 6,339,656 hogs, being 2,000,000 more than ever received before in one year. It required 129,916 stock cars to transport this vast number of hogs from the farms of the West and Northwest to the stock yards of Chicago. These hogs arranged in single file, would form a connecting link between Chicago and Pekin, China.

Of the large number of hogs received, five millions of them were slaughtered in Chicago. The aggregate amount of product manufactured from these hogs was 918,000,000 pounds. The capacity of the houses engaged in slaughtering operations in Chicago is 60,000 hogs daily. The number of hands employed in these houses is from 6,000 to 8,000. The number of packages required in which to market the year's product is enormously large, aggregating 500,-000 barrels, 800,000 tierces and 650,000 boxes.

There has been within the stock yards of the city, during the year 1878, 1,036,066 cattle. These were gathered from the plains of Oregon, Wyoming and Utah, and the grazing regions of Texas, as well as from all the Southern, Western and Northwestern States and Territories and from the East as far as Ohio. If these cattle were driven from Chicago southward, in single file, through the United States, Mexico, and the Central American States into South America, the foremost could graze on the plains of Brazil, ere the last one had passed the limits of the great city.

Not only does Chicago attract to its great market the products of a continent, but from it is distributed throughout the world manufactured goods. Every vessel and every train headed toward that city are heavily ladened with the crude products of the farm, of the forests, or of the bowels of the earth, and every ship that leaves her docks and every train that flies from her limits are filled with manufactured articles. These goods not only find their way all over our own country but into Europe, Asia, Australia, Africa, South America, Mexico, and the Islands of the sea; indeed, every nook and corner of the globe, where there is a demand for her goods, her merchants are ready to supply.

The wholesale trade for the year 1878 reached enormous figures, aggregating $280,000,000. Divided among the leading lines, we find there were sold of dry goods, $95,000,000 worth. The trade in groceries amounted to $66,000,000; hardware, $20,000,000; boots and shoes, $24,000,000; clothing, $17,000,000; carpets, $8,000,000; millinery, $7,000,000; hats and caps, $6,000,000; leather, $8,000,-000; drugs, $6,000,000; jewelry, $4,500,000; musical instruments, $2,300,000. Chicago sold over $5,000,000 worth of fruit during the year, and for the same time her fish trade amounted to $1,400,-000, and her oyster trade $4,500,000. The candy and other confectionery trade amounted to $1,534,900. This would fill all the Christmas stockings in the United States.

In 1852, the commerce of the city reached the hopeful sum of $20,000,000; since then, the annual sales of one firm amount to that much. In 1870, it reached $400,000,000, and in 1878 it had grown so rapidly that the trade of the city amounted during that year to $650,000,000. Her manufacturing interests have likewise grown. In 1878, her manufactories employed in the neighborhood of 75,000 operators. The products manufactured during the year were valued at $230,000,000. In reviewing the shipping interests of Chicago, we find it equally enormous. So considerable, indeed, is the commercial navy of Chicago, that in the seasons of navigation, one vessel sails every nine minutes during the business hours; add to this the canal-boats that leave, one every five minutes during the same time, and you will see something of the magnitude of her shipping. More vessels arrive and depart from this port during the season than enter or leave any other port in the world.

In 1831, the mail system was condensed into a half-breed, who went on foot to Niles, Mich., once in two weeks, and brought back what papers and news he could find. As late as 1846, there was often but one mail a week. A post-office was established in Chicago in 1833, and the postmaster nailed up old boot legs upon one side of his shop to serve as boxes. It has since grown to be the largest receiving office in the United States.

In 1844, the quagmires in the streets were first pontooned by plank roads. The wooden-block pavement appeared in 1857. In 1840, water was delivered by peddlers, in carts or by hand. Then a twenty-five horse power engine pushed it through hollow or bored logs along the streets till 1854, when it was introduced into the houses by new works. The first fire-engine was used in 1835, and the first steam fire-engine in 1859. Gas was utilized for lighting the city in 1850. The Young Men's Christian Association was organized in 1858. Street cars commenced running in 1854. The Museum was opened in 1863. The alarm telegraph adopted in 1864. The opera-house built in 1865. The telephone introduced in 1878.

One of the most thoroughly interesting engineering exploits of the city is the tunnels and water-works system, the grandest and most unique of any in the world; and the closest analysis fails to detect any impurities in the water furnished. The first tunnel is five feet two inches in diameter and two miles long, and can deliver 50,000,000 gallons per day. The second tunnel is seven feet in diameter and six miles long, running four miles under the city, and can deliver 100,000,000 gallons per day. This water is distributed through 410 miles of water mains.

Chicago river is tunneled for the passage of pedestrians and vehicles from the South to the West and North divisions.

There is no grand scenery about Chicago except the two seas, one of water, the other of prairie. Nevertheless, there is a spirit about it, a push, a breadth, a power, that soon makes it a place never to

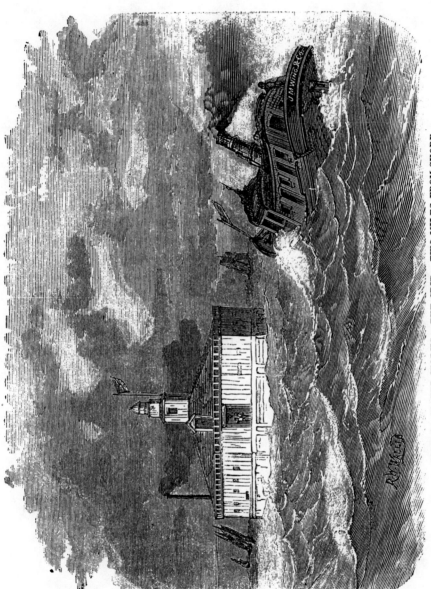

CHICAGO WATER WORKS—THE CRIB—TWO MILES FROM SHORE.

be forsaken. Chicago is in the field almost alone, to handle the wealth of one-fourth of the territory of this great republic. The Atlantic sea-coast divides its margins between Portland, Boston, New York, Philadelphia, Baltimore and Savannah, but Chicago has a dozen empires casting their treasures into her lap. On a bed of coal that can run all the machinery of the world for 500 centuries; in a garden that can feed the race by the thousand years; at the head of the lakes that give her a temperature as a summer resort equaled by no great city in the land; with a climate that insures the health of her citizens; surrounded by all the great deposits of natural wealth in mines and forests and herds, Chicago is the wonder of to-day, and will be the city of the future.

STATES OF THE UNION.

THEIR SETTLEMENT, ORIGIN OF NAME AND MEANING, COGNOMEN, MOT-
TOES, ADMISSION INTO THE UNION, POPULATION, AREA, NUMBER OF
SOLDIERS FURNISHED DURING THE REBELLION, NUMBER OF REPRE-
SENTATIVES IN CONGRESS, PRESENT GOVERNORS, ETC., ETC., ETC.

Alabama.—This State was first explored by LaSalle in 1684, and settled by the French at Mobile in 1711, and admitted as a State in 1817. Its name is Indian, and means " Here we rest." Has no motto. Population in 1860, 964,201; in 1870, 996,992. Furnished 2,576 soldiers for the Union army. Area 50,722 square miles. Montgomery is the capital. Has 8 Representatives and 10 Presidential electors. Rufus W. Cobb is Governor; salary, $3,000; politics, Democratic. Length of term, 2 years.

Arkansas—Became a State in 1836. Population in 1860, 435,-450; in 1870, 484,471. Area 52,198 square miles. Little Rock, capital. Its motto is *Regnant Populi*—" The people rule." It has the Indian name of its principal river. Is called the " Bear State." Furnished 8,289 soldiers. She is entitled to 4 members in Congress, and 6 electoral votes. Governor, W. R. Miller, Democrat; salary, $3,500; term, 2 years.

California—Has a Greek motto, *Eureka*, which means " I have found it." It derived its name from the bay forming the peninsula of Lower California, and was first applied by Cortez. It was first visited by the Spaniards in 1542, and by the celebrated English

navigator, Sir Francis Drake, in 1578.   In 1846 Fremont took
possession of it, defeating the Mexicans, in the name of the United
States, and it was admitted as a State in 1850.   Its gold mines
from 1868 to 1878 produced over $800,000,000. Area 188,982 square
miles.   Population in 1860, 379,994.   In 1870, 560,247.   She gave
to defend the Union 15,225 soldiers.   Sacramento is the capital.
Has 4 Representatives in Congress.   Is entitled to 6 Presidential
electors.   Present Governor is William Irwin, a Democrat; term,
4 years; salary, $6,000.

Colorado—Contains 106,475 square miles, and had a population
in 1860 of 34,277, and in 1870, 39,864.   She furnished, 4,903
soldiers.   Was admitted as a State in 1876.   It has a Latin motto,
Nil sine Numine, which means, "Nothing can be done without
divine aid."   It was named from its river.   Denver is the capital.
Has 1 member in Congress, and 3 electors.   T. W. Pitkin is Governor; salary, $3,000; term, 2 years; politics, Republican.

Connecticut—*Qui transtulit sustinet*, "He who brought us over
sustains us," is her motto.   It was named from the Indian Quon-
ch-ta-Cut, signifying "Long River."   It is called the "Nutmeg
State."   Area 4,674 square miles.   Population 1860, 460,147; in
1870, 537,454.   Gave to the Union army 55,755 soldiers.   Hartford is the capital.   Has 4 Representatives in Congress, and is
entitled to 6 Presidential electors.   Salary of Governor $2,000;
term, 2 years.

Delaware.—"Liberty and Independence," is the motto of this
State.   It was named after Lord De La Ware, an English statesman, and is called, "The Blue Hen," and the "Diamond State."   It
was first settled by the Swedes in 1638.   It was one of the original
thirteen States.   Has an area of 2,120 square miles.   Population in
1860, 112,216; in 1870, 125,015.   She sent to the front to defend
the Union, 12,265 soldiers.   Dover is the capital.   Has but 1 member in Congress; entitled to 3 Presidential electors.   John W.
Hall, Democrat, is Governor; salary, $2,000; term, 2 years.

Florida—Was discovered by Ponce de Leon in 1512, on Easter
Sunday, called by the Spaniards, Pascua Florida, which, with the
variety and beauty of the flowers at this early season caused him to
name it Florida—which means in Spanish, flowery.   Its motto is,
"In God we trust."   It was admitted into the Union in 1845.   It has
an area of 59,268 square miles.   Population in 1860, 140,424; in

1870, 187,756. Its capital is Tallahassee. Has 2 members in Congress. Has 4 Presidential electors. George F. Drew, Democrat, Governor; term, 4 years; salary, $3,500.

Georgia—Owes its name to George II., of England, who first established a colony there in 1732. Its motto is, " Wisdom, justice and moderation." It was one of the original States. Population in 1860, 1,057,286; 1870, 1,184,109. Capital, Atlanta. Area 58,·000, square miles. Has 9 Representatives in Congress, and 11 Presidential electors. Her Governor is A. H. Colquitt, Democrat; term, 4 years; salary, $4,000.

Illinois—Motto, "State Sovereignty, National Union." Name derived from the Indian word, *Illini*, meaning, superior men. It is called the "Prairie State," and its inhabitants, "Suckers." Was first explored by the French in 1673, and admitted into the Union in 1818. Area 55,410 square miles. Population, in 1860, 1,711,951; in 1870, 2,539,871. She sent to the front to defend the Union, 258,162 soldiers. Capital, Springfield. Has 19 members in Congress, and 21 Presidential electors. Shelby M. Cullom, Republican, is Governor; elected for 4 years; salary, $6,000.

Indiana—Is called "Hoosier State." Was explored in 1682, and admitted as a State in 1816. Its name was suggested by its numerous Indian population. Area 33,809 square miles. Population in 1860, 1,350,428; in 1870, 1,680,637. She put into the Federal army, 194,363 men. Capital, Indianapolis. Has 13 members in Congress, and 15 Presidential electors. J. D. Williams, Governor, Democrat; salary, $3,000; term, 4 year.

Iowa—Is an Indian name and means "This is the land." Its motto is, "Our liberties we prize, our rights we will maintain." It is called the "Hawk Eye State." It was first visited by Marquette and Joliet in 1673; settled by New Englanders in 1833, and admitted into the Union in 1846. Des Moines is the capital. It has an area of 55,045, and a population in 1860 of 674,913, and in 1870 of 1,191,802. She sent to defend the Government, 75,793 soldiers. Has 9 members in Congress; 11 Presidential electors. John H. Gear, Republican, is Governor; salary, $2,500; term, 2 years.

Kansas—Was admitted into the Union in 1861, making the thirty-fourth State. Its motto is *Ad astra per aspera*, "To the stars through difficulties." Its name means, " Smoky water," and

is derived from one of her rivers.   Area 78,841 square miles.
Population in 1860, 107,209; in 1870 was 362,812.   She furnished
20,095 soldiers. Capital is Topeka.   Has 3 Representatives in Congress, and 5 Presidential electors.   John P. St. John, Governor;
politics, Republican; salary, $3,000; term, 2 years.

Kentucky—Is the Indian name for "At the head of the rivers."
Its motto is, "United we stand, divided we fall."   The sobriquet
of "dark and bloody ground" is applied to this State. It was first
settled in 1769, and admitted in 1792 as the fifteenth State.   Area
37,680.   Population in 1860, 1,155,684; in 1870, 1,321,000.   She
put into the Federal army 75,285 soldiers. Capital, Frankfort.
Has 10 members in Congress ; 12 Electors.   J. B. McCreary,
Democrat, is Governor; salary, $5,000; term, 4 years.

Louisiana—Was called after Louis XIV., who at one time
owned that section of the country.   Its motto is "Union and Confidence."   It is called "The Creole State."   It was visited by La
Salle in 1684, and admitted into the Union in 1812, making the
eighteenth State.   Population in 1860, 708,002; in 1870, 732,731.
Area 46,431 square miles.   She put into the Federal army 5,224
soldiers. Capital, New Orleans.   Has 6 Representatives and 8
Electors.   F. T. Nichols, Governor, Democrat; salary, $8,000;
term, 4 years.

Maine.—This State was called after the province of Maine in
France, in compliment of Queen Henrietta of England, who owned
that province.   Its motto is *Dirigo*, meaning "I direct."   It is
called "The Pine Tree State."   It was settled by the English in
1625.   It was admitted as a State in 1820.   Area 31,766 square
miles.   Population in 1860, 628,279; in 1870, 626,463; 69,738 soldiers went from this State.   Has 5 members in Congress, and 7
Electors.   Selden Conner, Republican, Governor; term, 1 year;
salary, $2,500.

Maryland—Was named after Henrietta Maria, Queen of
Charles I. of England.   It has a Latin motto, *Crecite et multiplica-
mini*, meaning "Increase and Multiply."   It was settled in 1634,
and was one of the original thirteen States.   It has an area of 11,-
124 square miles.   Population in 1860 was 687,049; in 1870, 780,-
806.   This State furnished 46,053 soldiers. Capital, Annapolis.
Has 6 Representatives, and 8 Presidential electors.   J. H. Carroll,
Democrat, Governor; salary, $4,500; term, 4 years.

Massachusetts—Is the Indian for " The country around the great hills." It is called the " Bay State," from its numerous bays. Its motto is *Ense petit placidam sub libertate quietem*, " By the sword she seeks placid rest in liberty." It was settled in 1620 at Plymouth by English Puritans. It was one of the original thirteen States, and was the first to take up arms against the English during the Revolution. Area 7,800 square miles. Population in 1860, 1,231,-066; in 1870, 1,457,351. She gave to the Union army 146,467 soldiers. Boston is the capital. Has 11 Representatives in Congress, and 13 Presidential electors. Thomas Talbot, Republican, is Governor; salary, $5,000; term, 1 year.

Michigan—Latin motto, *Luebor*, and *Si quæris peninsulam amœnam circumspice*, " I will defend "—" If you seek a pleasant peninsula, look around you." The name is a contraction of two Indian words meaning "Great Lake." It was early explored by Jesuit missionaries, and in 1837 was admitted into the Union. It is known as the " Wolverine State." It contains 56,243 square miles. In 1860 it had a population of 749,173; in 1870, 1,184,059. She furnished 88,111 soldiers. Capital, Lansing. Has 9 Representatives and 11 Presidential electors. C. M. Croswell is Governor; politics, Republican; salary, $1,000; term, 2 years.

Minnesota—Is an Indian name, meaning " Cloudy Water." It has a French motto, *L'Etoile du Nord*—" The Star of the North." It was visited in 1680 by La Salle, settled in 1846, and admitted into the Union in 1858. It contains 83,531 square miles. In 1860 had a population of 172,023; in 1870, 439,511. She gave to the Union army 24;002 soldiers. St. Paul is the capital. Has 3 members in Congress, 5 Presidential electors. Governor, J. S. Pillsbury, Republican; salary, $3,000; term, 2 years.

Mississippi—Is an Indian name, meaning "Long River," and the State is named from the " Father of Waters." The State was first explored by De Sota in 1541; settled by the French at Natchez in 1716, and was admitted into the Union in 1817. It has an area of 47,156 square miles. Population in 1860, 791,305; in 1870, 827,-922. She gave to suppress the Rebellion 545 soldiers. Jackson is the capital. Has 6 representatives in Congress, and 8 Presidential electors. J. M. Stone is Governor, Democrat; salary, $4,000; term, 4 years.

Missouri—Is derived from the Indian word " muddy," which

more properly applies to the river that flows through it. Its motto is *Salus populi suprema lex esto*, "Let the welfare of the people be the supreme law." The State was first settled by the French near Jefferson City in 1719, and in 1821 was admitted into the Union. It has an area of 67,380 square miles, equal to 43,123,200 acres. It had a population in 1860 of 1,182,012; in 1870, 1,721,000. She gave to defend the Union 108,162 soldiers. Capital, Jefferson City. Its inhabitants are known by the offensive cognoman of "Pukes." Has 13 representatives in Congress, and 15 Presidential electors. J. S. Phelps is Governor; politics, Democratic; salary, $5,000; term, 4 years.

Nebraska—Has for its motto, "Equality before the law." Its name is derived from one of its rivers, meaning "broad and shallow, or low." It was admitted into the Union in 1867. Its capital is Lincoln. It had a population in 1860 of 28,841, and in 1870, 123,993, and in 1875, 246,280. It has an area of 75,995 square miles. She furnished to defend the Union 3,157 soldiers. Has but 1 Representative and 3 Presidential electors. A. Nance, Republican, is Governor; salary, $2,500; term, 2 years.

Nevada—"The Snowy Land" derived its name from the Spanish. Its motto is Latin, *Volens et potens*, and means "willing and able." It was settled in 1850, and admitted into the Union in 1864. Capital, Carson City. Its population in 1860 was 6,857; in 1870 it was 42,491. It has an area of 112,090 square miles. She furnished 1,080 soldiers to suppress the Rebellion. Has 1 Representative and 3 Electors. Governor, J. H. Kinkhead, Republican; salary, $6,000; term, 4 years.

New Hampshire—Was first settled at Dover by the English in 1623. Was one of the original States. Has no motto. It is named from Hampshire county in England. It also bears the name of "The Old Granite State." It has an area of 9,280 miles, which equals 9,239,200 acres. It had a population in 1860 of 326,073, and in 1870 of 318,300. She increased the Union army with 33,913 soldiers. Concord is the capital. Has 3 Representatives and 5 Presidential electors. N. Head, Republican, Governor; salary, $1,000; term, 1 year.

New Jersey—Was named in honor of the Island of Jersey in the British channel. Its motto is "Liberty and Independence." It was first settled at Bergen by the Swedes in 1624. It is one of the orig-

inal thirteen States. It has an area of 8,320 square miles, or 5,324,-
800 acres. Population in 1860 was 672,035; in 1870 it was 906,096.
She put into the Federal army 75,315 soldiers. Capital, Trenton.
Has 7 Representatives and 9 Presidential electors. Governor,
George B. McClelland, Democrat; salary, $5,000; term, 3 years.

New York.—The "Empire State" was named by the Duke of
York, afterward King James II. of England. It has a Latin motto,
Excelsior, which means "Still Higher." It was first settled by the
Dutch in 1614 at Manhattan. It has an area of 47,000 square
miles, or 30,080,000 acres. The population in 1860 was 3,880,735;
in 1870 it was 4,332,759. It is one of the original thirteen States.
Capital is Albany. It gave to defend our Government 445,959
men. Has 33 members in Congress, and 35 Presidential electors.
Governor, L. Robinson, Democrat; salary, $10,000; term, 3 years.

North Carolina—Was named after Charles IX., King of France.
It is called "The Old North," or "The Turpentine State." It was
first visited in 1524 by a Florentine navigator, sent out by Francis
I., King of France. It was settled at Albemarle in 1663. It was
one of the original thirteen States. It has an area of 50,704 square
miles, equal to 32,450,560 acres. It had in 1860 a population of
992,622, and in 1870, 1,071,361. Raleigh is the capital. She
furnished 3,156 soldiers to put down the Rebellion. Has 8 members in Congress, and is entitled to 10 Presidential electors. Z. B.
Vance, Democrat, is Governor; salary, $5,000; term, 4 years.

Ohio—Took its name from the river on its Southern boundary,
and means "Beautiful." Its motto is *Imperium in Imperio*—
"An Empire in an Empire." It was first permanently settled in
1788 at Marietta by New Englanders. It was admitted as a State
in 1803. Its capital is Columbus. It contains 39,964 square
miles, or 25,576,960 acres. Population in 1860, 2,339,511; in 1870
it had 2,665,260. She sent to the front during the Rebellion 310,-
654 soldiers. Has 20 Representatives, and 22 Presidential electors.
Governor, R. M. Bishop, Democrat; salary, $4,000; term, 2 years.

Oregon—Owes its Indian name to its principal river. Its motto
is *Alis volat propriis*—"She flies with her own wings." It was
first visited by the Spaniards in the sixteenth century. It was settled by the English in 1813, and admitted into the Union in 1859.
Its capital is Salem. It has an area of 95,274 square miles, equal
to 60,975,360 acres. It had in 1860 a population of 52,465; in

1870, 90,922. She furnished 1,810 soldiers. She is entitled to 1 member in Congress, and 3 Presidential electors. W. W. Thayer, Republican, is Governor; salary, $1,500; term, 4 years.

Pennsylvania.—This is the "Keystone State," and means "Penn's Woods," and was so called after William Penn, its original owner. Its motto is, " Virtue, liberty and independence." A colony was established by Penn in 1682. The State was one of the original thirteen. It has an area of 46,000 square miles, equaling 29,440,-000 acres. It had in 1860 a population of 2,906.215; and in 1870, 3,515,993. She gave to suppress the Rebellion, 338,155. Harrisburg is the capital. Has 27 Representatives and 29 electors. H. M. Hoyt, is Governor; salary, $10,000; politics, Republican; term of office, 3 years.

Rhode Island.—This, the smallest of the States, owes its name to the Island of Rhodes in the Mediterranean, which domain it is said to greatly resemble. Its motto is " Hope," and it is familiarly called, " Little Rhody." It was settled by Roger Williams in 1636. It was one of the original thirteen States. It has an area of 1,306 square miles, or 835,840 acres. Its population in 1860 numbered 174,620; in 1870, 217,356. She gave to defend the Union, 23,248. Its capitals are Providence and Newport. Has 2 Representatives, and 4 Presidential electors. C. Vanzandt is Governor; politics, Republican; salary, $1,000; term, 1 year.

South Carolina.—The Palmetto State wears the Latin name of Charles IX., of France (Carolus). Its motto is Latin, *Animis opibusque parati*, " Ready in will and deed." The first permanent settlement was made at Port Royal in 1670, where the French Huguenots had failed three-quarters of a century before to found a settlement. It is one of the original thirteen States. Its capital is Columbia. It has an area of 29,385 square miles, or 18,806,400 acres, with a population in 1860 of 703,708; in 1870, 728,000. Has 5 Representatives in Congress, and is entitled to 7 Presidential electors. Salary of Governor, $3,500; term, 2 years.

Tennessee—Is the Indian name for the " River of the Bend," *i. e.* the Mississippi, which forms its western boundary. She is called "The Big Bend State." Her motto is, " Agriculture, Commerce." It was settled in 1757, and admitted into the Union in 1796, making the sixteenth State, or the third admitted after the Revolutionary War—Vermont being the first, and Kentucky the second. It has an area of 45,600 square miles, or 29,184,000 acres. In 1860 its population numbered 1,109,801, and in 1870, 1,257,983. She furnished 31,092 soldiers to suppress the Rebellion. Nashville is the capital. Has 10 Representatives, and 12 Presidential electors. Governor, A. S. Marks, Democrat; salary, $4,000; term, 2 years.

Texas—Is the American word for the Mexican name by which all that section of the country was known before it was ceded to the United States. It is known as "The Lone Star State." The first settlement was made by LaSalle in 1685. After the independence of Mexico in 1822, it remained a Mexican Province until 1836, when it gained its independence, and in 1845 was admitted into the Union. It has an area of 237,504 square miles, equal to 152,002,-560 acres. Its population in 1860 was 604,215; in 1870, 818,579. She gave to put down the Rebelion 1,965 soldiers. Capital, Austin. Has 6 Representatives, and 8 Presidential electors. Governor, O. M. Roberts, Democrat; salary, $5,000; term, 2 years.

Vermont—Bears the French name of her mountains *Verde Mont*, "Green Mountains." Its motto is "Freedom and Unity." It was settled in 1731, and admitted into the Union in 1791. Area 10,212 square miles. Population in 1860, 315,098; in 1870, 330,551. She gave to defend the Government, 33,272 soldiers. Capital, Montpelier. Has 3 Representatives, and 5 electors. Governor, H. Fairbanks, Republican; term, 2 years; salary, $1,000.

Virginia.—The Old Dominion, as this State is called, is the oldest of the States. It was named in honor of Queen Elizabeth, the "Virgin Queen," in whose reign Sir Walter Raleigh made his first attempt to colonize that region. Its motto is *Sic semper tyrannis*, "So always with tyrants." It was first settled at Jamestown, in 1607, by the English, being the first settlement in the United States. It is one of original thirteen States, and had before its division in 1862, 61,352 square miles, but at present contains but 38,352 square miles, equal to 24,545,280 acres. The population in 1860 amounted to 1,596,318, and in 1870 it was 1,224,830. Richmond is the capital. Has 9 Representatives, and 11 electors. Governor, F. W. M. Halliday, Democrat; salary, $5,500; term, 4 years.

West Virginia.—Motto, *Montani semper liberi*, "Mountaineers are always free." This is the only State ever formed, under the Constitution, by the division of an organized State. This was done in 1862, and in 1863 was admitted into the Union. It has an area of

23,000 square miles, or 14,720,000 acres.   The population in 1860 was 376,000; in 1870 it numbered 445,616.   She furnished 32,003. Capital, Wheeling.   Has 3 Representatives in Congress, and is entitled to 5 Presidential electors. The Governor is H. M. Mathews, Democrat; term, 4 years; salary, $2,700.

Wisconsin—Is an Indian name, and means "Wild-rushing channel."   Its motto, *Civitatas successit barbarum,* "The civilized man succeeds the barbarous."   It is called "The Badger State." The State was visited by the French explorers in 1665, and a settlement was made in 1669 at Green Bay.   It was admitted into the Union in 1848.   It has an area of 52,924 square miles, equal to 34,511,360 acres.   In 1860 its population numbered 775,881; in 1870, 1,055,167.   Madison is the capital.   She furnished for the Union army 91,021 soldiers.   Has 8 members in Congress, and is entitled to 10 Presidential electors.   The Governor is W. E. Smith; politics, Republican; salary, $5,000; term, 2 years.

ILLINOIS INSTITUTE FOR DEAF AND DUMB.

The first class of unfortunates to attract the notice of the legislature were the deaf mutes. The act establishing the institution for the education of these unfortunates was approved by Gov. Carlin, Feb. 23, 1839, the asylum to be located at Jacksonville. The original building, afterward called the south wing, was begun in 1842, and completed in 1849, at a cost of about $25,000. A small portion of the building was ready for occupancy in 1846, and on the 26th day of January, of that year, the Institution was formally opened, with Mr. Thomas Officer as principal. The first term opened with but four pupils, which has increased from year to year, until the average attendance at the present time is about 250.

ILLINOIS INSTITUTE FOR THE INSANE.

In response to an appeal from the eminent philanthropist, Miss D. L. Dix, an act establishing the Illinois Hospital for the Insane, was approved by Gov. French, March 1, 1847. Nine trustees were appointed, with power to select a site, purchase land, and erect buildings to accommodate 250 patients. On the 1st of May the board agreed upon a site, 1¼ miles from the court-house in Jacksonville. In 1851 two wards in the east wing were ready for occupancy, and the first patient was admitted Nov. 3, 1851. In 1869 the General Assembly passed two acts creating the northern asylum for the insane, and the southern asylum for the insane, which was approved by Gov. Palmer, April 16, 1869. Elgin was selected as a location for the former, and Anna for the latter. The estimated capacity of the three asylums is 1,200 patients. In addition to the State institutions for the insane, there are three other asylums for their benefit, one in Cook county, which will accommodate about 400 patients, and two private institutions, one at Batavia, and one at Jacksonville.

ASYLUM FOR FEEBLE-MINDED.

The experimental school for feeble-minded children, the first institution of its kind in the North-west, was created by an act approved, Feb. 15, 1865. It was an outgrowth of the institution for deaf and dumb, to which idiots are frequently sent, under a mistaken impression on the part of parents, that their silence results from inability to hear. The selection of a site for the building was intrusted to seven commissioners, who, in July, 1875, agreed upon the town of Lincoln. The building was begun in 1875, and completed three years later, at a cost of $154,209. The average attendance in 1878 was 224.

THE CHICAGO CHARITABLE EYE AND EAR INFIRMARY.

The association for founding this institution was organized in May, 1858, and Pearson street, Chicago, selected for the erection of the building. In 1865 the legislature granted the institution a special charter, and two years later made an appropriation of $5,000 a year for its maintenance, and in 1871 received it into the circle of State institutions; thereupon the name was changed by the substitution of the word Illinois for Chicago. The building was swept away by the great fire of 1871, and three years later the present building was completed, at a cost of $42,843.

THE SOUTHERN ILLINOIS NORMAL UNIVERSITY

Is located at Carbondale. This University was opened in 1874, and occupies one of the finest school edifices in the United States. It includes, besides a normal department proper, a preparatory department and a model school. The model school is of an elementary grade; the preparatory department is of the grade of a high school, with a course of three years. The normal course of four years embraces two courses, a classical and a scientific course; both make the study of the English language and literature quite prominent.

THE ILLINOIS INDUSTRIAL UNIVERSITY,

Located at Urbana, was chartered in 1867. It has a corps of twenty-five instructors, including professors, lecturers and assistants, and has an attendance of over 400 pupils. It comprises four colleges (1) Agriculture, (2) Engineering, (3) Natural Science, (4) Literature and Science. These colleges embrace twelve subordinate schools and courses of instruction, in which are taught domestic science and art, commerce, military science, wood engraving, printing, telegraphy, photographing and designing. This institution is endowed with the national land grant, and the amount of its productive fund is about $320,000. The value of its grounds, buildings, etc., is about $640,000. It is well supplied with apparatus, and has a library of over 10,000 volumes.

HISTORY OF PIKE COUNTY.

CHAPTER I.

EARLY SETTLEMENT.

INTRODUCTORY.

We now begin to chronicle the history of one of the largest and wealthiest, as well as the oldest, counties in the great State of Illinois. To say that our task is a most difficult one will only be expressing the sentiment of all who have attempted the compilation of local history. Only such persons can fully appreciate the embarrassment arising from the multiplied perplexities that are continually crowding around the local historian. We shall seek to make this a record as detailed and accurate as accessible data will permit. Of course it will be impossible to gather up all of the fragmentary facts of the three-score years of the county's history, of most which no written record was ever made, and many even important facts have slipped through the meshes of memory never to be recalled. Doubtless when the early pilgrim reads, or has read to him, historical items recorded in this volume, it will rekindle in memory recollections of kindred facts, not given us, and that otherwise would have been forever cast into the darkness of oblivion. Records of these items should be made as they are brought to light, that the future historian may have the greater abundance of material from which to compile.

Truth and accuracy will be our motto, yet that some errors will occur in names and dates, and even in statements, cannot be denied. Studious care will be taken, however, to avoid as many such inaccuracies as possible.

The face of the country of this county, save that portion bordering on the Mississippi and Illinois rivers, is mostly rich, rolling prairie, watered by Bay, McGee, Six Mile, Honey, Pigeon and McCraney's creeks, with their numerous and small tributaries, along which are extensive bodies of timber.   The farmers have planted artificial groves extensively over the prairie, which has had the effect of ameliorating the climate, by keeping the winds of an open country from the surface of the earth.   By the energy and enterprise of the citizens of this county, it has been transformed from the native wilderness into one of the most attractive portions of the State, if not of the West.   It is claimed that there is no spot on the face of the earth capable of sustaining a denser population than the Military Tract; and those familiar with this beautiful portion of our State know that Pike county is not excelled by any other within its boundary.   That this county contains as intelligent, enterprising and thrifty agriculturists as probably can be found elsewhere in the same breadth of territory in the United States, few will deny.   Fine barns, with all the modern improvements, comfortable dwellings, lawns, gardens, out-houses, etc., are to be found on every hand; towns and cities have sprung up as if by magic, and every knoll is graced by a church edifice or school building.

The natural resources of Pike county, as above alluded to, for agricultural and manufacturing purposes, and marketing, give to the farmers and manufacturers of the county superior advantages. The agricultural interests of the county are well advanced.   Indeed, it may be said that Pike is the great agricultural county of Illinois. The soil is mostly rich prairie loam, and has great productive qualities.   It is mostly divided into farms of medium size, from 80 to 320 acres; but few large farms are to be found.   The benefit of this is apparent by the increased population and a better cultivation. The staple crops of cereals are corn, wheat and oats, which generally yield abundantly.   This is the condition of Pike county at present. How different when Ebenezer Franklin, with his family, located within its borders!   Then these prairies were a vast wilderness covered with a rank growth of prairie grass, and much of the land now under a high state of cultivation was covered with heavy forests.   At that time the native red men roamed unmolested over the flowery prairies and through dark forests.

We wish to quote in this connection the eloquent, just and appropriate tribute paid to Pike county by Hon. Wm. A. Grimshaw in his "Centennial Address."   It speaks in praiseworthy, yet truthful, descriptive terms of both people and county:

"The citizens of this county have always been marked for a love of our national Government, for participation in all State measures to promote the common good of Illinois.   With one brief exception, the period of the 'vigilance committee,' local government has always been of an orderly character.   The brief excitement of that period led to more efficient laws for the protection of society, and thus good came out of evil.   No fratricidal strife, no display of brothers in battle array with deadly cannon and all the dread habiliments of war, are portrayed here.   The life of our citizens has been with few exceptions that of peaceful farmers and townsmen, busy in the affairs of domestic life. Thus your historian has no startling tales to tell.

"Still as the current of your own gentle river, Illinois, with a few swells in the stream of life, when wars waged beyond the limits of the present county called off our men to war, has been the life of your people. Industry has prevailed. Education has had its marked influence, and the holy gospel, taught in its beauty and simplicity, has pervaded every walk in life. Crime has, notwithstanding, been perpetrated, to be brought generally to condign punishment. Such is generally the end of those who violate the laws, human and divine.

"This county, once embracing the fairest portion of the once Eden-like State of Illinois, yet retaining within her limits land beautiful to look upon, desirable to inhabit, and famed for her fair daughters, her gallant sons, prosperous farmers and mechanics, able professional men and legislators, her present territory equal yet almost to some of the old thirteen States, owes much, if not all, of this to the patriotism and foresight of the Revolutionary fathers.

"Contemplate the vastness of Pike county as she was when organized by the act of the Legislature of 1821, in these words:

SECTION 1.—Be it enacted by the People of the State of Illinois represented in the General Assembly, That all that tract of country within the following boundaries, to wit: beginning at the mouth of the Illinois river and running thence up the middle of said river to the fork of the same, thence up the south fork of said river until it strikes the State line of Indiana, thence north with said line to the north boundary line of this State, thence west with said line to the western boundary line of this State, and thence with said line to the place of beginning, shall constitute a separate county to be called Pike.

"To repeat the extent of the boundaries: On the south, begin at the junction of the Illinois and Mississippi rivers, then follow the Illinois to the fork of the same, meaning the Kankakee, thence to the line of the State of Indiana, thence north and west embracing the territory from Chicago, following on the line of Wisconsin to the Mississippi river, including the famed lead mines of Galena, and to the channel of the Mississippi, thence descending to the place of beginning.

"First note the beautiful, still gliding river, the Illinois, then observe the majestic Father of Waters; traverse all this territory, great in extent, formerly the home of savage tribes of Indians, the land marked by the tread of the buffalo and dotted over with the graves and mounds, the relics of extinct races, the fierce brute creation and game and fish abounding, prairies illimitable, adorned with flowers of gorgeous hues, fruits delicious in profusion and great variety, forests of vast size filled with gigantic trees and of many species, rivers bounding unfettered by man's contrivances; then no locks and dams existed thereon, fish in myriads were the dwellers in those rivers,—and these all existed in 1821, when Pike county was struck off by name from the older settlements and the few counties then existing in Illinois.

"Pike county has been the mother of States to the west of Illinois. Having a pioneer population of an enterprising turn, large numbers have emigrated together to Oregon, Texas and California and other remote points, following the star of empire. Many estimable farmers who once lived in Pike have gone further east in Illinois and settled in the prairie counties.

"The health of this county is almost invariably good excepting in lowlands where some malarious disease comes on at times. Longevity exists to a marked degree and children fairly swarm. Prosperity and fine crops are the general results of industry."

ANTE-PIONEER HISTORY.

Before proceeding further in detailing the immediate history of the county, we desire to mention a few important facts relative to the earliest history of this section of the State. In 1673 the great French explorers, Marquette and Joliet, passed down the Mississippi and up the Illinois in their canoes, on their first famous voyage down the great Father of Waters. Seven years later, Jan. 3, 1680, LaSalle, with his little band of Frenchmen, came down the Illinois river as far as Peoria lake, landed upon the opposite shore, and erected a fort—Fort Creve-cœur. This fort was soon evacuated and destroyed, yet the enterprising Frenchmen continued among the Indians as traders. They exerted no perceptible civilizing influence, however, upon the red-skins: indeed, by life and inter-marriage among them, they became in all respects more and more like them, until their identity was almost lost.

Year after year rolled by until almost a century and a half had passed since LaSalle stepped ashore from his skiff, before the aborigines who occupied the territory embraced within the present boundary of Pike county were molested by the encroachments of the white man. Generation after generation of natives appeared upon the wild scenes of savage life, roamed the forest and prairie, and glided over the beautiful, placid Illinois and Mississippi rivers in their log and bark canoes, and passed away. Still the advance of civilization, the steady westward tread of the Anglo-Saxon, disturbed them not. The buffalo, deer, bear and wolf roamed the prairie and woodland, the Indian their only enemy. But nature had destined better things for this fertile region. She had been too lavish in the distribution of natural advantages to leave it longer in the peaceable possession of those who had for centuries refused to develop, even in the slightest degree, any of her great resources. She accordingly directed hitherward the footsteps of the industrious, enterprising pioneer; and so fertile was the soil and so beautiful the flowers, so sparkling were the streams and shady the groves, that, in advance of all the surrounding country, the pioneers sought and settled the timber land and prairie of Pike county.

The thrilling scenes through which the pioneer settlers passed in the settlement of this portion of Illinois must ever awaken emotions of warmest regard for them. To pave the way for those who followed after them, to make their settlement in the West a pleasure, they bore the flood-tide wave of civilization; they endured all, suffered all. But few of these spirits now survive; they have passed away full of years and honors, leaving their children, and children's children and strangers to succeed them and enjoy the fruits of the toil, privations and savings of their long and eventful lives.

> Life with them is o'er, their labors all are done,
> And others reap the harvest that they won.

Too great honor cannot be accorded them, and we regret that we have not the data to speak more fully and definitely of them, their personal experiences, their lives and their characters.

FIRST AMERICAN SETTLEMENTS.

Coming on down through the years for over a century, we wish to speak of the first American settlements in the State, as an introductory to the more immediate history of the original Pike county.

The first settlement made within the borders of the great State of Illinois by citizens of the United States was in 1784, when a few families from Virginia founded a small colony or settlement near Bellefontaine, in Monroe county. The next American settlement was made in St. Clair county, two of which were made prior to the year 1800.

The first American settlers in Illinois were chiefly from Kentucky, Virginia, Pennsylvania, North Carolina, Tennessee and some from Maryland. Some of these had served with Gen. Clark, who conquered the country from the British in 1778. This whole people did not number more than 12,000 in 1812, but with the aid of one company of regular soldiers defended themselves and their settlements against the numerous and powerful nations of Kickapoos, Sacs, Foxes, Pottawatomies and Shawnees, and even made hostile expeditions into the heart of their country, burning their villages and defeating and driving them from the territory.

When the State was admitted in 1818 the settlements extended a little north of Edwardsville and Alton; south along the Mississippi to the mouth of the Ohio; east in the direction of Carlysle to the Wabash, and down the Wabash and Ohio to the conjunction of the Ohio and Mississippi. Such was the extent of the settlement in Illinois when the Territory was clothed with State honors.

There were but 15 organized counties represented in the convention to frame the first Constitution. These were St. Clair, Randolph, Madison, Gallatin, Johnson, Edwards, White, Monroe, Pope, Jackson, Crawford, Bond, Union, Washington and Franklin. The last three were the youngest counties, and were formed in 1818.

ORIGINAL PIKE COUNTY.

Pike county was the first or second county organized after the State was admitted into the Union. It was erected Jan. 31, 1821, and included all of the territory west and north of the Illinois river, and its south fork, now the Kankakee river. At the first election in Pike county after its organization only 35 votes were polled, even though it did extend over the entire northern part of the State, and out of which more than fifty counties have since been organized.

A "Gazetteer of Illinois and Wisconsin," published about 1822, says that the county "included a part of the lands appropriated by Congress for the payment of military bounties. The lands constituting that tract are included within a peninsula of the Illinois and the Mississippi, and extend on the meridian line (4th), passing through the mouth of the Illinois, 162 miles north. Pike county will no doubt be divided into several counties; some of which will become very wealthy and important. It is probable that the section about Fort Clark (now Peoria) will be the most thickly settled. On the Mississippi river, above Rock river, lead ore is found in abundance. Pike county contains between 700 and 800 inhabitants. It is attached to the first judicial circuit, sends one member to the House of Representatives, and, with Greene, one to the Senate. The county-seat is Cole's Grove, a post town. It was laid out in 1821 and is situated in township 11 south, in range 2 west of the fourth principal meridian; very little improvement has yet been made in this place or vicinity. The situation is high and healthy and bids fair to become a place of some importance."

Thus the historian of three-score years ago speaks of Pike county as it was in its original magnitude and wildness. How changed is the face of the country since then! Who could have foretold its future greatness with any degree of knowledge or certainty!

We deem it within the province of this work to speak of the earliest settlement of all this vast region. Much of it was settled prior to that portion contained within the present boundaries of the county, and as it was for many years a part of Pike county it is proper we should refer to it, briefly, at least.

The earliest history and the first occupation of the original Pike county are enshrouded in almost impenetrable obscurity. After the lapse of more than three-quarters of a century, the almost total absence of records, and the fact that the whites who visited or lived in this region prior to 1820 are all dead, render it impossible now to determine with any degree of certainty the name of him who is entitled to the honor of being recorded as "first settler." Perhaps the first man who sojourned within the Military Tract lived in what is now Calhoun county. He went there about 1801, and lived for years before any other settler came, and remained alone and unknown for a long time after the first pioneers moved into that section. His home was a cave dug out by himself, and was about a quarter of a mile from the Mississippi river. In 1850 the boards of his cave floor were dug up and the ground leveled. Who he was or where he came from was known only to himself, for he refused all intercourse with the settlers.

The next settlers, perhaps, were French trappers and half-breeds who formed quite a large colony on the Illinois river near the Deer Plains Ferry, Calhoun county. These remained there until the great high water of 1815 or 1818, which drove them away. Andrew Judy lived at this point at a very early day. Major Roberts settled in Calhoun county in June, 1811. He came from Ohio. John Shaw came into that county at a very early day and was one of the leading men in the organization of Pike county, and for some time was County Commissioner. He settled at Gilead, the site of the original county-seat of Pike county. He was the most noted and influential man in his day of all in all this region. He carried on farming, stock-raising, and conducted a store, and engaged in politics very largely. His influence was so great that he was able to rule the county indirectly, which he did for many years. He was denominated the "Black Prince," on account of his having great sway over the community. It is said that he had control over a large band of half-breeds, with which and his numerous other henchmen he controlled the elections, and carried every measure he desired. He forged deeds, even by the quire, doctored poll books, etc. So great was his influence and at the same time so injurious to the settlers that the public issue was gotten up in its politics, of "Shaw," or "Anti-Shaw," and not until there was a great and united struggle that John Shaw lost his supremacy.

There was a man by the name of Davison who was found living as a hermit a few miles above the mouth of Spoon river on its banks by the first settlers in Fulton county. He was a physician and a man of culture and refinement. How long he had resided there before discovered by the whites is not known, but evidently for many years, as the shrubbery and trees that he had planted had grown quite large. He was selected as one of the first grand jurors for the Circuit Court of Pike county. He refused all intercourse with the whites, and about 1824 put his effects in a canoe, paddled down Spoon river and up the Illinois to Starved Rock, where he lived in obscurity until he died, which was a few years afterward.

In 1778 the French made a settlement at the upper end of Peoria lake. The country in the vicinity of this lake was called by the Indians *Pim-i-te-wi*, that is, a place where there are many fat beasts. Here the town of Laville de Meillet, named after its founder, was started. Within the next twenty years, however, the town was moved down to the lower end of the lake to the present site of Peoria. In 1812 the town was destroyed and the inhabitants carried away by Captain Craig. In 1813 Fort Clark was erected there by Illinois troops engaged in the war of 1812. Five years later it was destroyed by fire. Some American settlers, however, early came into this neighborhood. These were mostly soldiers of the war of 1812 who had been given bounty-land for their services and had come to possess it. An old veteran of that war by the name of Wm. Blanchard came to Peoria in 1819, soon moved over the river into Tazewell county, and in 1830 moved just over the line into Woodford, and is still living there, perhaps the oldest living settler north of the mouth of the Illinois river.

The first permanent settlement by the whites in all Northwestern Illinois, of which any record or reliable knowledge now remains, existed about 1820 on the banks of the river now known as the Galena. This river was then known as Feve, or Bean river. The Indian name for the river was Mah-cau-bee, the fever that blisters, and was named from the fact of the Indians having small-pox here. Hundreds of the natives died and they gave the names of Big Small-Pox river and Little Small-Pox river to the streams upon which they lived. The former was changed by the whites to the more pleasant name of Fever river; the smaller is still known as Small-Pox creek. Galena was known as "Fever River Settlement," and we find frequent mention of it in the old Commissioners' Court records. John S. Miller, who was perhaps the first settler there, and Moses Meeker, perhaps the next, often applied to the court at Cole's Grove for licenses, recommendations to the Governor to be appointed Justice of the Peace, etc.

Fever river was also known in an early day by the name of Bean river, from the French name, Riviere au Feve, given it by the early traders and adventurers. This section of country is referred to in the "Gazetteer of Illinois and Missouri," a work published in 1822 and now very rare, as follows:

"*Bean river* (Riviere au Feve, Fr.), a navigable stream of Pike county, emptying into the Mississippi three miles below Cat-Fish creek, and 20 miles below Dubuque's mines, and about 70 above Rock river. Nine miles up this stream a small creek empties into it from the west. The banks of this creek, and the hills which bound its alluvium, are filled with lead ore of the best quality. Three miles below this on the banks of Bean river is the Traders' Village, consisting of ten or twelve houses or cabins. At this place the ore procured from the Indians is smelted and then sent in boats either to Canada or New Orleans. The lands on this stream are poor, and are only valuable on account of the immense quantities of minerals which they contain."

In the same work Chicago is simply mentioned as "a village of Pike county, containing 12 or 15 houses and about 60 or 70 inhabitants." Fort Dearborn had been built there in 1804, but so far was it in the wilderness that when the massacre of the garrison in 1812 occurred many days elapsed before it was known to the nearest white settlement. There was also a fort and military garrison on the Mississippi river where Warsaw is now located. This was known as Fort Edwards, and the name occurs frequently in the old records of Pike county. One of the main wagon-roads, and one upon which the Commissioners expended much time and money, was known as the Fort Edwards road.

By 1820 to 1825 many settlements had sprung up through Central Illinois, but scarcely before 1830 was there any considerable num-

ber of whites living north of the north line of the present boundary of Pike county. It is true, prior to that Adams, Fulton and
Schuyler counties had been organized, but they were very thinly
populated. By 1830 and after the close of the Black Hawk war in
1832 and the expulsion of the Indians the northern part of the
State settled up quite rapidly.

THE FIRST SETTLEMENT OF PIKE COUNTY AS IT IS AT PRESENT.

We now come to a period in the history of the settlement of this
county when we will restrict ourselves to the present boundaries of
Pike county. The few broken references to the settlement of the
Military Tract and Northern Illinois we offer as a slight historic
token to the grand old original Pike county—to Pike county as it
was in its primitive days. They are brief and scattering, but,
owing to the fact, as previously remarked, that there are no records
extant, and that the earliest pioneers have passed away, it is impossible to give more, other than to elaborate and enlarge on the facts
already stated, which we will not do for want of space.

Prior to the coming of the first settler to Pike county there had
often been French traders, hunters and travelers passing through
the native forests and crossing the wild and beautiful prairies. They
pitched their tent for the night, and amid the vast wilderness,
inhabited only by wild beasts and the native red man, rested their
weary limbs only to move at the early dawn. The first individual
of whom we have account, and this is traditionary, that settled in
Pike county as it is, or who made it his home for any considerable
time, was J. B. Teboe (Tibault), a Canadian Frenchman. He came
somewhere during the period between 1817 and 1819, and occupied
a cabin on the banks of the Illinois river, situated on what is now
section 33, Flint township. There is no doubt this man was in that
locality prior to 1820. He lived as a hunter, and for a time we
think ran a ferry, but whether he is entitled to the honor of being
termed the "first settler" we very much doubt. He, it seems,
tilled no land and made no permanent abode, nor had a family. He
was killed at Milton in 1844.

FRANKLIN AND SHINN THE FIRST SETTLERS.

The man who may properly be denominated the first settler of
Pike county was Ebenezer Franklin. He came to the county in
March, 1820, and first stopped upon the northwest quarter of section 27, half a mile east from where Atlas was afterward located
and up "Jockey Hollow." He brought with him his family, consisting of his wife, son and three daughters, besides a Mr. Israel
Waters. This gentleman afterward moved to Adams county.
When Franklin first came he found no neighbor with whom he
could stop until he had reared his cabin. He was obliged to pitch
his tent and gather his family around him in his tented mansion
provided with the meager and rude furniture he brought with him

and what he constructed after his arrival. There is no doubt the family suffered from the chilling winds of early spring, but they were sturdy pioneers and withstood the privations and hardships as became true pioneers. He resided in his tent until May, when he erected a rude log cabin.

The next settler to come in after Franklin was Daniel Shinn. He came from Batavia, Ohio, and arrived about the last of April, 1820. On his way here he stopped at Edwardsville, where he left most of his large family, which consisted of a wife and eight children: Benjamin, John, Eliza, Hannah, Mary, Phebe, Daniel and Nancy. John Webb, now living five miles east of Pittsfield, then only six years of age, came with them. Mr. Webb is now the oldest living settler in the county by four years, that is, he came to the county four years prior to any other man now living in the county. Mr. Shinn was the first man who brought a wagon into Pike county, probably the first to the Military Tract. He settled near Mr. Franklin, and the two lived in tents until May, when they both erected cabins, aiding one another in their labors. Mr. Shinn with two of his sons cleared a piece of ground and planted three acres of corn. It took but comparatively little labor to raise grain, but to have it ground or prepared for food was a hard task. At this early day there were no mills within reach of these early pilgrims. The first mill they had to go to was a horse-mill run by John Shaw in Calhoun county. Mr. Franklin erected his cabin upon the southeast quarter of section 22, Atlas township, or what is now Atlas, three-fourths of a mile from Atlas and about 150 yards north of where the road has since run. Many years ago, even, the place was covered with a spindling growth of young trees.

Mr. Shinn located as a near neighbor to Mr. Franklin. He became a great wolf-hunter, prompted by the fact of his being unable to raise stock, owing to their ravages. He lost 200 pigs by that rapacious animal, and resolved to make war upon them. He finally succeeded in raising fine hogs by shutting them up in a close log stable from their earliest pighood.

The Shinn family were originally from New Jersey. On their way West they stopped for awhile at Cincinnati, where they followed gardening. After a long and useful life Mr. Shinn died at a little over 70 years of age, while on a visit to his daughter at Pittsfield in 1852. He took an active part in the early history of the county.

THE COMING OF THE ROSSES.

In the year 1820 there also came, from Pittsfield, Mass., the Rosses: William (Col.), Clarendon, Leonard (Capt.), and Henry J. (Dr.); also Samuel Davis, Wm. Sprague and Joseph Cogswell, all settling in or near Atlas .Leonard had been Captain in the war of 1812, and William obtained his title afterward by having been appointed Colonel of Illinois militia. Davis was a bee-hunter, who built for himself and large family a log cabin on section 16. Two years afterward he moved into Missouri. Most of these men brought their families to their new homes the following February, having previously left them at Alton. Mr. Cogswell was from Berkshire, Mass.

The Rosses in coming West had a tedious journey. They came by flat-boats down the Alleghany and Ohio rivers, and by wagons from Shawneetown to Upper Alton, where at that time but one house existed, occupied by Major Hunter. Here they left their families, and coming northward, they found an Indian camp at the mouth of the Illinois river, where they split puncheons and laid them across two canoes and thus safely carried over their wagons. The horses were made to swim alongside. Continuing up the Mississippi bottom they marked the trees as they went, for there were no roads and nothing to guide them but an occasional Indian trail. They arrived at section 27 in township 6 south and 5 west, "at last," whence, according to tradition, the name "Atlas." Some wished to name the place "Charlotte," after a certain lady in the company. This beautiful land of prairie and timber charmed the immigrants, and they at once set to work their energies and constructed a camp to shelter themselves while preparing quarters for their families. They hurried up four rough log cabins, knowing that Indians were numerous and that probably not more than five white men were within 50 miles of them east of the Mississippi.

SEELEY, M'GIFFIN AND NEWMAN.

James M. Seeley, father of Dr. Seeley, of Pittsfield, came to this county about this time. Charles McGiffin and Levi Newman settled on this side of the Mississippi river opposite Louisiana on a slough called "McGiffin's Slough," but not known by that name now: but they had no families. McGiffin died two years afterward and Newman moved over into Morgan county.

JOHN AND JEREMIAH ROSS, BROWN, WOOD AND KEYES.

In 1821, John and Jeremiah Ross, brothers of the preceding, Rufus Brown, John Wood (afterward State Governor) and Willard Keyes arrived at Atlas. Here Brown kept a tavern, but he and these two Rosses and Mr. Wood removed to Adams county. When they first came to Pike county Wood and Keyes first settled on the 16th section just below New Canton and kept bachelor's hall on the bank of a creek, subsequently named "Keyes" creek, after one of these men. They had a few hogs, two yoke of oxen and a small iron plow, by which latter they broke up a piece of ground before building a cabin. In three or four years they sold out and went to Adams county, where Wood founded the city of Quincy. He was then a young man, vigorous and ambitious. One day he, with William Ross, the founder of Atlas, and Capt. Ross, the Sheriff of Pike county, were traveling over the country north and west of this county, but then within its borders. When nearing the Mississippi river he told his companions to follow him and he would show them where he was going to build a city. They went about a mile off the main trail when they reached the present site of the city of Quincy. The view presented to the trio of sturdy frontiersmen was a magnificent one. The hand of the white man had never touched the soil, or disturbed the beautiful decorations of nature. Below them swept the Father of Waters yet unburdened by steam navigation. Mr. Wood tried to show his companions the advantages the location had, but Mr. Ross, thoroughly interested in building up his own town of Atlas and so sanguine of its future greatness, that the beautiful and excellent location selected by Mr. Wood was completely overshadowed by that enjoyed by his village. Mr. Wm. Ross congratulated his young friend and hoped he would make of his town a success, but he despaired of it ever amounting to much, for, as he remarked to the Governor, "It's too near Atlas."

OTHER SETTLERS.

In 1821 there also came to the county James McDonald, who settled opposite Louisiana, on Sny Island, and kept a ferry. He opened the first farm on the road between Atlas and Louisiana, but floods drowned him out. He was from Washington county, N. Y., and his family consisted of himself, wife and four daughters. The next spring he was found dead at his ferry, supposed to have been murdered. Joseph Jackson afterward married his widow.

In the summer of 1821, Garrett Van Deusen came to the county and settled on the Illinois river near the old Griggsville Landing. He was the first settler on the east side of the county except two transient French families, who had located some distance below. He erected the second band-mill in the county, the first having been put up by Col. Ross, at Atlas.

THE "SICKLY SEASON."

The summer of 1821 sorely tried the hearts of the sturdy settlers in and about Atlas. That was a sickly season and scarcely a family but followed some of its members to the newly made cemetery, until over one-half the entire population were numbered with the dead. The prevailing cause of the visitation of such a calamity to the settlers was the malaria emanating from the vegetable decay of the newly broken prairie and the decomposition of immense quantities of fish in the ponds below the town. The victims of this dreadful malady were laid in coffins made from bass-wood puncheons, hollowed out and consigned to earth in a grave-yard near Franklin's first location, and about 400 yards west of Shinn's. The bones and dust of 80 persons now lie buried there, and at present there is not a stone or head-board, or any signs whatever of its being a cemetery. There was no physician nearer than Louisiana during this scourge, and with this fact, and taking into consideration the poor facilities the settlers had for providing for and nursing the sick, it remains no wonder that so many died.

During this year Col. Ross built a small brick house, the first in the county. Two years afterward he erected a much larger brick structure adjoining it.

FIRST PUBLIC IMPROVEMENTS.

This year also the first court-house in the county was built. Daniel Shinn took the contract for cutting and hauling the logs, at $6, and for $26 he got out the puncheons and finished the building. It was completed without nails or iron in any shape. It was 16 by 18 feet in dimensions, with one door and two windows, the door on the east side, one window on the south side and another on the west side; desks made of puncheons; chimney outside; and the clapboards of the roof held on with weight-poles and knees. There were no trees around the house, but plenty of hazel-brush in the vicinity.

This year the first school was taught in the county, by John Jay Ross, son of Capt. Leonard Ross. It was kept in the court-house, and the names of his pupils were, so far as remembered, Orlando, Charlotte, Schuyler, Mary Emily and Elizabeth Ross, Benjamin, John, Eliza and Phœbe Shinn, John Webb, Frederick and Eliza Franklin, Jeremiah and William Tungate, James, Laura and Nancy Sprague. James W. Whitney taught the next school, which was also at Atlas.

A FEW MORE OF THE EARLIEST PILGRIMS.

About this time Dexter Wheelock and wife settled at Atlas, where for a time he kept a hotel and a general store. He had been a drummer in the war of 1812, and was an active and generous man. He died many years ago, and his son, John G. Wheelock, has been a prominent citizen of the county.

The spring of 1822 two brothers named Buchanan settled at "Big Spring." A Mr. Allen (father of Lewis) came to the county this year, and was probably the first settler in the neighborhood of Milton. His wife was a sister of the celebrated Daniel Boone. An old gentleman named Clemmons also settled about this time near Milton, where his sons now reside. Joel Moore, now living two miles north of Pittsfield, on Bay creek, was the first settler on that stream.

This year Mr. Franklin sold out his place near Atlas, to Col. Ross, for $30 or $40, and removed to a point a little south of Pittsfield, where Mr. Allen now lives; he sold out here again ere long to Mr. Goodin, and located near Milton, on a prairie called after him, "Franklin's Prairie;" and this home too he subsequently sold, removing this time to Perry. He died in Milton in 1878.

Mr. Hoskins (father of John) came to the county soon after the Ross family.

FIRST WHITE CHILD BORN IN THE COUNTY.

The first white person born in this county was Nancy Ross, daughter of Col. Wm. Ross, born May 1, 1822. She died Nov. 18

of the same year at Atlas. Some say, however, that there was a white person born in this county some time previous to this; how true that is we cannot state authoritatively.

TRIP TO LOUISIANA.

The first settlers suffered much from want of provision, as well as from the loneliness of their wilderness homes. During the year 1822, Franklin and Shinn, getting out of provisions, started to Louisiana for a supply. On arriving at the river they gave the customary signal for the ferryman to come over after them, but could not make him hear. Being strong and fearless they undertook to swim the great river, even with their clothing on. They buffeted the waves well for a time, and made good progress, but unfortunately Mr. Shinn took the cramp, and came near drowning, and would have drowned if it had not been for his companion's presence of mind. Franklin, by beating him, got him out of the cramp. In order to make further progress, however, they were compelled to divest themselves of their clothing. After a long, hard and dangerous struggle they finally landed upon the Missouri shore, about three-quarters of a mile below town, but void of clothing. They made their presence known, however, and were soon furnished with clothing.

CRIMINAL DROWNED.

During this same year (1822) a man by the name of Franklin, not Ebenezer, stole a gun from a Mr. Hume. In making away with it in his haste he was unfortunate enough to lose it while swimming McGee's creek. He was pursued, caught, and in a very summary trial before Col. Ross, Justice of the Peace, was sentenced to have 25 lashes laid upon his bare back. This punishment being inflicted (and we are told he bore it nobly), he was given his liberty. He soon committed another crime, however, was caught, but broke from custody. The pioneers were full of pluck, and when they set out to accomplish anything they generally did it, at whatever price. He was tracked to Fort Edwards (now Warsaw) and again captured. They had no jail or place to confine such a cunning fellow with any safety; so it was determined to send him to the jail at Edwardsville. Constable Farr and John Wood (ex-Governor) took charge of him to convey him to Edwardsville. Knowing he would take advantage of every opportunity to escape, they lashed him to the back of a mule, by tying his feet underneath. They came to a creek on their journey, and the young man thinking that an excellent opportunity to escape, plunged in, even against the threatenings of his escort. He heeded them not, but yelled back that he would "go to h—l and kick the gate open for them." The water was high and before the mule had reached the farther shore he went down beneath the waves, carrying with him his rider. Both were drowned. Franklin's body was rescued and buried upon the bank of the creek. When Messrs. Farr and Wood returned to Atlas, Col. Ross asked them where their prisoner was, they had returned so quickly. "Oh, we've drowned him," was their indifferent reply. "You have to account for him in some way according to law, you know," said Col. Ross. "Oh, yes," they again replied, "we've drowned him." Franklin's bones were some time afterward taken up and wired together by Dr. Vandeventer, and the skeleton is now in the possession of his family at Versailles, Ill.

BISSELL, HUSONG, NICHOLAS AND MATTHEWS.

In 1823 Alfred Bissell came to the county and located at New Hartford, or rather, nearly a mile north of the present town. Mr. Bissell raised the first apples in Pike county. He finally sold out to a Mr. Brown, some of whose family still reside upon the place. Daniel Husong came to the county the same year, also an old man by the name of Nicholas, who was the first settler near Highland. Another gentleman, Mr. John Matthews, who was considerably advanced in life, the father of B. L. Matthews, and the grandfather of Col. Matthews, came and located north of Griggsville.

After this period settlers came in rapidly, and it is quite impossible for us to note the advent of each one. That will be done to a very great extent in our township histories.

FIRST FOURTH-OF-JULY CELEBRATION.

The first Fourth-of-July celebration ever held in Pike county, and probably in the Military Tract, was held at Atlas in 1823. Col. Ross thus speaks of it in a letter written at the time to a friend in the East, which is still preserved: "July 4, 1823.—The first celebration of the Fourth of July was held in Atlas, Pike county, Ill. Oration delivered by Nicholas Hanson, of Albany, N. Y. The Declaration of Independence was read. There was an audience of about fifty persons, who afterward partook of an excellent dinner prepared by Rufus Brown at his tavern. The audience marched in procession after dinner. A jolly good time was had drinking toasts, etc., and 'all went merry as a marriage bell;' this being the first celebration ever held in Pike county, or in this Military Tract."

This Rufus Brown, spoken of, subsequently removed to Quincy, where he built a log house on the lot where the Quincy House now stands. After living in Quincy for a time, he pulled up and moved further West, and has since died.

FIRST JAIL AND VISIT OF THE INDIANS.

1824.—This year the first jail at Atlas was built. Daniel Husong hewed the logs and Daniel Shinn did most of the work on the building. The door was four inches thick. Wrought spikes were used, and for hinges bars were employed which were as thick as a man's arm. The only window was a hole about the size of a pane of glass. The logs were a foot square and "scotched" down, and the place for ushering in prisoners was in the roof. It was a good jail, however,—even better, some think, than the jail at Pittsfield some years ago. The old Atlas jail building is still in existence, but has been removed to near the Levee and is considerably dilapidated.

This year old Keokuk and 500 of his men, on their way to fight Indians below St.·Louis, stopped on the Sny near Atlas, over night, and had a war dance. They had sent to the whites at Atlas a notice in advance that they intended them no harm. Keokuk was a fine-looking man, it is said, while Black Hawk, who also frequently visited this region, was rather a small man, with one eye.

FIRST MALE CHILD BORN IN THE COUNTY.

Nov. 11, 1824, Marcellus Ross was born, a son to Col. Wm. Ross at Atlas, the first white male child born in Pike county. It is stated, however, in Mr. Grimshaw's historical sketch, that a son to Ebenezer Franklin was born before this, and still others say that a son was born before this date in the family of Mr. Ward. In the proceedings of the Old Settlers' Association it is stated that Rev. John Hopkins, of New Hartford, was born in Pike county May 30, 1822; that he attended school at Atlas when there were but five scholars, and that he bound after the first reaper in the county. In July, 1836, Col. William Ross and family removed to Pittsfield, where he remained until his death, and where Marcellus still resides.

COL. BARNEY.

In 1826 there came to Atlas, from Berkshire, Mass., that eminent man, Col. Benjamin Barney, who still survives, residing at Barry. He "was a man of great physical powers, of strong natural sense, benevolent, patriotic, not learned in book lore, but wise in that which made him a leader in trying times; was sober, industrious and always at his post. His tales of early adventure are marvelous, and yet undoubtedly true."—Grimshaw. He was born in September, 1795, emigrated first to Sandusky, O., and afterward was one of the first five settlers in Seneca county in that State. In Ohio he married Minerva Harris, who died in 1849. He was the first blacksmith in Pike county, and probably the first in the whole Military Tract. He made the first plow ever made in this county, and was for a long time known as "the county blacksmith." He was induced to stop at Atlas mainly on account of his being offered the position of Deputy Sheriff by Capt. Ross, the newly elected Sheriff. Col. Barney bore a prominent part in the Black Hawk war, and his life has all along been so identified with the history of Pike county that his name will occur frequently in this volume.

BARRY

COL. BARNEY'S TRIP TO CARROLLTON.

During this age of quick transit we often speak of mail "facili-ties," but for pioneer times it would be more appropriate to say mail "difficulties." It must be borne in mind that it cost 25 cents for the early pilgrims who came to this country to get a letter from their friends in the East or South, and then the mails came only at long intervals. Col. Barney relates a bit of experience as a mail-carrier in early day, which is quite thrilling.

There had been no mail received at Atlas for about six weeks. The Illinois river was high, and filled with running ice so that it was impossible to cross it with any degree of safety. Capt. Ross was postmaster at Atlas, the only place in the county where there was a postoffice, and he as well as the other settlers were exceed-ingly anxious to get the mail from Carrollton, the point from which the Pike county mail was brought. Carrollton is on the east side of the river and 40 miles distant from Atlas. Postmaster Ross had made liberal offers to induce some one to go after the mail, but none had yet succeeded in getting it. The six dollars he had offered was a great motive, and at least three men at different times had attempted the trip, but could get no further than the Illinois river, and would return discouraged. At last, becoming exceedingly anxious to hear from the outside world, Mr. Ross made the very liberal offer of ten dollars to any one who would carry the mail to Carrollton and return with the mail from that point. This offer was made Saturday night, and Col. Barney resolved to attempt to win the prize. It must be remembered that in those primitive times ten dollars was considered a large amount of money; and the Colonel said, when he returned and got his money, that he felt as though he was rich enough to start a bank.

Mr. Barney was up before day Sunday morning getting ready for the trip. His wife prepared a lunch of corn-cake and venison for him to take with him and eat upon the way; but unfortunately he forgot it when he left home. He had traveled but a few miles ere it began to snow. The large flakes began to fall thicker and faster, and the wind began to blow and soon the storming elements were raging around him with great fury. He quickened the pace of his horse and finally arrived at the Illinois river at a point where there had been a ferry and where he intended to cross. The man who had conducted the ferry had recently died, leaving a family of wife and several small children. They lived in a rude cabin upon the western bank of the river; the widowed mother lay sick and near death's door; they were without medicine, food or care, and suffering untold misery. The Colonel put his horse in the smoke-house attached to the cabin, which was so small that the horse could not turn around in it. He then hired a lad who was there at this time to assist him over the river. After much difficulty he reached the eastern bank and started off on his trip to Carrollton on foot.

14

The Atlas mail was small, yet he found great difficulty in making his way through the deep snow. He at last reached his destination, got the mail and started homeward. Before leaving Carrollton, however, he called upon the doctor and reported the condition of the woman at the ferry. The physician said he had been down to the river two or three times on his way to visit her but could not get over, and had concluded that she was dead. He gave the Colonel some medicine for her, and the kind lady at the post-office gave him a large package of provisions also to take to the distressed woman. This package weighed about 16 pounds, and with the mail, which was quite large and consisted mostly of military matter, he started on foot for the river. It was dusk when he arrived in the river bottom. To add to the already great peril in which he found himself, a large pack of wolves, about 50 in number, followed him, some of them yelping furiously. The bolder ones would approach closely and gnarl at the lone footman, whom they were eager to make a meal of. He would frighten them off by slapping his hands on the mail-bags, making a loud, sharp noise. This he did repeatedly, and perhaps it was the only way he could get through safely, as he had no fire-arms or weapons of any kind. He reached the river only to find difficulties more complicated: he could not get over. He hallooed, but in vain. He got into an old boat which lay fastened in the ice out from the shore, and lay down, thinking he would be compelled to remain there during the night. He soon found himself shivering with cold, and would certainly freeze to death if he remained there longer. He aroused himself, got a pole and finally worked his way over the river, from cake to cake of the floating ice, though a dangerous task it was. He remained over night at the cabin and gave the widow the medicine and provision sent her. These relieved her present wants, but she continued to decline, and shortly afterward died.

The Colonel at last reached Atlas, with the long-looked-for mail. He made the settlers joyous with the letters brought from their friends and was himself made happy by the receipt of ten dollars, which he had certainly well earned.

DROWNING OF JAMES WARD.

In the spring of 1826, James Ward, who had settled about four miles south of Atlas near Six-Mile creek, and whose farm lay partly on the bluff and partly in the bottom, made a trip to Fort Clark, now Peoria, and other settlements in that direction in company with Col. Ross, on an electioneering tour, or to view some land. On arriving at Crooked creek on their return, just above a drift of flood-wood, Mr. Ward ventured to cross, but was drowned. Mr. Ross, thus left in a wilderness with the shades of night fast hovering around him, and the gloom cast over him by the loss of his companion, wandered on down the stream, not daring to cross and not desiring to stop. Soon he saw a light in the distance and followed on down until he came to the cabin of a lone hunter. Here he was taken in, provided for and kept for the night. In the morning the body was recovered and buried upon the bank. The horse had made the shore and was found fastened to a tree by his bridle being caught in a limb. A year or so afterward the bones of the drowned man were taken up and re interred with Masonic honors.

COL. ROSS' KEEL-BOAT.

In 1826 Col. Ross built a keel-boat called "The Basket," which was hauled down to the Sny and launched. It would hold about 50 tons, and in this craft the Colonel shipped the produce of the neighborhood, as beef, pork, hides, etc. He used to pack about 400 head of cattle every season. Dressed beef was only two and a half cents a pound. Dealers had the hide and tallow as their reward for killing and dressing. They sold their beef in the South, New Orleans generally, for five dollars a barrel, tallow ten cents a pound, dry hides five cents, and green hides two and a half cents a pound. To get their boats over sand-bars they would unload the barrels, roll them over the bars and then reload. On one trip it required one whole day to get over a distance of twelve miles.

A FEW OCCURRENCES OF 1826.

Capt. Hale, a Missionary Baptist minister, came to the county in the summer of 1826, but at this time several other ministers were also preaching in Pike county, as Messrs. Garrison, Medford and Lewis Allen. Mr. Medford was a smart man, and had a circuit extending from Rushville to some point in Calhoun county. Capt. Hale probably organized the first Baptist Church in the county.

This year also the first store building in the county was erected, by Col. Ross at Atlas. It was built of hewed logs, and in dimensions was 16 feet square. The principal part of a merchant's stock those days was whisky.

In the fall of 1826 the first whisky made in the county was manufactured by Mr. Milhizer, a Pennsylvania Dutchman, although it is also claimed that Mr. Blair, spoken of a little further on, erected the first distillery; but his distillery was erected in 1829 or 1830. Mr. Milhizer made but one barrel of whisky.

Soon after his arrival Col. Ross put up a band-mill by which he could grind four or five bushels a day, but he soon built a larger mill which, with four good horses, would grind from 25 to 30 bushels a day. Settlers from even 25 miles above Quincy used to come to this mill. Good fine flour, however, was brought from Cincinnati, O., but this costly article was used only on occasion of visits from friends, or on Sunday when the family thought they could stand the expense of such a luxury. For most of their milling at this period the settlers in this section went to St. Louis, Mo. There was no Alton then.

The first coal burned in Pike county was from Pittsburg, Pa., and used by Benj. Barney in his blacksmith shop in 1826. During the summer of 1827 there was a great deal of rain, and the streams rose higher than they ever did afterward until 1851. The Sny Carte was navigable for steam-boats at least as far up as Atlas, as Col. Ross proved to the astonishment of many. He had three steam-boats in his service, and one of them in particular, the "Mechanic," came up to a point directly opposite Atlas. Its arrival was announced by the firing of guns.

The first wheat raised in Pike county was raised this year by Col. Ross and Mr. Seeley, and it was also the first wheat ground within the limits of the county.

This year came Benjamin B. Barney, no relation of Col. Barney. Endeavoring to trace their relationship one day the Colonel said he was from Massachusetts, when Benjamin B. replied with an oath, "Oh, if you are a Yankee you are no connection of mine." This Benjamin B. Barney bought Col. Ross' horse-mill and kept it a long time, probably until it was worn out or finally abandoned.

1827.

In the vicinity of Atlas, Henry Long, from Baltimore city, settled about the year 1827. During a residence of many years, until his decease on his farm, he was a useful citizen and upright man. He reared a second numerous family of intelligent and educated children. His son, Jesse Long, has been a Supervisor of Atlas township, and resides on the old homestead of his father. Nathan Watson, now living about five miles south of Pittsfield with his son Job, came to the county in 1827. During this year or some time previously, there came to Atlas, James M. Seeley, who was for 12 years (1828—'40) noted as the honest, easy Sheriff of Pike county. It was his duty to collect revenue. If a man was not ready to pay his tax, Seeley paid it and trusted him. Mr. S. had a numerous family, of whom Dr. E. M. Seeley, who was a surgeon during the late war, was one; another was Dr. David Seeley, who was an early settler of Texas, where he died.

1828.

Among the many prominent citizens now living who came to the county in 1828, was James Ross, who introduced and used the first cradle in the county for cutting wheat. It was a great curiosity to the pioneers, but a familiar thing to him, as he was from Pennsylvania where cradles were common. He equipped and ran the first turner's lathe and cabinet-shop in Pike county. This shop was in one end of the first clerk's office building in Atlas. His shop was burned out here. He is now closing his long and eventful life in Pittsfield. Even when he was 60 years of age he was a fine dancer and could whistle almost equal to the flute. It has always been interesting to hear him tell stories of pioneer times.

This year a saw and grist mill was built at Rockport by James McMurphy and son, who used limestones for burrs. They also built a flat-boat which they ran to Galena in their trade. At this time there were but three steam-boats on the Mississippi river.

This year Wm. Montgomery Blair, a New-Light minister, came with his family to Kinderhook. His son Montgomery, now living at Barry, was then 19 years of age. The family emigrated originally from Kentucky to Ohio, then to Indiana and lastly to this county. When they arrived here, however, they found that several other families had preceded them in this part of the county, namely, an old hermit named Peter Harper, a refugee from justice, having come here from Indiana. He was at Kinderhook. To the north of where Barry now stands were David Edwards and Edward Earle, and to the south lived Samuel Gary, on section 30, then the Jackson family and Mr. Howard and John Milhizer. Harper lived at Kinderhook until his death.

Mr. Blair built the first log cabin at Kinderhook, and the next year he built the first mill in this part of the county, and also a distillery, which is said by some to be the first in the county. Although this gentleman made considerable whisky, the distillery had finally to be abandoned on account of there not being grain enough raised in the country to make the business pay. He sometimes made as high as two or three barrels of whisky per day by a process known as "steam distilling." Wheat at this time was only three "bits" a bushel, and Mr. Blair kept a stock on hand for two or three years waiting for a better market. Milling was so difficult to obtain that several days were generally wasted by persevering parties lingering around the mill to see that their grist was ground in its proper turn, or in frequent visits to the mill. At this period beef and pork were only one and a half cents a pound. A large three-year-old steer would bring only ten dollars.

About this period Benj. Matthews, a lad of 18 years, settled in the northern part of the county.

1829 AND ONWARD.

By this time the immigrants had become so numerous and the events of history so complicated that they cannot be very well grouped by years either in the memories of old settlers or in written history.

The second court-house was built in 1829 by Elijah Petty and Col. Ross, contractors, at a cost of $650. About this time the clerk's office building was erected in Atlas. It was a double log building, and one end was occupied by James Ross as a cabinet shop. This building was totally destroyed by fire one night during the winter of the big snow, as referred to further on. Many of the earliest records were thus lost, and many others would have been burned but for the great exertions and bravery of Mr. James Ross.

John Barney, now residing at Pittsfield, is a brother of Col. Benj. Barney, and came to the county in 1830. Soon after the county-seat was removed to Pittsfield, Mr. John Barney was elected treas-

urer, which office he filled with fidelity for a number of years. All
the money raised and expended for the construction of the present
court-house and the first Pittsfield jail passed through his hands.
It being once charged that he was a little behind with the public
funds, an investigation was instituted, which resulted in showing that
instead of his being in debt to the county, the county was owing him
over a hundred dollars.

Fielding Hanks settled in Pike county in 1830, and was probably the first tanner here.

CHAPTER II.

EARLY SETTLEMENT—CONTINUED.

THE WINTER OF THE BIG SNOW.

We now come to the winter of the deep snow, 1830-'1. The snow of that winter commenced falling Nov. 10, and did not all go away until the following April, yet the largest fall of snow did not begin until the 29th of December. This was the heaviest snow that ever fell in Illinois within the memory of the oldest settler of this part of the State. According to the traditions of the Indians as related to the pioneers, a snow fell from 50 to 75 years before the settlement by the white people, which swept away the numerous herds of buffalo and elk that roamed over the vast prairies at that time. This tradition was verified by the large number of bones of these animals found in different localities on the prairies when first visited by the whites. The deep snow is one of the landmarks of the pioneer. He reckons, in giving dates of early occurrences, so many years before or so many after the deep snow. He calculates the date of his coming, his marriage and birth of his children from it, and well might it make a lasting impression upon their minds.

In the northern portion of the county the snow at first was about three feet deep on a level, and as it settled a crust formed on the surface. The winter was also unusually cold, and this, in connection with the snow covering the mast and other food of wild animals, resulted in starving and freezing to death most of the game, as deer, wild hogs and turkey. The deer, indeed, had been rendered scarce by the sweeping fires of the preceding autumn which the Indians had set out. After all this, however, there was but very little suffering among the citizens of this county. They had plenty of meat and hulled corn, and with this simple fare they were content. What wild game there was alive in the forest was easily caught, on account of their reduced condition and the depth of the crusty snow which impeded their progress in the chase. Col. Ross chased down two deer with a horse, and caught and killed them by hand. The men got out of liquor, however, and this was their greatest privation; but their suffering on this account was probably more imaginary than real. On the 18th of February two men who had engaged to chop some wood for Col. Barney backed out of their agreement when they found he had no whisky.   Mr. Barney, recollecting that a neighbor owed him a pint of whisky on a bet made at some former time, induced the men to go to work by offering them a treat.   This whisky being the last in the neighbor's demijohn had some drug in it, but that "did not hurt the liquor any," as it was so scarce and costly, it being worth $1.25 a gallon.   Clothing was also a little scarce, as the new comers into the new country had but very few sheep.   For most of their substantial clothing the pioneers of these times had to depend upon home-made material.

In the northern part of the county the snow was so deep as to cover the ears of the outstanding corn and make it very difficult to gather.   Joshua Woosley, who, on account of the two preceding years being very favorable, inadvertently let his stock of corn on hand get quite low, gave men three bushels a day for picking corn; and it was surprising how much of the article these hardy pioneers would gather amid such surroundings.   Twenty men in four days gathered 2,500 bushels.

During the spring a freshet came with the melting snow, and the waters of the Sny undermined the mills at Rockport so that they sank down.   Col. Ross had 50 or 60 men at work there nearly all spring filling up the places washed out.

During this winter the clerk's office building at Atlas was burned down.   Col. Ross first discovered fire breaking out in that end of the structure where "Jimmy" Ross had his cabinet-shop, and raised the alarm; but the wind was blowing fiercely and nearly all was lost.   This building was not more than five rods from Col. Barney's residence, and he and "Jimmy" succeeded in rescuing some of the papers and records of the office, which but few of the other citizens seemed to care but little about.   Many such things grow valuable with the lapse of time, and doubtless many more papers might have been saved which would render this history more complete.

The year 1831 was also marked by a freeze in August which nearly ruined the corn crop before it was sufficiently mature, and consequently the following spring the farmers had to send to Kentucky for seed corn, paying for it on its delivery $3 a bushel.   Boats came up the river about one a week, and their arrival was always the occasion of joy or disappointment.   The settlers, however, got all the seed corn they wanted, those who were flush being willing to divide with their less fortunate neighbors and trust them, depending upon the success of their next crop for pay.   Shipping on the Mississippi at this period was limited to only three steam-boats between St. Louis and Galena, and whatever freighting was done by flat and keel boats, which were poled, rowed, sailed, cordelled and towed.

THE FIRST NEGRO SETTLERS.

"Free Frank," a colored man, arrived in Hadley township, this county, in the spring of 1831, with his wife Lucy and three children.   They were originally from Kentucky and had spent the preceding winter in Greene county, Ill. This family were the first settlers in that township, and none others arrived for two years. To conform to the custom of the age the Legislature gave Free Frank the surname of McWorter, and he was ever afterward known as Frank McWorter. He was a live, enterprising man, and laid out the town of New Philadelphia, which once had great promise of making a good town. He had bought his own freedom and that of his wife and many of his children, and left provision in his will to buy grandchildren, which was carried out by his son, Solomon McWorter. Frank died about the year 1857, at 77 years of age. His wife died in her 99th year in 1871. Mr. McWorter was born in North Carolina, his wife in Virginia. They were both members of the Baptist Church and led exemplary lives. By industry and economy they left a valuable farm to their heirs. A large and respectable settlement of their descendants now exists around the old home.

In 1832 or 1833 a colored man came to the southern part of the county known by the name of "Bob," who wanted to marry a white girl, the daughter of a Mr. Guernsey. This aroused the indignation of the whites, and as soon as he saw the citizens after him he took to his heels and ran away so fast that "50 men couldn't catch him!"

NUMEROUS SETTLERS.

Before the Black Hawk war there came to this county, settling in various parts, besides those we have mentioned and many others, Hawkins Judd, Geo. W. Hinman, Stephen R. Watson, Garrett Van Deusen, Daniel Clingensmith, N. E. Quinby, M. Branson and Horace Horton. Messrs. Hinman and Judd were County Commissioners with Col. Barney when they bought of the United States for $200 the quarter section of land upon which Pittsfield was located. They are now dead. Mr. Van Deusen, an eccentric Knickerbocker Dutchman, was a Justice of the Peace and likely one of the earliest settlers east of Pittsfield on Blue river, and was the originator of a queer device to crack corn, operated something after the manner supposed to be in vogue in the days of Adam and Eve. He used the stream of Blue river at a narrow place, and by catching and confining the water therefrom in a hollow tree or trough, open at the end up stream and closed at the lower end, he worked a swinging vessel which was suspended over a mortar to crack Indian corn. The process was to let the trough fill with water nearly to overflowing, when by its weight it would descend, dashing the pestle into the mortar and crushing the corn. The pestle being adjusted some distance from the end of the trough up stream, the water spilled beyond the mortar, and the machine adjusted itself for another beat at the corn. Col. N. E. Quinby was a lawyer. Mr. Clingensmith settled in the northern part of the county: he died in 1835. Capt. Horton was a jolly tar from Connecticut, an energetic man and a good settler. He came in 1832 and located above Rockport. Branson and Watson, the latter a tailor, settled at Atlas.

THE YEAR OF THE BLACK HAWK WAR.

Chronologically we have now arrived at the period of the Black Hawk war, and the connection of Pike county with that epoch will be given in the chapter upon that war. No county perhaps took a more active and decided part in this struggle of the pioneers with the Indians than this county. Almost as soon as it was known that soldiers were wanted Pike county had filled her quota. In an early day Indians were quite numerous here, but we have no record of any depredations being committed by them other than petty theft. The Sacs and Foxes made their headquarters along the Sny for many years, where they were often visited by Black Hawk and Keokuk. At or near Atlas the whites often saw them in their war dances. These Indians however gave the settlers of Pike county very little trouble. Indeed they sometimes evinced some title to the epithet "noble." As for example, when a squaw was at one time sick of a fever and was nursed and doctored by a white family at Atlas until she got entirely well to the surprise of her Indian friends, they were very thankful and showed their gratitude in many ways.

In this connection we may relate a little anecdote characteristic of early times. John Jay Ross and a Mr. Filer thought they would have some fun one day by frightening Mr. Young and his family who resided at Atlas, and in the vicinity of his house they imitated the noise and whoop of Indians so perfectly that Mr. and Mrs. Young thought they were surrounded by blood-thirsty red-skins. They were greatly frightened and chugged their children into a small cellar which was not large enough for themselves to get into. They ran out into the mustard patch and remained there until the afternoon of the next day, so scared were they, before they dared to return to the house and liberate their suffering children.

JAMES W. WHITNEY.

A very noted character in the earliest days of Pike county was James W. Whitney, more generally known as "Lord Coke," on account of his knowledge of law. He was teacher of the second school at Atlas, but having no family or permanent home he can scarcely be denominated a "settler." He was the first Circuit and County Clerk, and held many local offices. He was a native of Massachusetts, a man of considerable education, having some knowledge of Latin. He came to Illinois before it was a State and resided at or near Edwardsville. Not much is known of his former life, as he was always very taciturn when the subject was introduced. It is said that there was a hidden sorrow in his former life which was a delicate matter to touch upon. He wrote a very peculiar hand, which would indicate that he was an oddity. At first sight one would have taken him to be a well-preserved preacher or schoolmaster of the days of the earlier Adamses. His dress was plain and even homely; his hair was sparse and all combed to the back of his head, and often tied with a buckskin string or old black shoe-string as a cue. Pecuniarily he was not prosperous, and he was very indifferent with respect to his dress. He made his journeys generally afoot and alone, putting up where night found him, with some friend, and his acquaintance was very extensive. He was always welcomed by the lonely pioneers, as he was a kind of gazetteer, bringing them the news when newspapers were scarce. He lived sometimes alone in a log cabin and sometimes he made the city of Quincy his headquarters.

"Lord Coke" was also known as the "Speaker of the Lobby," as he was the leader of that branch of the Legislature for many years. When theaters and shows were rare, the citizens, judges and legislators at Vandalia were all agog to witness the convening of the Lobby. It was a great event. A throng would assemble, and after some ceremony "Lord Coke" would mount the stand and call the house to order. He would deliver his annual message, which would be received with cheers and laughter. Many hits and jokes were embodied in the message. Sometimes the satire was very broad, and at one time he hurt his standing with the Supreme Court by a farcical account of a meeting represented to have been held by that Court and leading members of the Bar to "exterminate the varmints of the State." He presided over the "Lobby" with magisterial sway, and when mock heroics moved the man he would be a very important personage. The "Lobby" was organized by appointing subordinate officers and numerous committees, whose titles and functions would be of the most ludicrous character; and the members composing the same would be in physical form, public standing and personal bearing the most opposite of that position and character. For example, Col. Thos. Mather, President of the State Bank of Illinois, was a man short in stature but of great rotundity of person, quiet in demeanor; Judge Thomas Brown and Jesse Thomas, jr., were fine, portly gentlemen. Such as these "Lord Coke" would announce, and that in print, as the most suitable members of "the committee on gymnastics and ground and lofty tumbling." Many reports of these committees would be submitted which would be in accord with their burlesque titles. These reports were often written by "Lord Coke" himself, and there was a broad personality in them rather Hudibrastic.

At the Bar "Lord Coke" was not successful, as there was a want of practical sense in his applications and his law was often obsolete. He died Dec. 13, 1860, between 83 and 85 years of age.

OTHER PROMINENT CHARACTERS.

Parvin Paullin, a native of New Jersey, came in mature years to this county, served one term as a Representative in the Illinois Legislature, and was Probate Judge, discharging always his duty with honor and efficiency. He died many years ago.

Ephraim Cannon was an early settler of Pike county, and for a time Sheriff.

Robert and Joseph Goodin and Fisher Petty were amongst the noted men of Highland. Petty was a County Commissioner at Pittsfield; Mr. Murphy was the first County Surveyor; and Joseph Goodin was County Surveyor thereafter and a good officer. He was living a few years ago in Missouri.

John George Nicolay, an illustrious representative of Pike county education, was born in Germany, and came to this county an obscure boy; being very studious he became highly self-educated; learned the printer's trade in Pittsfield; married Miss Bates of that place; he edited the *Free Press* for a short time, and when O. M. Hatch was elected Secretary of State Mr. N. was his clerk for two years at Springfield; read law in Abraham Lincoln's office, and on the election of Mr. Lincoln to the Presidency of the United States he became one of his private secretaries; subsequently he was Consul to Paris, and is now Marshal of the Supreme Court of the United States, which is a life office or a tenure during good behavior.

John Hay, son of Dr. Hay, of Warsaw, and nephew of Milton Hay, next mentioned, and for some time a resident of Pittsfield, was a companion of Mr. Nicolay in the study of law in Mr. Lincoln's office at Springfield and in being private secretary of the President. While in Pittsfield he published "Pike County Ballads," a collection of capital pieces of poetry, among the most noted of which are " Banty Tim," " Little Breeches " and " Bludsoe."

Milton Hay, now ranking high as a lawyer at Springfield, resided in Pittsfield in his earlier days as an attorney at law. He has since been in a Constitutional Convention and in the Legislature of the State.

Major Charles J. Sellon we can claim as a son of Pike county, his parents having been the present wife of Col. D. B. Bush, by her former husband, Rev. John Sellon, an Episcopal clergyman who once owned St. Ann's Church, New York city, and was a wealthy man, and whose sister was the wife of Sir Benjamin Brodie, the eminent English physician. Charles J. was brought up principally in the family of Col. Bush, was in the Mexican war (in the battle of Buena Vista), and during our late war was Major of an Illinois regiment; was editor of the Springfield (Ill.) *Journal*; still later on the Peoria *Transcript*. He died in 1862.

"Aunt" Roby Ross, still living at Barry, in her 92d year, came with her people to Atlas. She was born Sept. 27, 1789, in Rensellaer county, N. Y., and was first the wife of Clarendon Ross and afterward of his brother Capt. Leonard Ross. Clarendon Ross was the first man who died in the county and Captain Ross is long since dead. Aunt Roby's memory is still clear, and she relates many interesting experiences and events of early times. Her house was the stopping place for many people; she has fed as many as a hundred in a day. She would arrange tables out of doors made of clapboards placed upon sticks, supported by stakes driven in the ground. In that day they had an abundance of meat, vegetables and sometimes fried cakes and crab-apple sauce. Mrs. Ross's son Schuyler, by her first husband, died at the age of 20, in 1832, at Atlas.

Merrill E. Rattan, the first Postmaster at Pittsfield, long since dead, was also Probate Judge. He kept a hotel on the same lot where the Oregon House now stands. Wm. Watson, once a Probate Judge, is still living in Pittsfield. As a business man Mr. Watson was ever foremost and has accumulated some property. Robert R. Greene and his cousin Austin Barber opened and carried on the first large store in Pittsfield. These gentlemen are both yet living in that town. Mrs. G. was one of the earliest and highly respected school-teachers. Mr. Barber was for a period County Clerk.

Wm. A. Grimshaw came to Pike county in 1833. For his biography see history of Pittsfield township. John U. Grimshaw, cousin of the former, settled near Pittsfield in 1834, and afterward moved to town and for many years was an active merchant. He died many years since. Jackson Grimshaw, a brother of William A., was a resident of Pittsfield for 14 years, then of Quincy, Ills., where he died in December, 1875.

Belus and Egbert Jones, brothers, were old settlers. Belus was never a lawyer, but a pettifogger, who hung on to "Lord Coke"(J. W. Whitney) like a bobtail to a kite. At court time it was said, "No court till Coke and Belus come."

Major James Tolbert, an old Virginian, was an officer in the 17th Illinois Militia at an early day. He was an early settler of Pike county.

Lyman Scott, an early settler, married a daughter of Leonard Ross. He was for a time one of the owners of a former mill at Rockport. He was a pushing business man. Many years ago he went to Kansas and is now dead.

John Neeley, an early County Commissioner, removed to Texas and has since died.

John Lyster, at times a Justice of the Peace, was an early settler in the Meredith and Neeley neighborhood near the Illinois river, now Detroit township.

David Dutton early settled in the vicinity of Pleasant Vale, once County Commissioner, a prosperous farmer, and peculiar in his ways. He has long since deceased.

Among the early settlers of Pike county was Mrs. Nancy M. Heath, who taught the first school in Pittsfield in the winter of 1834. She had 14 scholars, taught in a rented house and boarded herself. Her terms were $3 per scholar for 12 weeks. The names of her patrons were Jonathan Pike, Col. Johnson, Wm. Watson, Ephraim Cannon, James McNary, Wm. Grimshaw, Dr. Worthington, Mr. Davis, and John Turnbull. Her maiden name was Dunbar, and she was born Jan. 1, 1791, the first white child born in Cincinnati; was brought up by Gov. McArthur, of Ohio; in 1813 she married Dr. Jonathan Heath, who was born on the south bank

of the Potomac, Morefield, Hardy county, Va. She came to Naples
Morgan county, in 1825, taught school there, and came to Pittsfield in
1834. The school-house, which was also their dwelling, was a small
hewed-log house rented of Mr. Turnbull. She has had six children,
five girls and one son, all dead. Mrs. Heath is still living in Pittsfield, but has had feeble health for many years. Her daughter,
afterward Mrs. A. V. Wills, also taught school with her.

Dr. Hezekiah Dodge emigrated from Virginia to Bayville, this
county, in an early day. In his physical structure he was "long,
lean and lank, and moved upon a spindle shank."

Mr. Gray, an early settler and prominent citizen of the county,
was Sheriff about 1851; was Postmaster at Barry, and afterward for
many years his home has been in Pittsfield.

Joshua Woosley, an early settler of Hadley township, has been
Sheriff, and taken quite an active part in the politics of the county.
He is still a man of great activity, living on the old homestead.

Among many other pioneers of Pike county we would mention,
Henry R. Ramsey, Jacob Hodgen (father of Dr. John Hodgen),
Charles T. Brewster, W. B. Grimes, D. B. Bush, Elias Kent Kane
(nephew of the celebrated Elisha Kent Kane, the Arctic explorer),
all of whom have been more or less prominent in the history of this
county. A little anecdote concerning Mr. Kent, who settled
in Montezuma township in 1836, we cannot forbear to relate here.

He went out deer-hunting one day, soon scaring up three large
deer, which ran around him in a circle about 300 yards distant. He
stood watching them with cocked gun in his hands, not knowing
why he did not shoot; but subsequently learned from friends that
he must have had the "buck ague."

Many other names of early settlers will appear in the histories of
the respective townships.

Among the sons of Pike county who have departed to other fields
of glory, are: Ozias M. Hatch and Alexander Starne, both of Pittsfield, then of Griggsville; both have run about the same career in
this county, having been Clerks of the Circuit Court, members of
the Legislature, and Secretaries of State; and both are now residents of Springfield, in prosperous circumstances. Mr. Starne left
Philadelphia in 1836, "with the intention of getting so far away
from home that he never could get back again," and he chose the
beautiful section of country called Pike county for his permanent
home. He relates many amusing stories concerning the olden
times, clock peddlers, abolition riots, Dr. Dix's first land purchase
and trip to the grist-mill.   •

Among other numerous settlers in various parts of the county
we would name the following: Rev. John Shinn, one of the early
preachers of the county, settled just west of Phillips' Ferry; then
came David Johnson, who bought the farm owned by him. He
settled there in 1828, and for many years was Surveyor of the
county. Near him was Richard Wade; the next two who came
were a Mr. Bateman and Andrew Phillips. Geo. W. Hinman, an

early prominent man, came in 1829. Joel Moore was the first settler north of Atlas toward Griggsville. Nathan W. Jones, a resident of Griggsville, was a well-known early settler. Abel Shelley, the Bradburys, Charles and Martin Harrington were also prominent pioneers. Boone Scholl, the founder of Perry, which was laid out first as " Booneville," was an early settler.

In concluding our personal mention of early settlers, we quote the following from Mr. Grimshaw's " Centennial Address:"

" Alfred Grubb, once called the ' Little Bay Horse,' for his sprightliness, was a good Sheriff and a County Judge. Thomas Orr, noted as a grand juror for many long years, was respected by all. Thomas Hull, a good farmer and remarkable for his active piety. These all leave numerous descendants of respectability. The Blairs (father and several sons), all good men, were in the vicinity of Barry before Pittsfield was laid out. William, son of the senior, was a marked member of the Illinois Legislature, and an upright and useful man. He is long dead. Montgomery Blair was once a member of the Constitutional Convention of 1847. Harvey Blair is yet alive, and is an estimable farmer.

" It is impossible in this sketch to notice all the early settlers; some have emigrated, others have died. At court time at an early day in Pittsfield, Samuel Gibson, Henry Kent, George Gibson, Sam'l Sitton, Esquire Hayden, the Tucker brothers would be seen, and Wm. Johnson, James Johnson, John and Jacob Heavener. The latter dressed in the homeliest garb, with his long rifle as bosom friend. James Johnson was a conspicuous man. Both of these men were possessed of great nerve and endurance, and made great havoc amongst the deer. Small " varmint " they despised. Sam'l G. Sitton survives in his 75th year; and on June 29th, 1876, he cut on his own farm an acre of wheat with a sickle and bound it up on that day, and the next day was at Pittsfield as spry as usual. Harvey Dunn, of Chambersburg, was an old settler, and in 1847 was a member of the Constitutional Convention of Illinois. He was a very unassuming but intelligent, honest man; but is long dead. Stephen R. Gray, venerable and respected in years, yet lives. He was Sheriff about 1851. He is an early settler and resided at or near Barry, and was at one time Postmaster thereat. Hamilton Wills is yet as happy as ever, jolly in person, comfortable in business, an old settler in Pittsfield, as a Justice of the Peace in former years useful and respected. Richard Kerr, of Pleasant Hill township, was an old farmer, a leading whig, and represented Pike county in the Legislature for one term. He died many years since, esteemed by all, leaving many relatives in Pike.

" Bonaparte Greathouse, of Milton, was County Commissioner at an early day, a man of great worth and a good farmer. He is long dead and left surviving him a numerous family. Several of his sons are practitioners at law. Sam'l L. Crane, now venerable in years, was a very early settler of Morgan county, Ill., and has filled acceptably with perfect integrity the office of Postmaster at

Pittsfield. He is now in private life. He is the father of that useful son, resident of Pittsfield, James H. Crane, who has been Circuit Clerk of Pike county, yet lives here, and is a Deputy Clerk in the office of Geo. W. Jones, our present and efficient popular circuit clerk. Wm. B. Grimes yet lives in Pittsfield. He was an able and honest County Clerk for one term, succeeding Wm. Steers, who was a good and worthy officer; and his successor is Jonathan L. Frye, who was a son of an honest miller, Jonathan Frye. James McWilliams, venerable for his years, influential in his town of Griggsville, has been a Representative of the county in the Legislature and often a Supervisor of Griggsville township. Daniel D. Hicks, now the esteemed Cashier of the First National Bank, is an old resident of Pittsfield and has honorably filled several offices. He was once Sheriff of the county. During his term of office a riot took place one election day in Pittsfield, when many wild boys who had been good soldiers in the Mexican war took a most active part in the riot, calling out, 'We are some punkins.' By aid of a posse of the people, called by Hicks, the riot was put down."

MR. HINMAN'S LETTER.

We copy the following very excellently prepared historical article from the Griggsville *Reflector* of July 1, 1876. It was prepared by Asa Hinman, son of the veteran pioneer, George W. Hinman. It so clearly portrays various features of the county's history, and knowing that it will be accepted as from a reliable source, we make no alterations in it, but present it as from the pen of Mr. Hinman:

"In 1829, I think Oct. 14th, my father, George W. Hinman, crossed the Illinois river at Phillips' Ferry with his family to make a permanent residence in Pike county. He drove out to the foot of the mound upon which the town of Griggsville now stands, and stopped with a man by the name of Bateman, who had made a small improvement and laid claim to the S. W. quarter of sec. 14, T. 4. S., 3 W., which my father soon afterward bought and occupied. This was on the main traveled route from Phillips' Ferry to Quincy and Atlas, the county-seats of Adams and Pike, the two routes parting on top of the mound in what is now called Quincy Avenue. The first settlement on the road, which was then known as the Atlas trail, after passing the site where Griggsville was afterward built, was seven miles out on Bay creek, where Joel Moore had settled some two or three years before. He emigrated from North Carolina, and, as I have understood, served in the army of the United States for the land he lived upon. The next settlement was Col. Seeley's, twelve miles farther and three miles from Atlas, on the trail to Quincy. It was thirty miles to the first house, where lived John Wiggle, a German, who formed the nucleus for the large German settlement that afterward settled in that part of Adams county.

"I believe Atlas was the only laid-out town in Pike county at

PERRY

that time. At Phillips' Ferry there was a small settlement. I will name those I remember: Nimrod Phillips, Dr. Bennett, first owners of the ferry, Tebo & McWorthy. One and a half miles up the road lived Charles Hazelrig, the only blacksmith in the eastern part of the county.

"The settlement on the road west from the ferry was David Johnson's, who settled on the farm owned for a long time by the Rev. John Shinn and now the property of E. S. Parker. Mr. Johnson settled there in 1828. He was surveyor in this county for many years. Near this place on the north side of the road lived Richard Wade. The next two settlements were Bateman, of whom I have spoken, and Andrew Phillips, who lived just east of Marshall's blacksmith shop. Dr. Phillips lived one and a half miles south of town on the farm now owned by Davis. North of town lived Marshall Kee, John Matthews, father of B. L. Matthews, and grandfather of Col. Matthews, Abel Shelly, Wm. Wilkerson, Sam Holaway, Abraham Scholl, Sam Chenoweth, and an old gentleman by the name of Ayers. All these I have named were men of families; and none to my knowledge now remain but David Johnson, who still lives in the town of Perry, and is badly crippled with rheumatism, but otherwise is in good health. Many of their children and grandchildren yet remain in the county.

"Although the immediate descendants of these old pioneers grew up without an opportunity to get an education, many of them are, yes, I may say most of them, are noble, high-minded men and women, and are generally among the foremost to make a sacrifice to secure for their children a substantial education; and while on this subject I will say, if there was a school-house in the county I was not aware of its location. The first school-house near Griggsville was built in 1831. It was located a little northeast of town, a small log cabin, stick-and-clay chimney, the floor laid from slabs split from lind logs, and the seats made of some material mounted on wooden legs. For light, one log was cut out of the building, a hewn slab put under this opening and paper pasted over it in cold weather; then with a rousing log fire, Webster's speller, the Testament, sometimes the Life of Washington, sometimes Jack Downing, Robinson Crusoe, or whatever happened to be in the library at home, and a few copies of Daboll's or Pike's arithmetic, and a long 'gad' or two, Master Robert Rankin used to 'teach the young idea how to shoot.' Some of my young friends no doubt will laugh at my description of our educational privileges in those days, but this happened less than half a century ago and within less than half a mile and in sight of that fine school-house that so adorns the town and adds so much to your educational privileges. My description of this one will answer with very little variation all the first schools in this part of the county.

"The next settlements to those already mentioned were along the bluff near Chambersburg and a few in the neighborhood of Detroit. The first settlers were poor, honest and brave, always kind to

15

friends and ready to resent an insult, but rarely with any weapon only such as nature furnished them with.

"The first settlements were nearly entirely confined to the edge of the timber where small fields could be cleaned and plowed with one yoke of oxen or a span of horses, the prairie sod being tough, requiring heavy teams to plow it.

"At this time game was very abundant. Deer, turkeys, prairie chickens, quail, raccoon, opossum and skunk were here in immense numbers. The buffalo had disappeared, but from the amount of horns and bones that lay bleaching on the prairies they must have been here in vast numbers.

"At this time occasional bands of Indians would come in to hunt, but the settlers would form into companies, shoulder their rifles and march out to their camps and drive them away.

"Now, I can imagine some of my young friends would like to know how these poor settlers lived and what kind of houses they had, how they dressed themselves, and many other questions. Well, I have told you game was plenty; so was wild honey; the land productive and every man and boy who was large enough knew how to use the rifle and bring down the game. And up to the winter of 1830–'1 the winters had been very mild. Flax grew well, and cotton for the first few years did well. The women had all been raised to spin, weave and manufacture all the clothing that was needed in the family; but a large portion of the men dressed deer-skins and made themselves pants and coats, or what they called hunting-shirts. Some wore moccasins made of the same material, others would buy leather and manufacture shoes for their own family, or perhaps some neighbor would become quite an expert at cobbling, and besides doing all the shoe work for his own family, would do also a good deal for his neighbors; and I have seen women that could make quite a respectable shoe. The men would frequently manufacture caps for themselves and boys from the skins of foxes, coons and muskrats. Honey, at that day, was almost the only sweetening, besides maple sugar, that was used. Very little tea and coffee were used. Cows were cheap and the rich and nutritious grass caused them to produce choice milk and butter. Everybody used milk in those days. Potatoes, squashes, pumpkins and the various vegetables were securely stored for winter. The people had no money; they made but very few debts and very little dealing at the stores. What they did was mostly trade in furs, peltries and beeswax; and some of the oldest settlers would have a little surplus to sell to new comers.

"It was several years before there was any grain shipped from this part of the country. The only means of transportation was a keel-boat owned and run by Ira Kellogg from Naples to St. Louis. It would make a trip once in five or six weeks. Naples was the only trading point for all the east side of the county. All the mills I can think of now that were then in Pike county, were Johnson's little grist and saw mill, two miles above Chambersburg, built in

1830 or 1831, Van Deusen's little corn-cracker on Blue river, that would grind from one to two bushels per hour according to the stage of water, and Barney's horse-mill, some four or five miles from where Pittsfield now stands. As these mills did not accommodate half the settlers, hand-mills, mortars and pestles were resorted to, and quantities of hominy were used during the winter season.

"Now, for the habitations. Well, they were all built of logs after the fashion of the school-house I described. All had fire-places and only one room. The cooking was done in iron vessels on and around the log fire. If the weather was cold, the family large, or company in, which very frequently happened, the wood was piled on so as to raise the heat and cause all hands to sit back to give the cooks room to work. In at least two corners of the cabin would be one-legged bedsteads, made by boring two holes at right angles into the logs and two to correspond into a single post to receive the outer ends of the two rails. Clapboards, being laid across, formed quite a convenient bedstead; and besides these I have often seen a loom and spinning-wheel in use in the same cabin. This state of affairs would often last for years before another room would be added.

"At the time of which I write, settlements were not very rapid. The land was not in market. Congress had passed an act that all actual settlers who had lived for one year upon the public lands were entitled to enter or buy 160 acres at any time before the land was offered at public sale, which was in the fall of 1830; but very few of the settlers had any money to buy the land upon which they lived. The land office for this district was at Edwardsville, at which place a loan office was opened by Mason & Co. They would loan $200 to a settler which would pay the Government for 160 acres of land, the settler giving mortgage on the land and personal security for the payment of the $200 with 35 per cent. interest.

"Soon after this, settlements became more frequent, many of the new comers bringing some money with them. Many of the old settlers who had borrowed money at the enormous rate of interest referred to, sold their land and improvements, thereby enabling them to pay the mortgage and have some money left to buy another tract of unimproved land. The most of these early settlers were from the Southern States. Very few of them had ever had many advantages of an education; and, coming into a new country, where for several years schools were unknown, and then for several years more the only schools we had being gotten up by the individual efforts of the poor settlers, we see how limited their education must have been. We had no school fund then, no law to levy tax for school purposes, and school-houses were built by individual effort, and teachers hired in the same way. Books and papers were very scarce. I think the nearest paper published in the State was at Vandalia, the seat of Government at that time. Our postoffice was at Naples, in Morgan, now Scott, county, where we paid twenty-five cents postage on a letter.

"With these limited advantages nearly all the children of that day grew to be men and women with but little education, or what is considered so at the present day. And let me say to my young friends, when you feel disposed to laugh at the speech, orthography, or grammar of old fogies who have come up from those days, just laugh and feel good, and then remember them with gratitude for the many sacrifices and noble efforts they have made to secure to you the grand educational advantages you now enjoy under our free-school system.

"In December, 1830, snow fell to the depth of three feet on a level and drifted in many places to eight or ten feet. This was kept up by snow-falls until the middle of March. This has been known and referred to as the winter of the deep snow. During this winter vast numbers of deer, turkey and other game died, or were killed by thoughtless hunters. During these early settlements wolves were very abundant and very destructive on pigs and sheep. This county had a great many snakes, of which the rattlesnake was the most numerous and dangerous, persons and animals being frequently bitten by them, causing the most intense pain and occasionally producing death. The habits of these reptiles were to gather up late in the fall at some rocky bluff or other place where they could make their way underground beyond the reach of frost and remain there until warm weather in May, when they crawled out and lay around in the sun a few days and then dispersed for miles over the surrounding country. During the time of their coming out in May we used to visit their dens and kill them in large numbers. This practice, in the course of a few years, greatly lessened their numbers, but still, in some localities a few remain.

"In the fall of 1830, if my recollection is right, we had the first preaching, by a Methodist minister named Hunter, whose circuit or mission covered all the territory south of Rushville and Warsaw, lying between the Illinois and Mississippi rivers. He went around this circuit once in four weeks. The preaching place for a little society that was formed in the neighborhood of Griggsville was at my father's house, on the S. W. quarter of sec. 14, T. 4 S., R. 3 W.

"ASA HINMAN."

MR. GARRISON'S LETTER.

In 1876, when F. M. Grimes was preparing the history of Montezuma township, he received the following very descriptive letter from Z. A. Garrison, of Oregon:

"Fifty years ago I with my father and his family crossed the Illinois river in a small hand ferry-boat at Meacham's Ferry, where Montezuma now stands. We went west four miles and settled in the timber, a pretty country abounding with game of all kinds. Deer, turkey and bees were very plenty. The Indians were our most numerous neighbors, being about twenty to one white man. In the winter of 1829 and 1830, the deep snow fell, which was four feet on a level. The summer following I was tending the ferry for Solomon Seevers at Montezuma and saw the first steam-boat that ploughed the Illinois river. It was a small stern-wheeler. When opposite the ferry the wheel rolled up so much grass that it could not turn, and the men had to cut it loose and pole her through the grass. There was but one water mill in the county and that was on Big Blue. It was a tub-wheel and a very faithful one it was. When it got one grain cracked it would jump upon another with a powerful vim and crack it too. The nearest store in the county was kept by Col. Ross at Atlas. Women wore homespun cotton dresses, and deer-skin moccasins. Men and boys dressed in buckskin from head to foot, and on the head a coon or fox skin cap; ate hog and hominy, lived sociably and enjoyed each other's company with true friendship."

COUNTY—SEAT MOVED TO PITTSFIELD.

By the year 1831 it was seen that the county-seat could not long remain at Atlas, and a movement was started to fix its future and permanent location. The Legislature of the following winter authorized the appointment of three commissioners to locate the permanent seat of justice, which commissioners were Hawkins Judd, Geo. W. Hinman and Benj. Barney. After thoroughly canvassing the situation they chose that beautiful site, centrally located in the county, whereon the present town of Pittsfield stands. The parties who wished to make the best of the situation had not the necessary $200 to enter the land with. It was difficult to borrow it anywhere in the county except of the Ross family, and they were interested in Atlas and opposed to Pittsfield. Of course some ill-feeling was engendered, and Mr. Hinman and Col. Barney got so mad they swore they "would never hold office again," and the Colonel has kept his word. They signed a note and obtained the money of Col. Ross, had the ground surveyed, let the building of the court-house to a Mr. Burke, and the commissioners held court in it in the fall of 1833, and the next spring the Circuit Court was held there. The Commissioners favoring the location were elected by a handsome majority at the next election, showing how the people of the county felt on the subject.

THE BEAUTIFUL PRAIRIES.

The large prairies of the county presented a most beautiful sight before they were settled. The following very descriptive lines on "The Prairies of Illinois," by Capt. Basil Hall, graphically portrays their beauty in their wild and native state:

"The charm of prairie exists in its extension, its green, flowery carpet, its undulating surface, and the skirt of forest whereby it is surrounded; the latter feature being of all others the most significant and expressive, since it characterizes the landscape, and defines the form and boundary of the plain. If the prairie is little, its greatest beauty consists in the vicinity of the encompassing edge of forests, which may be compared to the shores of a lake, being intersected with many deep, inward bends, as so many inlets, and at intervals projecting very far, not unlike a promontory or protruding arm of land. These projections sometimes so closely approach each other, that the traveler passing through between them may be said to walk in the midst of an alley overshadowed by the forest, before he enters again upon another broad prairie. Where the plain is extensive, the delineations of the forest in the distant background appear as would a misty ocean beach afar off. The eye sometimes surveys the green prairie without discovering on the illimitable plain a tree or bush, or any other object save the wilderness of flowers and grass, while on other occasions the view is enlivened by the groves dispersed like islands over the plain, or by a solitary tree rising above the wilderness. The resemblance to the sea which some of these prairies exhibit is really most striking. In the spring, when the young grass has just clothed the soil with a soddy carpet of the most delicate green, but especially when the sun is rising behind a distant elevation of the ground and its rays are reflected by myriads of dew-drops, a more pleasing and more eye-benefitting view cannot be imagined.

"The delightful aspect of the prairie, its amenities, and the absence of that sombre awe inspired by forests, contribute to forcing away that sentiment of loneliness which usually steals upon the mind of the solitary wanderer in the wilderness; for, although he espies no habitation, and sees no human being, and knows himself to be far off from every settlement of man, he can scarcely defend himself from believing that he is traveling through a landscape embellished by human art. The flowers are so delicate and elegant as apparently to be distributed for mere ornament over the plain; the groves and groups of trees seem to be dispersed over the prairie to enliven the landscape, and we can scarcely get rid of the impression invading our imagination, of the whole scene being flung out and created for the satisfaction of the sentiment of beauty in refined men.

"In the summer the prairie is covered with tall grass, which is coarse in appearance, and soon assumes a yellow color, waving in the wind like a ripe crop of corn. In the early stages of its growth it resembles young wheat, and in this state furnishes such rich and succulent food for cattle that the latter choose it often in preference to wheat, it being no doubt a very congenial fodder to them, since it is impossible to conceive of better butter than is made while the grass is in this stage.

"In the early stages of its growth the grass is interspersed with little flowers,—the violet, the strawberry-blossom, and others of the most delicate structure. When the grass grows higher these disappear, and taller flowers, displaying more lively colors, take their place; and still later a series of still higher but less delicately formed flowers appear on the surface. While the grass is green these beautiful plains are adorned with every imaginable variety of color. It is impossible to conceive of a greater diversity, or discover a predominating color, save the green, which forms a beautiful dead color, relieving the splendor of the others. In the summer the plants grow taller, and the colors more lively; in the autumn another generation of flowers arises which possesses less clearness and variety of color and less fragrancy. In the winter the prairie presents a melancholy aspect. Often the fire, which the hunters annually send over the prairies in order to dislodge the game, will destroy the entire vegetation, giving to the soil a uniform black appearance, like that of a vast plain of charcoal; then the wind sweeping over the prairie will find nothing which it might put in motion, no leaves which it might disperse, no haulms which it might shake. No sooner does the snow commence to fall than the animals, unless already frightened away by the fire, retire into the forests, when the most dreary, oppressive solitude will reign on the burnt prairies, which often occupy many square miles of territory."

PRAIRIE FIRES.

Fires would visit the grassy plains every autumn. The settlers who had pushed out from the timber took great precaution to prevent their crops, houses and barns from being destroyed, yet not always did they succeed. Many incidents are related of prairie fires. The great conflagrations were caused either accidentally, or designedly from wantonness, or with a view of bewildering the game. The fire often spread further than it was intended it should. Wherever were extensive prairie lands, one-half was burned in the spring and the other half in the autumn, in order to produce a more rapid growth of the naturally exhuberant grass, destroying at the same time the tall and thick weed stalks. Violent winds would often arise and drive the flames with such rapidity that riders on the fleetest steeds could scarcely escape. On the approach of a prairie fire the farmer would immediately set about "burning back," —that is, burning off the grass close by the fences, that the larger fire upon arriving would become extinguished for want of aliment. In order to be able, however, to make proper use of this measure of safety, it was very essential that every farmer should encompass with a ditch those of his fences adjoining the prairie. When known that the conflagration could cause no danger, the settler, though accustomed to them, could not refrain from gazing with admiration upon the magnificent spectacle. Language cannot convey, words cannot express, the faintest idea of the splendor and grandeur of such a conflagration during the night. It was as if the pale queen of night, disdaining to take her accustomed place in the heavens, had dispatched myriads upon myriads of messengers to light their torches at the altar of the setting sun until all had flashed into one long and continuous blaze.

The following graphic description of prairie fires was written by a traveler through this region in 1849:

"Soon the fires began to kindle wider and rise higher from the long grass; the gentle breeze increased to stronger currents, and soon fanned the small, flickering blaze into fierce torrent flames, which curled up and leaped along in resistless splendor; and like quickly raising the dark curtain from the luminous stage, the scenes before me were suddenly changed, as if by the magician's wand, into one boundless amphitheater, blazing from earth to heaven and sweeping the horizon round,—columns of lurid flames sportively mounting up to the zenith, and dark clouds of crimson smoke curling away and aloft till they nearly obscured stars and moon, while the rushing, crashing sounds, like roaring cataracts mingled with distant thunders, were almost deafening; danger, death, glared all around; it screamed for victims; yet, notwithstanding the imminent peril of prairie fires, one is loth, irresolute, almost unable to withdraw or seek refuge."

INCIDENTS OF PIONEER LIFE.

The amusements of the pioneers were peculiar to themselves. Saturday afternoon was a holiday in which no man was expected to work. A load of produce might be taken to " town " for sale or traffic without violence to custom, but no more serious labor could be tolerated. When on Saturday afternoon the town was reached, " fun commenced." Had two neighbors business to transact, here it was done. Horses were " swapped," difficulties settled and free fights indulged in. Blue and red ribbons were not worn in those days, and whisky was free as water; twelve and one-half cents would buy a quart, and thirty-five or forty cents would buy a gallon, and at such prices enormous quantities were consumed. Go to any town in the county and ask the first pioneer you meet, he will tell you of notable Saturday-afternoon fights, either of which to-day would fill a column of the *Police News*, with elaborate engravings to match. Indeed, fights on Saturday in the villages and settlement centers were so customary that when a Saturday passed with no fight in the neighborhood, it was the occasion of considerable remark for weeks.

Rough, ready to fight, as these pioneers were, their latch-string was always out. No stranger ever stopped at their cabins without receiving a hearty welcome.

The settler in the early days was not only hospitable but also philanthropic, and never neglected an opportunity to aid a neighbor. House-raisings were his special delight. Let a new-comer arrive in the neighborhood and all were ready to help him. One would send a bushel or two of potatoes, another a piece of meat, another some other article that could be used to eke out the larder; but when the new-comer had his logs cut and all ready for the raising, then the fun commenced. Teams, men, axes, all were on the ground at an early hour, logs were hauled, scored, one side hewed, it may be, and before night willing hands had erected a residence as comfortable and commodious as any in the settlement, and at night was ready for the "house-warming," where dancing was kept up until the "wee short hours," and where all enjoyed themselves in a manner unknown to the people of to-day. Let a neighbor get sick in the fall, as frequently occurred, and some neighbor would inaugurate a "chopping bee" or corn-gathering, for his benefit, when all his fall work would be done in a day,—corn gathered and cribbed, wood chopped and hauled, and everything put in good shape for the winter. After the day's labors were completed, song and dance were in order, and until morning, perhaps, the younger members of the community would keep up their hilarity.

The only amusements of the pioneers had a hospitable, kindly core and were connected with some helpful act for needy neighbors. It was not only in amusements, but in all other acts of life that this kindliness was manifested, as instances which living witnesses can testify to will illustrate.

TRADE.

The earliest commercial transactions carried on in this, county were but neighborhood exchanges, in great part. True, now and then a farmer would load a flat-boat with beeswax, honey, tallow and peltries, with perhaps a few bushels of wheat or corn or a few hundred clapboards, and float down the Illinois or Mississippi river to St. Louis, or even to New Orleans, where he would exchange his produce for substantials in the way of groceries and a little ready money, with which he would return by some one of two or three steam-boats then running; or if the period of the trip was before the advent of steam-boats he would turn his load into cash and come home on foot.

After the advent of steam-boats a new system of commerce sprang up. Every town would contain one or two merchants who would buy corn, wheat and dressed hogs in the fall, store them in warehouses on the river at some of the "landings," and when the river opened in the spring would ship his winter's accumulations to St. Louis, Cincinnati or New Orleans for sale, and with the proceeds visit New York and lay in six months' supply of goods. So far as the farmer was concerned in all these transactions money was an unknown factor. Goods were always sold on twelve months' time and payment made with the proceeds of the farmers' crops. When the crops were sold and the merchant satisfied the surplus was paid out in orders on the store to laboring men and to satisfy other creditors. When a day's work was done by a working man his employer would say, "Well, what store do you want your order on?" and the order was always cheerfully accepted.

Hogs were always sold ready dressed. The farmer, if forehanded, would call in his neighbors some bright fall or winter morning to help "kill hogs." Immense kettles filled with water had been boiling since dawn. The sleds of the farmer covered with loose plank formed a platform for dressing, and a cask or half hogshead, with an old quilt thrown over the top, was prepared in which to scald. From a crotch of some convenient tree a projecting pole was rigged to hold the dead animals. When everything was arranged the best shot of the neighborhood loaded his trusty rifle and the work of killing commenced. To make a " hog squeal " in shooting or " shoulder-stick," i. e., run the point of the knife used into the shoulder instead of the cavity of the breast, was a disgrace. As each hog fell the " sticker " mounted him and plunged a long, well-sharpened knife into his throat, and others caught him by the legs and drew him to the scalding tub now filled with hot water, into which a shovel-full of good green-wood ashes had been thrown. The cleaners now took the departed porcine, immersed him head first into the scalding tub, drew him back and forward a time or two, tried the hair, and if it would " slip " easily the animal was turned and the other end underwent the same process. As soon as taken from the water the scrapers with case-knives went to work and soon had the animal denuded of hair, when two stout fellows would take it up between them and a third man to manage the " gambrel " (which was a stout stick about two feet long, sharpened at both ends to be inserted between the muscles of the hind legs at or near the hock joint), the animal would be elevated to the pole and the entrails removed by some skillful hand.

When the work of killing was completed and the hogs had time to cool, such as were intended for domestic use were cut up, the lard tried out by the women of the household, and the surplus taken to town to market. In those days almost every merchant had, at the rear end of his place of business or at some convenient neighboring building, a " pork-house," and would buy the pork of his customers and of such others as would sell to him, and " cut " it for market. This gave employment to a large number of hands in every village cutting pork—work which lasted all winter; also to a large number of teams hauling to the river, and coopers making pork barrels.

Prices of pork then were not so high as at present. Thousands of hogs dressed for market have been sold in this county at $1.25 to $1.50 per hundred pounds: sometimes they were sold by the dozen, bringing from $12 to $18 per dozen, owing to size and quality. When, as the county grew older and communications easier between the seaboard and the great West, prices went up to $2 and $2.50 per hundred pounds, the farmers thought they would always be content to raise pork at such a fine price.

There was one feature in this method of buying pork that made any town in Pike county a paradise for the poor man in winter. " Spare-ribs, " " tender loins, " " pigs' heads " and " feet " were not considered of any value, and were given freely to all who asked. If a barrel were taken to any pork-house and salt furnished, the barrel would be filled and salted down with tender loins or spare-ribs for nothing. So great in many cases was the quantity of spare-ribs, etc., to be disposed of, that they would be hauled away in wagon loads and dumped in the woods out of town.

In those days if wheat brought half a dollar per bushel the farmer was satisfied. A good young milch-cow could be bought for from $5 to $10, and that payable in work.

Those might truly be called close times, yet the citizens of the county were accommodating, and no case of actual suffering for the necessaries of life was known to exist before each vied with the other to relieve it.

PREACHING OF THE GOSPEL.

The early settlers were not entirely without preaching. Says an old pioneer on this subject: "The ministers of the gospel of the Savior of the world hunted us up and preached to what few there were; therefore, we did not degenerate and turn heathen, as any community will where the sound of the gospel is not heard. I shall not give their names, though sacred in memory, for they were not after the fleece, but after the flock, because they had but little to say about science and philosophy, but spoke of purer things."

In speaking of the early preachers Col. Wm. Ross, in a letter read before the first meeting of the Old Settlers' Association, said: "Among my early recollections are the faithful services rendered by pioneer ministers of the gospel, among whom the name of Brother Trotter is familiar. He rendered faithful services as a minister of Christ, and was well received by all Christian denominations as a liberal-minded Christian and a noble man."

Rev. W. D. Trotter, the gentleman above referred to, was present at this meeting, and reviewed the hardships and trials of the early settlers of Pike county to the great entertainment of the audience. He had been a missionary in this county as early as 1830. He exhibited a balance sheet of his receipts and expenditures during the year 1832–'3, in what was then called Blue River Mission. He received from the mission $88; the conference paid him $12 in addition, making his salary $100 for his services for the year.

Hon. Wm. A. Grinshaw delivered the oration of the occasion and referred to this subject in the following language: "We all worship God according to the dictates of our own conscience, and under our vine and fig tree. When Brother Trotter, who is now present, venerable with years and revered for piety, or old Father Wolf, now gathered to his fathers, blessed for his good deeds, came around to his appointment, all of every religion and no one religion turned out to meeting in the woods or the log school-house, or at a settler's home; we had no fine churches in those days. Mormons puzzled the unwary by their startling pretense at new revelations. Or, if disappointed by the regular minister, old Father Petty would recite in prayer Belshazzar's feast in trembling tones of piety."

In early day when public gatherings were occasions of great excitement and means of conveyance rare the people would walk a great way to church. Girls have been known to walk six miles to church, to "meeting" as it was termed in those days. Persons very often would ride horseback, two or three on a horse, and go ten or fifteen miles in this way, bringing along their bread and cheese.

Until public buildings were erected meetings would be held in private houses, as they were offered by their owners, or in groves.

EDUCATION.

Though struggling through the pressure of poverty and privation the early settlers planted among them the school-house at the earliest practical period. So important an object as the education of their children they did not defer until they could build more comely and convenient houses. They were for a time content with such as corresponded with their rude dwellings, but soon better buildings and accommodations were provided. As may readily be supposed, the accommodations of the earliest schools were not good. Sometimes schools were taught in small log houses erected for the purpose. Stoves and such heating apparatus as are now in use were unknown. A mud-and-stick chimney in one end of the building, with earthen hearth and fire-place wide and deep enough to take in a four-foot back-log, and smaller wood to match, served for warming purposes in winter and a kind of conservatory in summer. For windows, part of a log was cut out in either side and may be a few lights of eight-by-ten glass set in, or just as likely as not the aperture would be covered over with greased paper. Writing benches were made of wide planks, or likely puncheons, resting on pins or arms, driven into two-inch auger-holes bored into the logs beneath the windows, Seats were made out of puncheons, and flooring of the same material. Everything was rude and plain, but many of !America's greatest men have gone out from just such school-houses to grapple with the world and make names for themselves, and have come to be an honor to their country. Among these we can name Abraham Lincoln, our martyred President, one of the noblest men ever known to the world's history. Stephen A. Douglas, one of the greatest statesmen of the age, began his career in Illinois teaching in one of these primitive school-houses.

Things are changed now. We no longer see the log school-house. Their places are filled with handsome frame or brick structures, which, for elegance and beauty of design, rival those of older settled countries; and in place of the "masters" who were "looked up to" as superior beings, and were consulted on all matters of law, physic and religion, there are teachers of liberal culture, intelligent and progressive, many of whom have a broad and comprehensive idea of education, and regard their labor as something more than merely teaching in order to make a living,—more than a knowledge of a great number of facts in the great universe of mind and matter. It means culture, the developing and disciplining of all the faculties of the human mind. It is the comprehension of the entire being of man. And the school or teacher who takes charge and care of the young should provide the means and methods for carrying forward the process in all departments of their complex nature, physical, mental and spiritual.

EARLY MILLING.

One of the greatest difficulties encountered by the early settlers was in having their milling done. By a liberal application of enterprise and muscle they experienced but little trouble in producing an abundance of the cereals, but having it converted into breadstuff was a source of much hard labor. The hand-mill introduced was a great improvement over the mortar or tin grater, a description of which is given elsewhere in this volume. Then the band-mill was introduced.

John Shaw ran a horse-mill for a time in Calhoun county, where the earliest settlers sometimes went, but it appears he soon abandoned it. Wm. Ross then started one at Atlas. The burrs of this mill were limestone, and it is said that in every bushel of meal ground in this mill there would be a peck of stone dust. Many of the settlers had to travel long distances to mill, and then often wait for several days before they could get their grist.

After the large mill was built at Rockport it was the great center for milling for all this section of country.

MORMONS.

The Mormons first settled at "Mormontown," about three miles east of Pittsfield, in 1839, and by 1845 there were 300 voters in that settlement. They were quiet and harmless. On the building of Nauvoo most of them removed to that place. They tried to work some miracles about Pittsfield, but not with very signal success. We heard of but one crime committed by them during their career in this county, and that was not particularly a Mormon crime. A man among them named Benj. Sweat was convicted of passing counterfeit gold : was caught at Jacksonville. He was very poor and excited the sympathies of the people, and a petition was presented for his release, which was granted.

COTTON.

In pioneer times a little cotton was raised in the Military Tract, and as late as 1861 and 1862 there was cotton raised in Pike county. Lindsay Dilworth, living eight miles from Pittsfield, raised 17 pounds from three rows, each 100 feet long. One-half of it was frost-bitten : the remainder was white and fine-fibered. In 1862 Wm. Ross, jr., raised some very good cotton.

ASIATIC CHOLERA.

While this scourge wrought great devastation in some sections of the United States in 1848-'9, Pike county almost escaped its ravages. In and about Pittsfield Dr. Comstock, DeWitt St. John, David Ober and wife, Mr. Main, Alvin Hash's wife and several strangers died, and at Kinderhook there were 15 or 20 cases of the disease. It seemed to have got out into the county from Louisiana, whither it had been brought by steamers from the lower Mississippi.

STATE IMPROVEMENTS.

The celebrated internal improvement system inaugurated by the State in 1836-'7 did not give Pike county any railroads or canals, or even promise any; but an appropriation of several thousand dollars was made, which was economically expended in the improvement of highways. Commissioners were appointed, men were hired to superintend the work, and wagon roads were made evener or improved from Quincy through the northeastern part of the county, from Pittsfield to Florence, and one from Griggsville to the Illinois river. These works were completed, however, by county and township aid.

ORIGIN OF NAMES OF CREEKS.

McCraney's creek, formerly called "McDonald's creek," by the Government survey, was named after McCraney, who was the first settler upon its banks. He was a man of great endurance and a skillful sportsman. One day he chased down a gray wolf with his horse, when he placed one foot upon the animal's neck and with the other succeeded in breaking his legs so that he could get something with which to completely dispatch him.

Hadley creek was named after Col. Levi Hadley, an early settler.

Dutch Church creek was named after a rocky bluff near its bank which is supposed to resemble an old Dutch church in the city of Albany, N. Y. Keyes creek was named after Willard Keyes.

Ambrosia creek was named from the purity of its waters.

Two-Mile creek was named from its crossing the bluff two miles from Atlas.

Six-Mile creek is six miles below Atlas.

Bay creek was so called from the bay into which it runs.

FIRST THINGS IN PIKE COUNTY.

The first settler in Pike county was Ebenezer Franklin, who also cut the first tree and built the first log cabin, in 1820.

The first white person born in the county was Nancy, daughter to Col. Wm. Ross, at Atlas, May 1, 1822, who died Nov. 18, the same year.

Marcellus Ross, now living one mile east of Pittsfield, was the first white male child born in Pike county.

The first death in the county was that of Clarendon Ross, at Atlas.

Daniel Shinn brought the first wagon into the county in 1820.

Col. Benj. Barney was the first blacksmith in the county, erecting his shop at Atlas in 1826. He also burned the first coal in the county, it having been shipped from Pittsburg, Pa.

James Ross brought and used the first grain cradle here, in 1828.

James Ross also equipped and ran the first turner's lathe and cabinet shop, at Atlas, in 1828.

Col. Wm. Ross built the first brick house in the county, at Atlas, in 1821.

He also erected the first store building, at Atlas, in 1826, and also the first grist-mill, a band-mill, at Atlas, about the same time.

Fielding Hanks was the first to follow tanning in Pike county.

The first Circuit Court was held at Coles' Grove, Oct. 1, 1821.

The first Court at Atlas was held "the first Thursday after the fourth Monday in April," which would be May 1, 1823.

The first court-house within the present limits of Pike county was built at Atlas in 1824.

The first jail was erected at Atlas in 1824.

The first school was taught at Atlas by John Jay Ross in 1822.

The first Church was organized in the Ross family at Atlas prior to 1830. It was Congregational.

The first church building in Pittsfield was the Congregational, and built by Col. Ross.

Capt. Hale, a Baptist minister, probably organized the first Baptist church in Pike county.

The first library was founded at Atlas, about 1833–'4.

The first Fourth-of-July celebration was held at Atlas in 1823.

The first political meeting was held in Montezuma township in 1834, when Col. Ross, who was running for the Legislature, made a speech. About 50 voters were present, besides boys. No nominations or appointments were made.

The first whisky distilled in the county was manufactured by Mr. Milhizer in 1826.

The first wheat was raised by Col. Ross and Mr. Seeley near Atlas, which was also the first ground in Pike county and made into biscuit. The flour was bolted through book muslin.

The first apples were raised by Alfred Bissell, near New Hartford, and the first at Pittsfield by Col. Wm. Ross.

The first man hung in the Military Tract was a Mr. Cunningham, at Quincy.

The first man executed in Pike county was Bartholomew Barnes, at Pittsfield, Dec. 29, 1872.

The first State Senator elected from Pike county was Col. Wm. Ross.

The first County Commissioners were Capt. Leonard Ross, John Shaw and Wm. Ward.

The first County Treasurer was Nathaniel Shaw, appointed in 1821.

The first County and Circuit Clerk was James W. Whitney.

T. L. Hall, of Detroit tp., taught the first singing school, at Atlas.

The first Justices of the Peace were Ebenezer Smith and Stephen Dewey, appointed in 1821.

The first Constable was Belus Jones, appointed in 1821.

The first Masonic lodge was held up-stairs, at the house of Col. Ross, in Atlas, between 1830 and 1834. The desk used on the occasion is still in the possession of Marcellus Ross. It is a plain box, strongly built, fifteen inches square and two and one-half feet high, and contains two shelves. In one side is a door swung on hinges.

WHAT THE PIONEERS HAVE DONE.

Pike county is a grand county, in many respects second to none in the State, and in almost everything that goes to make a live, prosperous community, not far behind the best. Beneath its fertile soil is coal enough to supply the State for generations; its harvests are bountiful; it enjoys a medium climate and many other things that make them a contented, prosperous and happy people; but the people owe much to those who opened up these avenues that have led to their present condition and happy surroundings. Unremitting toil and labor have driven off the sickly miasmas that brooded over swampy prairies. Energy and perseverance have peopled every section of the wild lands, and changed them from wastes and deserts to gardens of beauty and profit. When but a few years ago the barking wolves made the night hideous with their wild shrieks and howls, now is heard only the lowing and bleating of domestic animals. Only a half century ago the wild whoop of the Indian rent the air where now are heard the engine and rumbling trains of cars, bearing away to markets the products of the soil and the labor of its people. Then the savage built his rude huts on the spot where now rise the dwellings and school-houses and church spires of civilized life. How great the transformation! This change has been brought about by the incessant toil and aggregated labor of thousands of tired hands and anxious hearts, and the noble aspirations of such men and women as make any country great. What will another half century accomplish?

There are few, very few, of these old pioneers yet lingering on the shores of time as connecting links of the past with the present. What must their thoughts be as with their dim eyes they view the scenes that surround them? We often hear people talk about the old-fogy ideas and fogy ways, and want of enterprise on the part of the old men who have gone through the experiences of pioneer life. Sometimes, perhaps, such remarks are just, but, considering the experiences, education and entire life of such men, such remarks are better unsaid. They have had their trials, misfortunes, hardships and adventures, and shall we now, as they are passing far down the western declivity of life, and many of them gone, point to them the finger of derision and laugh and sneer at the simplicity of their ways? Let us rather cheer them up, revere and respect them, for beneath those rough exteriors beat hearts as noble as ever throbbed in the human breast. These veterans have been compelled to live for weeks upon hominy and, if bread at all, it was bread made from corn ground in hand-mills, or pounded up with mortars. Their children have been destitute of shoes during the winter; their families had no clothing except what was carded, spun, wove and made into garments by their own hands; schools they had none;

Col. William Ross

churches they had none; afflicted with sickness incident to all new countries, sometimes the entire family at once; luxuries of life they had none; the auxiliaries, improvements, inventions and labor-saving machinery of to-day they had not; and what they possessed they obtained by the hardest of labor and individual exertions; yet they bore these hardships and privations without murmuring, hoping for better times to come, and often, too, with but little prospects of realization.

As before mentioned, the changes written on every hand are most wonderful. It has been but three-score years since the white man began to exercise dominion over this region, erst the home of the red man, yet the visitor of to-day, ignorant of the past of the county, could scarcely be made to realize that within these years there has grown up a population of 50,000 people, who in all the accomplishments of life are as far advanced as are inhabitants of the counties of older States. Schools, churches, colleges, palatial dwellings, beautiful grounds, large, well-cultivated and productive farms, as well as cities, towns and busy manufactories, have grown up, and occupy the hunting grounds and camping places of the Indians, and in every direction there are evidences of wealth, comfort and luxury. There is but little left of the old landmarks. Advanced civilization and the progressive demands of revolving years have obliterated all traces of Indian occupancy, until they are only remembered in name.

In closing this chapter we again would impress upon the minds of our readers the fact that they owe a debt of gratitude to those who pioneered Pike county, which can be but partially repaid. Never grow unmindful of the peril and adventure, fortitude, self-sacrifice and heroic devotion so prominently displayed in their lives. As time sweeps on its ceaseless flight, may the cherished memories of them lose none of their greenness, but may the future generations alike cherish and perpetuate them with a just devotion to gratitude.

16

CHAPTER III.

ORGANIC HISTORY.

THE MILITARY TRACT.

At the close of the war between the United States and England in 1812 our Government laid off a tract of land in Illinois for the soldiers who participated in that war. The land thus appropriated was embraced in the region between the Mississippi and the Illinois rivers, and south of the north line of Mercer county. Its northern boundary, therefore, ran east to Peru on the Illinois river, and a little south of the middle of Bureau and Henry counties. To it the name " Military Tract " was given, and by that name this section is still known. Within this boundary is embraced one of the most fertile regions of the globe. Scarcely had Congress made the proper provisions to enable the soldiers to secure their land ere a few of the most daring and resolute started to possess it. There were only a few, however, who at first regarded their " quarter-section " of sufficient value to induce them to endure the hardships of the pioneer in its settlement and improvement. Many of them sold their patent to a fine " prairie quarter " in this county for one hundred dollars, others for less, while some traded theirs for a horse, a cow, or a watch, regarding themselves as just so much ahead. It is said that an old shoemaker, of New York city, bought several as fine quarters of land as are in Pike county with a pair of shoes. He would make a pair of shoes for which the soldier would deed him his " patent quarter" of land. This was a source of no little trouble to the actual settlers, for they could not always tell which quarter of land belonged to a soldier, or which was " Congress land " and could be pre-empted. Even when a settler found a suitable location known to be " patent land," with a desire to purchase, he experienced great difficulty in finding the owner, and often did not find him until he had put hundreds of dollars' worth of improvements on it, when the patentee was sure to turn up. Many of the early settlers presumed that the owner never would be known; but in many instances, after a patent quarter-section was made valuable by improvement, the original patent would be brought on by some one, who would oust the occupant and take possession, sometimes paying him something for his improvements and sometimes not. Many holders of patents had no pity. This condition of affairs presented a temptation to merciless "land-sharks," who would come into this section and work up cases, ostensibly for the original patentees, but really for their own pockets. The most notorious of these was one Toliver Craig, who actually made it a business to forge patents·and deeds. This he carried on extensively from 1847 to 1854, especially in Knox and Fulton counties, and to some extent in Pike. He had forty bogus deeds put on record in one day at Knoxville. He was arrested in New York State, in 1854, by O. M. Boggess, of Monmouth, and taken to the jail at Cincinnati, Ohio, where he attempted suicide by arsenic; but at the end of the year he was released on bail.

PIKE COUNTY.

As a part of the Territory of Illinois in 1790 all of that portion of Illinois south of what is now Peoria was made a county and named St. Clair, in honor of Gen. St. Clair, Governor of the Northwestern Territory. Cohokia was the county-seat of this county. In 1812 that part of Illinois Territory above St. Louis was created into a county called Madison, with Edwardsville as the county-seat. Illinois was admitted as a State in 1818, and in 1821 all that part of Madison county between the Mississippi and Illinois rivers was organized into a county and named Pike. Its name was chosen in honor of Gen. Pike, of the war of 1812. The tract of country now known as Pike county was surveyed by the Government in the years 1817–'9, and soon afterward attracted attention on account of its natural advantages for commerce, fertility of soil and abundance of water. It is the oldest county in the Military Tract, and one of the largest, containing 510,764 acres, or 800 square miles, in 23 townships. The following is a copy of the act organizing the county :

AN ACT TO FORM A NEW COUNTY ON THE BOUNTY LANDS. APPROVED JAN. 31, 1821.

SECTION 1. Be it enacted, etc., that all that tract of country within the following boundaries, to wit: Beginning at the mouth of the Illinois river and running thence up the middle of said river to the fork of the same, thence up the south fork of said river until it strikes the State line of Indiana, thence north with said line to the north boundary line of this State, thence west with said line to the west boundary line of this State, and thence with said line to the place of beginning, shall constitute a separate county to be called Pike.

SEC. 2. Be it further enacted that there shall be appointed the following persons, to wit: Levi Roberts, John Shaw and Nicholas Hanson, to meet at the house of Levi Roberts, in said county, on or before the first day of March next, to fix the temporary seat of justice of said county, the said seat of justice to be south of the base line of said county.

SEC. 3. Be it further enacted, etc., that the citizens of Pike county be hereby declared entitled in all respects to the same rights and privileges that are allowed in general to other counties in the State.

SEC. 4. Be it further enacted, etc., that said county of Pike be and form a part of the first judicial circuit.

This act to take effect and be in force from and after its passage.

COUNTY-SEAT LOCATED.

The following act was passed at the next session of the Legislature :

AN ACT DEFINING THE BOUNDARIES OF 'PIKE COUNTY, AND FOR OTHER PURPOSES.   APPROVED DEC. 30, 1822.

SECTION 1. Be it enacted by the people of the State of Illinois represented in General Assembly, that the county of Pike shall be bounded as follows, to wit: On the north by the base line; on the east by the Illinois river; on the west by the Mississippi; and all the rest and residue of the territory, composing the county of Pike before the passage of this act, shall be attached to, and be a part of, said county until otherwise disposed of by the General Assembly of this State.

SEC. 2. Be it further enacted, etc., for the purpose of fixing the permanent seat of justice of said county, the following persons be and the same are hereby appointed Commissioners, to wit: Garrett VanDusen, Ossian M. Ross, John M. Smith, Daniel Ford and Daniel Shinn, who, after being duly sworn by some judge or justice of the peace of this State, faithfully and impartially to discharge the duties imposed upon them by this act, shall meet at the house of John Shaw, in said county, on or before the first day of March next, and proceed to determine on the permanent seat of justice of said county, and designate the same, taking into consideration the condition and convenience of the people, the future population of the county, and the health and eligibility of the place; and they are hereby authorized to receive as a donation for the use of said county any quantity of land that may be determined on by them, from any proprietor that may choose to offer such donation of land; which place, so fixed and determined upon, the said Commissioners shall certify, under their hands and seals, and return the same to next Commissioners of Court in said county, which shall cause an entry thereof to be made upon their books of record.

SEC. 3. Be it further enacted, etc., that the said Commissioners shall receive, as a compensation for their service, the sum of two dollars per day for each day by them necessarily spent in discharging the duties imposed upon them by this act, to be allowed by the Commissioners of the Court, and paid out of the county treasury.

Pursuant to that portion of the above act as relating to locating the county-seat, the Commissioners made their report to the County Commissioners at their March term of Court, 1823, and presented the Court with a deed from William Ross and Rufus Brown for an acre of land upon section 27, Atlas township.

COUNTIES CUT FROM PIKE.

When Pike county was organized it embraced all of that country between the Illinois and Mississippi rivers, and extended east along the line of the main fork of the Illinois, the Kankakee river, to the Indiana State line and on to the northern boundary of the State, including the country where Rock Island, Galena, Peoria and Chicago now are. It was indeed a large county, and embraced what is now the wealthiest and most populous portion of the Great West. The extensive lead mines of Galena had not yet been discovered, and Chicago was only a trading and military post. The Commissioners of Pike county, as will be noticed in the following chapter, exercised full authority, so far as the duties of their respective offices were concerned, over all this vast region.

Settlers soon began to locate here and there in the Military Tract. Two years had scarcely passed ere the few settlers east of the fourth principal meridian and north of the base line desired a county, and appealed to the Legislature for power to organize one. Ossian M. Ross, the founder of Lewistown, Fulton county, and one of the prime movers in the organization of that county, was at that time a member of the County Commissioners' Court of Pike county. The following is an abstract of the act referred to:

An act approved Jan. 28, 1823, forming the county of Fulton out of all the attached part of Pike, beginning where the fourth principal meridian intersects the Illinois river, thence up the middle of said river to where the line between ranges five and six east strikes the said river, thence north with the said line between ranges five and six east, to the township line between townships nine and ten north, then west with said line to the fourth principal meridian, then south to the place of beginning; and all the rest and residue of the attached part of the county of Pike east of the fourth principal meridian shall be attached to Fulton county.

Jan. 13, 1825, Schuyler county was cut off from Pike and Fulton, and included all that country within the following boundaries: " Commencing at a place where the township line between townships two and three south touches the Illinois river, thence west on said line to the range line between ranges four and five west, thence north from said line to the northwest corner of township three north, range one west, thence east on said township line to the Illinois river, thence down the said river to the place of beginning."

The same year an act was passed forming new counties. Those formed were Adams, Hancock, McDonough, Warren, Mercer, Henry, Putnam and Knox. Their boundaries were fixed by the act of Jan. 30, 1825. Calhoun county was cut off from Pike county and organized in 1825.

GENERAL REVIEW.

No whites settled north of Alton for agricultural purposes prior to 1819. During that year and the next there was a sufficient number of settlers to organize a county. Accordingly the Legislature of 1820–'1, as above seen, organized the county of Pike, which then included all of the State of Illinois between the Illinois and Mississippi rivers. The county-seat was first fixed at Coles' Grove, adjoining the locality of Gilead, afterward the county-seat of Calhoun county. This place was named after Edward Coles, Governor of Illinois.

We copy the following topographical sketch of Pike county from " Peck's Illinois Gazetteer," published in 1834, as giving an idea of the county at that early date:

" Pike county is the oldest county in the Military Tract, and was erected from Madison and other counties in 1821. It then embraced the whole county northwest of the Illinois river, but by subsequent formation of new counties it is now reduced to ordinary size, containing twenty-two townships, or about 800 square miles. It is bounded north by Adams, east by Schuyler and the Illinois river, south by that river and Calhoun, and west by the Mississippi. Besides the Mississippi and Illinois rivers, which wash two sides, it has the Sny Carte slough, running the whole length of its western border, which floats steam-boats to Atlas at a full stage of water. Pike county is watered by the Pigeon, Hadley, Keyes, Black, Dutch Church, Six-Mile and Bay creeks, which flow into the Mississippi; and Big and Little Blue, and the North and West Forks of McGee's creek, which enter into the Illinois. Good mill-sites are furnished by these streams.

"The land is various. The section of country, or rather island, between the Sny Carte slough and the Mississippi, is a sandy soil, but mostly inundated land at the spring flood. It furnishes a great summer and winter range for stock, affording considerable open prairie, with skirts of heavy bottom timber near the streams. Along the bluffs and for two or three miles back the land is chiefly timbered, but cut up with ravines and quite rolling. Far in the interior and toward Schuyler county excellent prairie and timber lands are found, especially about the Blue rivers and McGee's creek. This must eventually be a rich and populous county.

"In Pleasant Vale, on Keyes creek, is a salt spring twenty feet in diameter, which boils from the earth and throws off a stream of some size, and forms a salt pond in its vicinity. Salt has been made here, though not in great quantities.

"In the county are seven water saw-mills, four grist-mills, one carding-machine, five stores, and a horse ferry-boat across the Mississippi to Louisiana."

HANSON AND SHAW.

The State Constitution, adopted on the admission of Illinois into the Union in 1818, prohibited slavery in this State. Owing to this fact many of the early immigrants coming West, who were from the slave States of Virginia and Kentucky, passed right through this garden of Eden into Missouri. An effort was made, therefore, to so amend the Constitution as to permit slavery in this State that it might be more attractive to settlers, and the sequel showed that Illinois had a narrow escape from the dreadful evils of slavery. When the necessary preliminary resolution was offered in the Senate it was ascertained that the requisite two-thirds vote to pass the resolution for the call of a convention to amend the Constitution could be obtained and to spare; but in the House they needed one vote. At first it was strenuously argued that the two-thirds vote meant two-thirds of the two Houses in joint convention; but the opponents were too powerful in their argument upon this point. The majority, however, was not to be foiled in their purpose. Another mode presented itself: all that was required was courage to perpetrate a gross outrage on a recalcitrant member. There had been a contested election case from Pike county. The sitting member decided by the House to be entitled to the seat was Nicholas Hanson, and the contestant, John Shaw, the "Black Prince." Hanson's vote had been obtained for the re-election of Jesse B. Thomas, strongly pro-slavery, to the United States Senate; but further than this he would not go. Shaw, who favored the convention project, was now discovered to be entitled to the seat. A motion was thereupon made to reconsider the admission of Hanson, which prevailed. It was next further moved to strike out the name of Hanson and insert that of Shaw. During the pendency of the resolution a tumultuous crowd assembled in the evening at the State House, and after the delivery of a number of incendiary speeches, inflaming the minds of the people against Hanson, they proceeded through the town (Vandalia) with his effigy in a blaze, accompanied with the beating of drums, the sound of bugles, and shouts of "Convention or death." A motion to expel Hanson and admit Shaw was adopted, and the latter awarded the majority by voting for the convention resolution, which thus barely passed. The night following, a number of members of both Houses entered their solemn protest against this glaring outrage of unseating Hanson, both with the object intended and the manner of perpetrating it. Many reflecting men, earnest in their support of the convention question, condemned it, and it proved a powerful lever before the people in the defeat of the slavery scheme. The passage of the convention resolution was regarded as tantamount to its carriage at the polls.

The pro-slavery party celebrated their triumph by an illumination of the town, and the procession, accompanied by all the horrid paraphernalia and discordant music of a *charivari*, marched to the residence of Governor Coles, and the quarters of the chief opponents of the measure, where they performed with their demoniac music to annoy and insult them.

The convention resolution was finally defeated by 1,800 majority at the polls.

It is thus seen how Pike county gave the casting vote on the slavery question in this State in 1820.

MARQUETTE COUNTY.

The counties now bounding Pike on the north are Adams and Brown; but in 1841 there was a county struck off from the east side of Adams and called Marquette. Columbus, being more centrally located in Adams county, became ambitious for the county-seat, but as Quincy was too powerful against this project, the eastern portion of Adams county was struck off by an act of the Legislature in order that the ambition of Columbus might be satisfied and become a county-seat. No attempt was made to organize the county until 1846, when Quincy again proved too powerful for them, and the following Legislature repealed the act defining the boundaries of the county.

COUNTY-SEAT CONTEST.

In 1842–'3 an effort was made to divide the county, the new county-seat to be at Barry. Dr. Thomas Worthington was a mem-

ber of the State Senate, and Wm. Blair of the House, each representing the interests of his section of the county. The bill introduced
by Mr. Blair proposed to divide the county by a line running
north and south through its extent; but, after the presentation
of many petitions and remonstrances, and a period of considerable excitement, the bill failed to pass the House. In 1850 the
county was divided into 19 townships, and organized under the township organization law of the Constitution of 1848. Under this
mode the county is at present conducted. And that was the end
of this little fight. The county remains, therefore, to the present
day as it was outlined by the Legislature of 1825. In the fall of
1846 the effort was renewed. Meetings were held in various parts
of the county, and speeches were made on both sides of the question; but public interest soon died down.

CHAPTER IV.

IMPORTANT LABORS OF THE COUNTY COMMIS-
SIONERS' COURT.

FIRST MEETING.

The first meeting of the County Commissioners' Court of Pike county was held April 24, 1821. There were present Leonard Ross, John Shaw, and William Ward, the three Commissioners. After the Court was organized, Stephen Dewey was appointed Clerk *pro tem*, in the absence of James W. Whitney, the Clerk. The records give but little information in regard to the organization of the county. They begin with unqualified statements, and record the acts of the honored Court with greatest simplicity.

The first business before the Court was an application for a license to sell spirituous liquors made by Belus and Egbert Jones. The license was granted upon the payment of $3 into the newly made treasury by the Joneses.

Belus Jones was then appointed Constable for the county of Pike. The liquor traffic evidently was not great enough to employ the entire time of the two gentlemen, and as the newly organized county needed a Constable, Mr. Jones' services were solicited in that capacity.

The county must needs have a Treasurer; accordingly Nathaniel Shaw was appointed to this important office. The Court then adjourned to meet at 7 o'clock A. M., April 25.

According to adjournment the Commissioners assembled upon the morning of the 25th. The first business presented to the consideration of the Court was an application for license to sell liquors presented by Thomas Ferguson. The Court seemed to possess a willingness to encourage the liquor business within the newly made county, as they granted Mr. Ferguson license for $2.50. Why they should grant him a license for 50 cents less than they charged the Joneses, we can not tell. Perhaps an increase of business and flattering prospects enabled them to reduce the " tax."

Ebenezer Smith and Stephen Dewey were then recommended " as fit and suitable persons for the Governor to commission Justices of the Peace." The Court then adjourned until June.

SECOND MEETING.

Monday, June 4, 1821, the date set for the convening of the Court, John Shaw appeared and opened Court, but there not being a quorum present the Court was kept open until 4 o'clock in the afternoon, when all of the Commissioners appeared and took their seats. Upon the following day James W. Whitney, who had been appointed Clerk of the Court, although we find no record of his appointment, "appeared in open Court and took the several oaths required by law, and gave bond in the penal sum of $1,000, and tendered Levi Roberts and Rigdon C. Fenton his securities, who were accepted and approved by the Court."

TAVERN LICENSE.

At the June term, 1821, Nathaniel Hincksley was granted license " to keep a tavern. "

A tavern in those days was a combination of an inn and a saloon. The proprietor, however, did not expect to derive any great revenue from the hotel, but looked to his liquors for an income. Many of these " taverns " were the smallest of log cabins. Here and there all over the country, sometimes miles from any other cabin, they might be found. Some of them were indicated to be such by signs nailed to a post, tree, or to the side of the cabin. These were of the rudest make and design. Some simply had the word "entertainment" scrawled upon them, while others, more explicit, read "entertainment for man and beast." Some were still more definite and said simply " whisky and oats. " The storms of a half century, the advancement of civilization, the culture of the age, have all combined to transform these rudest of signs, scribbled by an uncultured pioneer upon hewn boards, into gilded and glittering letters artistically traced upon French-plate glass.   •

The name by which the place was known where liquor was vended was shortly after this changed from "tavern" to "grocery" or "groggery," and subsequently assumed the appellation of "saloon;" and finally, that coming into disrepute, many have adopted the more modern title of "sample room," "hall," "garden," etc.

The following schedule of "tavern rates" was then established to govern Hincksley :

Victuals, per meal,..	25 cents
Horse keeping, per night,........	37½ "
Lodging, per night,..	12½ "
Whisky, per half pint,....................................	12½ "
Rum and gin, per half pint, ...	25 "
French Brandy, per half pint,.............................	50 "
Wine, per half pint,...	37½ "

JOHN KINZIE JUSTICE OF THE PEACE FOR PIKE COUNTY.

Upon motion of Abraham Beck, Esq., John Kinzie was recommended to the Governor of Illinois as a fit and suitable person for

Justice of the Peace for Pike county. This gentleman was the well-known first settler of Chicago, and at that time resided there, it then being in this county. It must be remembered that Pike county at that time spread over a vast territory, and embraced all of the northern part of the State. Yes, though unlearned in law and unacquainted with science and literature, the Commissioners held jurisdiction over a large district; and that they conducted the public affairs rightly, and built a firm and solid foundation upon which the future prosperity and greatness of this portion of our beloved State should rest, can not be gainsaid. This is plainly evident from the unparalleled strides made in agricultural and mechanical progress; from the hundreds of thousands of busy inhabitants now dwelling within this territory; and from the vast stores of wealth accumulated solely from resources within it. Those great and unconcealed wonders reflect honor and credit each day upon their founders; and as days and years multiply, when the same territory over which they presided shall be teeming with millions of earnest and energetic people, then will great honors and more exultant praise and adoration be expressed for the brave, sturdy pioneers who explored and opened up a region so prolific, and founded a community that for genius, enterprise and wealth will in the near future out-rank many older settled countries, and indeed will vie with many kingdoms of the earth. Then these vast prairies will be cultivated as a garden. Every forest tree and woodland will be utilized, and populous cities with numerous factories and vast stores of commerce may be numbered by the score. Then will the modes of travel be superior to the remarkable railroad facilities of to-day, and transport the increased products with greater facility. Indeed, everything will then be as different and as superior to what they are at present as the things of to-day are as compared with those of fifty years ago. Our readers may regard this as wild and unreasonable speculation, as wholly visionary; but they are only the conclusions deduced from a careful study of history, of a comparison of what has been accomplished, with certain advantages, with the results that the superior advantages now enjoyed will as certainly accomplish.

THE POOR.

One of the first acts of the noble-hearted Commissioners was to make provisions for their poor. The pioneers were generous and liberal to a fault when it came to provide the necessities of life to those more unfortunate in their midst. June 5, 1821, Baxter Bradwell and Joel Bacon were appointed overseers of the poor.

RECORD BOOK.

A record book was then ordered to be purchased, for which $3.00 was given. This is a common paper-covered blank book of about 200 pages, and at the present time the price would be considered high if the book were sold at half that amount.

LAYING OUT ROADS.

For many years the petitions for roads occupied a very large proportion of the Court's time and attention, and consumed more space
to record than all other proceedings.   They are similar in construction, and it would be useless, and worse, to speak of them as often
as they occur.   We will only give a specimen of these applications
and the mode of dealing with them.   The records read as follows:
"A petition of sundry inhabitants of this county was presented
praying that a road may be laid out from McDonald's Ferry on the
Mississippi river, the nearest and best course to the Illinois river to
meet a road that may be laid out from thence to Vandalia."   The
prayer was granted, and Daniel Shinn, Clarendon Ross and Ebenezer Franklin were appointed a committee to view and ascertain
where said road should be located.

Upon the 3d of July of the same year the committee reported
and their report was: "Accept as far as the north line of section 27
of township 6 south, in range 5 west [Atlas township], that being
as far as said Commissioners were able to proceed, owing to the excessive growth of vegetation; and it is further ordered that the time
for viewing and laying out the remainder of said road shall be extended until after the vegetation shall be destroyed by frost."

Five days' work upon this road was required of each man who
lived within two and one-half miles of it.   This rule also applied
to other roads laid out in those primitive times.   One dollar was
allowed for each day a man labored more than that.

A petition was also presented for a road from Ferguson's Ferry
on the Illinois river, to Fort Edwards, upon the Mississippi river.
Again we find "a petition presented by sundry citizens, Oct. 4,
1821, for a road from Fort Clark (now Peoria) to the mouth of the
Illinois river."   Accordingly James Nixon, John Shaw and Ebenezer Smith were appointed a committee to view the road from the
house of Ebenezer Smith to Fort Clark.

FERRY LICENSE.

June 6, 1821, a license was granted James McDonald "to keep
a ferry upon the east bank of the Mississippi river, opposite to the
town of Louisianaville, on condition of his paying a tax of one dollar, besides Clerk's fee, and on his entering into bonds according
to law, and that the following rates of ferriage be established, to
wit : "

For a single person,......................... 25	cents
For a single horse,.. 25	"
Every head of cattle over one year old,... 25	"
Every hog, sheep or goat,................................... 6¼	"
Every four-wheeled carriage,............................1 00	"
Every hundred weight of dead lumber,.................. 6¼	"
Every two wheeled carriage,............................ 75	"

MILITIA PRECINCTS.

Among the pioneers "training" or "muster day" was one which was looked forward to with feelings of pleasure. It was necessary to have a well organized militia to repel any invasions of the Indians which at that time were numerous through this section of the country. The Commissioners' Court, in its official capacity, took note of this, and accordingly, June 6, they "ordered that the militia of this county be organized into a regiment, and all that part of the county lying south of the township line between townships 8 and 9 compose the first company district; and all north of that line to the base line compose the second company district ; and all north of the base line be and compose the third company district. Baxter Broadwell, Wm. Metz and Rigdon C. Fenton were appointed Judges of election in the first company district; Wm. Keyes, Peter D. Moyer and Clarendon Ross were appointed judges of election in the second company district; Ossian M. Ross, Dr. Davison and Amos Eveland, as judges of election in the third company district. An election was then called for June 30, 1821, to select officers for the various companies. The base line, which runs east and west upon a parallel with Beardstown, was made the dividing line between the two militia battalions of the regiment of Pike county. The battalion south of the base line was the first, and the one north the second, battalion.

INDIAN TRAILS.

A sum not to exceed ten dollars was appropriated " to defray the expenses of opening and clearing out the old trace from the head or upper end of Salt Prairie to the lower end of Sni Carte Prairie, and five dollars for opening and cleaning out the old trace from the lower end of Sni Carte Prairie to Ross settlement." Further on in the records we find these orders rescinded, and at the same time Joel Bacon and James Levin were ordered credited with the amount of their road tax for having opened the said "trace." These traces were old Indian trails, but having been deserted for newer ones were unfit for travel.

SUNDRY ACTS.

John Shaw was paid $5.00 for his services as an interpreter at the October term of the Circuit Court during the trial of two Indians for murder. These 'were Shonwennekek and Pemesan, who are spoken of in connection with this trial more fully in the chapter upon the criminal record.

Ossian M. Ross was then recommended to the Governor as a suitable person for Justice of the Peace in Pike county. Mr. Ross at this time lived where Lewistown, Fulton county, now stands. He was with one exception the first settler of that county, and was the founder of Lewistown.

There was no jail in the county at this time, and at the October term, 1821, "Nathan Shaw was given $22.50 for guarding Indian prisoners." These, we presume, were the two Indians referred to above, and who were on trial for murder. The same amount, and for the same purpose, was given to Christopher Long.

Jan. 10, 1822, "Abner Eads, of Peoria, made application for license to keep a tavern in the house where he now resides, which is granted on him paying $1.50."

Jan. 12, 1822, the Sheriff was paid $50 for his salary for the year. Mr. Whitney was given $30 for his services as Circuit Clerk, and $30 as Clerk of the Commissioners' Court, and $50 for his salary as Judge of Probate.

Jan. 12, 1822, John Shaw was paid $8 for locating the county-seat, and Levi Roberts $4 for like services.

Abraham Beck, Judge of Probate, died, and Jan. 12, 1822, the administrator of his estate was paid $16.60 as salary while he was Judge.

FIRST INQUEST.

The official papers of the inquest held over the body of James McDonald were ordered filed. McDonald ran a ferry across the Mississippi river at Louisiana. It is supposed he was murdered at his landing during the winter. He was found lying dead upon the ice one day by two men on their way to Louisiana. They went to his ferry, but found him dead, and evidences of a long and severe scuffle all around him, as if he had been struggling for life in a hand-to-hand combat. The tracks of two men led from this place across to Louisiana, and it was generally supposed they were the men who killed McDonald, although nothing in a legal way was ever done with them.

TREASURER'S FIRST REPORT.

The first report made by a County Treasurer of Pike county was made March 5, 1822. We give it in full:

Cash received into the Treasury..........................	$765
Cash paid out under order of Court.........................$701.28½	
Treasurer's compensation................................. 38.25	
	$739.53½
Balance in Treasury.................................	$25.47

ROSS' TAVERN.

Ossian M. Ross was then granted a license to keep a tavern at his house. He lived where the city of Lewistown now is. The same schedule which regulated other "Public Inns" or "Tavern-Keepers" were adopted to regulate him.

David W. Barnes, O. M. Ross and Daniel Sweetland were appointed trustees of the school section, tp. 5 north, R. 3 east, which is Lewistown tp., Fulton Co. These gentlemen lived in Lewistown, and were its first settlers.

ELECTION PRÉCINCTS.

June 5, 1822, the county was divided into three election precincts. All that part of the county lying north of the township lines, between towns 4 and 5 south and west of the Illinois bluffs, and all north of the base line, was the first precinct. Election was ordered in this precinct at the house of O. M. Ross, and that gentleman was appointed judge of election. All that part of the county lying north of township lines between towns 9 and 10 south, and west of Illinois bluffs and north of the base line, was made another precinct, and the "polls ordered opened at the house of Rufus Brown and Daniel Whipple, Leonard Ross and Wm. Ross, judges." "The remainder of the county was made another precinct, and election held at county-seat, and John Shaw, Stephen Dewey and Amos Bancroft, judges."

DAVENPORT'S TAVERN.

June 6, 1822, it was ordered that a license to keep a tavern at or near Fort Armstrong, be granted to George Davenport for $3.00. This place was on the lower end of Rock Island. Mr. Davenport was the man who kept the trading post at Fort Armstrong, and in honor of him Davenport, Iowa, was named. The generous Commissioners permitted Davenport to charge higher rates for "entertainment" than they did those nearer to the borders of civilization.

NEW COMMISSIONERS.

An election was held in August, 1822, for selecting three new Commissioners. Those chosen were David Dutton, James M. Seeley and Ossian M. Ross. Much trouble appears to have grown out of this election, as we find the election of the three honorable gentlemen was contested, and evidently very strongly, too. The contestants were Ebenezer Smith, James Nixon and William Metz. The case was appealed to the Circuit Court, Judge John Reynolds presiding. He decided in favor of the contestants. We cannot tell upon what grounds they contested the rights of Dutton, Seeley and Ross to take their seats as Commissioners, but from what we can glean from the indefinite records they did not comply with the law in taking the oath of office, as the contestants claimed. These were merely technical grounds, but the law must be complied with to the letter. Smith, Nixon and Metz held a term of Court Sept. 3 and 4, 1822, but transacted no business of importance. The other gentlemen called Court for Oct. 10, but no quorum was present. Another session was held Oct. 24. Commissioners Dutton and Seeley being present. We find recorded upon the following day "a certificate of the Hon. John Reynolds setting forth the result of the contested election." This decision was the result of a second hearing of the case by the Judge, and is as follows:

"State of Illinois, ss:—Upon a second and full examination of the documents transmitted to me in relation to the contested election of the Sheriff, Coroner and County Commissioners for the county of Pike; and being satisfied that the certificates heretofore given by me of the election of Rigdon C. Fenton as Sheriff, Joel Bacon as Coroner and Ebenezer Smith, William Metz and James Nixon as County Commissioners, was given without sufficient consideration, I do hereby revoke the said certificates, and do now certify that Leonard Ross was duly elected Sheriff, Daniel Whipple, Coroner, and James M. Seeley, David Dutton and Ossian M. Ross County Commissioners for Pike county in said State.

"Given under my hand and seal this 4th day of September, 1822.
"JOHN REYNOLDS,
" Justice of the Supreme Court of said State, and presiding in the first Judicial Circuit."

Thus, after a long and hotly contested trial, the Judge reversed his former decision and reinstated Seeley, Dutton and Ross, as well as the Sheriff and Coroner, whom he had decided were not legally and rightfully entitled to hold the positions to which they claimed they had been elected.

CLERK'S OFFICE.

We find the following quaint item on record, which is in reference to renting an office for the County and Circuit clerks . "John Shaw, having proposed to lease the county the building in Coles' Grove, adjoining the one now occupied by Rigdon C. Fenton, for the term of one year, to be occupied as a Clerk's office, for the sum of $6\frac{1}{4}$ cents, and to be repaired by the county, under the direction of said Shaw, and to suit his convenience."

COUNTY-SEAT MOVED TO ATLAS.

Evidently a little rivalry had sprung up between the settlements at Atlas and Coles' Grove, the latter of which had been the county-seat up to this time (1823). Atlas was the most important town in the county, and it became ambitious to have the county buildings located there, which it finally secured. Pursuant to an act of the Legislature, approved Dec. 30, 1822, "to fix upon and locate the permanent seat of justice for Pike county," the commission appointed made their report at the March term of the Commissioners' Court, 1823, and presented a deed from William Ross and Rufus Brown for one acre of land, which was given as an inducement for the county to locate its seat of justice there. The report reads as follows :

"The Commissioners appointed to fix upon and locate the permanent seat of justice of Pike county have attended to the services assigned them, and do report that they have fixed the permanent

James M Williams

GRIGGSVILLE

seat of justice of said county upon section 27, town 6 south, range 5 west, and have taken a deed of the proprietor of one acre of land on which to erect the public buildings, which is particularly described in said deed, and that they have named the seat of justice Atlas.

"JOHN M. SMITH,
"DANIEL MOORE,
"DANIEL SHINN."

NEW COMMISSIONER.

An election was held March 18, 1823, to select a County Commissioner to fill vacancy occasioned by O. M. Ross, resigning. The county of Fulton, where Mr. Ross lived, having just been formed, and he chosen Sheriff, Amos Bancroft was elected to fill the vacancy.

DIFFICULTY IN SELECTING COUNTY-SEAT.

It appears that some dissatisfaction arose from the selection made by the Commissioners for a county-seat. We presume that the feeling was then as now in this and all other counties. More than one place, settlement or town, think it is the most suitable and proper place for the county-seat. In relation to the difficulty at this time we find the following statement on record : " Nicholas Hanson and Leonard Ross presented a report of certain persons appointed by an act of the Legislature as Commissioners to locate the permanent seat of justice for Pike county, and moved to have said report filed and recorded, which said motion for the reasons following : 1st, The authority given by the act aforesaid was a special joint authority and should have been strictly pursued ; 2d, It happens that but three out of five Commissioners acted in the location of the county-seat, when the law gave no power to a majority to act ; 3d, That said Commissioners did not return and present their report at or before the time prescribed by law for the return of said report ; 4th, That the legal and qualified County Commissioners were in session at the time prescribed by law for the return of said report. And for the reasons aforesaid this Court does adjudge and decide that the proceedings of said Commissioners to locate the permanent county-seat of Pike county are void, and that the temporary seat of justice of said county still remains at Coles' Grove."

This decision was finally reversed, as seen from the following order made at the June term of the Court in 1824: " The doings of this Court at a special term held on 26, 27 and 28 of January last, and also doings of this Court at last March term be, and the same are hereby, confirmed and established, except a contract entered into with John Shaw for the purpose of leasing a house, the rent of which was 6¼ cents, in Coles' Grove, which contract is by mutual consent released and dissolved; and also an order of adjudication respecting the county-seat, which order is revoked and rescinded."

17

Thus, according to the selection made by the commission appointed for that purpose, the county-seat was moved from Coles' Grove, now in Calhoun county, to Atlas.

COUNTY DIVIDED INTO TOWNSHIPS.

Upon the 28th of January, 1824, the county of Pike was divided into three townships by the Court, as follows: That part commencing at the mouth of the Illinois river, thence up the said river to the north line of the first tier of sections above the north line of town 8 south, thence running on said line west to the Mississippi river, thence down said river to place of beginning, constituted Coles' Grove township. That part embraced within the boundary beginning at the northeast corner of section 36 of township 7 south, on range line between ranges 4 and 5 west, thence along said range line north to the north line of the county, thence west to the Mississippi river, thence down said river to a point directly west of the place of beginning, thence to the place of beginning, which composed Atlas township. That part of the county within the following limits was known as Franklin township: Commencing on the Illinois river one mile north of the north line of township 8 south, thence up the said river to the base line, thence along said line to the range line between ranges 4 and 5 west, thence south running on the said range line to the northwest corner of section 31, of town 7 south, and range 4 west, thence along the north line of said section 31, and said first tier of sections north of town 8 south, to the place of beginning, together with all of the attached part of Pike county lying north of the aforesaid boundaries.

Thus it will be seen that these were exceedingly large townships. They embraced several counties, and extended over one of the fairest portions of this great State. These divisions were made for the convenience of the settlers in voting, making roads, etc., yet from the extended size of each township we can see that many of the early voters had to travel many miles to cast his ballot.

FEARLESS COMMISSIONERS.

During the year the Commissioners pursued the even tenor of their way, granting petitions for roads, ferries, tavern licenses and election precincts; appointing and removing officers with an inflexibility of purpose that is really amusing. When they investigated a matter there were no palliating circumstances to screen the delinquent, but the judicial guillotine cut off official heads with a refreshing impartiality. Negligent officers feared the power of the "triple C" more than Damocles feared the hair-suspended sword. They simply and plainly said "Go," and the official hesitated not but went at once, and that was the end of it.

In reference to this subject we find the following quaint document on record under date of July 29, 1824:

"It appearing to this Court that the Clerk for some time past has not resided at the county-seat, nor kept the records and papers belonging to the county at this place; and the Court having considered the facts and the law arising upon the case, does adjudge and determine that the said office of Clerk is now vacant, and that for the aforesaid cause James W. Whitney, the Clerk, be and is hereby removed from office."

We suppose that Whitney remained at Coles' Grove after the county-seat had been removed to Atlas, and the inconveniences of having the county offices and officials scattered over the country in that wise would not be endured longer by the strict, law-abiding Court.

The Court assembled upon the following day, and not yet having selected a clerk, appointed Mr. Whitney Clerk *pro tem.* It appears that the Commissioners had nothing personally against Mr. Whitney, for the very next act of the Court was to recommend him to the Governor as a fit and proper person to be appointed County Surveyor, to fill the vacancy having occurred by the removal of Stephen Dewey out of the county. This man Dewey, the first Surveyor of Pike county, laid out the town of Lewistown, Fulton county, where he shortly afterward removed and served for many years as Circuit and County Clerk, and did efficient work in the organization and establishment of that county.

It appears that the Court could find no suitable person to take charge of the Clerk's office, for upon July 30, two days after Mr. Whitney was so summarily removed from office, he was re-instated. Perhaps a compromise was made between the Court and Mr. Whitney. It is more than likely that he was compelled to move to the county-seat in order to receive again the patronage of the Court. He served until April 27, 1825, when he resigned and George W. Britton was appointed in his stead. Whitney was indicted for malfeasance in office, and the suit was withdrawn on condition he would resign.

NEW JUSTICES OF THE PEACE.

At the September term, 1824, in compliance with a petition from the citizens on and near Fever river (now Galena) and the lead mines, John Connelly, Moses Meeker and John S. Miller were recommended as proper persons for the Governor to commission Justices of the Peace of Pike county. These men were the very earliest settlers in northern Illinois, and of whom we speak more fully in a former chapter. April 27 of the following year Chas. D. St. Traine was recommended for the same office.

COURT-HOUSE.

The little temporary log court-house first built in Atlas soon became too small to accommodate the Court and county officers, so the building of a new court-house was discussed and determined upon by the honorable Court, as is evinced by the following order :

" Notice is hereby given that on the 25th day of June instant, at the court-house in Atlas, Pike county, Illinois, at 2 o'clock, P. M., will be let to the lowest bidder the building of a court-house so far as is hereinafter expressed : To be 40x30 feet on the floor and 20 feet high, two stories; to be built of brick, the two side walls below to be one and a half brick thick, the other walls to be one brick thick. The outside to be finished complete with doors and windows; the lower floor to be laid with brick or tile, fire-places and partitions, except the partition of the grand jury room, to be done with a plain wooden cornice. The Commissioners reserve one bid for the county. Plans to be shown and further particulars made known at time and place of sale.

" N. B.—County orders to be given to undertakers on interest until paid. It is proposed to give the job of procuring the stone and mortar for building separate from the other part or parts, all of which is to be completed by the first day of January, A. D. 1827. Sufficient securities will be required."

The contract for furnishing stone and mortar was struck off to Daniel Shinn and Joseph Petty for $200. The main contract was given to Leonard and William Ross at $1,260.

It appears, however, that the building of this fine structure was never carried to completion. The building rose in its magnificent proportions only in the visions of the honorable Commissioners. It was evidently too fine and expensive for the times.. They rented an office for the County and Circuit Clerks, which in the winter of 1830–'31 burned down.

Nothing further was done, according to the records, toward the building of a new court-house until April 7, 1829, when the subject was again before the Court for its consideration. The Court then ordered the contract for the erection of a building of the following dimensions and description to be let: "Said house to be 30 feet long by 18 feet wide, to be two stories high,—the lower one nine feet and the upper one eight feet high. To be covered and enclosed in a good, workmanlike manner. To leave and case two outside doors in the lower story, and also six windows in the same, and six windows in the upper story. To put in joists and sleepers for the upper and lower floors, putting them down loose so as to serve as floors. To be underpinned with six pillars, to be substantially made of stone, placing one at each corner of the house and one under each side in the middle; all to be done in a good, workmanlike manner. The undertaker to give bond with good and sufficient security in double the sum at which the same shall be stricken off for prompt and faithful performance of his contract. The contractor shall receive his pay out of the first moneys which shall come into the treasury not otherwise appropriated."

The records continue as follows: " The court next proceeded to sell the building of said court-house to the lowest bidder, and after sufficient notice was given thereof, and the same for a long time exposed, it was stricken off to James Rice for the sum of $493, that being the lowest sum bid therefor."

James Rice failed to furnish the required security for the faithful performance of his contract, and accordingly June 1, 1829, the Sheriff was ordered to again " put up at public auction and sell the building of the same to the lowest bidder, with the addition to the former plan of six feet in length and six feet in breadth." They further altered the plans upon the 6th of June, upon which day they met for the purpose of letting the contract for building it. They made the following alterations: " There shall be ten stone pillars, 18 inches above the surface of the ground, six windows in the lower story with 16 lights in each window, 8 by 10, and 8 windows in upper story with 12 lights in each window, 8 by 10."

The contract was " struck off " to Elisha Petty for $600. William Ross went upon his bond for $1,200. Mr. Petty was subsequently allowed $42.28 for extra work.

The court-house was accepted by the Court Sept. 7, 1829.

COUNTY-SEAT RE-LOCATED.

It appears that the location of the county-seat at Atlas was not entirely satisfactory to every person, as we find an election was held in March, 1827, to select commissioners to re-locate the county-seat. David Dutton, Joel Meacham and William Meredith were chosen for this work. That any definite move was made by these gentlemen toward selecting another site for the county-seat we are not aware; the records are silent as to anything done by these gentlemen. By the year 1832 the subject of changing the county-seat from Atlas, however, was freely discussed. It was desired to have it more centrally located. The Legislature of 1832–'3 appointed a commission to re-locate the county-seat. These gentlemen made their report in April 13, 1833, which is as follows:

" We, the undersigned, having been appointed commissioners to change and re-locate the seat of justice of the county of Pike by the Legislature of the State of Illinois, by an act approved Feb. 22, 1833, beg leave to report to your honorable body now in session, that after being duly sworn in conformity with said act, did, on the 9th day of April, 1833, enter upon the duties assigned us by said act, by examination of said county of Pike, having a due regard to the present as well as the future settlement and prospective growth of said county, have selected and located the southeast quarter of section 24, in township 5 south, and range 4 west of the fourth principal meridian, as the county-seat of the county of Pike, said county-seat to be known and designated by the name of Pittsfield.
" April 17, 1833.

" SAMUEL ALEXANDER,
" EARL PEIRCE,
" JOHN W. STERNE."

Each of these gentlemen was paid $36 for his services.

The town was platted and a sale of lots held April 15, 1833. The records proceed as follows: " The amount of notes and cash, after paying Wm. Ross, Esq., $200 borrowed of him to enter the quarter section on which the town of Pittsfield is located; the expenses to Alexander Peirce and Sterne $108, for locating said seat of justice; also, for advertising sale of lots, paying for the survey of the same, making plat and all the expenses of the Commissioners'

Court, which have accrued in and about the location, sale of lots, laying off the town, etc., leaves the amount of $901.88, which sum is delivered over to the Treasurer as a special fund for the purpose of erecting public buildings." Thus it will be seen that the county purchased the land upon which the business and much of the residence portion of the town of Pittsfield now stands for the sum of $200. The new town having been surveyed, large hard-wood stakes were driven, designating the corner of each lot, and being also the only guide to the location of streets.

April 15 was the day appointed for the first sale of lots at public auction. The settlers assembled from all parts of the county upon the site of the proposed village, each anxious to become the owner of a town lot. This and subsequent sales were held, and lots seem to have met with a ready sale at fair prices, which is the best evidence that the pioneers were not only enthusiastic in sentiment in relation to the bright prospects and future greatness of the town they were building, but were also willing to lend all the material aid in their power to the consummation of the desired end.

Another sale of lots was held Oct. 28, 1833, from which the county realized $1,150.74 cash, and notes to the amount of $876.73. Another sale was held June 4, 1834, when 38 lots were sold, realizing $1,060 cash, after deducting $67 as expenses, and $704 worth of notes. Another sale was had Monday, May 2, 1836, when 102 lots were sold for $9,354.50. Another, Oct. 6, 1837, when 28 lots brought $4,110.

THE CLERK RESIGNS.

The following document appears upon pages 121 and 122 of 2d volume of County Commissioners' Court records. It is the resignation of William Ross, as Clerk. He had served the county in that capacity faithfully and ably for a decade, and now as he is about to leave he writes his old associates the following resignation:

ATLAS, Sept. 1, 1834

To the Hon. Benj. Barney, Geo. W. Hinman and Andrew Phillips, County Commissioners for the County of Pike, and State of Illinois :

GENTLEMEN:—The period will soon arrive in which it will become my duty to resign to you the office I hold on the appointment of your Court, on account of my having been elected a member of the next General Assembly of this State. To hold both offices is incompatible with the Constitution of our State and contrary to my wishes. I will therefore for the purpose of giving the Court time to select my successor, propose to make this my resignation of the office of Clerk of your Court, to take effect on the 25th day of November, 1834.

In doing this, I beg of you to do me the justice to be assured that in presenting myself as a candidate at the late election, which has terminated in the necessity of my withdrawing my services from you, it is not without a strict regard to all the considerations which I conceive bind a dutiful citizen to his country. I have been influenced by no ambitious motives ,or self-aggrandizement; but my sole object has been to restore and sustain the dignity of our country.

Permit me here to remark that it is a source of great pleasure to me that during a period of about ten years which I have had the honor to serve this county in several important offices, I have been so fortunate as to discharge those duties to the satisfaction of my fellow-citizens generally.

Relying upon the guidance of that Being which controls the destinies of man, I hope and trust that I may be be permitted to retain that continuation of confidence which has been so recently manifested toward me until my latest breath.

With sentiments of great personal consideration,

I remain, yours sincerely,

W. Ross, C. C. C. C. P. C.

AD QUOD DAMNUM.

This was a process to secure a mill site. In those early times the milling of the country was of no little importance. Mills were of such great public necessity that they were permitted.to be located upon any person's land, if the miller thought the site desirable. Sites along the streams were selected for water-power. A person looking for a mill-site would follow up and down the stream for the desired location, and when found he would go before the Commissioners' Court and secure a writ of *ad quod damnum*. This would enable the miller to have the adjoining land officially examined and the amount of damage for making the dam was secured.

The old records contained numerous applications for these writs. We quote one only as a specimen of others:

" On application of Wm. Ross, and previous notice having been given of his intention, by publication on the door of the court-house for four weeks preceding the sitting of the Court, it is ordered that a writ of *ad quod damnum* issue, directed to the Sheriff of the county, commanding him to summon twelve good and lawful men of his county to meet on the southeast quarter of section 18, in township 6 south, and range 5 west, to locate and set apart by metes and bounds so much of the said quarter section, not exceeding three acres, as they shall think necessary for the purpose of erecting a dam across the Sny Carte for a water grist and saw-mill."

FIRST COURT-HOUSE AT PITTSFIELD.

The county-seat having been re-located, a town laid out, lots sold, business houses and dwellings being erected, it became the duty of the Court to have a court-house built in the new town. Accordingly, Tuesday, June 4, 1833, the contract for building a court-house at Pittsfield was let to Israel N. Burtt, he agreeing to erect the structure for $1,095. This he speedily did, and the old building still stands upon the street at the corner of the alley, facing and just north of the Public Square. It is a frame building, in a good state of preservation, and is occupied by Mr. Heck as a bakery and grocery.

PRESENT COURT-HOUSE.

Two years had scarcely rolled by ere the building of a new court-house was begun to be agitated. Some of the more aristocratic thought the county should have a finer court edifice, one more in keeping with the wealth and progress of the county. It is true the county had grown rapidly in population and wealth. Notice, therefore, was given by the Court that plans for a new building would be received. Upon the 5th day of February, 1836, the Court accepted the plans that were presented by Benjamin L. Osborne, and gave him a premium of $20 for the plans.

The county not owning desirable ground, as it was thought, upon which to locate the contemplated structure, the Court appointed James Johnson, James D. Morrison and William Watson agents to procure by purchase or exchange a suitable piece of ground. This committee accordingly procured of Daniel B. Bush a part ot lot 6, block 5, being the whole front of said lot upon the Public Square, running back 100 feet, for which they gave Mr. Bush a part of lot 8, block 5. This location was not satisfactory to all parties, and quite a bitter war arose as to where the court-house should stand. It was at last decided that it should be located upon the center of the Public Square.

At the September term, 1836, Wm. Ross, Uriah Brown and James Johnson were appointed agents upon the part of the county to contract for the erection of a court-house, "said building to be placed in the center of the Public Square, and not to cost over $15,000." These gentlemen entered into contract with Benjamin T. Osborne, George D. Foot and Judson Clement for the erection of the court-house for the sum of $15,000. Daniel D. White, Henry Caswell and Lyman Beeman were appointed a committee to superintend its erection.

The construction of the court-house was pushed rapidly on, and Dec. 8, 1838, it was delivered over to the Sheriff, though in an unfinished condition. It was used for court purposes in this way for a time before completion. By June, 1839, it was completed, and Foot, Clement and Osborne were paid the balance due them in county orders, upon which the county paid 12 per cent. interest.

This structure still stands and is in use to-day. It is located in the center of a small square, which is set with many large and beautiful trees. The main upper room is used for circuit court purposes. Besides this room there are two other smaller ones, one of which is occupied by the State's Attorney, the other a jury room. Upon the main floor there is a hall-way running through the building from north to south. Upon either side of this are offices for the county officials. ·Upon the west side are the County Judges, Sheriff's and School Superintendent's offices, and upon the opposite side are the offices of the County Treasurer and Surveyor.

This building when erected was among the finest and largest court-houses in the West, and for many years it stood foremost among the public buildings of Illinois, and was pointed to with pride, not only by the citizens of Pike county, but by those throughout Central Illinois. It stood as a monument of the enterprise of the pioneers of this section, and was one of the grandest evidences of the prosperity of the newly settled State. It stands to-day as solid as when first built. Every stone and brick is in its place, and every timber has stood the storms of nearly half a century unshaken. Around this old building cluster pleasant recollections of the long-ago. Within its storm-beaten walls have been heard pleas as rich in eloquence as were ever presented to judge or jury. Within those old walls, made sacred by time and the memories of ·

some of the grandest characters and most gifted men known in the history of Illinois, many a scene full of historic interest has occurred, which, could we accurately picture, would be read more as a romance than prosaic history. What numbers of trembling and downcast prisoners have stood before the learned tribunal within the old upper room, to plead "Guilty," or "Not Guilty!" Then the long, hotly-contested trial came; witnesses examined and cross-examined; the wrangle and wordy wars between the lawyers; the appeal to the jury and addresses, which for logic, eloquence, touching, sympathetic eloquence, have not been excelled in all the broad land. How many times have the twelve jurors, sworn to be impartial, filed into their little secret room, to consult and decide the fate of the prisoner at the bar! Then how often have the joyous words come forth, "Not Guilty!" But, again, how very many have stood before the Judge to hear in measured tones their sentence! Sometimes it was thought Justice was outraged; that the Judge, jury and Prosecuting Attorney had prostituted their high positions, violated their sworn duty, and made easy the escape for culprits; yet, taking it all in all, the goddess of justice has shed no more tears over insults to her holy and righteous charge here than she has at any other judgment-bar in the State. Law and justice have almost always been vindicated, and the offender punished.

Could these old walls speak and tell us of the eloquent and effective pleadings of Lincoln, Baker, Richardson, McDougal, Browning, Bushnell, Manning, Walker and others, or of the learned decisions of Douglas, Young, Thomas and Walker, that they have listened to, how eagerly we would seek them! We do not forget that at the present time justice is as swiftly vindicated as ever before; that the Pike county Bar is at its maximum in point of legal ability. It takes the mazes of time to add the luster of fame to the labors and character of most men. That which is of the past, or of the future, we are wont to believe possesses more merit than that which we have with us. Thus it is with the legal lights of to-day.

Just west of the court-house and within the Court Square stands the "fire-proof." This building contains the offices of the Circuit and County Clerks, and was erected in 1854. It was first ordered built upon the northwest corner of the Square, but that order was rescinded and it was decided to erect it "near the west gate of the Public Square, upon the south side of the walk, the south side ranging with the south side of the court-house, the west end 24 feet from the fence of the Public Square."

FENCE AROUND THE SQUARE.

Speaking of the fence around the Public Square calls to mind an order of the Court of June, 1845, giving the President and Trustees of Pittsfield permission to fence the Public Square and plant within the enclosure ornamental or shade trees. Heretofore, we presume, there was neither fence nor shrubbery in the vicinity of the court-house, save the hazel-brush that stood in its native growth within the Square. Here, we are told that Wm. R. Peters often fed his cattle.

We find in the records of the Board of Supervisors that in April, 1854, that body appropriated $200, on condition that the town of Pittsfield should appropriate a like amount, to build a fence around the Public Square, "ten feet inside of present fence, and put hitching posts where the fence stood."

FIRST JAIL AT PITTSFIELD.

Necessarily, as faithful historians, we are compelled to mar the pleasant progress of this chapter by reference to prison bars. It seems as the county advanced in wealth and population the evil principle kept pace with it; and as immaculate and good as the pioneer fathers undoubtedly were, even among them there were wicked and vicious characters. The old log jail at Atlas never was a very strong or secure one, and prisoners were continually escaping. When the county-seat was moved to Pittsfield, it was determined to build a good, substantial jail. Accordingly the contract for building a jail was let to M. E. Rattan, March 5, 1835, for a prison to cost $3,889. The building was to be 28x36 in size, two stories high, and to be made of stone. It appears that considerable time was employed in its erection, for we find it was not received by the county until June, 1839, when Mr. Rattan was allowed $300 for the extra work performed.

A NEW REGIME IN CHOOSING COMMISSIONERS.

Heretofore the terms of office of all three of the Commissioners had expired at the same time, being elected for two years; but in 1838 a new rule was adopted, in compliance with an act of the Legislature. Now they were to be elected for three years and one retire every year, thus leaving two experienced men in office. For the first terms, however, one of them should serve only one year, another two, and the third three years. On convening at the fall term of this year they drew lots to decide the term each should serve. Three pieces of paper, upon which were written "one year," "two years," "three years," respectively, were thrown together, and each Commissioner drew one. John W. Burch drew "one year," Alfred Grubb, "two years," and John Neeley "three years."

POOR FARM.

At the December term, 1843, the Court provided a farm for the poor of the county, and instead of "letting out" or "selling" the paupers as heretofore, they were obliged to go to that farm. The first pauper of whom we find mention on the records was Joseph Moore. He died in June, 1830. Green Street was the next one mentioned.

LAST MEETINGS.

The Commissioners' Court continued to manage the affairs of the county until 1849, when the new Constitution of the State went into effect, which abolished this time-honored Court. Before adjourning finally, however, it ordered a vote to be taken for or against township organization, and then adjourned till "court in course," but never re-assembled.

CHAPTER V.

GEOLOGY.*

A large proportion of the upland of Pike county was originally heavily timbered, but there are several small prairies in the central and northern portions. It is a well-watered county, and the valley of the Mississippi is from 8 to 12 miles wide, most of it lying on the Illinois side. More than one-fifth of the area of the county lies in this valley. The general level of the uplands may be estimated at from 200 to 300 feet above the great water courses, with no very well-defined water-shed. The soil on the timbered lands is generally a chocolate-colored clay loam, becoming lighter in color on the banks of the streams and in the vicinity of the river bluffs.

The geological structure of this county is somewhat peculiar, and the strata exposed within its limits comprise the upper part of the Niagara limestone, the whole series of Lower Carboniferous limestones except the Chester group, and a limited thickness of Coal Measures, with the usual surface deposits of Loess and Drift. The most northerly outcrop of Devonian beds is in Calhoun county. The Loess and Drift measure 40 to 100 feet in thickness in Pike county, the Coal Measures 20 to 60, St. Louis limestone one to 30, Keokuk group 100 to 125, Burlington limestone 150 to 200, Kinderhook 100 to 120, and the Niagara limestone one to 50.

The Niagara limestone is found only in the southwest part of the county, where its main outcrop is at the base of the bluffs between Rockport and the south line of the county and for a short distance up Six-Mile creek. It contains a few fossils at the outcrop near Pleasant Hill, among which are Trilobites and a few shells. At Mr. Wells' place, N. W. ¼ sec. 17, Pleasant Hill township, the buff-colored magnesia beds of this group are exposed about 10 feet in thickness, and the rock has been quarried for building-stone. On the S. E. ¼ sec. 8 there is an exposure of about 22 feet of this limestone, the lower 10 feet being a gray, even-bedded limestone, and the upper 12 feet a buff-colored magnesian

*Abstracted from State Geological Report by Prof. A. H. Worthen.

rock, closely resembling the rock from the Grafton quarries. It is the prevailing rock at Pleasant Hill, where it forms a limestone bench about 30 feet high, above the road, at the base of the bluffs. Two miles north of Pleasant Hill, on a branch of Six-Mile creek, the upper part of this limestone is exposed in the bed of the creek.

KINDERHOOK GROUP.

One of the best exposures of this group in this county is just above Kinderhook: whence the name. It is at the point of the bluff, and comprises 2C feet of Loess, 15 of Burlington limestone, 6 of thin-bedded, fine-grained limestone, 36 of thin-bedded sandstone and sandy shales, and 40 feet of clay and sandy shales, partly hidden. Fossil shells are found in the sandstone. This group is also well exposed at Rockport and two miles below Atlas, and somewhat exposed at the base of the Illinois river bluffs. Almost everywhere in the county the Burlington limestone overlies the group, which determines the topographical features of the region also underlaid by the shales and gritstones of the group.

BURLINGTON LIMESTONE.

This limestone forms the bed rock over fully one-half the uplands. It is from 50 to 100 feet in thickness, and its best exposures are among the river bluffs. It is a rather coarse-grained, gray stone, interspersed with brown layers, and is largely composed of the fossilized remains of crinoids and mollusks. In the Mississippi bluff, near the north line of the county, 40 feet or more of the lower portion of this limestone is exposed, forming the upper escarpment of the bluff, and consisting of alternate beds of gray and brown limestone, usually in regular and tolerably thick beds. It has fossils, and has been extensively quarried on Big Blue creek for building purposes. On the eastern side of the county the most northerly outcrop of this limestone is near Griggsville Landing, where the cherty beds of the upper division of this rock are exposed at the base of the bluff. The outcrop here is about 50 feet thick. It appears about the same at Montezuma, and is seen exposed at points all along these bluffs. It is well exposed on Bay creek, forming the main portion of the bluffs along this stream from near Pittsfield to the southeast corner of the county. It is the most important of all the limestones exposed in this county, both as regards extent of exposure and its economical value. As a building stone it is not equal to the magnesian beds of the Niagara group, as found near Pleasant Hill, but is nevertheless very durable. It can be found over half the county.

KEOKUK GROUP.

This group lies just above the Burlington limestone, and outcrops over a large portion of the northern and northeastern parts of the county, where it is frequently found immediately beneath the Coal Measures. The St. Louis group, which should properly intervene, was worn away before the coal epoch. It consists of light gray and bluish gray cherty limestones at the base, which closely resemble the upper beds of the Burlington limestone. Some of the limestone strata are as crinoidal in their structure as the Burlington, but they are usually more bluish gray in color. There is usually a series of cherty beds, 10 to 30 feet in thickness, separating the main limestones of the two groups, which may properly be regarded as transitional. The upper division consists of lime-clay shales and thin-bedded limestones, containing geodes lined with crystallized quartz, chalcedony, calcite, dolomite, crystals of zinc blende and iron pyrites. The pyrites is usually in minute crystals implanted on quartz.

This division may be seen a mile and a half southeast of Griggsville, and where it first appears beneath the Coal Measures the geodes are imbedded in a ferruginous sandstone, which perhaps represents the conglomerate usually lying at the base of the Coal Measures. This indicates that before or during the formation of this conglomerate the shales originally inclosing the geodes were swept away, and the geodes were then enclosed in sand which subsequently hardened. These geode-bearing limestones are exposed near Perry Springs, where the waters derive their mineral ingredients from these beds. At Chambersburg, the limestones of this group form the bed of McGee's creek. Other prominent exposures of these limestones are at Griggsville Landing, on Hadley's creek, near Huntley's coal-bank, etc. From this stratum much good building stone has been quarried.

ST. LOUIS GROUP.

On the banks of McGee's creek only are indications of the presence of this group. The beds exposed here consist of brown magnesian limestone and shales, 20 to 30 feet thick. A mile and a half northwest of Perry quarries have been opened in these beds, and about three miles north of Perry Springs they are again exposed, overlaid by shale, the whole being about 20 feet in thickness.

COAL MEASURES.

The coal formation occupies but a limited area in the central and northern portions of this county, underlying the whole of New Salem township, and a portion only of the four surrounding townships. The thickness does not probably exceed 60 feet. The following are the principal points where coal has been dug in Pike county:

Huntley's, N.W. ¼ sec. 15, Hadley township; coal 16 to 24 inches thick, overlaid by about 6 inches of black shale.

Huntley's new bank, N.W. ¼ sec. 10, Hadley township; bed 6 feet thick, with a parting of clay shale in the middle, about 2 inches in thickness. The coal in the upper part of this seam is rather soft, and contains considerable iron bisulphide. The lower division affords a harder and better coal and rests upon a gray fire clay 2 feet or more in thickness.

Three miles east of Barry coal has been dug on a small branch south of the Philadelphia road; and a mile further south there is a blue clay shale 25 to 30 feet thick exposed along the creek which intersects the river bluffs near New Canton. It contains septaria and tuten-mergel, and closely resembles the shale over the coal at Huntley's mine.

From this point the western boundary of the Coal Measures trends southeastwardly to Houseworth's coal bank, two miles and a half northwest of Pittsfield, on N.W. ¼ sec. 16, Pittsfield township. Coal about 18 inches thick, overlaid by about three feet of dark blue shale, passing upward into sandy shale 10 feet more.

Four miles west of Griggsville, coal is found on Mr. Dunham's place. It is 14 to 20 inches thick, overlaid by about two feet of fossiliferous black shale. This seam of coal outcrops on S. E. ¼ sec. 11, same township, and in the ravines between Griggsville and Philadelphia, via New Salem.

A half mile south of Griggsville coal has also been worked, the seam being 18 to 24 inches thick.

On Lazarus Ross' place, a mile and a half northwest of Perry Springs, some indications of coal may be seen in the bluffs of the middle fork of McGee's creek.

QUATERNARY SYSTEM.

A broad belt of alluvial bottom lands, 6 to 12 miles wide, skirts the whole western border of Pike county. The deposit consists of alternations of clay, sand and loam, in quite regular strata, but of variable thickness. The soil is exceedingly fertile, and where they are above high water, they constitute the most productive and valuable lands in the county. A large proportion of this land was originally prairie, but now there are many belts of heavy timber skirting the small streams intersecting these bottoms.

On the east side of the county there is very little bottom land from the south line of the county to the north line of Flint township, where it begins to widen, and thence to the north line of the county the Illinois bottoms are 2 to 5 miles wide; but they are too low and wet for cultivation. A portion of them are heavily timbered with cottonwood, sycamore, soft maple, elm, ash, hackberry, honey locust, linden, black walnut, water oak, hickory, etc.

LOESS.

The river bluffs on both sides of the county are capped with this formation, which ranges from 10 to 60 feet or more. It always overlies the Drift, where both are present, and hence is of more recent origin. It generally consists of buff or brown marly clays or sands, usually stratified, and often so coherent as to remain in vertical walls 20 or 30 feet high when cut through. From 75 to

80 per cent. of it is silica, 10 to 15 per cent. alumina and iron peroxide, 3 to 4 per cent. lime, and 1 to 2 per cent. magnesia. In the vicinity of Chambersburg the Loess is 60 to 70 feet thick. Everywhere it furnishes a light, porous sub-soil, which is admirably adapted to the growth of fruit trees, vines and small fruits. In some places it contains a variety of fossil shells which present the usual bleached and water-worn appearance of the dead shells of our ponds and bayous. It also affords a variety of chalky lumps and masses which assume many imitative forms, as of potatoes and the disks called "clay-stones" in New England. It also gives origin to the bald knobs so frequently met with along the river bluffs, and is often rounded into natural mounds which have been very generally used by the Indians as burial places. The bones of extinct animals are often found in the marly beds of this formation, along with land and fresh-water shells.

DRIFT.

This deposit consists of variously colored clays containing gravel and boulders. It underlies the Loess, and hence is not visible along the bluffs. In the interior of the county it is often penetrated by well-diggers. It thins out toward the bluffs. At the base of the Drift near Barry there is a bed of clean, yellow flint gravel, partially cemented by iron oxide into a ferruginous conglomerate.

ECONOMICAL GEOLOGY.

Pike county has an abundance of building stone. The Niagara limestone near Pleasant Hill furnishes a buff magnesian rock, in very regular beds, fully equal in quality to that of Grafton and Joliet. Part of the stone in the public-school building at Pittsfield was brought from Joliet, while stone just as good and beautiful was outcropping within ten miles of that town. "A want of the knowledge of this fact," says Mr. Worthen, "has probably cost the citizens of Pike county far more than their proportion of the entire cost of the geological survey of Illinois."

The Burlington limestone, which outcrops over a wide area in this county, will furnish an unlimited supply of excellent building stone. It is probably not less than 150 feet thick. The more flinty portions are the best material for macadamizing roads. Near Montezuma is a 10-foot bed of excellent dimension stone. Similar beds are exposed on Big Blue creek four miles southeast of Pittsfield, where they are 40 feet thick, containing masses two to four feet in thickness. On the west side of the county it forms an almost continuous outcrop, 10 to 40 feet thick, along the river bluffs; and on the east side of the county it also forms a continuous outcrop in the bluffs from Griggsville Landing south.

The lower portion of the Keokuk limestone is fully as useful as the preceding. Excellent quarries are worked two miles north of Griggsville on the south fork of McGee's creek. The stone is com-

Hutson Martin

DERRY TP

posed almost entirely of the joints and plates of crinoids, cemented together by a calcareous paste.

The St. Louis group, although limited in extent, furnishes some good building stone, mostly found in Perry township and vicinity, as already described.

The coal deposits in this county are all, except at Huntley's place, too thin for profitable working. Where surface "stripping," however, can be done, it pays to mine the thinner deposits. Huntley's is probably a local deposit, a "pocket," which will soon be exhausted.

No mineral ore, except a little iron, has been found in Pike county.

The Burlington and Keokuk groups furnish the best of material for quick-lime. The St. Louis group, which is generally preferred, is very limited.

Good hydraulic limestone for cement can be obtained from the Kinderhook group.

Fire clay, which usually underlies the coal, can be mined with the coal to advantage. The brown clays of the Drift and the Loess furnish superior material for brick.

For marble the bed of oolitic conglomerate of the Kinderhook group at Rockport furnishes a stone capable of a fine polish and makes a beautiful variegated marble ; but the bed, so far as examined, is rather thin for profitable working. Some of the sub-crystalline beds of the Burlington limestone also receive a high polish and make a fine ornamental stone.

The Perry mineral springs, three in number, issue from the upper part of the Keokuk limestone which underlies the valley and outcrops along the bluffs. The principal ingredients of the water here are the bi-carbonates of lime and magnesia, the silicate of potash and soda and the carbonate of potash. For further account of these springs see history of Perry township in this volume.

There are a few small caves in Pike county, two near Barry, into one of which one can enter a distance of 550 feet and the other 400 feet. In early day panthers were known to inhabit these caves. In Pearl township, on land owned by Judge Atkinson, the railroad employees of the Chicago & Alton company were blasting rock in 1871 or 1872, when they discovered a small cave in which were found lime carbonate drippings in the form of stalagmites and stalactites. Many of these are of imitative forms and can be imagined to be petrified human beings or animals. An exaggerated account of this cave was published in the Pittsfield papers at the time, which led many people to believe something wonderful was found at the place.

18

CHAPTER VI.

ZOOLOGY.

QUADRUPEDS.

Of the species of native animals that once roamed the flowery prairies and wild forests of Pike county, but few of the smaller remain, and none of the larger. Of the latter we cannot even find a specimen preserved in taxidermy. The buffalo which grazed upon the verdant prairies has been driven westward. With or before it went the beaver, elk, badger, panther, black wolf and black bear. Some animals that were quite numerous have become very rare, such as the gray fox, the catamount, otter, lynx, and the beautiful Virginia deer.

There still remain many of the different species, mostly inhabiting the country adjacent to the Illinois and Mississippi rivers and a few of the other larger streams. These are, however, fast disappearing, and ere long will be known only in history, as are the deer, the beaver, and the bison. Among those still to be found here are the gray wolf, which is numerous in some parts, the opossum, raccoon, mink, muskrat, the common weasel, the small brown weasel, skunk, woodchuck, or Maryland marmot, prairie mole, common shrew mole, meadow and deer mouse, and the gray rabbit. Of squirrels there are the gray timber squirrel, the fox, chipmunk, the large gray prairie squirrel, the striped and the spotted prairie squirrel, and the beautiful flying squirrel. The dark-brown and the reddish bat are common. Other small animals have been found here which have strayed from other localities.

BIRDS.

Of the 5,000 existing species of birds many have sojourned in this county, some temporarily and others for a considerable time. Many migratory species come only at long intervals, and therefore but little is known of them.

There is not a more fascinating study than that afforded by our feathered friends. Their free movements through seemingly boundless space, the joyous songs of many, and the characteristic tones of all, their brilliant colors, their lively manners, and their wonderful instincts, have from earliest ages made a strong impression on the minds of men, and in the infancy of intellect gave rise to many peculiar and mysterious associations. Hence the flight of birds was made the foundation of a peculiar art of divination. Religion borrowed many symbols from them, and poetry many of its ornaments. Birds avail themselves of their powers of wing to seek situations adapted for them in respect to temperature and supply of food. The arrival of summer birds is always a welcome sign of advancing spring, and is associated with all that is cheerful and delightful. Some birds come almost at the same date annually; others are more influenced by the character of the season, as mild or severe.

Pike county is highly favored, compared with any county north of it, as the Virginia red-bird and cedar-bird remain here during the winter, and the indigo-bird is here in its season. Parroquets also used to abound in this region.

The following list is as nearly correct as can be compiled from the available information upon the subject:

Perchers.—This order of birds is by far the most numerous, and includes nearly all those which are attractive either in plumage or in song. The ruby-throated humming-bird, with its exquisite plumage and almost ethereal existence, is at the head of the list. This is the humming-bird which is always the delight of the children, and is the only one found in Illinois. The chimney swallow, easily known from other swallows by its very long wings and forked tail, and which is a true swift, is quite numerous. Of the whip-poorwill family there are two representatives,—the whippoorwill proper, whose note enlivens the forest at night, and the night-hawk. The belted kingfisher, so well known to the school-boy, is the only member of its family in this region. At the head of the fly-catchers is the king-bird, the crested fly-catcher and the wood pewee.

Sub-order of *Singers—Thrush family.*—Of this family are the robin, the wood thrush, Wilson's thrush, the blue-bird, the ruby-crowned and the golden-crested wren, tit-lark, the black and the white creeper, blue yellow-backed warbler, yellow-breasted chat, worm-eating warbler, blue-winged yellow-warbler, Tennessee warbler, and golden-crowned thrush. *Shrike family.*—This family is represented by the great northern shrike, red-eyed fly-catcher, white-eyed fly-catcher, the blue-headed and the yellow-throated fly-catcher. *Swallow family.*—This family of birds are very numerous in Pike county. Among them are the barn swallow, white-bellied swallow, bank swallow, cliff swallow, and purple martin. *Wax-wing family.*—The cedar-bird is the representative of the wax-wing in America. *Mocking-bird family.*—The genera of this family are the cat-bird, brown thrush, the house and winter wren. *Finch and Sparrow family.*—The snow bunting and Smith's bunting appear only in winter. The purple finch, the yellow-bird and the lark finch inhabit this county. Of the passerine genus of this family are the Savannah sparrow, the field and the chipping sparrow, the black snow-bird, the tree sparrow, the song sparrow, the swamp and the fox-colored sparrow, the black-throated bunting, the rose-breasted gros-beak and the ground robin. *Titmouse family* is represented by the chickadee and the tufted titmouse. *Creeper family.*—There are two specimens of this family,—the white-bellied nut-hatch and the American creeper. *Skylark family.*—This melodious family is represented here by only the common skylark of the prairie. *Black-bird family.*—The rusty black-bird, the crow black-bird, the cow-bird, the red-winged black-bird, the meadow lark, the orchard and the Baltimore orioles of this family, are the most beautiful and brilliant of birds that inhabit this region. *Crow family.*—The blue-jay and the common crow comprise the species of this family.

Birds of Prey.—This order of birds comprises all those, with few exceptions, which pursue and capture birds and other animals for food. They are mostly of large size, the females are larger than the males, they live in pairs, and choose their mates for life. Most raptorial birds have disappeared. Among them are the golden eagle, which was always rare but now no longer seen here; the bald eagle, or properly the white-headed eagle, once quite common, now . scarce. Some well-preserved specimens of this genus are in the county. This eagle enjoys the honor of standing as our national emblem. Benjamin Franklin lamented the selection of this bird as emblematical of the Union, for its great cowardice. It has the ability of ascending in circular sweeps without any apparent motion of the wings or the tail, and it often rises in this manner until it disappears from view; when at an immense height, and as if observing an object on the ground, it sometimes closes its wings and glides toward the earth with such velocity that the eye can scarcely follow it, causing a loud rustling sound like a violent gust of wind among the branches of the forest. The *Hawk family* has eight or nine species, some but seldom seen, others common. The turkey-buzzard has almost, if not quite, disappeared. Of the owl genera are several species, though all are but seldom seen because of their nocturnal habits. Among them are the barn owl, the screech owl, the long and the short eared owl, the barred owl, and the snowy owl, the latter being the rarest.

Climbers.—But few of this order remain in the county, the most common of which are the woodpeckers. Of the various kinds are the golden-winged, the pileated, the hairy, the downy, the yellow-bellied, red-bellied and the red-headed. At an early day the Carolina parrot, generally called the "parrokeet," was often seen, but he has now entirely deserted this section. The yellow and black-billed cuckoos are occasionally seen.

Scratchers.—This order contains but few genera in this county. The wild turkey, the choicest of game, has almost entirely disappeared, and was the only one of its family that ever sojourned here. In an early day they were in abundance. *Grouse family.*—The chiefest among this family is the prairie chicken, which, if not carefully protected, must ere long follow the wild turkey, never to return. The ruffled grouse, wrongfully called "pheasant," has of late made its appearance. It is quite fond of cultivated fields, and, if properly protected and encouraged until it becomes fairly settled, will make a fine addition to the game, and fill the place of the prairie chicken. *Partridge family.*—The fate of that excellent bird, the quail, is only a question of a short time. *The Dove family.*— The wild pigeons continue to make their semi-annual visits, but not in such vast numbers as years ago. Acres of forest were so often filled at night with these birds that the breaking of boughs and the flying of pigeons made a noise that could be heard for miles, and the shot of a sportsman's gun could not be heard at a distance of ten feet. Highly interesting is the description by Audubon of the enormous flights which he observed on the Ohio in the fall of 1813; they obscured the daylight and lasted three days without interruption. According to a very moderate estimate of his, each flight contained the stupendous number of one billion, one hundred and fifteen thousand million, one hundred and thirty-six thousand pigeons. These flights caused a general commotion among the entire rural population. Desirous of booty and anxious lest their crops should be spoiled, the farmers, arming themselves with rifles, clubs, poles, torches and iron pots filled with sulphur, proceed to the resting places of the birds. The work of slaughter being accomplished everybody sat down among mountains of dead pigeons, plucking and salting the birds which they selected, abandoning the rest to the foxes, wolves, raccoons, opossums and hogs, whole herds of which were driven to the battle-field. The plaintive notes of the Carolina dove, commonly known as the turtle-dove, are still heard.

Swimmers.—This order of birds, which formerly frequented this county in large numbers, have almost disappeared. They are migratory, and in their usual season would appear coming from the north or south, as winter passes into summer or summer into winter. *Diver family.*—The great northern diver, or loon, sometimes visits this section, but inhabits the frigid zone. *Gull family.*—Of this family are Wilson's tern and silvery gull. *Pelican family.*—The rough-billed pelican was the only genus of this family that ever stopped in Pike county, and it has now altogether ceased to make its visits here. *Cormorant family.*—The double-crested cormorant, or sea raven, has been seen here. *Duck family.*—This family of migratory birds visited the ponds and streams of this county in large numbers before it became so thickly settled, both on their northern and southern passage, but now mostly confine themselves to the Illinois and Mississippi, where large numbers are found. This family furnishes most game for sportsmen and for the table. There are the wood-duck, the big black-headed duck, the ring-necked duck, the red-head, the canvas-back, the dipper, the shell-drake or goosander, the fish-duck, the red-breasted, and the hooded merganser, the mallard and the pintail, the green-winged and the blue-winged teal, the spoonbill and the gadwall, the baldpate, the American swan, the trumpeter swan and the white-fronted goose.

Waders.—Probably less is known of this order of birds than of any other, because of their shyness and solitary habits. They frequented the marshes, but cultivation has drained their favorite haunts. *Crane family.*—The whooping crane, always rare, is now never seen. The sand-hill cranes stop on their journeys north and south. *Heron family.*—The great blue heron or crane, least bittern, the green heron, night heron and the American bittern, compose those of this family visiting this region. *Ibis family.*—The glossy ibis has been seen here. *Plover family.*—The golden plover, the killdeer and the king plover comprise this family known here. *Phalarope family.*—The Wilson's and the red phalarope have frequented the swamps of this county. *Snipe family.*—Various birds of this family have been common in and around the swamps of this county. Among them were Wilson's snipe, grey or red-breasted snipe, the least and the semi-palmated sandpiper, the willet, the tell-tale, the yellow-leg, the solitary sandpiper, the spotted sandpiper, the field plover, long-billed curfew, the common rail, the clapper rail or mud hen, and the coot.

Reptiles.—All of the species of this class that ever inhabited this region are still to be found here except the poisonous snakes. The rattlesnake, of the genus Crotalus, is of a yellowish-brown color, and has a series of horny joints at the end of the tail, which make a rattling sound. These were the most venomous of all snakes found here, and were numerous in the early settlement. There are two kinds, the bandy, or striped, and the prairie rattlesnake, the latter being still occasionally found. The copperhead was always rare. Among the harmless snakes are the water-snake, the garter-snake, the bull-snake, the milk-snake, the black-snake, and the blue racer.

Many reptiles found here are erroneously called lizards, but are salamanders and other like innocent creatures. Lizards are never found in this county. Among the tortoises or turtles are found the map turtle, the snapping and the soft-shelled turtle. Of the batrachian, or naked reptiles, there are a few, and, though loathsome to sight and touch, are harmless. The toad, the bull-frog, the leopard-frog, the tree-toad, with some tailed batrachia, comprise the most of this order. The Illinois river bull-frog is as large as a man's head, often much larger, and his deep bellowing can be heard for a mile or more.

FISHES.

Although fishes are the lowest class of vertebrates, their varied forms and colors, which often rival those of precious stones and burnished gold, the wonderful power and velocity of some, the wholesome food furnished by many, and the exciting sport of their capture, combine to render fishes subjects of great interest to the

casual observer, as well as to the amateur and professional natural-
ist. The number of known species of fishes is about ten thousand.
The waters of this county are quite prolific of the finny tribe. The
commerce in fish has become quite extensive along the Illinois and
Mississippi. *Sickle-backed family.*—This family furnishes the
game fish, and are never caught larger than four pounds in weight.
The varous genera found here are the black bass, goggle-eye, the
croppy, or big black sun-fish, and the two common sun-fish. *Pike
family.*—There are but two species of this family,—the pickerel,
weighing from five to twenty-five pounds, and the gar pike. *Sucker
family.*—Of this tribe are the buffalo, red-horse, white-sucker, two
species of black-suckers, mullet ranick. Fish of this family are
found in all the streams of the county. They abound wherever
there is water. *Cat-fish family.*—Of this voracious family the
channel cat-fish, the mud cat-fish and two species of the small cat-
fish inhabit the waters of this county, and are caught ranging in
weight from one to thirty pounds.

The shovel-fish is yet abundant, and its flesh, as well as its general appearance, resembles that of the cat-fish.

Besides these varieties there are the chub, silver-sides, and fresh-
water herring, and large numbers of other species denominated
minnows, which are found in the smallest spring branches, as well
as the larger streams.

CHAPTER VII.

BOTANY.

Persons coming to the West for the first time in their lives are deeply impressed with the high and rolling character of our prairies, which they had before always imagined low and level; and this feature of the prairie, combined in early days with its beautiful, dreamy covering of flowering plants and grassy verdure in spring and summer, inspired one to sing:

> A billowy ocean with green carpet spread,
> Which seems almost too neat for man to tread!
> With glittering stars of amaryllis white,
> With violets blue and roses red and bright,
> With golden cinquefoil, star-grass, buttercups,
> With dazzling cardinal flowers and painted-cups,
> And lone but cheerful meadow larks to sing,
> This grassy sea appeared in smiling spring.
> In summer came the stately compass-plant,
> As if to guide the wandering immigrant.
> Then asters, golden-rods and wild sunflowers
> O'erspread the vales in labyrinthine bowers.
> Thus nature, clad in vesture gold and green,
> Brought autumn in and closed the floral scene.

Also the beautiful, clean-cut hills of our forests present a tasteful view scarcely ever witnessed in the East. But at the present day both our prairie and our timber are under either cultivation or pasturage, and blue grass, white clover and a large number of introduced weeds from the East have taken the place of the original flora. Industrially this cultivation is a gain, but poetically it is a loss. Only in the most retired situations can many interesting plants be found which used to be abundant. Several species of prairie clover, false wild indigo, rosin-weed, mountain mint, loosestrife, etc., have almost disappeared with the original prairie, while a few of the modest strawberry, star-grass and blue-eyed grass remain with us as sweet reminiscences of the past.

Nearly all the plants growing spontaneously in cultivated or waste grounds are "introduced;" that is, they have been brought here by white settlers,—unintentionally, of course, with reference to most of the weeds. In the timbered sections no particular weed is on the increase in the present decade, but in the prairie section, the garden parsnip, common thistle, rich weed (in artificial groves), toad flax, wild lettuce, and oxybaphus (a four-o'clock plant) are increasing rapidly; and along the railroads several sand plants are making good headway, as sand-bur, polanisia, ox-eye daisy, etc.

Before settlement by the whites the prairie was mostly covered by two or three kinds of grass. Several other kinds grew in patches here and there, notably the Indian grass and blue joint, which grew very tall. In wet places grew "slough" grass and many sedges, and along the channeled sloughs abounded several species of golden-rod, aster and wild sunflower, which in the latter part of summer and in autumn formed waving yellow stripes across the prairie, and were peculiarly charming. They seemed to have a sedative effect upon the feelings.

About 2,300 species of plants are found within the United States, 1,600 of which can be found in Illinois, and about 950 in Pike county. We now give a list of all the common plants growing spontaneously in Pike county, and some of the most interesting rare ones, excepting mosses, mushrooms, etc.; and we name all the trees and shrubs, rare as well as common. We give the English names, following Gray's Manual, fifth edition, mainly, in respect to names, and altogether with respect to the order in which the families range. By the way, we make a few corrections of popular errors as to names. Some names, even in the books, are applied to two or more different plants, as sycamore, button snake-root, black snakeroot, goose-grass, hair-grass, loosestrife, etc. Also, every plant has several names,—communities differing widely in this regard. We endeavor to select the most common name as we can judge from Gray's Botany.

Crowfoots.—Common virgin's bower, a vine, and Pitcher's virgin's bower, a half vine, are occasionally found : the leather-flower, a cultivated vine bearing large, blue flowers, is of the same genus. The Pennsylvanian, Virginian and wood anemones occur here and there. Liver-leaf ("liver-wort") is common on forest hillsides. Rue anemone, and the early, the purplish and the tall meadow-rues are common in the woods. The true buttercups of the East are not found here, but the most common flower corresponding to them is the creeping crowfoot. The small-flowered, the hooked, the bristly and the early crowfoots also occur. Isopyrum grows in moist, shady places. Marsh marigold is common in early spring, growing in mud supplied with fresh water : in the East they are called "cowslips" and sometimes used for greens. Water plantain spearwort, growing in mud, and yellow water crowfoot, growing in water and with the submersed leaves finely divided, are seen occasionally. Wild columbine, so easily recognized by its resemblance to the cultivated species, abounds in the margins of the woods ; so also two species of wild larkspur. Yellow puccoon is very scarce. White baneberry is occasionally seen in the deep woods.

Custard-Apple Family.—The papaw is common along the Illinois river. It fruits better in Calhoun county than Pike, being of a more modern growth here. This is a fragile bush, with large leaves, bearing fruit about the size and appearance of short, thick, green cucumbers, which have a pulp like the banana.   To " learn" to like them one must merely taste of them at times far apart.

Moonseed Family.—Canadian moonseed is abundant in the woods.   It is a smooth, twining vine like the morning-glory, with a beautiful, round, yellow root, which has a tonic-bitter taste, and is sometimes called sarsaparilla.   The true wild sarsaparilla belongs to the Ginseng family.

Barberry Family.—May-apple is abundant and blue cohosh somewhat rare.

Water Lilies.—The pond, or white water lily, is abundant in large, open ponds in the river bottoms, and the yellow water, or frog lily, growing in shallow, stagnant water, is scarce, as is also the yellow nelumbo, a similar plant.

Poppy Family.—The well-known blood-root is the only representative of this family growing wild in this country.

Fumitory Family.—The celebrated Dutchman's breeches is the only member of this family in our woods.   Bleeding heart is of the same genus.

Mustard Family.—Marsh cress is common ; lake cress, growing in water, is sometimes seen; and horse-radish flourishes beyond the bounds of cultivation.   Pepper-root, an early-flowering plant, is common in the dense forest.   Two varieties of spring cress are frequent.   Two species of the delicate little rock cress are also frequent.   Hedge mustard is the most common mustard-like weed that grows on cultivated and waste grounds.   Tansy mustard is rare.   Black mustard, the type of this family, flourishes on cultivated and waste grounds.   White mustard is very rare at the present day.   Shepherd's purse is abundant early in the season,— a weed everywhere : its seed-pod is triangular, somewhat inflated, and in shape resembles a shepherd's purse of the olden time.   Wild peppergrass is common in late summer : seed-pods, wafer-form. Whitlow grass grows in sandy ground.   To the Mustard family belong the radish, turnip and cabbage of our gardens.

Caper Family.—Polanisia, a fetid pod-bearing plant, is common on sandy ground, and is extending along the railroads where sand and gravel are deposited.

Violets.—Common blue violet is abundant, the other kinds more rare, namely, hand-leaf, arrow-leaved, larkspur, bird-foot, downy yellow, etc.   Heart's-ease belongs to this order.

Rock-Rose Family.—Frost-weed grows in sandy soil, and pinweed on dry ground.

St. John's-worts.—Two or three rare species are found in this county.

Pink Family.—Starry campion, sleepy catchfly, corn cockle, sandwort, long-leaved stitchwort and forked chickweed are found here and there.   Common chickweed and three species of mouse-ear chickweed and bouncing bet are more common.   Carpet weed is common on the sand; it grows in the form of a bunchy lamp-mat.

Purslane Family.—Akin to the beautiful portulaca is our universal purslane, often called " pursley." Spring beauty belongs to this family. It is one of our earliest spring flowers, and may be distinguished by the plant's having but two leaves, long and narrow and somewhat fleshy. The flower is a light rose color, with deeper veins.

Mallows Family.—Common, or low mallows and velvet-leaf, or Indian mallows are very abundant. The latter is a tall, pestiferous weed about our fields, with seed-vessels resembling poppy-bolls. Sida and bladder ketmia, or flower of an hour, are common. To this order belong the hollyhock and okra, in cultivation.

Linden Family.—Bass-wood, known as lin among Southern people, is the only member of this family growing here.

Geranium Family.—Wild crane's-bill is common in early spring, having a solitary, rose-colored flower on the summit. Carolina crane's-bill is rather rare. Spotted and pale touch-me-nots are common in moist, shaded places, growing in dense patches. The balsamine of cultivation is of the same genus. Yellow wood-sorrel is everywhere, and here and there the violet wood-sorrel prevails to some extent. This is erroneously called " sheep-sorrel." Sheep, or field sorrel grows on sandy or gravely ground, has lance-shaped and pointed leaves, obscure flowers, and seeds like pie-plant or yellow-dock, while wood-sorrel grows mostly in clay soil, has three leaflets like clover, showy flowers, and seeds in a pod. The two sorrels belong to different orders, but have a similar taste.

Rue Family.—The northern prickly ash, a common shrub in our woods but growing scarcer. and the still rarer hop-tree, are the only members of this family in Pike county. Garden rue is of the same order, or family.

Cashew Family.—In America this would seem to be rather the sumac family. The smooth sumac is common everywhere, fragrant sumac abundant in sandy ground, and poison ivy is common along fences—some places abundant. The latter is a coarse, woody vine with innumerable rootlets, and has three leaflets to each leaf, with these leaflets sometimes partly divided. When the plant is young it can be distinguished from box-elder by the latter having a white " bloom " on the stem; and at all times it can be distinguished from Virginia creeper (American ivy, an innocent plant) by the latter having five leaflets to each leaf, and the whole leaf in shape like that of buckeye.

Vine Family, that is, the grape-vine family.—Virginia creeper, just described, is as abundant as any weed. The winter, or frost grape is common, but the summer grape, a delicious fruit, is very scarce, if indeed it can be found at all in this county. It used to be abundant, but the vines have been destroyed by reckless grape gatherers.

Buckthorn Family.—The noted red-root, or New Jersey tea, a

shrub in the margin of prairies and to some extent in all other situations, is the only representative of this family here, and it is becoming rarer by the encroachments of cultivation and pasturage.
The leaves make very good tea.

Staff-tree Family.—The climbing bittersweet and waahoo are
all there are of this family in our limits.   The former is a smooth,
woody vine, common in the woods, climbing by simply twining,
and bearing orange-colored berries in clusters, often called wax-
work and used in ornamentation.   This vine is often called simply
bittersweet, but the true medical bittersweet is a very different
plant, scarcely a vine at all, and not growing wild in this county.
The waahoo, or burning-bush, is a real bush of about the size and
proportions of a plum-tree; its twigs have four white lines, and its
crimson fruit in autumn after the leaves have fallen are very showy.
The flowers are dark purple.

Soapberry Order includes the Maple, Bladdernut and Soapberry
(proper) families.   Of the maples the most common are the sugar and
the white.   The latter is one of the soft maples, the red maple of other
sections of the United States being the other.   The red does not
grow in this county.   Box-elder is sometimes called ash-leaved
maple, and belongs to this family.   The American bladdernut is a
tree-like shrub about 10 feet high, producing large three-lobed, inflated seed pods.   The Ohio buck-eye is common in the river bottoms.

Milkworts.—Seneca snakeroot and two other species of milkwort
are found in this region.

Pulse Family.—This large family is characterized by having
seeds in pods like beans and peas, which are members of the family.
The first in the list, according to the books, are the clovers,—red
and white.   Two other species of this genus occur, indeed, but are too
rare to enumerate here.   Then the white sweet clover, more recently
escaped from cultivation; then two species of prairie clover, almost
extinct.   Goat's rue, false indigo (Amorpha) and lead plant abound
on dry, sandy loam in river bottoms.   The common locust was introduced here, but this is too far north for it to be hardy enough to
withstand our winds and the borer.   A honey-locust occurs here
and there.   One milk vetch is frequent.   Six species of tick trefoil
abound.   These are those plants in the woods bearing "pods" of
triangular, flat burs.   Two species of bush clover are found here.
One vetch (tare) and one marsh vetchling, ground-nut, kidney bean,
false indigo (Baptisia) and wild senna are found here and there.
Hog peanut, called wild pea or bean by some, abounds everywhere
in the woods.   Red-bud is an ugly little tree except in the spring
before the leaves appear, when the whole top is of a beautiful
purplish-red from the blossoms.   Partridge pea is abundant "in
spots," grows like a weed in low places, 20 inches to 2 feet high,
has leaves like a locust, and bears a very large yellow flower.
The sensitive plant may be found within the bounds of this county,

but if so, it is very scarce. Kentucky coffee-tree is rare. It is famous for its beautiful compound leaves and glossy beans.

Rose Family.—Most of our fruits come from this family, as the apple, peach, plum, cherry, strawberry, etc. The wild plum (yellow or red) is becoming very scarce. The wild black cherry is abundant; the choke-cherry is a shrub found occasionally. Nine-bark, common meadow-sweet and goat's-beard are species of spiræa frequently found. Agrimony is a coarse herb occasionally found, having leaves resembling those of the strawberry and bearing a kind of drooping bur; plant about two feet high. One species of avens is very common; three other species are found. Common cinquefoil, or five-finger, resembles the strawberry very closely, and abounds in dry soil. Norwegian cinquefoil has similar leaves, but the plant is coarse and grows three feet high; not common. Another species is also found. One species of wild strawberry abounds in retired situations; it was common over the original prairie. The blackberry and the raspberry prevail here as elsewhere, but their sylvan territory is narrowed to close limits by the encroachments of man. Of the roses proper the dwarf wild rose is the most common, but its territory is also very limited now-a-days. The early wild rose occurs. Three species of red haw (hawthorn) occur, and two varieties of one species. The black, or pear, thorn is the most common, with two varieties, then the scarlet-fruited thorn, and lastly the cockspur thorn. The crab-apple is well known.

Saxifrages.—Two or three species of gooseberry are common; swamp saxifrage and a species of alum-root are sometimes met with.

Orpine Family.—Ditch stonecrop is common during wet seasons.

Evening Primrose Family.—Common evening primrose, enchanter's nightshade, and one species of willow-herb, are common; seed-box, water-purslane, sun-drops and two other species of false loosestrife occur occasionally.

Loosestrife Family.—One species not infrequent.

Gourd Family.—The wild balsam-apple is a vigorous, herbaceous vine, bearing bur-like fruit, about cultivated grounds, and the one-seeded star cucumber flourishes in the shaded river bottoms.

Parsley Family.—This family is characterized by having their seed-bearing tops like those of parsnips. Most of the poisonous plants growing in this country belong to this family. Two species of black snakeroot prevail in this county. Parsnip itself is becoming a common weed in open but protected places; and there may be found here and there the cow parsnip, cowbane, meadow parsnip, spotted cowbane, rattlesnake master, two species of water parsnip, honewort, chervil, two species of sweet cicely, poison hemlock. Of the whole family the most poisonous are the spotted cowbane and poison hemlock.

Ginseng Family.—Ginseng, on account of its popular medical qualities, has been pretty well thinned out. The true wild sar-

saparilla (a plant of the appearance of a large ginseng) is sometimes found, and spikenard is common in the forest ravines.

Dogwoods.—The most common dogwood is the white-berried, or
panicled cornel; next the rough-leaved, the alternate-leaved, the
flowering, the silky, and lastly the red-osier.

Honeysuckle Family.—Common elder is becoming too abundant. Yellow honeysuckle is common. Horse gentian, or fever-
wort, is a forest weed bearing 5 to 10 yellow berries in a circle
around the stem at every place where the two opposite leaves are
attached. The true black haw is scarce, but sheep-berry, which is
generally called black haw, is common.

Madder Family.—Two species of the small bed-straw are
abundant, and the sweet-scented is common, while occasionally
may be found cleavers, or goose-grass. Wild liquorice occurs
rarely. These herbs are all of a flax-like appearance, having several beautiful little leaves in a whorl at each joint. Button bush
is common in wet ground.

Composites.—This order is by far the largest of all. Its flowers
are compound, that is, there are several, sometimes many, small
flowers crowded close together in a head, as sunflower, lettuce,
dandelion, aster, chrysanthemum, May-weed, etc. Their time of
flowering is generally late in the season.

Iron-weed is common on flat ground: its summit in August is
a beautiful royal purple. Four species of button snakeroot (one
called also blazing star) are abundant on protected original prairie,
and occur nowhere else. Five species of thoroughwort grow here,
that called boneset being abundant. The species called trumpet, or
Joe-Pye weed, is a tall, interesting weed, with 3 to 6 leaves in each
whorl, that is, at each joint. Kuhnia is not rare; it resembles
boneset. Mist-flower grows in our limits. Of the asters there are
about 30 species growing within this county, about half of them
very common. The flowers have a starry appearance: hence the
name. The most remarkable of them is the New England aster,
a large purple flower along the roadsides in September. Five
species of fleabane, similar to the asters in appearance, are common, namely, horse-weed, which is abundant on waste and cultivated grounds, Robin's plantain, common fleabane, and two daisy
fleabanes, one of them called also sweet scabious. About 18
species of golden-rod can be found in this county, only half of them
common, however. The most abundant is the Solidago Canaden-
sis. From these much honey is made by bees in September. Four
species of rosin-weed used to prevail on the original prairie, but
their territory is very limited at the present day. The most noted
of them has divided leaves, and is also called compass plant, or
polar plant, the leaves having once been thought to point north
and south. They do indeed stand with their faces somewhat parallel, but they are just as apt to have their edges toward other points
of the compass. One species of rosin-weed has undivided leaves,
large and rough, and is called prairie dock. This and the compass

plant flourish on flat prairie soil which is not pastured. The species called cup-plant grows along the banks of channeled sloughs. The leaves join together at the base so as to form a cup. It is a very large weed. Parthenium, a similar plant, is not rare. Ragweed is the most common weed we have along the roadsides: called also hogweed, Roman wormwood, etc. Great ragweed is the largest weed that grows in this country. Common along fences. Cocklebur is on the increase. We have a State law "providing" for their destruction. Ox-eye, Lepachys and six species of cone-flower are almost common. Six species of wild sunflower flourish along fences in unfrequented situations. They are tall weeds, but not troublesome. One kind has tuberous roots and is really an artichoke. Three species of tickseed occur in this county. The true Spanish needle does not grow here, but three species of its genus abound here, especially during wet seasons, namely, common and swamp beggar-ticks and the larger bur-marigold. The smaller bur-marigold is found in shallow running water. Fetid marigold is abundant in dry situations along the wagon roads. When struck, even lightly, it yields a rank aromatic odor: called also false dog-fennel. Sneezeweed, which looks somewhat like a Spanish needle, is abundant during wet seasons and exceedingly scarce at other times. Mayweed, or dog-fennel, every one is familiar with. So with yarrow. The ox-eye daisy, or white-weed, a vexatious weed in the East, is just beginning to creep in along the railroads. Biennial wormwood is a common but harmless weed in waste places. Common and plantain-leaved everlasting are common. Fire-weed abundant. Golden rag-wort here and there in the spring. The famous Canada thistle is seldom seen: the common thistle abounds more and more. Two other species are common, growing very tall. Burdock is a Composite. Dandelion belongs in this connection. Wild lettuce and false or blue lettuce are common milky weeds, growing very tall. Two species of sow-thistle, comparatively harmless, are modestly on the increase.

Lobelias. —The celebrated medical lobelia, or Indian tobacco, flourishes along our garden fences. The great lobelia, or blue cardinal flower, is abundant in moist ground. The cardinal flower is the most showy, dazzling-red flower we have growing wild: found in wet ground and on the banks of sloughs. A small and slender species of lobelia is common in protected situations.

Campanula, or Bellflower Family.—The tall bellflower is common. Venus's looking-glass is found here and there. "Bluebells" do not belong here: they are the smooth lungwort, belonging to the Borage family.

Ebony Family.—Persimmon, or date plum; rather scarce, but more abundant farther south.

Plantain Family.—The common plantain of our door-yards. Four other species of this family may occur in this county, but they are exceedingly rare.

Primrose Family.—Two species of loosestrife (Lysimachia) occur.

Figwort Family.—Mullein, toad-flax ("butter-and-eggs"), figwort, beard-tongue, two species of Gerardia, two species of lousewort and cow-wheat, are common, while monkey-flower, hedge hyssop, false pimpernel, purslane and corn speedwell are sometimes seen. Toad-flax has persistent roots like witch-grass and threatens to become a pest. The snap-dragon of our gardens is a fig-wort.

Vervains.—Verbenas belong to this order. The most abundant plant belonging to this family, and growing wild, is the hoary vervain; next are the bracted (prostrate), the white, or nettle-leaved, and the blue. They all prefer dry, waste grounds, and are much inclined to hybridize. Fog-fruit is abundant in sandy ground along the rivers.

Mint family.—Common are wood sage, or American germander, wild mint, bugle-weed, American pennyroyal, and hedge nettle, two species. Motherwort, catnip, heal-all, and wild mint are abundant. Here and there are water horehound, mountain mint, horse-mint, blephilia (two species), giant hyssop (two species), false dragon-head, or lion's-heart, mad-dog skullcap and one other species of skullcap. Ground ivy, or gill-over-the-ground, is abundant about dwellings. What is generally called "horse-mint" in the West is "wild bergamot" according to the books, while wild mint is often taken for peppermint. True peppermint, spearmint, and horehound are scarce within our limits. South of the Illinois river horehound takes the place of catnip along the fences and roadsides. Salvia, sage and Mexican sage are cultivated plants belonging to this order.

Borage Family.—Hairy and hoary puccoon, smooth lungwort, stick-seed, beggar's lice and common hound's-tongue are common; all other species rare. Comfrey belongs to this family. Smooth lungwort is often called "blue-bells." It is common in early spring about door-yards and along fences near dwellings. Common hound's-tongue flourishes along the roads; flowers a dull purple, appearing in early summer. Beggar's-lice is a species of hound's-tongue.

Water-leaf Family.—Ellisia appears in cool, shady places, and resembles small tomatoes in leaf and fruit.

Polemoniums, or Phloxes.—Greek valerian, paniculate, hairy and divaricate phlox are frequent. The true wild sweet-William is very rare.

Convolvulus, or Morning-glory Family.—The most common plant of this order growing spontaneously beyond the bounds of cultivation is hedge bindweed, or Rutland beauty. Eight species of dodder ("love-vine") may be found, all rare except one. It appears like orange-colored thread growing on the tops of weeds.

Nightshade Family.—To this family belong Irish potatoes, tomatoes, egg-plant, bitter-sweet, tobacco and Jerusalem cherry. The most common weeds of this family are jimson-weed, horse-nettle

W.R. Wills Sen.

PITTSFIELD T.P.

("bull nettles"), common or black nightshade and two species of ground-cherry. The white-flowered jimson-weed (Datura Stramonium) is called common stramonium or thornapple by Dr. Gray, while the purple-flowered he calls purple thornapple.

Gentians.—One beautiful species of American centaury, American Columbo and several species of gentian are found within our limits, but all of them are scarce. "Horse gentian" belongs to the Honeysuckle family.

Dogbanes.—Spreading dogbane in the borders of thickets and Indian hemp (Amsonia) on the river banks are common.

Milkweeds.—Common milkweed, or silkweed, is common; has large, boat-shaped pods of glistening cotton. Swamp milkweed is also common. Butterfly weed, or pleurisy-root, whorled milkweed and two species of green milkweed occur not rarely.

Olive Family.—It would seem more natural to us Westerners to call this the Ash family, as we have no members of this order about us except the five species of ash,—white, black, blue, red and green, the white being the most common. Some of these kinds are difficult for the beginner to distinguish.

Birthworts.—Wild ginger is common in deep, wooded ravines. The leaf is kidney-shaped, plant but few inches high, and the root tastes like ginger.

Four-o'clock Family.—Oxybaphus is rapidly increasing along the railroads, and in low, sandy places.

Pokeweeds.—The common poke with its purple-juiced clusters of berries is well known.

Goosefoots.—Lamb's-quarters, or pigweed, a common weed in our gardens, is the type of this order. Beet and spinach belong here. Next in abundance to lamb's-quarters are oak-leaved goosefoot, maple-leaved goosefoot, Jerusalem oak and Mexican tea. Wormseed is a fetid plant belonging to the genus goosefoot. Orache is becoming abundant in the towns and cities.

Amaranths.—The cultivated coxcomb, globe amaranth and prince's feather (red, chaffy spikes) illustrate the characters of this family. Pigweed is one of the most common weeds in cultivated ground. The pigweed of the last paragraph should be called goosefoot only, or lamb's-quarters. White pigweed, generally known in the West as "tumble-weed," is abundant in some fields. Amarantus blitoides has recently become very abundant in our towns. At a little distance it resembles common purslane. Acnida and Froelichia are common in sandy soil near the rivers.

Buckwheat Family or Knotweeds.—Goose-grass is the most ubiquitous member of this order, forming a carpet in every dooryard. A taller variety with wider leaves also abounds under the shade trees about the premises. Two species of smart-weed, mild water-pepper, water Persicaria and two other species of knotweed are all common. Out of 14 species of what appears to be smart-weed, only two are biting to the taste. Arrow-leaved tear-thumb, black bindweed and climbing false buckwheat are common vines.

19

Pie-plant, "yellow dock" and sheep-sorrel represent another division of the knotweed family. The most common member of this division in Pike county is curled, or "yellow" dock; then follow sheep-sorrel (abounding in sandy soil), pale, water, swamp and bitter docks.

Laurel Family,—Sassafras is common along the bluffs and bottoms of the rivers. Spice bush is also found in Pike county.

Sandal-wood Family.—Bastard toad-flax rather scarce.

Spurges.—Spotted spurge, an herb growing more prostrate than all others, on cultivated ground; milky; no visible flowers. Three other species of spurge are almost common. Three-seeded Mercury, known in former years to inhabit only the dark forest, has followed to our city residences where it can find a similar situation. Croton is common near the rivers; an insignificant little herb.

Nettle Order.—Of the Elm family are the white and the slippery elm and the hackberry,—the first mentioned abundant, the other two scarce. Of the Bread-fruit and Fig family is the red mulberry, which is scarce. Of the Nettle family proper are the true nettle (rare), wood nettle (common), richweed, pellitory, hemp and hop. Richweed, or clearweed, like the Mercury of the last paragraph, has followed man to his artificial groves and is very abundant on flat ground under heavy shade-trees, in some places. It is remarkable that botanists have placed in this order the Osage orange tree of our hedges, the bread-fruit tree of the far-off Pacific isles, the fig and the banyan, and the poison upas of the East Indies.

Plane-Tree Family.—"Sycamore," or button-wood, or American plane. The true sycamore of Europe is a different tree.

Walnut Family.—Black and white walnut (butternut) are well known. Three species of shell-bark and two of smooth-bark, besides pecan in the river bottoms, are common in this country. The list comprises the shag-bark, the western shell-bark, the mockernut or white-heart, the pig-nut or broom, bitter-nut or swamp hickories, and the pecan. The latter used to be abundant in the river bottoms, but the larger trees having been cut out for both the timber and the fruit, most of the pecan growth now is too young to produce much fruit.

Oak Family.—This family comprises not only the oaks but also the chestnut, beech, hazel-nut and iron-wood. Some of the oaks hybridize so much that it is difficult to keep track of the species and varieties. White oak, of course, takes the lead here as elsewhere, but the black jack is about as abundant. The latter is usually the "second growth," and is as good as hickory for firewood. Bur-oak, scarlet oak and black oak (yellow-barked, or quercitron) are common. Laurel or shingle oak, yellow chestnut oak and red oak are occasionally met with. Laurel oak is so called on account of the shape of its leaves, and is also called shingle oak, on account of its being so good in pioneer times for clapboards. Two species of iron-wood flourish here. They belong to different genera, one having seeds in clusters of involucres resembling hops: hence it is called hop hornbeam. The other iron-wood or hornbeam is also called blue or water beech.

Birch Family.—The red, or river birch is sometimes found along the rivers and creeks.

Willows.—The most common willow, as well as the largest, is the black; then the prarie, glaucous, heart-leaved, shining and long-leaved. The black and the shining willows have tough twigs which are very brittle at the base. Several other species of willow occur, but are rare. The quaking asp, or American aspen, the cotton-wood, balm-of-Gilead, Lombardy poplar and silver-leaf, or white poplar, are well known.

Arum Family.—Indian turnip (Jack-in-the pulpit) abundant; skunk cabbage common in wet places supplied by spring-water; sweet flag and green dragon very rare.

Duckweeds.—One species common on the surface of ponds. It does not take root in the earth.

Cat-tails.—Common cat-tail (a kind of flag) and a species of bur reed occur in wet places.

Pondweeds.—Several species grow throughout this country. They grow in or under water.

Water-Plantain Family.—Arrowhead (two species, with several variations) is abundant. Has large, arrow-shaped leaves and white flowers in threes, and grows along the sloughs. Water plantain is sometimes found : grows in same situation as last.

Amaryllis Family.—The star-grass is common. It is a modest little grass-like plant, putting forth its conspicuous, yellow, 3-petaled flowers in June.

Iris Family.—The larger blue flag is becoming rare. The blue-eyed grass looks like the star-grass just mentioned, except that the flowers are white or pale blue.

Yam Family.—Wild yam-root is a green vine sometimes seen in the woods.

Smilax Family.—Common green-brier, Smilax hispida and carrion flower are all not very rare.

Lily Family.—Purple trillium, or three-leaved nightshade, is abundant: flowers in May. One other species of trillium sometimes occurs. Bellwort is an early flower in the woods. Smaller Solomon's seal and false spikenard are common. Wild orange-red lily is common in the margins of prairies which are not pastured and have never been broken. White dog's-tooth violet and great Solomon's seal are reported here. It is another early-flowering plant of a similar appearance to the last and in similar situations. Squill (eastern quamash, or wild hyacinth) is said also to be found in this county. Wild garlic, having tops like our garden top-onions, and wild leek are common in low places not pastured.

Rush Family.—The bog-rush is a very common, yellowish, grass-like herb along roads and paths, especially those leading through the forest ; but it is also found to some extent in all other situations.

Pickerel-weed Family.—Water star-grass, growing under running water in the forest brooks, is common.

Spiderworts.—Common spiderwort is common.

Sedges.—There are three or four dozen species of sedge growing within the limits of any one county, but they are all unimportant plants. They have a grass-like appearance, but can readily be distinguished from the grasses by their having triangular stems and bur-like tops (seed clusters), while the grasses have round or roundish stems. What is generally called lake grass along the rivers is a true sedge, and its English name is great bulrush. It is by far the largest of the sedges. The river club-rush is next in size.

Grasses.—Blue grass takes the lead for prevalence and utility. Next, two species of fox-tail. Besides these the most common grasses are white grass, rice cut grass, Indian rice or water oats, timothy, rush grass (two species), bent grass, wood reed-grass, dropseed (two genera); reed bent-grass, blue joint grass, porcupine grass, fresh-water cord-grass, Koeleria, Eatonia (two species), melic grass, fowl meadow grass and its congener, Glyceria fluitans, low spear-grass, red top, Eragrostis (three species), fescue (two species), chess, Bromus ciliatus, reed (a tall, broom-corn-like grass growing in dense fields in the swamps of the river bottom), hordeum pratense (a kind of wild barley), two species of lyme-grass or wild rye, bottle-brush grass, reed canary grass, Paspalum, wire grass, eight species of panic-grass, among them two kinds of tickle-grass and one old-witch grass, crab-grass and barn-yard grass, sand-bur (in sand) and two species of beard-grass. About two dozen other kinds of grass can be found in the county, but they are all very rare.

Horse-tails.—Scouring rush and common horse-tail (especially along railroads) are common : two other species scarce.

Ferns.—Maiden-hair, brake, a spleenwort, a shield fern, a bladder-fern and the sensitive fern are common in the order here named, while one species of flowering fern and two or three other ferns may be found.

CHAPTER VIII.

ARCHÆOLOGY.

Perhaps no district of country in the West contains more traces of that pre-historic people known to us only as the "Mound-Builders" than the district between the Illinois and the Mississippi rivers. There is scarcely a township of land in this section which does not contain more or less of these traces, and in some of them are works which in extent and character will compare with any in the West.

The mounds in this county are evidently of three classes : sacred mounds, which were used for the sacrificial fires; burial mounds, which were erected over the last remains of important personages; and mounds which were used for domestic habitations. These were probably residences similar to those of some tribes of our present Indians. First, poles or logs set up in a circle, then covered with brush or grass, and the whole with earth to a considerable extent. The sacrificial mounds always contained burnt earth, burnt bones, and frequently, too, the charred bones of human beings. In the burial mounds only the bones of a few persons are found, probably of some chief and his immediate family, and usually near them are utensils of the kitchen, arrows, pottery, and such articles as were most prized in life by the departed.

In some localities immense shell-heaps exist, while it is not uncommon to find in the mounds shells from the sea, notably the conch-shell and sea-periwinkles, the latter very common. Implements of both hardened copper and copper in a soft state are often found, and a metal resembling iron in texture and color, but hard enough to cut glass and which resists the action of almost all the acids.

That these mounds were not erected by the same race as our present Indians is at once apparent from the bones of the latter being of a reddish hue, while those of the Mound-Builders are of a different shade and much larger.

It is our opinion that the Mound-Builders were a pastoral people, who had made considerable progress in civilization. In the winter, doubtless, they drove their flocks and herds to the bluffs and rich, sheltered bottoms where they could obtain shelter, and in the summer they drove them to the prairies for pasturage. Doubtless, like the Chinese of to-day, they esteemed their native hills sacred and sought to be buried there, no matter where the iron hand of Death overtook them; and their friends, respecting this desire, were in the habit of bringing the bones of each family or tribe to these sacred burial places, after they had been stripped of their flesh, for permanent burial.

Perhaps some future archæologist will delve among these ruins and find a key to the mystery of the Builders, of whom we to-day know next to nothing; and unless some means are taken by the Government or societies organized for the purpose, and these measures at no distant day, they will have become so far obliterated by the plow and by unskilled diggers that the slight clues they contain will be buried in oblivion greater than now enshrouds the history of their builders.

A few years ago some of the prominent gentlemen of Pike county interested themselves in organizing an "Archæological Society," but of late the interest seems to have abated very perceptibly, and the Society so enthusiastically organized can now scarcely be said to be in existence.

The gentlemen proposing to organize an "Antiquarian Society" met at the court-house in Pittsfield, May 24, 1873, when Dr. T. Worthington was called to the chair and R. H. Criswell appointed secretary. They organized the "Pike County Antiquarian Society," and the permanent officers elected at this meeting were, President—Wm. A. Grimshaw; Vice Presidents—Wm. McAdams, Esq., Dr. E. S. Hull, of Madison county, Capt. W. H. Reed, of Calhoun county, Dr. T. Worthington, of Pike, Dr. A. Mittower, of Pike, Richard Perry, of Pike, H. J. Harris, of Pike, C. L. Obst, of Pittsfield, Archæologist Artist; Dr. Thos. Aiton, Secretary; Wm. R. Archer, Treasurer.

W. B. Grimes, Dr. Mittower and C. L. Obst were appointed a committee to solicit contributions to the cabinet of the Society, and invite the exhibition of such relics as owners are unwilling to part with, the object being to obtain possession of evidences and traces of the people of antiquity, their implements and usages as far as practicable.

A letter was read before the Society from Mr. McAdams, of Waterville, Jersey county, May 18, 1873, as follows:

"I see in the papers a call for a meeting in Pittsfield on the 24th inst., to organize a society with a view of further investigation and more perfect knowledge of relics and ancient remains near the Illinois and Mississippi rivers. I have for the last 15 years, during my leisure hours, been making some investigations of the mounds and tumuli of Jersey and Calhoun counties. There is not perhaps in all the West a section richer or more interesting in its great numbers of relics of an almost unknown race of people who once inhabited this country. No thorough investigation has been made. Already many of them have been destroyed by the cultivation of new fields. Before many years the majority of them will be obliterated, or so defaced that the original plan of construction will be lost. There should be a society like the one you propose to organize, not only for the purpose of investigation but also for the purpose of making some record of their work. Comparatively little is known of the mounds of Jersey and Calhoun, although I have visited many of them and collected quite a number of interesting relics.   Yours truly,

"WM. MCADAMS."

The second week in June, 1873, the Society made an excursion to the southern part of the county and spent several days among the numerous mounds in that locality, where they found many relics of the aborigines, among which were arrow heads, fish-spears, stone knives and hatchets, earthen vessels of various kinds, copper kettles, stone pipes, shell and copper beads, silver ear-rings, silver buckles, etc. Nearly all these articles were found imbedded in the mounds with human bones, pieces of pottery, etc., generally at a depth of about three feet below the surface. In some cases stone vaults containing bones and other relics were discovered a few feet beneath the surface. The members of the Society who went on that excursion say they had a most enjoyable trip and consider themselves well repaid for their trouble.

In the summer of 1873, Col. D. B. Bush presented to the Society for its museum Indian trappings of great value. Thos. James, of Martinsburg, presented a large lot of beautiful beads and amulets from the Big Mound of Sacramento valley, Cal.; also, moss, peat, cinnabar and Chinese corn, etc.—all from California. Col. S. S. Thomas presented a rare and beautiful specimen of *coquine* and concrete shells from St. Augustine, Florida. In September of the same year, Col. A. C. Matthews contributed to the museum one beaked saw-fish (*Pristis*) from Matagorda Island, Texas; autograph letter of Henry Clay, dated Oct. 5, 1829, Ashland, Ky.; pass of Lieut. Gen. S. B. Buckner, C. S. A.; one copy of army correspondence; also coin and fossils. Geo. H. French presented a stone mortar from Pilot Bluff, Illinois river; E. N. French, specimens of columnar limestone; Hon. J. M. Bush presented one copy of the *Massachusetts Centennial*, published at Boston, Sept. 5, 1789, about four months after the inauguration of President Washington; Hon. W. A. Grimshaw presented books as follows: American volume, Ancient Armeca; Lines of Humboldt; two volumes of Smithsonian Institute Reports, 1865–'6; two volumes of History of Wisconsin; stone and flint implements, bone needle and specimens of pottery. Patrick Halpin presented specimens of American and Italian marble.

In December, Mr. R. Perry contributed specimens of silicious and ferruginous conglomerate; Dr. A. McFarland, a very nice human skeleton, five bottles containing in alcohol specimens of ophidian, all indigenous to Pike county, and also one containing tænia; Thos. Williams, seven beautiful flint implements; and N. W. Kibler, a very large tooth of a pachyderm.

Feb. 21, 1874, Geo. Bell, Thos. Bloomer, Hiram Horton and G. S. Pennington found remains of five human skeletons in the Mississippi bluffs on the farm of Mrs. L. B. Lyon at the mouth of Dutch creek hollow. One skull measured 26 inches from the top of the cranium around under the lower jaw. Indeed, many more skeletons are in these bluffs. Several wagon-loads of rock had been thrown over these remains. The heads appeared to be laid toward a common center of about three feet space. One skull contained a rock which had doubtless been thrown there when the remains were buried. The bones were very brittle and difficult to secure in their integrity from among the roots. There are seven of these mounds in Mr. Horton's field, in a semi-circle, all containing human remains. Also a species of pottery has been found there.

In the southeast part of Pearl township about a mile from the Illinois river two copper vessels were once found, one smaller than the other, under some flat stones which had been plowed up, and a little lower down stone coffins were found in a field where they had been plowing; but these "remains" were probably left there by early French explorers.

Mr. C. L. Obst, photographer in Pittsfield, who is a fine archæologist and the virtual founder of the "Pike County Antiquarian Society," has a splendid collection; namely, 100 varieties of flint implements, four varieties of stone hatchets, four of wedges, varieties of stone disks of various materials, as iron ore, sandstone, granite and greenstone, four varieties of plummets, mostly iron ore, two of hammers, pestles, round stone for clubs, eight kinds of pipes, iron ore and greenstone chisels, plowshares and hoes, a large variety of pottery, drills and mortars, bone of the pre-historic bison, sinkers, weights, etc., etc. Mr. Obst has also a good collection of geological specimens.

The museum of the Society is in the Public Library room over the postoffice in Pittsfield, but the association is not active at present and their collection of relics seems neglected.

CHAPTER IX.

IMPORTANT LABORS OF THE BOARD OF SUPERVISORS.

COUNTY COURT.

In 1847 a State election was held for members of the Constitutional Convention, which Convention prepared and submitted to the people a new Constitution, which was adopted by a large majority. By this Constitution, in place of the Commissioners' Court a County Court was organized in each county. This Court consisted of a County Judge, and, if the Legislature saw proper to so order it, two Associate Justices. This the Legislature favorably acted upon. The last meeting of the County Commissioners' Court was held November, 1849. After the transaction of such business as properly came before them, they adjourned until court in course, but never re-assembled.

On the first Monday of December of the same year the first regular term of the County Court was held. The duties of the Court in a legislative capacity were precisely the same as those of the County Commissioners' Court. In addition to the legislative power the members of this Court were permitted to exercise judicial authority, having all the rights and privileges of Justices of the Peace, together with all probate business. This Court consisted of a County Judge and two Associate Justices. The Judge and Associate Justices acted together for the transaction of all county business, but none other. The Justices had an equal vote with the Judge, and received the same salary while holding Court, which was $2 per day. Two of the three constituted a quorum.

The County Judge who served under this regime was James Ward. The Associate Justices were Joshua Woosley and William P. Harpole.

TOWNSHIP ORGANIZATION.

The Constitution of 1847 provided for township organization in those counties desiring it. (Hons. Wm. R. Archer and Wm. A. Grimshaw, both of this county, were members of the Convention framing this Constitution.) The question of organizing according to this provision soon began, of course, to agitate the people of Pike county, and the controversy grew bitter,—the bitterest indeed that this more than usually peaceful community ever indulged in. Immigrants from the East were familiar with the workings of township legislation and management, and desired to perpetuate their home institution in the West; but the other citizens of the county were afraid that the introduction of the measure would necessitate an increase of office holders, useless expenses and many unforeseen vexations. The Judges in office were all opposed to the innovation,—so much so indeed that they continued to hold Court even after the great victory of the innovators in carrying the county by 1,563 votes against 317, and the election of new members. For a short time the county had two legislatures at once. The vote was taken at the general election of November 6, 1849, at which election Peter V. Shankland was elected County Clerk on this hotly contested issue, and Stephen R. Gray Sheriff. Both these gentlemen were Democrats, in favor of township organization. Indeed, as a matter of curiosity, but of no political significance, we may state that the fight on both sides was nearly all done by the Democrats, the Whigs taking but little part.

An election was held in November, 1849, to vote " for " or "against " township organization, which resulted in favor of the measure. This was met with bitter opposition however, and an appeal was taken to the Circuit Court by Samuel L. Crane. The law was decided to be constitutional, and the election a fair one.

The Board of Supervisors of Pike county first assembled April 8, 1850, this being one of the first counties in the State to organize under the township mode.

There were present at this meeting the following members: Montgomery Blair, Barry; Hazen Pressy, Washington; Archibald Brooks, Chambersburg; David Preble, Salem; Wilson Adams, Hardin; Wm. Ross, Newburg; Thos. Hull, Kinderhook; A. W. Bemis, Martinsburg; R. C. Robertson, Milton; James M. Seeley, Atlas, and John McTucker, Hadley. Supervisor Blair was elected temporary Chairman and Col. Ross chosen Chairman. The Board then adjourned to re-assemble April 23, 1850. There were present at this the second meeting the following gentlemen: Wm. Ross; Archibald Brooks; Darius Dexter, Perry; Amos Hill, Griggsville; David Preble; John McTucker; Montgomery Blair; Jesse Seniff, Detroit; Thomas Hull; A. W. Bemis; J. M. Seeley; J. T. Hyde, Pittsfield; R. C. Robertson; Wilson Adams; Hazen Pressy; and James Talbot, Pleasant Vale.

The County Court, when in session in 1849, appointed a committee to divide the county into townships. This committee made their report to the Board of Supervisors, which is as follows:

" We, the undersigned, Commissioners appointed by the honorable the County Court at the December term, 1849, to divide Pike county into towns or townships pursuant to the declared wish of the citizens of said county, decided by a majority of votes given for and against township organization at an election held on Tuesday

after the first Monday in November, 1849, under and by authority
of an act to provide for township and county organization, and may
organize whenever a majority of votes of said county at any general election shall so determine, respectfully report that, after mature deliberation and hearing the views and consulting the wishes
of the people through delegations appointed by the different precincts, they have unanimously agreed upon the following division
boundaries and names, and report the same as organized :

"JOHN LYSTER,
"S. R. GRAY,
"JOHN K. CLEVELAND.

"Commencing at the northeastern corner of the county and
making fractional townships 3 s., 1 and 2 w., a town by the name
of Chambersburg; Congressional township 3 s., 3 w., Perry; 3 s.,
4 w., Fairmount; 4 s., 7 w., and fractional of 4 s. and 8 w., Kinderhook; 4 s., 6 w., Barry; 4 s., 5 w., Hadley; 4 s., 4 w., New
Salem; 4 s., 3 w., Griggsville; fractional township 4 s., 2 w., Flint;
fractional township 5 s., 2 w., Detroit; Congressional township 5 s.,
2 w., Newburg; 5 s., 4 w., Pittsfield; 5 s., 5 w., Washington; 5 s.,
6 w., and the fractional townships 5 s., 7 w., and 5 s., 8 w., and 6
s., 7 w., Pleasant Vale; 6 s., 5 w., 6 s., 6 w., 7 s., 5 w. and 7 s., 8
w., Atlas; 6 s., 4 w., Martinsburg; 6 s., 3 w., Hardin; 6 s., 2 w.,
Milton; fractional township 7 s., 2 w., Pearl; 7 s., 3 w., Spring
Creek; and 7 s., 4 w., Pleasant Hill."

Subsequently the Board of Supervisors were notified by the
State Auditor that the names of Washington and Milton must be
changed, owing to other townships in the State bearing those
names. On motion of Supervisor Robertson the name of Milton
was changed to Montezuma; and on motion of Supervisor Pressly
that of Washington to Derry.

In 1876 the fractional part of township 4 s., 8 w., and heretofore
a part of Kinderhook township was organized into a separate township and named Levee. In 1879 that part of Atlas township in
town 7 s., 5 w., was organized into a separate township and named
Ross.

JAIL.

At the April meeting, 1863, the Board of Supervisors resolved
to build a new jail, the cost of which should not exceed $15,000. Su-
pervisors Gray, Dimmitt, Smitherman, Roberts, Dennis, Adams
and Shields were appointed a committee to carry out the decisions
of the Board, and they authorized a sub-committee to visit jails of
other counties and procure plans and specifications for consideration
and adoption by the above committee; and also with full power to
appoint, if they see proper, a sub-committee as acting superintend-
ents of the erection of said building; and also the said committee
was given power to dispose of the old part of the present jail, together with the lot, and to purchase a more suitable lot whereon to
erect the new building.

At a meeting held Tuesday, Sept. 16, 1863, Supervisor Dennis offered a resolution to increase the appropriation for the building of the jail and Sheriff's residence from $15,000 to $25,000. Supervisor Hollis moved that the appropriation be $20,000. His motion was lost, and Mr. Dennis' was adopted.

The jail building, of which we give a cut in this volume, was completed in due time, and now stands an honor to the county.

SUPERVISORS.

Below we give a full list of all the Supervisors from the time the county was organized under the township law till the present time, by years, together with the name of the chairman and the township each member is from:

1850.

William Ross, Newburg, *Chairman.*

Archibald Brooks, Chambersburg.
Darius Dexter, Perry.
Amos Hill, Griggsville.
David Preble, New Salem.
John McTucker, Hadley.
Montgomery Blair, Barry.
Jesse Seniff, Detroit.
Thomas Hull, Kinderhook.
A. W. Bemis, Martinsburg.
J. M. Seeley, Atlas.

J. F. Hyde, Pittsfield.
R. C. Robertson, Milton (Montezuma).
Wilson Adams, Hardin.
Hazen Pressy, Washington, Derry.
James Talbot, Pleasant Vale.
William Turnbull, Flint.
William Morrison, Fairmount.
Thomas Barton, Pleasant Hill.
J. P. Stark, Spring Creek.

1851.

William Ross, Newburg, *Chairman.*

Amos Hill, Griggsville.
Thomas Odiorne, Atlas.
Hazen Pressy, Derry.
William Morrison, Fairmount.
William Turnbull Flint.
Thomas Barton, Pleasant Hill.
William Grammar, Hadley.
John Lyster. Detroit.
Worden Willis, Pleasant Vale.
Montgomery Blair, Barry.

Darius Dexter, Perry.
D. H. Gilmer, Pittsfield.
R. C. Robertson, Montezuma.
William Adams, Hardin.
Harvey W. McClintock, Martinsburg.
David Preble, New Salem.
J. P. Stark, Spring Creek.
Thomas Hull, Kinderhook.
Constantine Smith, Pearl.
Peter Karges, Chambersburg.

1852.

H. R. Ramsay, Atlas, *Chairman.*

James Brown, Chambersburg.
Darius Dexter, Perry.
David Preble, New Salem.
John E. Ayres, Fairmount.
M. B. Churchill, Kinderhook.
S. K. Taylor, Derry.
D. H. Gilmer, Pittsfield.
M. J. Noyes.
Amos Hill, Grigsville.
John Lyster, Detroit.

William Turnbull, Flint.
H. W. McClintock, Martinsburg.
E. C. Thurman, Pleasant Hill.
William Grammar, Hadley.
B. F. Brownell, Barry.
S. Grigsby. Pleasant Vale.
Richard Robertson, Montezuma.
A. Main, Hardin.
. ohn P. Stark, Spring Creek.

1853.

William Turnbull, *Chairman.*

James Brown, Chambersburg.
William Dustin, Atlas.
Daniel Fisher, New Salem.
Thomas Hull, Kinderhook.
Harlow Huntley, Hadley.
Tyre Jennings, Barry.
B. L. Matthews Perry.
H. T. Mudd, Pittsfield.
Constantine Smith, Pearl.

William E. Smith, Spring Creek.
Cornelius Sullivan, Martinsburg.
Jonathan Frye, Detroit.
Dennis Leary, Montezuma.
William Kinman, Griggsville.
Samuel G. Sitton, Hardin.
William C. Crawford, Fairmount.
L. H. Stone, Pleasant Hill.
F. A. Landrum, Derry.

1854.

J. S. Roberts, Martinsburg, *Chairman.*

James Brown, Chambersburg.
Calvin Greenleaf, Flint.
Jonathan Frye, Detroit.
Dennis Leary, Montezuma.
Constantine Smith, Pearl.
B. L. Matthews, Perry.
James Winn, Griggsville.
B. F. Westlake, Newburg.
John Heavener, Hardin.
Wm. E. Smith, Spring Creek.

Daniel Fisher, New Salem.
Henry T. Mudd, Pittsfield.
L. H. Stone, Pleasant Hill.
Wm. Grammar, Hadley.
Jethro Petty, Derry.
Wm. Dustin, Atlas.
Tyre Jennings, Barry.
Charles T. Brewster, Pleasant Vale.
S. B. Gaines, Kinderhook.
Wm. C. Crawford, Fairmount.

1855.

B. F. Westlake, Newburg, *Chairman.*

John Loer, Chambersburg.
Wm. Thackwray, Flint.
D. Leary, Montezuma.
Constantine Smith, Pearl.
B. L. Matthews, Perry.
James Winn, Griggsville.
Wilson Adams, Hardin.
Wm. C. Smith, Spring Creek.
Wm. C. Crawford, Fairmount.
Daniel Fisher, New Salem.
H. T. Mudd, Pittsfield.

John S. Roberts. Martinsburg.
John Ray, Pleasant Hill.
Joseph P. Smith, Hadley.
J. S. Vertrees, Perry.
Simon K. Taylor, Derry.
Tyre Jennings, Barry.
Thos. Odiorne, Atlas.
Charles T. Brewster, Pleasant Vale.
S. B. Gaines, Kinderhook.
R. C. Allen, Detroit.
Nicholas Hobbes, Fairmount.

1856.

J. S. Roberts, Martinsburg, *Chairman.*

John Loer, Chambersburg.
Jonathan Frye, Detroit.
Wm. Wheeler, Pearl.
O. M. Hatch, Griggsville.
Joseph G. Colvin, Hardin.
Wm. H. Love, Fairmount.
Daniel D. Hicks, Pittsfield.
Alex. Hemphill, Pleasant Hill.
Josiah Long, Atlas.
Daniel Pyle, Flint.

Edwin Wooley, Montezuma.
John L. Gaine, Perry.
B. F. Westlake, Newburg.
Wm. E. Smith, Spring Creek.
Wm. F. Hooper, New Salem.
Richard Hayes, Hadley.
James Wallace, Pleasant Vale.
A. Landrum, Derry.
John P. Grubb, Barry.

1857.

John W. Allen, Detroit, *Chairman.*

B. B. Metz, Chambersburg.
Joseph G. Pyle, Flint.
Spencer Hudson, Montezuma.
Constantine Smith, Pearl.

Wm. F. Hooker, New Salem.
Daniel D. Hicks, Pittsfield.
Joshua Butler, Martinsburg.
Alex. Hemphill, Pleasant Hill.

Thos. Reynolds, Perry.
Alfred Gordon, Griggsville.
B. F. Westlake, Newburg.
J. G. Colvin, Hardin.
John H. Brewer, Fairmount.
Wm. E. Smith, Spring Creek.

Richard Hayes, Hadley.
John L. Underwood, Derry.
Jesse Long, Atlas.
J. R. Williams, Barry.
James Wallace, Pleasant Vale.
M. B. Churchill, Kinderhook.

1858.

Wm. Turnbull, Flint, *Chairman.*

Harvey Dunn, Chambersburg.
Jonathan Frye, Detroit.
E. N. French, Montezuma.
Hiram Hess, Pearl.
Thos. Reynolds, Perry.
James Winn, Griggsville.
B. F. Westlake, Newburg.
Adam Puterbaugh, Hardin.
Wm. E. Smith, Spring Creek.
John H. Brewer, Fairmount.

Thos. Gray, New Salem.
Austin Barber, Pittsfield.
Joshua Butler, Martinsburg.
John G. Sitton, Pleasant Hill.
Wm. Grammar, Hadley.
John L. Underwood, Derry.
Sherman Brown, Atlas.
James B. Williams, Barry.
James Wallace, Pleasant Vale.
A. T. Love, Kinderhook.

1859.

John S. Roberts, Martinsburg, *Chairman.*

Wilson S. Dennis, Chambersburg.
James L. Thompson, Flint.
Jonathan Frye, Detroit.
Isaac S. Brown, Montezuma.
Constantine Smith, Pearl.
B. L. Matthews, Perry.
James Winn, Griggsville.
Benj. F. Westlake, Newburg.
Wilson Adams, Hardin.
Wm. E. Smith, Spring Creek.

John Vail Fairmount.
James C. Conkright, New Salem.
Isaac W. Jones, Pittsfield.
Thos. Barney, Pleasant Hill.
Wm. Grammar, Hadley.
Simon K. Taylor, Derry.
Sherman Brown, Atlas.
Richard St. John, Barry.
James Wallace, Pleasant Vale.
John G. Wheelock, Kinderhook.

1860.

John S. Roberts, Martinsburg, *Chairman.*

James H. Dennis, Chambersburg.
Jas. L. Thompson, Flint.
John W. Allen, Detroit.
E. C. Clemmons, Montezuma.
Hiram Hess, Pearl.
James Johns, Perry.
T. H. Dimmitt, Griggsville.
B. F. Westlake, Newburg.
J. C. Colvin, ardin.
Wm. E. Smith, Spring Creek.

John Vail, Fairmount.
Jas. C. Conkright, New Salem.
David A. Stanton, Pittsfield.
Alex. Parker, Pleasant Hill.
Wm. Grammar, Hadley.
James B. Landrum, Derry.
Sherman Brown, Atlas.
Lewis D. White, Barry.
Harrison Brown, Pleasant Hill.
John G. Wheelock, Kinderhook.

1861.

John S. Roberts, Martinsburg, *Chairman.*

J. H. Dennis, Chambersburg.
Geo. H. Sanford, Flint.
John W. Allen, Detroit.
Wm. B. Grimes, Montezuma.
Andrew N. Hess, Pearl.
Geo. W. Baldwin, Perry.
Thos. H. Dimmitt, Griggsville.
B. F. Westlake, Newburg.
Jos. G. Colvin, Hardin.
Wm. E. Smith, Spring Creek.

John Vail, Fairmount.
A. J. McWilliams, New Salem.
D. A. Stanton, Pittsfield.
A. J. Lovell, Pleasant Hill.
Wm. Grammar, Hadley.
Isaac Pryor, Perry.
J. G. Adams, Atlas.
John McTucker, Barry.
Perry H. Davis, Pleasant Vale.
John Aron, Kinderhook.

1862.

John S. Roberts, Martinsburg, *Chairman.*

James H. Dennis, Chambersburg.
Geo. H. Sanford, Flint.
Jonathan Frye, Detroit.
Geo. Underwood, Montezuma.
Andrew N. Hess, Pearl,
James W. Brown, Perry.
T. H. Dimmitt, Griggsville.
B. F. Westlake, Newburg.
J. G. Colvin, Hardin.
Wm. E. Smith, Spring Creek.

Wm. Morrison, Fairmount.
A. J. McWilliams, New Salem.
D. A. Stanton, Pittsfield.
L. H. Stone, Pleasant Hill.
Wm. Grammar, Hadley.
J. B. Landrum, Derry.
J. G. Adams, Atlas.
Henry Wallace, Barry.
P. H. Davis, Pleasant Vale.
John Aron, Kinderhook.

1863.

John S. Roberts, Martinsburg, *Chairman.*

James H. Dennis, Chambersburg.
Wm. Thackwray, Flint.
L. J. Smitherman, Detroit.
J. O. Bolin, Montezuma.
A. N. Hess, Pearl.
Augustus Akin, Perry.
T. H. Dimmitt, Griggsville.
Strother Grigsby, Newburg.
B. F. Westlake, Newburg.
J. G. Colvin, Hardin.
D. Hollis, Spring Creek.

Wm. Morrison, Fairmount.
A. J. McWilliams, New Salem.
S. R. Gray, Pittsfield.
A. Hemphill, Pleasant Hill.
Wm. Grammar, Hadley.
Thos. Harris, Derry.
J. G. Adams, Atlas.
Wm. P. Shields, Barry.
J. R. Thomas. Pleasant Vale.
John Aron, Kinderhook.

1864.

James H. Dennis, Chambersburg, *Chairman.*

Wm. Thackwray, Flint.
L. J. Smitherman, Detroit.
E. N. French, Montezuma.
A. N. Hess, Pearl.
Harvey Dunn, Jr., Perry.
Thos. H. Dimmitt, Griggsville.
Nathan Kelley, Newburg.
B. C. Lindsay, Hardin.
David Hollis, Spring Creek.
John Vail, Fairmount.

John Preble, New Salem.
N. A. Wells, Pittsfield.
J. S. Roberts, Martinsburg.
Alex. Hemphill, Pleasant Hill.
Wm. Grammar, Hadley.
Thos. S. Harris, Derry.
J. G. Adams, Atlas.
Wm. P. Shields, Barry.
James Wallace, Pleasant Vale.
John G. Wheelock, Kinderhook.

1865.

P. H. Davis, Pleasant Vale, *Chairman.*

Jas. H. Dennis, Chambersburg.
Wm. Turnbull, Flint.
L. J. Smitherman, Detroit.
Robert E. Gilliland, Montezuma.
A. N. Hess, Pearl.
John E. Morton, Perry.
T. H. Dimmitt, Griggsville.
Wm. J Ross, Jr., Newburg.
Samuel Heavener, Hardin,
David Hollis, Spring Creek.

John Vail, Fairmount.
Asahel Hinman, New Salem.
J. M. Bush, Pittsfield.
David Roberts, Martinsburg.
Alex. Hemphill, Pleasant Hill.
Wm. Grammar, Hadley.
Albert Landrum, Derry.
Wm Dustin, Atlas.
Wm. P. Shields, Barry.
John G. Wheelock, Kinderhook.

1866.

James H. Dennis, Chambersburg, *Chairman.*

William Turnbull, Flint.
L. J. Smitherman, Detroit.
George Marks, Montezuma.

James M. Ferry, Pittsfield.
R. A. McClintock, Martinsburg,
A. F. Hemphill, Pleasant Hill.

Joshua Hanks, Pearl.
John E. Morton. Perry.
T. H. Dimmitt, Griggsville.
Strother Grigsby, Newburg.
David Hollis, Spring Creek.
John Vail, Fairmount.
John Preble, New Salem.

William Grammar, Hadley.
Albert Landrum, Derry.
J. G. Adams, Atlas.
William M. P. Shields, Barry.
James Wallace, Pleasant Vale.
R. M. Murray, Kinderhook.

1867.

James H. Dennis, Chambersburg, *Chairman*.

James L. Thompson, Flint.
L. J. Smitherman, Detroit.
John O. Bolin, Montezuma.
Joshua Hanks, Pearl.
John A. Morton, Perry.
Thomas H. Dimmitt, Griggsville,
Strother Grigsby, Newburg.
Jos. G. Colvin, Hardin.
David Hollis, Spring Creek.
John Vail, Fairmount.

John Preble, New Salem.
George W. Jones, Pittsfield.
William M. McClintock, Martinsburg.
A. F. Hemphill, Pleasant Hill.
William Grammar, Hadley.
Albert Landrum, Derry.
J. G. Adams, Atlas.
M. Blair, Barry.
Perry H. Davis, Pleasant Vale.
Thomas McIntire, Kinderhook.

1868.

James H. Dennis, Chambersburg, *Chairman*.

William Anderson, Flint.
John W. Allen, Detroit.
James A. Brown, Montezuma.
Joshua Hanks, Pearl.
Harvey Thornbury, Perry.
T. H. Dimmitt, Griggsville.
Strother Grigsby, Newburg.
John C. Dinsmore, Hardin.
F. J. Halford, Spring Creek.
John Vail, Fairmount.

John Preble, New Salem.
George W. Jones, Pittsfield.
John Melton, Martinsburg.
William Grammar, Hadley.
Albert Landrum, Derry.
Montgomery Blair, Barry.
P. H. Davis, Pleasant Vale.
A. J. Lovell, Pleasant Hill.
J. G. Adams, Atlas.
R M. Murray, Kinderhook.

1869.

George W. Jones, Pittsfield, *Chairman*.

James H. Dennis, Chambersburg.
William Anderson, Flint.
John Lyster, Detroit.
James A. Brown, Montezuma.
David Hess, Pearl.
B. L. Matthews, Perry.
Noah Divilbiss, Perry.
T. H. Dimmitt, Griggsville.
B. F. Westlake, Newburg.
B. C. Lindsay, Hardin.
Frank J. Halford, Spring Creek.

T. M. Coss, Fairmount.
John Preble, New Salem.
Joseph Turnbaugh, Martinsburg.
J. B. Harl, Pleasant Hill.
William Grammar, Hadley.
Maberry Evans, Derry.
A. Simpkins, Atlas.
Montgomery Blair, Barry.
P. H. Davis, Pleasant Hill.
John Aron, Kinderhook.

1870.

George W. Jones, Pittsfield, *Chairman*.

Lewis Ham, Chambersburg.
William Anderson, Flint.
Samuel Hayden, Detroit.
James A. Brown, Montezuma.
George W. Roberts, Pearl.
B. L. Matthews, Perry.
T. H. Dimmitt, Griggsville.
Thompson J. Pulliam, Newburg.
Alvin Petty, Hardin.
F. J. Halford, Spring Creek.

Taylor M. Coss, Fairmount.
John Preble, New Salem.
John Brittain, Martinsburg.
A. J. Lovell, Pleasant Hill.
J. W. Burke, Derry.
William Dustin, Atlas.
M. Blair, Barry.
P. H. Davis, Pleasant Vale.
John Clutch, Kinderhook.

J. H. Strubinger

DERRY TP

1871.

George W. Jones, Pittsfield, *Chairman.*

Lewis Ham, Chambersburg.
William Anderson, Flint.
B. W. Flynn, Detroit.
James A. Brown, Montezuma.
George W. Roberts, Pearl.
Thomas Reynolds, Perry.
James McWilliams, Griggsville.
T. G. Pulliam, Newburg.
Francis Frye, Hardin.
T. J. Halford, Spring Creek.

William Morrison, Fairmount.
John Preble, New Salem.
Hardin Goodin, Martinsburg.
A. J. Lovell, Pleasant Hill.
William Grammar, Hadley.
William Dustin, Atlas.
James W. Burke, Derry.
Calvin Davis, Barry.
M. D. Massie, Pleasant Vale.
John Clutch, Kinderhook.

1872.

George W. Jones, Pittsfield, *Chairman.*

Lewis Ham, Chambersburg.
B. W. Flynn, Detroit.
William T. Dugdell, Montezuma.
G. W. Roberts, Pearl.
Thomas Reynolds, Perry.
James McWilliams, Griggsville.
Strother Grigsby, Newburg.
Francis Frye, Hardin.
David Hollis, Spring Creek.
William Corey, Fairmount.

John Preble, New Salem.
William Fowler, Martinsburg.
A. J. Lovell, Pleasant Hill.
William Grammar, Hadley.
J. W. Burke, Derry.
William Dustin, Atlas.
Calvin Davis, Barry.
M. D. Massie, Pleasant Vale.
John Clutch, Kinderhook.

1873.

Lewis Ham, Pittsfield, *Chairman.*

David Pyle, Flint.
B. W. Flynn, Detroit.
Milton Grimes, Montezuma.
George W. Roberts, Pearl.
Thomas Reynolds, Perry.
James McWilliams, Griggsville.
P. H. Cooper, Newburg.
Wright Hicks, Hardin.
F. J. Halford, Spring Creek.
William Corey, Fairmount.

Addison Cadwell, New Salem.
Lewis Dutton, Pittsfield.
William Fowler, Martinsburg.
A. J. Lovell, Pleasant Hill.
William Grammar, Hadley.
Thomas H. Coley, Derry.
Josiah Long, Atlas.
John P. Grubb, Barry.
John Horn, Pleasant Vale.
John Clutch, Kinderhook.

1874.

James H. Dennis, Chambersburg, *Chairman.*

William Turnbull, Flint.
William Douglas, Detroit.
A. J. Worcester, Montezuma.
Andrew N. Hess, Pearl.
Thomas Reynolds, Perry.
James McWilliams, Griggsville.
Nathan Kelley, Newburg.
Wright Hicks, Hardin.
C. C. Melton, Spring Creek.
William Corey, Fairmount.

Addison Cadwell, New Salem.
Lewis Dutton, Pittsfield.
Francis Fowler, Martinsburg.
A. J. Lovell, Pleasant Hill.
William Grammar, Hadley.
Maberry Evans, Derry.
J. G. Adams, Atlas.
Calvin Davis, Barry.
John B. Horn, Pleasant Vale.
John Clutch, Kinderhook.

1875.

William B. Grimes, Pittsfield, *Chairman.*

J. L. Metz, Chambersburg.
Austin Wade, Flint.
Henry Moler, Detroit.
A. J. Worcester, Montezuma.

Addison Cadwell, New Salem.
Thomas Aiton, Martinsburg.
A. J. Lovell, Pleasant Hill.
William Grammar, Hadley.

20

D. W. Miller, Pearl.
Thomas Reynolds, Perry.
James McWilliams, Griggsville.
J. H. Farrington, Hardin.
C. C. Melton, Spring Creek.
R. B. McLaughlin, Fairmount.

Maberry Evans, Derry.
J. G. Adams, Atlas.
Alex. White, Barry.
M. D. Massie, Pleasant Vale.
William Ross, Newburg.
R. M. Murray, Kinderhook.

1876.

A. J. Worcester, Montezuma, *Chairman.*

J. L. Metz, Chambersburg.
Joseph Wilson, Flint.
Henry Moler, Detroit.
G. W. Roberts, Pearl.
Z. Wade, Perry.
George Pratt, Griggsville.
C. P. Chapman, Newburg.
R. R. Pollock, Spring Creek.
R. B. McLaughlin, Fairmount.
Addison Cadwell, New Salem.
Wm. B. Grimes, Pittsfield.

Thomas Aiton, Martinsburg.
A. J. Lovell, Pleasant Hill.
William Grammar, Hadley.
Maberry Evans, Derry.|
Samuel Taylor, Atlas.
W. F. White, Barry.
R. M. Murray, Kinderhook.
John W. Brammell, Pleasant Vale.
J. H. Farrington, Hardin.
F. A. Douglas, Levee.

1877.

J. W. Burke, Derry, *Chairman.*

George Ham, Chambersburg.
Joseph Wilson, Flint.
David Stoner, Detroit.
Charles E. Bolin Montezuma.
A. N. Hess, Pearl.
Z. Wade, Perry.
George Pratt, Griggsville.
C. P. Chapman, Newburg.
Wright Hicks, Hardin.
W. R. Wilson, Spring Creek.
R. B. McLaughlin, Fairmount.

Addison Cadwell, New Salem.
Lewis Dutton, Pittsfield.
William Fowler, Martinsburg.
John S. Lockwood, Pleasant Vale.
William Grammar Hadley.
Samuel Taylor, Atlas.
W. F. White, Barry.
F. L. Zernberg, Pleasant Hill.
R. M. Murray, Kinderhook.
Marcus Hardy, Levee.

1878.

Calvin Davis, Barry, *Chairman.*

George Ham, Chambersburg.
Joseph Wilson, Flint.
W. T. Smith, Detroit.
C. E. Bolin, Montezuma.
G. W. Roberts, Pearl.
J. W. Grimes, Perry.
George Pratt, Griggsville.
C. P Chapman, Newburg.
J. H. Griffin, Hardin
M. W. Bogart, Spring Creek.
Dele Elder, Fairmount.

John Preble, New Salem.
Lewis Dutton, Pittsfield.
P. H. Sullivan, Martinsburg.
A. L. Galloway, Pleasant Hill.
H. L. Hadsell, Hadley.
T. H. Coley, Derry.
Samuel Taylor, Atlas.
J. S. Lockwood, Pleasant Vale.
Samuel Clark, Kinderhook.
Marcus Hardy, Levee.

1879.

J. C. Newton, Chambersburg.
David Pyle, Flint.
B. W. Flynn, Detroit.
N. D. McEvans, Montezuma.
G. W. Roberts, Pearl.
Z. Wade, Perry.
George Pratt, Griggsville.
C. P Chapman, Newburg.
George Main, Hardin.
C. C. Melton, Spring Creek.
Dele Elder, Fairmount.

Abel Dunham, New Salem.
H. S. Lloyd, Pittsfield.
P. H. Sullivan, Martinsburg
A. L. Galloway, Pleasant Hill.
Orrin Campbell, Hadley.
T. H. Coley, Derry.
C. B. Dustin, Atlas.
E. A. Crandall, Perry.
M. D. Massie, Pleasant Vale.
John Clutch, Kinderhook.
Marcus Hardy, Levee.

CHAPTER X.

BLACK HAWK WAR.

In November, 1830, 50 or 60 of the Sac and Fox tribes of Indians came down on a hunting excursion and camped on Bay creek. These tribes at that time were living on Rock river in the northern part of the State, and wished once more to visit the scenes of their former hunting-ground. Some little trouble occurred between these Indians and the whites on account of the disappearance of hogs in the neighborhood. The settlers turned out and caught some of the red men, tied them up and administered to them severe flagellations with withes, and they immediately left the country, never, with one or two exceptions, to return in a body to Pike county. This episode comes as near to anything of a warlike nature, especially a hostile collision with the Indians, as any that we have any record of occuring in Pike county.

In the fall of 1831 Black Hawk and his tribes appeared on Rock river, where they committed several petty depredations. The settlers of Rock River and vicinity petitioned Gov. Reynolds for aid, stating that " Last fall the Black Hawk band of Indians almost destroyed all of our crops, and made several attacks on the owners when they attempted to prevent their depredations, and wounded one man by actually stabbing him in several places. This spring they acted in a more outrageous and menacing manner." This petition represented that there were 600 or 700 Indians among them: it was signed by 35 or 40 persons. Another petition sets forth that " The Indians pasture their horses in our wheat-fields, shoot our cows and cattle and threaten to burn our houses over our heads if we do not leave." Other statements place the Indians at not more than 300.

According to these petitions, Gov. Reynolds in May, 1831, called for 700 mounted men. Beardstown was the designated place of rendezvous, and such were the sympathy and courage of the settlers that the number offering themselves was nearly three times the number called out. They left Rushville for Rock Island June 15, 1831; and on the 30th of the same month, in a council held for the purpose, Black Hawk and 27 chiefs and warriors on one part, and Gen. Edmund P. Gaines, of the U. S. army, and John Reynolds, Governor of Illinois, on the other part, signed a treaty of peace and friendship. This capitulation bound the Indians to go and remain west of the Mississippi river.

In April, 1832, in direct violation of the treaty above referred to, Black Hawk, with some 500 followers, appeared again upon the scene of action, and fear and excitement spread through the length and breadth of the State. To again drive them from the State, Gov. Reynolds called on the Militia April 16, 1832.

TROOPS RAISED IN PIKE COUNTY.

No sooner had volunteers been called for than every county and settlement throughout this portion of the State promptly responded. Nowhere, however, was such alacrity shown in answering the call as in Pike county. The hearts of the sturdy pioneers were easily touched by the stories of depredations by the Indians. These stories were doubtless greatly exaggerated, yet the frontiersmen who knew the subtlety and treachery of the red men well knew they could not be trusted; and almost any crime was expected of them.

Col. Wm. Ross, then Captain of the Pike County Militia Company, received word from the Governor on Friday, the 20th, and he immediately issued the following :

" COMPANY ORDERS.—The volunteer company of Pike county will meet at Atlas, on Monday, the 23d inst., ready to take up their march by sun-rise, except such part of the company as are living on the east side of said county, which part will meet the company at the house of William Henman, about four miles this side of Phillip's Ferry, on the same day, all with a good horse, and rifle, powder-horn, half pound of powder, and one hundred balls, with three days' provisions. The commanding officer of said company flatters himself that every man will be prompt to his duty.
[Signed,]   " W. Ross, Capt. 1st Rifles, Pike Co.
" April, 1832."

The Captain then called upon Benj. Barney at his blacksmith shop and told him of the nature of the order he had received, and for him to forthwith mount a horse and start out to notify the settlers to assemble immediately. Mr. Barney was engaged at his forge at the time, making a plow; but he straightway laid down hammer and tongs, untied his leathern apron, left his fire to smolder and die, and started immediately upon his mission. He first went to a man at the mouth of Blue creek; from thence he made a circuit of the county, appealing to all to assemble at Atlas without delay. He tells us that almost all of them left their work and started immediately.

The men having assembled at Atlas, the martial band began to discourse lively music to stir the patriotism of the militia-men to a high pitch so that they would enlist for the service. The music did not seem to "enthuse" them with as great a desire to enlist as their leaders had anticipated. Something more potent must be had; so two buckets of whisky were summoned to their aid; the men were formed in two lines facing each other, and wide enough apart to admit of two men walking up and down the line between them. Capt. Ross and Lieut. Seeley started down the line, each with a bucket of liquor; two boys followed with water, and then came the music. It was understood that those who would fall in after the music would enlist for service. By the time the third round was made 100 men were in line, which was even more than the quota of this county under that call. Wm. Ross was elected Captain and Benj. Barney, 1st Lieutenant. The company adjourned to meet at Griggsville on the following day at 10 o'clock A. M. The men went to their homes in various parts of the county to notify their families of their enlistment and to make slight preparations for their journey. We are told that with four or five exceptions, and those lived along the Illinois river, every man was at Griggsville by sunrise on the day appointed.

The company then started for Beardstown, the place of rendezvous for the troops in this part of the State. The Illinois river was very high and much difficulty was experienced in crossing it. The ferry would carry but six horses at a time; and while waiting for transportation the horses stood in mud up to their knees. It was a gloomy time and they had no liquor with which to cheer up the new volunteers. Capt. Ross was among the first to cross over, while Lieut. Barney remained with the men upon the western bank. Great dissatisfaction was being manifested by the men under Lieut. Barney, who were waiting in the mud and water to cross the river, all of whom did not get over until 11 o'clock that night. Lieut. Barney sent word to Capt. Ross to forward him a jug of whisky. This was done; a fire was built, striking it by the flint locks of their guns; the whisky was distributed, and once more the troops were in good spirits and ready for any hardship.

The Pike county troops arrived at Beardstown the next day, being the first company to reach that point. The Governor and some of the leading officers were already there. It was found that the Pike county company was too large; it accordingly was divided and formed into two companies. Lieut. Barney was chosen Captain of one of these, and Joseph Petty, Captain of the other. James Ross was elected 1st Lieutenant of Capt. Petty's company, and a Mr. Allen, of Capt. Barney's company. Capt. Ross was chosen Colonel and aid of the commanding General. It was he who appointed Abraham Lincoln, our martyr President, to the Captaincy of one of the Sangamon county companies in this war.

The troops marched from Beardstown to Rock Island, where they were mustered into the United States service by Gen. Zachary Taylor. At Fort Armstrong, which was at that point, there were then only about 50 United States troops. The Pike county volunteers, with others, then marched up toward Dixon on Rock river, the course the Indians had taken. They followed them for some days, but did not overtake them or encounter them in any engagement. During the entire campaign the Pike county troops did not meet the foe in battle array; not a leaden ball was shot at any of these men during the 50 days they were out. During this time they ran short of provisions, and sent to Chicago, but in that present great city, where millions of hogs are slaughtered annually and the greatest grain market in the world exists, they could not get a barrel of pork or of flour. The Pike county volunteers then went to Ottawa and shared with some troops at that point. They obtained rations enough there to last them about three days, when they marched on down the river to the rapids, where there was a boat filled with United States provisions. There they drew rations for their homeward march. Capt. Barney drew seven days' rations for his men, but Capt. Petty thought they would get home in three or four days, so only drew four days' rations, much to the regret of the hungry stomachs of his men, as it took them longer to get home than he had anticipated. The privates of this call received $8 a month, and were paid off that fall by United States agents, who came to Atlas.

THE STAMPEDE.

While in the northern part of the State four regiments of troops camped together, among whom were the men from this county. They formed a hollow square, upon the inside of which were the officers' tents. The horses, about 1,000 in number, were guarded in a corral outside of the square. In the dead hour of night, when not a light remained burning, and the slow tread of the faithful sentinel was the only sound that broke the silence, the horses became frightened and stampeded. In the wildest rage they dashed forward, whither they knew not ; they headed toward the camp of slumbering soldiers, and in all the mad fury of frightened brutes they dashed forward over cannon, tents and men, wounding several of the latter quite severely. The troops heard their coming and supposed each wild steed was ridden by a wilder and less humane red-skin ; the treacherous and subtle foe was momentarily expected and the frightened men thought they were now coming down upon them. They had all heard of the night attack upon the rangers at the famous battle of Tippecanoe, and feared a repetition of that night's bloody work. Capt. Barney, with quickness of thought and military skill, in a loud voice gave orders for his men to form at the rear of their tents. He hallooed lustily, and when he went up and down the line feeling his way he found every man in his place. The commanding officers hearing the Captain's orders and knowing there would be safety with his company if anywhere, ran to him. Fortunately the horses were riderless, which was soon discovered, and then the frightened men began joking. Col. De Witt joked Capt. Barney considerably about his hallooing so loud, when Gen. Taylor spoke up and said he was glad the Captain was so prompt to give orders for his men to form, as it showed a soldierly disposition ; besides, it let him know where he might go for safety.

A third company subsequently went from Pike county under

Capt. Hale and Lieut. David Seeley : about 50 men composed this company of mounted riflemen. They enlisted for three months and participated in the famous battle of Bad-Ax.

The people of this county were not disturbed by the Indians at this time, but so timid were they that they were easily frightened. The following incident is related by Samuel Clark, of Kinder-hook township. In 1832, during the Black Hawk war, a man while passing a neighbor's house heard the cries of a child who was in the house. He supposed the Indians were within committing their foul deeds, and accordingly raised the alarm that the Indians were there murdering all the members of the family, and everybody who came that way. This created the greatest consternation in the settlement, for the people had heard of the bloody deeds committed upon the settlers in the northern part of the State. The settlers fled for safety. Some went to the fort, others ran hither and thither they knew not where. One very large fleshy woman mounted a horse and rode in the direction of the fort at full speed. She came to a ditch about ten feet wide and as many feet deep; the horse halted, but she urged him to jump, which he did at great peril, but fortunately landed safely on the opposite side. After the people had become quite exhausted with running they learned that no Indians were near, but that the yells came from the child because his father was chastising it.

CHAPTER XI.

CRIMINAL RECORD.

INTRODUCTORY.

Since the two Indians, Shonwennekek and Pemesan, were indicted for murder, there have been 41 other indictments for this grave crime returned by the grand juries of Pike county, many of which included more than one individual. This represents a long and bloody calendar, a stain that every good citizen would have blotted out were it possible. It has been made by the blood of many victims, dyed in crimson never to be erased, and we only record what has occurred. Who can picture the agony of heart, the remorse, the anguish of mind, to say nothing of the physical pains caused by these bloody deeds ? Both the victim and his friends, as well as the perpetrator of the crime, have suffered untold misery.

Often has the deadly weapon been brought into use on the slightest pretext. A moment after he had taken the life of his victim and he had realized that his hands were stained with the life-blood of a fellow man, the perpetrator of the deed would have given everything he possessed or ever hoped for, and in some cases life itself, could he but recall the deed; but alas ! it is done, never to be undone. The feeling has not been thus in every instance where the bloody victim fell at the feet of the man-slayer, but frequently so. Sometimes the joy was great when he who sent the deadly messenger saw its work well done.

Among this long catalogue of criminals only one has ever suffered the extreme penalty of the law, and most of them have had light punishment. We begin with the first person indicted for murder, and give every indictment during the county's existence. There are a multitude of cases of murder or manslaughter of which we make no mention, as no indictments were made for want of sufficient evidence.

Pemesan and Shonwennekek.
(Two Indians.)

These Indians were indicted Oct. 2, 1821, at the very first term of Court held in Pike county, for the murder of a Frenchman. The evidence showing, however, that the shooting of the deceased was more an act of carelessness than of premeditated murder, the next morning the jury returned a verdict for manslaughter on the part of Pemesan, or "Traveler," and that Shonwennekek, or "Spice-bush," was not guilty. The Court had assigned Daniel P. Cook and Polemon H. Winchester as counsel for the Indians, and John Shaw and Jean Baptist Patelle were the sworn interpreters. No attorney for the people appears on record, but of course there must have been such an officer present. It appears that these Indians were out hunting one day, and when the Frenchman suddenly appeared in view in the distance they took him to be a deer or some other animal, and Pemesan immediately fired and killed him. No sooner was this done than they discovered their mistake, and Shon-wennekek proposed that they run away; but Pemesan argued that as it was an accident the whites would do them no harm. Thereupon they immediately surrendered themselves to a magistrate. Pemesan's punishment was a fine of 25 cents and imprisonment for 24 hours. He accordingly paid the fine and served out his sentence in a rail pen which was guarded for the occasion.

Charles Collins, James Whitly, Alfred Miller and James Stockton.

These parties were indicted for murder May, 2, 1843, but after their case was continued from term to term with hopes of arresting them, they were never found.

Winship Moreton

was indicted Sept. 10, 1841, but the following April his case was stricken from the docket.

John Bartholomew, et al.

were indicted April 5, 1848, for the murder of John Crewson, or Cruson, near the Mississippi river a few days preceding (March 29), while the latter was hauling a log for the rafting. He was shot beside his team. The others indicted with Bartholomew were Benj. Chouls and John Stipp. The two latter took a change of venue to Adams county, where a *nolle prosequi* was entered April 2, 1849. Bartholomew's case was continued from term to term until Sept, 12, 1853, when it was stricken from the docket.

John McGuyre

was indicted Sept. 5, 1849, for the murder of Wm. Bennett near Phillip's Ferry, Sept. 1, preceding. That day McGuyre went to the house of Mr. Pease where Mr. Bennett was and urged him to go gunning, but which, by the solicitation of Mr. Pease, he declined doing. McGuyre left and returned about sun-down, when Pease and Bennett were eating their supper, who invited him to partake ; he refused, saying, "G—d d—n you! I am tired waiting for you and am going to shoot you now." He immediately fired a load of buckshot, which struck Bennett in the face, killing him. McGuyre commenced reloading his gun with the declared intention of killing Pease, but the latter made his escape and raised the alarm. McGuyre ran away but was arrested on the 6th and taken before the Circuit Court then in session, and at first pleaded guilty; but after the consequence of such a plea was explained to him, he pleaded not guilty, and for want of time his case was continued to the next term of Court. McGuyre broke jail twice: the first time he was caught at McGee's creek, in crossing which he came very near being drowned, and the second time he got out through the wall, a stone having been removed by the aid of friends outside. This was effected without awaking a family which was asleep directly above. He has never been re-taken, and his case was finally stricken from the docket with leave to reinstate.

George Kesterson

was indicted for murder March 29, 1851, but for some reason was never brought to trial.

Philip Wilcox

was indicted Oct. 11, 1851, and he also was never tried.

Preston F. Groves

was indicted March 23, 1853, for the murder of Robert Carr, about 5 miles east of Pittsfield. Both these parties were married men and frequented a house of ill repute. Groves was tried and acquitted March 28, 1853.

Jonathan W. Hutchinson.

⸙ This man was indicted Nov. 27, 1854, for killing Francis P. Wells in Brown county. A change of venue had been taken from that county, his case was tried at Pittsfield, and after the jury was out several days it brought in a verdict of not guilty, Sept. 18, 1855.

Hugh W. Wren

was indicted Sept. 14, 1855, for manslaughter; about a fortnight afterward his bail was forfeited by his escape and his case was never brought to trial.

James Daniels

was accused of killing Newton Soules in Calhoun county in a saloon. Soules had burned his hair previously. Daniels was indicted in the Pike county Court Sept. 12, 1856; but Aug. 5, 1859, his case was discontinued.

Stephen Cole et. al.

were, according to the record, indicted for murder March 9, 1857.
In this suit it seems that no parties were ever brought to trial.

Robert Ellis.

This criminal was indicted April 14, 1860, for the murder of
Benj. F. Wade, Dec. 23 preceding, a little west of Detroit. Wade
broke Ellis' whisky bottle and a quarrel ensued which resulted in
the fatal affray in the yard of Francis Phillips. Ellis stabbed
Wade with a large pocket-knife. Ellis pleaded not guilty but was
convicted of manslaughter Nov. 24, 1860, and sentenced to one year
in the penitentiary.

Edwin C. Hendrick.

This party was indicted Aug. 10, 1860, for poisoning to death
Emeline Amanda Hendrick. He pleaded not guilty, was tried,
and, after the jury had two days' consultation, he was acquitted.

James Likes, Simon Likes, Lyman Likes, Philip Neal, Christopher Neal and Wm. Bothwick.

The indictment in this case, Nov. 23, 1860, was for the murder
of Samuel Macumber, an innocent man about 65 years of age,
living in Barry township, and who was killed Oct. 23, 1860. The
parties set upon their victim in cold blood and killed him with
clubs and stones. Macumber was a Baptist minister, who had
married the mother of the Neals, and it was alleged that he maltreated her in some way. After trial all the indicted parties were
acquitted Dec. 8, 1860, except Christopher Neal, who was convicted
of manslaughter and sentenced for life, and James Likes was
acquitted the next term of Court.

*Thomas Johnson, Fielding Johnson, John Hopkins, Andrew J.
Winsor, Mary Pearson, Julia Bell, Angeline Bell and Hampton
Winsor.*

These parties were indicted during the spring term of Court in
1863, for the murder of Andrew J. Pearson, in Flint township.
The victim, a farmer, was found murdered by hanging, and robbed.
November 18, 1862, Pearson started from his house in search of
some of his stock. Night came on and he did not return. Suspicion
was aroused, inquiries and search were made, and finally his body
was found in a ravine, a half mile from home, covered up with
leaves, brush, etc.: two hundred dollars in money had been taken
from his person. The robbers also went to his house, and, finding
no one at home, they entered it and took about seventy dollars more,
which they found in a bureau. They then took a good horse and
decamped. Of the above parties, some were directly accused by the

indictment, some impleaded with them, and severances were obtained. Some of them were desperadoes from Missouri; some of the parties took a change of venue to Brown county. The result of the whole prosecution was, that Thomas Johnson and John Hopkins were convicted of manslaughter April 27, 1863, and sentenced for life; Fielding Johnson was convicted of the same and sentenced for 20 years, and the rest were discharged.

During the trial the guilty criminals pleaded guilty of manslaughter, confessing as follows: They lived in Missouri, were rebels in Porter's army, which subsequently disbanded. They worked several days for a neighbor of Pearson's named Dimmitt, and spent several evenings at Mr. Pearson's house. This man and his wife, Mary (impleaded above), frequently quarreled. The night previous to the murder they had an unusually wicked altercation, after which Mrs. P. went into a fit. After coming out she told the accused that if they would kill Pearson she would give them a horse. The girls, Julia and Angeline Bell, her daughters by a former husband, also expressed the wish that they should kill him. The next morning they invited Pearson out for a walk and told him they were going to hang him. He said he did not blame them. Two of them held him up while the other adjusted the rope. He did not resist nor struggle. After he was dead they took sixty dollars from his pocket, carried it to the house and reported what they had done. All were rejoiced and gave the prisoners ten dollars apiece. Mrs. Pearson gave them a horse, asking them not to betray her, and they started for Missouri. The daughters asked for and received a lock of their hair for mementoes, and a parting kiss.

The young men were not over twenty years of age, did not look like criminals, and were said to be respectfully connected.

John W. Parks and Henry C. Price.

These parties were indicted Apr. 18, 1864, for the murder of Peter C. Staats, an old settler of Hadley township, on the road between New Salem and Maysville. Staats was twice shot in the back, one ball coming out at the breast. The accused took a change of venue to Adams county and were finally acquitted.

George Crow, alias Roselle,

was indicted April 19, 1864, for the murder of a Mr. Gard. May 21, following, he broke jail, and the shooting necessary to his capture June 11, in Greene county, resulted in his death the next day in jail.

Austin and Abraham Stevens

were, according to the records, indicted April 19, 1864, for murder, but it appears that there was never any trial of the case.

Wm. W. Moore and J. S. Wilson

were indicted the same day for being accessory after the fact of the murder. They moved their case to Brown county, and from the evidence elicited it appears that young Moore, only sixteen years of age, had killed John Ziff, living near Pittsfield. Mr. Moore's father and Ziff had a dispute about some wood which Moore had been cutting on land which Ziff claimed and which Moore had rented. Ziff struck Moore with an ax, knocking him down and then stamping upon him. The lad seeing his father in this condition, ran up and struck Ziff a blow upon the top of his head with the edge of an ax, thus literally cleaving his head clear to his shoulders.

Samuel Evans and Matthew Gilmer, Gilmore, or Gilman·

These men were indicted Nov. 29, 1864, for killing Cornelius Myers, Evans being a resident of Montezuma. They broke jail, and after several months Evans was recaptured in Tennessee. He took a change of venue to Brown county, where he was convicted of manslaughter and sentenced for twelve years in the State prison. There he became insane, and after his release he stole a horse, was arrested, and while in jail his insanity became so marked that he was finally sent to the asylum at Jacksonville.

Chas. Brummell or Brumble, etc.

This rascal, whose name was spelled half a dozen different ways, was indicted March 15, 1866, for the murder of Edward Garrison, of New Canton. The fatal deed was perpetrated by stabbing the victim with a pocket-knife. Sept. 19, 1867, he was convicted of the charge and sentenced to State prison for three years.

Name not Given.

Although not strictly within the purview of this chapter, we may mention here, as the parties were both residents of Griggsville, this county, that Dr. J. H. Caldwell, of that place, went to Texas in May or June, 1868, employing a young man to accompany him, who, on the 24th of June, murdered and robbed the doctor, but was summarily lynched by the infuriated people when the deed occurred.

Mc Wright Murray

was indicted for murder in 1869, but the case was ultimately stricken from the docket.

Joseph Daul and Anthony Scheiner.

These criminals were indicted April 20, 1869, for committing murder in Brown county, as the result of an affray connected with the burning of show tents at Mount Sterling. A change of venue was taken to Pike county, and after a two days' trial the chaps were sentenced to 15 years' hard labor.

Capt. Wm. H. Stout.

This man was indicted April 6, 1871, charged with the murder of a Mr. Kimball, at Cockle-bur slough, the preceding year. By change of venue his case was taken to the Brown county Court.

Samuel Douglas

was the homicide who beat to death James Sapp, June 12, 1871, near Pleasant Hill. At the first beating he left Mr. Sapp lying prostrate, and induced a Mr. McKenna to accompany him to the place, who tried to lift him up, when Douglas gave the poor victim several additional blows, from which he died a few days afterward. Douglas and McKenna were both arrested, but the latter was dismissed for want of evidence against him. Douglas was held for manslaughter, the indictment being made Oct. 12, 1871. He was convicted and sentenced Nov. 29, 1871, for six and a half years in the penitentiary.

John Shannahan.

Sept. 16, 1871, in Pleasant Vale township, Wm. Hall claimed that Shannahan had said something mean about him, and proceeded to assault him with a club. The latter warded off the blow, snatched the club from Hall, who then started to run away; Shannahan, however, soon overtook him, struck him on the head with the club, knocking him over into a gully senseless, and Shannahan tumbling down with him. Hall's ankle was broken in the fall, and he died soon afterward. Shannahan was arrested and committed to jail, where he suffered from a feeble constitution and a diseased leg, which had to be amputated. He was indicted by the grand jury, Oct. 12, 1871, but he died before the trial took place.

Bartholomew Barnes.

The only execution ever taking place in Pike county was that of Bartholomew Barnes, Dec. 29, 1871, in the Pittsfield jail-yard, for the murder of John Gresham in Calhoun county. The suit was first instituted in that county, and a change of venue being taken to this county, the case was called at the session of the Pike county Circuit Court Nov. 27, 1871; and after a thorough trial the traverse jury returned a verdict of guilty of murder in the first degree, and that he should suffer death by hanging. The particulars of the murder are well condensed in Judge Higbee's sentence given Dec. 6, as below. The court-house was crowded to overflowing with ladies and gentlemen to hear the sentence of death pronounced upon the young convict. At 10½ A. M. he was brought in to receive his sentence. Death-like stillness reigned within the room, as the Judge, in a solemn and impressive manner, addressed him, broken only by the prisoner, who, standing with brazen effrontery, gave vent occasionally to protests of innocence. The Judge said:

"In discharging the unpleasant duty required of me by the law, it seems proper that I should place on the files of this Court a brief statement of the facts and proofs which render it the duty of the Court to pronounce a judgment which is to deprive a human being of his life.

"By the record in this case it appears that you were indicted at the May term of the Calhoun Circuit Court, 1871, for the murder of John Gresham, and the case was brought here on a change of venue for trial; that there is no prejudice in this county which would injuriously affect your rights is sufficiently manifest by the fact that the crime for which you have been tried was committed in another county; and of the twelve jurors selected for your trial every one has stated under oath that he never heard of the case until called into the jury box.

"From the evidence it appears that somewhere about the first of February last, for some cause (which is not apparent) you became very much enraged against the deceased in the town of Pleasant Hill and threatened to whip him. When told by the town constable that that would not be permitted and that he would arrest you if you did not keep quiet, you said that you would see the deceased at same other time and tear his heart out. On the 27th day of February the deceased, his son (15 years of age) and yourself, were in Clarksville, Mo., and crossed the river on your return in the afternoon in the same boat, the deceased and his son within a wagon; and after the boat landed, as they were leaving the river for home, you asked the privilege of riding with them, to which the boy objected, his father being quite drunk at the time. You then said to them that if they would let you ride you would be quiet and peaceable; whereupon the deceased consented, and you got into the wagon and seated yourself on a board beside the deceased, the boy standing up in front driving. You had gone but a short distance when some words passed, but no blows or attempts to strike ensued, and you jumped out, saying, 'You d——d old son of a bitch!' At the time you jumped out the board on which the deceased was sitting tipped up and he fell out on the other side on his back near the wagon and near to a fence. You ran back to the wagon and to where the deceased lay, and turning your back to the fence, you seized the rails with which to steady yourself, and with the deceased still lying on his back immediately in front of you, with the heel of your boot you stamped his face, head and breast until you killed him. The evidence shows that in this brutal manner, and when the deceased was lying on his back perfectly helpless, in the presence of his son and another witness who was near by, you stamped from eight to ten times, breaking his nose, cheek-bone and jaw, and crushing out one eye, and forced the heel of your boot through his skull into his brain

more than an inch in depth, and so crushed and disfigured his face
that it could not be recognized by Dr. Thomas, who had lived a
near neighbor to deceased for 20 years.

"While engaged in this work of death, Mr. Oyler, who was a
short distance off and saw it all, hallooed and started to run to you.
On seeing him you jumped over the fence and started to run. You
were pursued and captured in a few minutes, and blood was found
all over the heel of your boot, with hair and whiskers still adhering
to it. Soon afterward you declared that you had not seen deceased
on that day.

"In answer to all this proof you produced a single witness, your
brother, who testified that in the fall of 1869 deceased made some
threats against you, which, so far as the evidence shows, he never
attempted to execute. Beyond this you offer no explanation or
justification of this dreadful crime.

"Upon this proof the jury have found you guilty of murder, and
their verdict declares that you shall suffer death by hanging. You
have been well defended by able attorneys, fairly tried, and, as it
seems to me, properly convicted; and it only remains now for the
Court to pronounce the judgment of the law, which is, to deprive
you of your life. Unpleasant as this duty is, I am not at liberty
to shrink from it. You have deprived John Gresham of his life by
a foul and brutal murder, and the law demands your life as the penalty. As the time which can be extended to you to prepare to
meet this dreadful punishment is limited by law, let me admonish
you not to spend it in vain efforts to arrest your doom, but rather
devote every moment of the time allotted you to prepare for the
final trial wherein injustice is never done and where all must
answer for every act of his life. It is the order of this Court, Bartholomew Barnes, that you be taken from here to the county jail of
this county and there confined until Friday, the twenty-ninth day
of December, 1871, and that between the hours of 10 o'clock A. M.
and 3. P. M. of said day, in said jail, and in the presence of the witnesses required by law, hanged by the neck until you are dead."

We take the following account of the execution from the *Old
Flag* of Jan. 4. 1872:

"The dreadful day having arrived, a large crowd gathered around
the jail, which increased constantly as the hour of execution approached. There was no disturbance, however, the anxiety of suspense seeming to pervade the throng and keep them quiet, and
waiting almost with suspended breath until the tragedy was over.
The execution was delayed until afternoon in order to give the
prisoner all the time possible. About half past one, or later, in
company with the physicians, the jury and others, we were admitted
to the Sheriff's room and waited the last preparations for the final
scene. The leave-taking of the brother and sister and relatives of
the prisoner we did not witness. At about a quarter past two the
great iron door leading from the Sheriff's room into the hall of the
jail was unbarred, and those in waiting entered the hall and took

PIKE COUNTY JAIL

places in front of the scaffold and waited with uncovered heads the appearance of the prisoner. We need hardly tell our readers there was stillness in that company and that all sound was hushed except the long-drawn breathings of men who knew they stood in the chamber of Death, that a living mortal man was soon to be his victim, and that a fellow being was within a few moments of eternity and judgment. There was the scaffold, rather a rough-looking structure, and of larger dimensions than we had expected to see; above it, from a pulley fastened to a beam, hung a rope apparently about half an inch in thickness, with knot and noose on the end of it.

"As we stood there contemplating the scene, and held our watch to note the time, some few remarks were made in a whisper and several times a reporter asked us, ' What time is it now ?' Seventeen minutes past two, eighteen minutes, nineteen minutes, each elapsing minute increasing the anxiety of suspense and expectation; twenty minutes, and the Sheriff and prisoner, accompanied with deputies and ministers, appeared on the corridor and descended one flight of steps and ascended the other which led to the scaffold. The prisoner was pale from long confinement, but we could not say that he flinched or quailed at the sight of the gallows or when standing on the platform. When his eyes first caught sight of scaffold and rope there was an expression of surprise which was momentary, and that was all. He was well dressed in a black suit with a fine shirt, white stockings and slippers, and looked like a gentleman. He was told to be seated on a seat of boards that had been prepared, which he did, Revs. Priestly and Johnsey, Methodist preachers, sitting on each side of him. They sat only for a moment when deputy Landrum told him to stand up, which he did. They both stood close to the grated window when the death warrant was read to him by Mr. Landrum distinctly, but with evident emotion, and was heard by the prisoner attentively, but without any manifestations whatever. When the reading was over and Mr. Landrum had folded the paper, ' Let us pray ' was announced, and a prayer was pronounced by Rev. Mr. Johnsey, which to our ear was somewhat peculiar if not poetical, the prisoner all the while uttering fervid ejaculations, such as, ' O Lord, have mercy on my soul!' On rising from his knees after the prayer he deliberately stepped forward, and taking the rope in his right hand, passed the noose into his left and seemed to take a careful look at it. He was then told, if he had any thing to say, to say it now. He hesitated a moment as if not fully comprehending what was meant; but upon being told a second time, he said, ' Well, I say that I believe all my sins have been pardoned; and I thank the jailor for his kindness to me, and I hope that no one will ever again be hung.' He was then told to take farewell of all; and having shaken hands with the ministers, Sheriff and attendants, he asked leave to pray once himself, and was told to do so, when, kneeling down with his face toward the window in the west, he said, as we understood, ' O Lord,

21

I pray thee to forgive my sins, to save my soul and take me to heaven,' repeating the petitions, as we thought, twice or more. He then arose and stepped forward on the trap, and the rope was put over his head and adjusted about his neck, and the black cap drawn over his face, his hands and feet having been previously tied, he all the while praying, ' O Lord, save my soul.''

"This was the most solemn and anxious moment of the execution, both to the doomed man and to the spectators. There stood a man on the immediate confines of two worlds, just ready to step into eternity and know the grand secret; only one moment more to live in this life.

" The cap was drawn over his face at twenty-five minutes past two; the elapsing seconds now seemed as long as minutes; the Sheriff and an attendant were the last to come down from the steps. The fatal lever which should spring the trap was at the bottom, concealed by a piece of carpet. ' What time is it now?' said the reporter to us. Twenty-five minutes and fifteen seconds past two, and quick as a flash the man who was standing on the scaffold and still saying, ' O Lord, save my soul,' dropped till his head hung more than six inches below. There was no noise more than the sudden tightening of the cord with a heavy weight would occasion. A trap door swung into a niche prepared to receive it and remained there. The rope had been perfectly tested and did not stretch the least. The fall was more than six feet. His neck had been instantly broken and all pain was over. The victim did not struggle at all. At the end of the first minute there was a slight motion of the feet and limbs, swaying slightly, which was continued until after the end of the second minute, and evidently caused by muscular contraction. At the end of three and a half minutes there was one violent and last contraction of muscle; shoulders heaved and the whole body was lifted up, and then relapsed and hung motionless; at the end of twenty minutes the doctors pronounced Barnes dead, and at the end of twenty-five minutes the body was cut down and laid out, while a further examination was made by the doctors, who pronounced his neck broken and his life to be extinct; at the end of thirty minutes from the time of the drop and within about five minutes of 3 o'clock he was placed in a coffin and at once carried out and delivered to his relatives to be taken to Pleasant Hill for burial."

The preparations for the hanging had been very complete, and there was not a single mistake or slightest failure in any particular; and Sheriff McFarland deserves praise for the manner in which he bore himself and performed his melancholy duties.

Barnes made a " confession " in which he insisted to the last that he did not mean to kill Gresham, and claimed that he was drunk and did not know what he was about. The warrant was printed it a very large plain hand by the pen of doctor J. J. Topliff, who was Circuit Clerk at the time.

John Barnes,

cousin of the preceding, was indicted Nov. 29, 1871, for the murder of McLaughlin, in Detroit, on the sixteenth of that month. The name of the murdered man was ascertained only by its being marked on his arm with India ink. Both the men had been in a saloon drinking and had had a quarrel about a red ball. McLaughlin shook his fist in Barnes' face and told him not to open his face again about it. He turned around, and when his eyes were averted Barnes jumped to his feet having a knife in his hand which he swung with great force, the blade striking McLaughlin's face and neck, severing the jugular vein and windpipe and completely cutting his throat. Barnes then made a back stroke which missed McLaughlin, who then staggered into a back room and fell dead. Barnes was immediately arrested and committed to the Pittsfield, jail where, sometime after his indictment, he gradually wasted away with pulmonary consumption and died.

Jack Connor, alias Wm. C. Walton, and Chas. Berry,

were indicted in the Pike Circuit Court Oct. 18, 1872, for manslaughter. April 11, 1873, Connor was acquitted and Berry was convicted and sentenced for one year.

Peter B. Ford.

On the night of May 3, 1872, George DeHaven, of Barry, was killed on a shebang boat just above Florence, by Peter B. Ford. Two disreputable women and two or three low-lived men were on board. "Tack," Henry Schaffner and DeHaven came on the boat, which was owned by the Fords. After drinking awhile Tack hauled open his coat and declared he was the best man on board, and attacked Elisha N. Ford. At the same time DeHaven sprang at Peter Ford with brass knuckles on one hand and a cocked revolver in the other, pointed at Peter's breast. Peter knocked the revolver aside and shot DeHaven, who died in about 20 minutes. Elisha and the two women were arrested, but after examination were discharged. Peter was also arrested, and indicted Oct. 21, 1872, for murder, was convicted, and "sent up" for 18 years. A motion for a new trial was made, but denied, and the sentence was executed.

James Ray and L. J. Hall.

At Pleasant Hill, June 22, 1872, L. J. Hall, a grocer, had a controversy with a Mr. McGinn, when a young man named James Ray interfered, knocking McGinn down with a beer glass and beating him and stamping upon him, Hall meanwhile keeping off all who would interfere. When the beating ceased McGinn was found dead. Hall then gave Ray some money, telling him to make his escape, which it seems he did most effectually. Hall was arrested, and examined, but acquitted of being an accessory. McGinn left a wife and eight children.

Matthew Harris and Thomas Stapleton.

At a place called the cut-off, on the Sny Levee, in the spring of 1873 were two large squads of men at work. The one working higher up the river received $2.00 per day to each man and those below received $1.75. After those above had completed their work, their employers told them they could go and work with those below if they were willing to work at the same rates. They all went to work, but after awhile became dissatisfied with the wages, threatened to strike, and made a good deal of disturbance. Their employers discharged several of the ring-leaders who still continued to make trouble. When pay-day arrived the strikers drank a great deal, came to the place of work and were determined, as they said, to clean out Harris, the time-keeper, and Stapleton, the "walking-boss." As the two latter were coming from the store after dinner, the mob of strikers fell upon them and Harris and Stapleton both fired at the first man, Pat Vaughan, killing him and slightly injuring another man. This proceeding deterred the rioters from any further aggressions. Stapleton and Harris were arrested, but to keep them safe from the rioters they were lodged in the jail at Pittsfield. They were indicted April 12 following, tried, convicted of murder, and July 1 both were sentenced to State prison for one year.

Andrew Hamilton.

Near Nebo, Feb. 5, 1875, a number of young people assembled at the house of Mrs. McKee, for the purpose of taking part in a dance. Among those present were Andrew Hamilton and Clifton U. Daniels, both young men and sons of well-known farmers in the vicinity. During the dance a quarrel arose between Hamilton and Daniels, when the former drew a revolver and shot Daniels in the neck at its juncture with the chest. The wounded man staggered against the wall and fell dead almost instantly. Hamilton immediately fled, and, so far as appears from the records, has never been captured.

John A. Thomas

was indicted Oct. 14, 1876, for murder, but three days afterward was acquitted.

John H. Mallory.

A man named Davis got to peeping around Mallory's house at night to see some girls, and Mallory, discovering the fact, ran out with a gun and shot Davis as he dodged behind a cedar bush, and killed him. This occurred at Barry. Mallory was indicted October 14, 1876, for manslaughter. The case dragged along in the Courts until April 6, 1878, when the accused was acquitted.

George Haskins.

About four miles northwest of Kinderhook a quarrel took place, March 4, 1877, between two young men, Geo. Haskins and a Mr. Simpkins, originating in a controversy about a dog biting a sister of Simpkins. A tussle ensued during which Simpkins was stabbed with a knife, and from the effects of the wound he shortly afterward died. Haskins was arrested, and April 10, 1877, he was indicted for murder; but the trial resulted in his conviction for manslaughter, and Oct. 19, following, he was sentenced to two years, imprisonment at hard labor. He was only nineteen years of age and Simpkins seventeen.

Henry A. Fowler.

This ruffian and a Mr. Hamilton were attending a dance near Nebo in the spring of 1878, where they drank and quarreled until Fowler cut Hamilton across the arm with a knife, and the latter bled to death. Fowler was arrested and April 6, 1878, was indicted for murder. Before his trial he escaped from jail, but voluntarily returned and delivered himself up. The trial resulted in his conviction and sentence to confinement in the State prison for two years.

Thomas McDonald.

James A. Brown was murdered near his own door in Montezuma March 11, 1878, shortly before daylight. Jan. 25 preceding he had been waylaid, drugged and robbed by two men in a small wood near his home, and lay exposed all night in a stupid condition until found the next morning, and was restored to consciousness with much difficulty. Thomas McDonald was afterward arrested and identified as one of those two men: the other culprit remained at large. Mr. Brown and his friends had feared that an effort would be made to prevent him (Brown) from appearing at a certain trial, and the tragedy just mentioned showed how well grounded their fears had been. For several nights preceding the murder noises had been heard in the vicinity of the residence of Brown, and he went armed. About 4 o'clock that morning (Monday) he stepped from his house to an out-house a few yards distant, taking his rifle with him. On his return a few minutes later, and when within two or three paces of the door, he was shot, the ball entering the back of the head and coming out toward the front. Hearing the report the family rushed out to find the victim lying where he fell, and in a few moments he ceased to live. Excitement became so intense that the Sheriff had to obtain assistance from the State Government to aid in keeping the peace. The excitement was greatly intensified by a report that the Sheriff intended to remove the prisoner from the Pike county jail to another county. McDonald was tried and found innocent. A full account of his case is given in the history of Pittsfield.

Colonel Williams.

A number of people gathered at the house of Monte Gant about ten miles south of Pittsfield, on Christmas eve, to have a dance, and were enjoying themselves in the usual way, when some of the boys asked Andrew Main (commonly denominated " Coon Main ") to call off a set. Main refusing, they said they could get along well enough without him. He thought this a good time as any to whip some of the boys, and, the quarrel continuing for some time, he commenced striking them. Main struck Williams, knocking him down. Williams then commenced stabbing at Main with his pocket knife. Main got hold of a long iron poker and commenced striking at Williams. About this time the landlord interfered and turned them from the house, when the latter and his brother Colonel immediately left and were followed by Main and two or three others. Then Colonel Williams shot Main with a revolver, and he and his brother immediately ran away, no effort being made at the time to arrest them. The wounded man then retured to the house, lay down on a bed, saying that Colonel Williams had shot him, and died about five hours afterward. Williams has been arrested, and is now in the Pittsfield jail awaiting trial.

Boyles,

a lad seventeen years of age, is also in jail for helping his brother to escape who had killed a companion with a pocket knife.

CHAPTER XII.

PIONEER LIFE.

LOG CABINS.

We shall, in this chapter, give as clear and exact a description of pioneer life in this county as we can find language to picture it in, commencing with the time the sturdy settlers first arrived with their scanty stores. They had migrated from older States, where the prospects for even a competency were very poor, many of them coming from Kentucky, for, it is supposed, they found that a good State to emigrate from. Their entire stock of furniture, implements and family necessities were easily stored in one wagon, and sometimes a cart was their only vehicle.

As the first thing after they arrived and found a suitable location, they would set about the building of a log cabin, a description of which may be interesting to the younger readers, and especially their descendants, who may never see a structure of the kind. Trees of uniform size were selected and cut into pieces of the desired length, each end being saddled and notched so as to bring the logs as near together as possible. The cracks were "chinked and daubed" to prevent the wind from whistling through. This had to be renewed every fall before cold weather set in. The usual height was one story of about seven or eight feet. The gables were made of logs gradually shortened up to the top. The roof was made by laying small logs or stout poles reaching from gable to gable, suitable distances apart, on which were laid the clapboards after the manner of shingling, showing two feet or more to the weather. The clapboards were fastened by laying across them heavy poles, called "weight poles," reaching from one gable to the other, being kept apart and in their place by laying pieces of timber between them called "runs," or "knees." A wide chimney place was cut out of one end of the cabin, the chimney standing entirely outside, and built of rived sticks, laid up cob-house fashion and filled with clay, or built of stone, often using two or three cords of stone in building one chimney. For a window, a piece about two feet long was cut out of one of the wall logs, and the hole closed, sometimes with glass, but oftener with greased paper pasted over it. A door-

way was also cut through one of the walls, and the door was made
of spliced clapboards and hung with wooden hinges. This was
opened by pulling a leather latch-string which raised a wooden
latch inside the door. For security at night this latch-string was
pulled in, but for friends and neighbors, and even strangers, the
"latch-string was always hanging out," as a welcome. In the interior, upon one side, was the huge fire-place, large enough to contain
a back-log as big as the strongest man could carry, and holding enough wood to supply an ordinary stove a week ; on either
side were poles and kettles, and over all a mantel on which was
placed the tallow dip. In one corner stood the larger bed for the
old folks, under this the trundle-bed for the children ; in another
corner stood the old-fashioned, large spinning-wheel, with a smaller
one by its side ; in another the pine table, around which the family
gathered to partake of their plain food ; over the door hung the
ever-trustful rifle and powder-horn; while around the room were scattered a few splint-bottomed chairs and three-legged stools ; in one
corner was a rude cupboard holding the table ware, which consisted
of a few cups and saucers and blue-edged plates, standing singly
on their edges against the back, to make the display of table furniture more conspicuous.

These simple cabins were inhabited by a kind and true-hearted
people. They were strangers to mock modesty, and the traveler,
seeking lodgings for the night or desirous of spending a few days
in the community, if willing to accept the rude offering, was always
welcome, although how they were disposed of at night the reader
may not easily imagine ; for, as described, a single room was made
to serve the purpose of kitchen, dining-room, sitting-room, bed-
room, and parlor, and many families consisted of six or eight members.

SELECTION OF HOMES.

For a great many years but few thought it advisable to attempt
farming on the prairie. To many of them the cultivation of the
prairies was an untried experiment, and it was the prevailing
opinion that the timber would soon become very scarce,—a fear
soon proven to be without foundation. Another obstacle that was
in the way for a great many years, was that no plows suitable for
breaking the prairie land could be had. The sod was very much
tougher then than it was in after years when the stock had pastured
the prairies and killed out the grass to some extent. It would be
astonishing to the younger residents to see the immense crops of
prairie grass that grew upon the fields which are to-day in such a
high state of cultivation. It grew in places six to twelve feet high.
It was these immense crops of grass that furnished the fuel for the
terrible fires that swept over the prairies during the fall. Then,
again, there was so much of the prairie land that was considered
too wet to be ever suitable for cultivation. Many of the older settlers now living well remember when farms that are now in the

highest state of cultivation were a vast swamp. There was another drawback in the settlement of the prairies, and that was the great labor and cost of fencing. But the principal reason for locating in the timber was that many of their cabins were poor, half-finished affairs, and protection from the driving storms was absolutely required. The timber also sheltered stock until such times as sheds and out-buildings could be erected. That the time should soon come when intelligent, enterprising farmers would see that their interest lay in improving prairie farms, and cease clearing fields, when there were boundless acres presenting no obstacle to the most perfect cultivation, argues nothing in the policy of sheltering for a time in the woods. In regard to the pioneers settling along the timber, we often hear remarks made as though the selection of such locations implied a lack of judgment. Those who are disposed to treat it in that manner are asked to consider carefully the above facts, when they will conclude such selection argued in their favor.

Clearing of timber land was attended with much hard labor. The underbrush was grubbed up, piled into heaps and burned. The large trees were in many cases left standing, and deadened by girdling. This was done by cutting through the bark into the wood, generally through the " sap," all around the trunk.

MILLING.

Not the least of the hardships of the pioneers was the procuring of bread. The first settlers must be supplied at least one year from other sources than their own lands. But the first crops, however abundant, gave only partial relief, there being no mills to grind the grain. Hence the necessity of grinding by hand power, and many families were poorly provided with means for doing this. Another way was to grate the corn. A grater was made from a piece of tin, sometimes taken from an old, worn-out tin bucket or other vessel. It was thickly perforated, bent into a semi-circular form, and nailed, rough side upward, on a board. The corn was taken in the ear, and grated before it got dry and hard. Corn, however, was eaten in various ways.

Soon after the country became more generally settled, enterprising men were ready to embark in the milling business. Sites along the streams were selected for water-power. A person looking for a mill-site would follow up and down the stream for a desired location, and when found he would go before the County Commissioners and secure a writ of *ad quod damnum*. This would enable the miller to have the adjoining land officially examined, and the amount of damage by making a dam was named. Mills being such a great public necessity, they were permitted to be located upon any person's land where the miller thought the site desirable.

The Hominy Block.—Before giving the particulars of the anecdote about to be related it would be well to describe the hominy block, for there are thousands in this county, doubtless, especially of the rising generation, who have never so much as heard of the

hominy block.   It consisted of a hole bored or burned in the end
of a log or stump, basin form, in which the corn was placed and
then pounded with an iron wedge, block of wood or a rolling pin.
Sometimes the pounding apparatus consisted of a long, heavy block
of wood attached to a spring-pole above, which lessened the labor of
preparing a meal.   The one we have in question consisted of a
burned-out place in the top of a stump, a heavy block or pole attached to a transverse spring-pole, but was run by water power
instead of the common way.   This hominy block was made and
owned by Amasa Shinn, who resided in or near Kinderhook township.   Mr. Shinn would fill the block with corn at night, set it in
motion, and by morning it would be pulverized and ready to be
made into bread for breakfast.   There came a time, however, when
Mr. Shinn and family preferred to fast, for at least one meal.
Squirrels were quite numerous in those days—far more than they
are at present—and one evening after Mr. Shinn had set his mill in
motion as usual, a squirred hopped upon the edge of the block and
began wistfully to scrutinize the corn below.   Finally he concluded
to have some; and while the hammer was up, jumped into the
block and began helping himself, when the huge pounder alighted
upon him.   During the remainder of the night the pounder kept
regularly descending into the block, thoroughly mashing and mix-
ing the squirrel and the corn.   When Mr. Shinn came down the
next morning for his meal he found a conglomerate of squirrel and
meal.

Many interesting and ludicrous incidents are related in reference
to going to mill, waiting for grists, etc., many of which are
greatly overdrawn.   Harrison Henry, now deceased, often related
an incident that, although untrue, was commendable for its witticism
and application to the mills of pioneer days.   He would tell the
story of himself in the following language: "I went to Mr. Everitt's mill (an overshot water-mill) one day, and remained until
night for my turn.   When my turn came Mr. Everitt filled
the hopper with corn, and taking me with him to the house, retired
for the night, leaving the mill to do the work alone.   During the
night I was awakened by the barking of Mr. Everitt's dog.   This
annoyed me not a little, but I finally fell asleep again.   In the early
morning when I awoke, I heard the almost steady barking of the
dog, and went down to the mill to learn what it was barking at.   On
arriving there I found that the dog had eaten all the meal and was
barking for more!   He would wait until a little meal would come
down, when he would ravenously lick it up, and then look up the
spout and bark for more!"   Mr. Henry would continue: "I don't
tell this incident to injure the mill, for it was a very good and faithful mill; it grinds away faithfully on one grain until it finishes it,
and then jumps right on to another."

NATIVE ANIMALS.

The wild animals infesting this county at the time of its settlement were the deer, wolf, bear, wild-cat, fox, otter, raccoon, wood-chuck or ground-dog, skunk, mink, weasel, muskrat, opossum, rabbit and squirrel; and the principal feathered game were the quail, prairie-chicken, and wild turkey. Several of these animals furnished meat for the early settlers; but their principal meat did not consist long of game. Pork and poultry were soon raised in abundance. The wolf was the most troublesome animal, it being the common enemy of the sheep. It was quite difficult to protect the sheep from their ravages. Sometimes pigs and calves were also victims of the wolf. Their howlings in the night would often keep families awake, and set all the dogs in the neighborhood to barking. Their yells were often terrific. Says one settler: " Suppose six boys, having six dogs tied, whipped them all at the same time, and you would hear such music as two wolves would make." To effect the destruction of these animals the county authorities offered a bounty for their scalps; and, besides, big hunts were inagurated for their destruction, and " wolf hunts " are prominent among the memories of the early settlers. Such events were generally turned into a holiday, and everybody that could ride a nag or stand the tramp on foot joined in the deadly pursuit. A large circuit was generally made by the hunters, who then closed on every side, driving the hungry wolves into the center of the corral, where they were despatched. The return home with the carcasses was the signal for a general turnout, and these " pleasure parties " are still referred to by old citizens as among the pleasantest memories of early life in Pike county. Many a hungry wolf has been run down on the prairies where now is located a town or a fine farm residence. This rare old pastime, like much of the early hunting and fishing the pioneers indulged in here, departed at the appearance of the locomotive.

BEE-HUNTING.

During the early settlement of this part of the State, one of the prevailing customs of the poineers was " bee-hunting." Often a small company would travel many miles into a wild, unsettled country, in search of the sweet, flavored honey of the wild bee. Large trees containing many gallons, and often a barrel, were frequently found by bee-bunters. The little, busy bees would be carefully watched as they flew heavily laden with the richest extract of the flowers that were purely native and unknown to the present generation. They always took a " bee-line " for their homes. This was a correct guide to the sturdy hunter, who had studied with care the ways of the bee and by their knowledge took advantage of the little insect. Once on the trail, good bee-hunters were almost certain to capture the rich prize. After the bee-tree was discovered it was no trouble to get possession of the honey. The tree was felled, and the hunters would rush for their booty ere it was lost by running out upon the ground.

MANNERS AND CUSTOMS.

The pioneer was more freely and heartily social with his friends, and cold toward his enemies, than we seem to be at the present day; and he showed what race he belonged to by his efforts to establish religious, philanthropic and educational institutions. The young folks, we have no doubt, found many ways of robbing old Time of loneliness. It would be unfair to suppose them, especially the ladies, destitute of fashionable aspirations, but the means for gaudy display were very much circumscribed in those days. The male attire consisted chiefly of buckskin, or homespun cloth,—we might add home-woven, the loom being far more common in or near their rude huts than the piano or organ. They were not, however, destitute of musical taste, and many of their vocal performances would compare favorably with our present choirs. We may safely say they sang with the spirit. Most of the ladies, also, wore homespun, which they manufactured from wool, flax, cotton, and the bark or lint of the nettle, colored with such ingredients as nature provided, without the aid of art. A few even adopted buckskin. How many yards of the latter article were required for a fashionable dress in those times, or in what particular style it was cut and trimmed, we are not informed, and must leave the ladies to draw their own conclusions. These dresses certainly were durable, and shielded the wearer in out-door exercises incident to the planting, attending and gathering of crops, in which pursuit the ladies in all new countries assist.

Another of the prevailing fashions was of that of carrying fire-arms, made necessary by the presence of roving bands of Indians, most of whom were ostensibly friendly, but like Indians in all times, treacherous and unreliable. These tribes were principally Pottawatomies. There were also in the northern part of the State several tribes of hostile Indians, ready at any time to make a murderous, thieving raid upon the white settlers; and an Indian war at any time was an accepted probability; and these old settlers to-day have vivid recollections of the Black Hawk and other Indian wars. And, while target practice was much indulged in as an amusement, it was also necessary for a proper self-defense, the settlers finding it necessary at times to carry their guns with them when they went to hoe their corn. In some instances their guns were stacked in the field and the laborers worked for a certain distance around them, and then moved the guns to a certain position and again proceeded with their work.

These were only a few of the hardships incident to pioneer life, which was largely made up of privations, inconveniences and dangers. They had few labor-saving machines and no reliable markets. Even communication by letter with their distant friends and relatives was rendered difficult for want of proper mail facilities, and sometimes for the want of money to pay the postage on the letters sent to them,—the postage then being twenty-five cents for a single letter, many of which remained in the office for weeks on account of the inability of the persons addressed to pay the postage.

MARKETS.

The earliest settlers of the county went to St. Louis with what little produce they had to sell, and the merchants bought all their goods in that city. Soon, however, Louisiana became a market, and produce was wagoned to that city and from there sent south on the river. There was at that time no sale for corn, or comparatively none, and wheat would bring but a small price; so that really there was no impetus given to the raising of grain of any sort, except for home consumption, until the advent of the railroad. At that time improvement began. The great resources of the county which had scarcely supplied more than home demand were then turned to supply the wants of thousands. That occasion, the advent of railroads, was the commencement of agricultural development. It was the commencement of the manufacturing institutions the county can now boast of; it was the building of her thriving cities and towns; indeed it was the beginning of progress.

One of the earliest steam-boats in the Illinois river trade was the steamer "Exchange," which plied between St. Louis and Peoria. She was familiarly known as "the Shingle Weaver," so called from the fact of her carrying upon her hurricane deck a machine for cutting shingles, which was operated by the machinery of the boat, cutting whenever the boat was in motion. Shingle timber would be obtained at the wood-yards along the river, and market found for the manufactured goods at St. Louis. This boat was an especial favorite with the people of this county, many of whom would, when desiring to take a trip by the river, wait for her coming, and most of the early stocks of goods for the eastern part of the county were shipped on her; she also carried most of the county's "beeswax" and other products to their market.

"When the first settlers came to the wilderness" says an old settler, "they all supposed that their hard struggle would be principally over after the first year; but alas! we looked for 'easier times next year' for about ten years, and learned to bear hardships, privation and hard living as good soldiers do. As the facilities for making money were not great, we lived pretty well satisfied in an atmosphere of good, social, friendly feeling, and thought ourselves as good as those we left behind when we emigrated West."

CHILLS AND FEVER.

One of the greatest obstacles to the early settlement and prosperity of this county was the "chills and fever," or "ague," or "Illinois shakes," as it was variously styled. This disease was a terror to new comers. In the fall of the year everybody was afflicted with it. It was no respecter of persons; everybody shook with it, and it was in every person's system. They all looked pale and yellow as though they were frostbitten. It was not contagious, but was a kind of miasma floating around in the atmosphere and absorbed into the system.   It continued to be absorbed from day to day, and week to week, until the whole body corporate became charged with it as with electricity, and then the shock came; and the shock was a regular shake, with a fixed beginning and an ending, coming on each day, or each alternate day, with a regularity that was surprising.   After the shake came the fever, and this "last estate was worse than the first."   It was a burning, hot fever and lasted for hours.   When you had the chill you couldn't get warm, and when you had the fever you couldn't get cool.   It was exceedingly awkward in this respect; indeed it was.   Nor would it stop for any sort of contingency.   Not even a wedding in the family would stop it.   It was imperative and tyrannical.   When the appointed time came around everything else had to be stopped to attend to its demands.   It didn't even have any Sunday or holidays. After the fever went down you still didn't feel much better.   You felt as though you had gone through some sort of collision and came out not killed but badly demoralized.   You felt weak, as though you had run too far after something, and then didn't catch it.   You felt languid, stupid and sore, and was down in the mouth and heel and partially raveled out, so to speak.   Your back was out of fix and your appetite was in a worse condition than your back.   Your head ached and your eyes had more white in them than usual, and altogether you felt poor, disconsolate and sad.   You didn't think much of yourself, and didn't believe other people did either, and you didn't care.   You didn't think much of suicide, but at the same time you almost made up your mind that under certain circumstances it was justifiable. You imagined that even the dogs looked at you with a kind of self-complacency.   You thought the sun had a kind of sickly shine about it.   About this time you came to the conclusion that you would not accept the whole State of Illinois as a gift, and if you had the strength and means, you picked up Hannah and the baby and your traps, and went back "yander" to Injianny, Ohio, or old Kaintuck.

> "And to-day the swallows flitting
> Round my cabin see me sitting
> Moodily within the sunshine,
>   Just inside my silent door,
> Waiting for the 'ager,' seeming
> Like a man forever dreaming;
> And the sunlight on me streaming
>   Throws no shadow on the floor;
> For I am too thin and sallow
>   To make shadows on the floor—
>   Nary shadow any more!"

The above is no picture of the imagination.   It is simply recounting what occurred in hundreds of instances.   Whole families would sometimes be sick at one time, and not one member scarcely able to wait upon another. One widow lady on the Illinois river informs us that she lost nine children from this dreaded disease!

COOKING.

To witness the various processes of cooking in those days would alike surprise and amuse those who have grown up since cooking stoves and ranges came into use. Kettles were hung over the large fire, suspended on trammels which were held by strong poles. The long-handled frying-pan was used for cooking meat. It was held on the fire by hand; or, to save time, the handle was laid across the back of a chair. This pan was also used for baking short-cake. A better article was a cast-iron spider, which was set upon coals on the hearth. But the best thing for baking bread was the flat-bottomed bake-kettle, of greater depth, with closely fitting cast-iron cover, and commonly known as the "Dutch oven." With coals over and under it bread and buscuit would quickly and nicely bake. Turkeys and spare-ribs were sometimes roasted before the fire, suspended by a string, a dish being placed underneath to catch the drippings.

IMPLEMENTS.

The agricultural implements used by the first farmers here would in this age of improvement be great curiosities. The plow used was called the bar-share plow. The iron point consisted of a bar of iron about two feet long, and a broad share of iron welded to it. At the extreme point was a coulter that passed through a beam six or seven feet long, to which were attached handles of corresponding length. The mold-board was a wooden one split out of winding timber, or hewed into a winding shape in order to turn the soil over. Sown seed was brushed in by dragging over the ground a sapling with a bushy top. In harvesting the change is most striking. Instead of the reapers and mowers of to-day, the sickle and cradle were used. The grain was threshed with a flail, or trodden out by horses or oxen.

WOMEN'S WORK.

The men were not called upon to endure alone all the hardships and labor of frontier life. The women also had their physical labor to perform, and much of it was quite arduous. Spinning was one of the common household duties. This exercise is one which few of the present generation of girls have ever enjoyed. The wheel used for spinning flax was called the "little wheel," to distinguish it from the "big wheel," used for spinning yarn. These stringed instruments furnished the principal music of the family, and were operated by our mothers and grandmothers with great skill, attained without pecuniary expense and with far less practice than is necessary for the girls of our period to acquire a skillful use of their costly and elegant instruments.

The loom was not less necessary than the wheel. Not every house, however, in which spinning was done had a loom; but there were always some in each settlement who, besides doing their own weaving, did some for others. Settlers, having succeeded in spite of the wolves in raising sheep, commenced the manufacture of woolen cloth; wool was carded and made into rolls by hand-cards, and the rolls were spun on the "big wheel." We occasionally find now, in the houses of the old settlers, one of these big wheels, sometimes used for spinning and twisting stocking yarn. They are turned with the hand, and with such velocity that it will run itself while the nimble worker, by her backward step, draws out and twists her thread nearly the whole length of the cabin. A common article woven on the loom was linsey, also called linsey-woolsey, the chain being linen and the filling woolen. This cloth was used for dresses for the girls and mothers. Nearly all the clothes worn by the men were also home-made. Rarely was a farmer or his son seen in a coat made of any other. If, occasionally, a young man appeared in a suit of "boughten" clothes, he was suspected of having gotten it for a particular occasion, which occurs in the life of nearly every man.

Not until the settlers had supplied themselves with the more useful articles of clothing and with edibles of various kinds, did wheat bread become a common article of food. It is true they had it earlier, but this was only served on extra occasions, as when visitors came, or on Sundays; and with this luxury they would have a little "store coffee." "The little brown jug" found a place in almost every home, and was often brought into use. No caller was permitted to leave the house without an invitation to partake of its contents.

PLEASURES OF PIONEER LIFE.

The history of pioneer life generally presents the dark side of the picture; but the toils and privations of the early settlers were not a series of unmitigated sufferings. No; for while the fathers and mothers toiled hard, they were not averse to a little relaxation, and had their seasons of fun and enjoyment. They contrived to do something to break the monotony of their daily life and furnish them a good, hearty laugh. Among the more general forms of amusement were the "quilting-bee," "corn-husking," "apple-paring," "log-rolling" and "house-raising." Our young readers will doubtless be interested in a description of these forms of amusement, when labor was made to afford fun and enjoyment to all participating. The "quilting-bee," as its name implies, was when the industrious qualities of the busy, little insect that "improves each shining hour" were exemplified in the manufacture of quilts for the household. In the afternoon ladies for miles around gathered at an appointed place, and while their tongues would not cease to play, their hands were as busily engaged in making the quilt; and desire was always manifested to get it out as quickly as possible,

GRIGGSVILLE

for then the fun would begin. In the evening the gentlemen came, and the hours would then pass swiftly by in playing games or dancing. "Corn-huskings" were when both sexes united in the work. They usually assembled in a large barn, which was arranged for the occasion; and when each gentleman had selected a lady partner the husking began. When a lady found a red ear she was entitled to a kiss from every gentleman present; when a gentleman found one he was allowed to kiss every lady present. After the corn was all husked a good supper was served; then the "old folks" would leave, and the remainder of the evening was spent in the dance and in having a general good time. The recreation afforded to the young people on the annual recurrence of these festive occasions was as highly enjoyed, and quite as innocent, as the amusements of the present boasted age of refinement and culture.

FURNITURE OF THE PIONEER CABINS.

The furniture of the cabin was as primitive as the occupants. In one corner—perhaps in two or three corners—were the bedsteads. These were your genuine "cottage bedsteads," made by boring one hole, say four feet from one corner of the cabin, into a "house-log," another hole, say six feet from the same corner, on another side; opposite these holes was set an upright post, usually a section from the body of a peeled sapling; in this post two holes would be bored at any desired height, and at right angles with each other; poles were inserted in these holes, making in this manner a square frame; over this frame was laid a covering of clapboards, or, as some denominated them, "shakes," and on top of this platform the bed was spread. The chairs were not exactly chairs, but three-legged stools or puncheon benches. The cupboard was literally a cupboard, being a puncheon supported by pins driven into holes in the house logs at some convenient corner. The boxes which had held the family dry goods while *en route* to the new country generally furnished the table, and a trough or troughs the meat and soap barrels. Hollow logs sawed into sections and provided with a puncheon bottom furnished a receptacle for meal, potatoes, beans, wheat, "and sich like truck"—to use the pioneer vernacular. The table was bounteously supplied with "samp," "lye hominy," "corn pone," honey, venison, pork, stewed pumpkin, wild turkey, prairie chicken and other game. Wheat bread, tea, coffee, and fruit—except wild fruit—were luxuries not to be indulged in except on special occasions, as a wedding or gala day. "Samp" was quite a frequent dish. It was made by burning a hole into some convenient stump in the shape of a mortar; this hole was filled with corn and pounded by a large pestle hung like the old-fashioned well-sweep pendent from a long pole, which was nearly balanced on an upright fork. This pole had a weight attached to one end and the pestle to the other; the weight would lift the pestle, while manual force was expected to bring it down. When the "samp" was pounded sufficiently, it was washed and boiled like rice.

22

The traveler always found a welcome at the pioneer's cabin. It was never full; although there might already be a guest for every puncheon, there was still "room for one more," and a wider circle would be made for the new-comer at the log fire. If the stranger was in search of land, he was doubly welcome, and his host would volunteer to show him all the "first-rate claims in this neck of woods," going with him for days, showing the corners and advantages of every "Congress tract" within a dozen miles from his own cabin.

To his neighbors the pioneer was equally liberal. If a deer was killed, the choicest bits were sent to his nearest neighbor, a half-dozen miles away, perhaps. When a "shoat" was butchered, the same custom prevailed. If a new-comer came in too late for "cropping," the neighbors would supply his table with just the same luxuries they themselves enjoyed, and in as liberal quantity, until a crop could be raised. When a new-comer had located his claim, the neighbors for miles around would assemble at the site of the new-comer's proposed cabin and aid him in "gittin" it up. One party with axes would fell and hew the logs; another with teams would haul the logs to the ground; another party would "raise the cabin"; while several of the old men would "rive the clapboards" for the roof. By night the cabin would be up and ready for occupying, and by the next day the new-comer was in all respects as well situated as his neighbors.

Saturday was a regular holiday, in which work was ignored and everybody went to town or to some place of general resort. When all were together in town, sport began. Of course whisky circulated freely and everybody indulged to a greater or less extent. Quarrels were now settled by hand-to-hand encounters; wrestling-matches came off or were arranged for the future; jumping, foot-racing, and horse-racing filled up the interval of time; and everybody enjoyed the rough sport with a zest unknown among the more refined denizens of the present day.

CHAPTER XIII.

It is not strange that among the pioneer settlers of any new country a deep-seated and sincere friendship should spring up that would grow and strengthen with their years. The incidents peculiar to life in a new country,—the trials and hardships, privations and destitution,—are well calculated to test not only the physical powers of endurance, but the moral, kindly, generous attributes of manhood and womanhood. Then are the times that try men's souls, and bring to the surface all that may be in them whether good or bad. As a rule there is an equality of conditions that recognizes no distinctions. All occupy a common level, and as a natural consequence a strong brotherly and sisterly feeling rise up that is as lasting as time. For "a fellow feeling makes us wondrous kind." With such a community there is a hospitality, a kindness, a benevolence, a charity unknown and unpracticed among the older, richer and more densely commonwealths. The very nature of the surroundings teaches them to feel each other's woe and share each other's joy. An injury or a wrong may be ignored, but a kindly, charitable act is never forgotten. The memory of old associations are always fresh. Raven locks may bleach and whiten, full, round cheeks become sunken and hollow, the fires of intelligence vanish from the organs of vision, the brow become wrinkled with care and age and the erect form bowed with accumulating years,—but the true friends of "long ago" will be remembered as long as life and reason endure.

The surroundings of pioneer life are well calculated to test the "true inwardness" of the human heart. As a rule the men and women who first settle in a new country,—who go in advance to spy out the land and prepare it for the coming people,—are bold, fearless, self-reliant and industrious. In these respects, no matter from what remote section or country they may come, there is a similarity of character. In birth, education, religion and language, there may be a vast difference, but imbued with a common purpose,—the founding and building of homes,—these differences are soon lost by association, and thus they become one people united by a common interest; and no matter what changes may come in after years the associations thus formed are never buried out of memory.

In pioneer life are always incidents of peculiar interest, not only to the pioneers themselves, but which if properly preserved, would be of interest to posterity; and it is a matter of some regret that "The Old Settlers' Association" was not formed years before it was, and that more copious records were not kept. Such an association with well kept records of the more important events, such as dates of arrivals, births, marriages, deaths, removals, nativities, etc., as any one can easily and readily see, would be the direct means of preserving to the literature of the country the history of every community, that to future generations would be valuable as a record of reference, and a ready and sure method of settling important questions of controversy. Such records would possess facts and figures that could not be had from any other source. Aside from this historic importance such associations serve as a means of keeping alive and further cementing old friendships and renewing among its members associations that were necessarily interrupted by the innovation of increasing population, cultivating social intercourse and creating a charitable fund for such of their old members as were victims of misfortune and adversity.

The subject of organizing an old settlers' society was brought up in the summer of 1869. In the *Pike County Democrat* of July 29, that year, the following significant passage occurs: "The time will come when the history of this county will be written. For that history, the meeting of such society will furnish the best material, and the parties now living attest the facts that will form a large portion of it." There was nothing definitely done toward the organization of this society until the summer of 1872, when some of the leading old settlers interested themselves in it. The first meeting was held on what is called Blue creek, Aug. 21, 1872. The meeting was called to order by Wm. Turnbull, of Flint, on whose motion Capt. B. F. Westlake was appointed temporary Chairman. Upon taking the chair Capt. Westlake stated in brief the object of the meeting, and for the purpose of effecting on organization he suggested the propriety of appointing a committee on permanent organization to report to the meeting at 1 o'clock, P. M. This committee consisted of Col. A. C. Matthews, Jas. H. Dimmitt and Wm. Turnbull. The meeting was then addressed by Rev. Mr. McCoy, after which an adjournmemt was had until 1 o'clock, P. M. After the dinner was dispatched the people were called together by the choir, discoursing most pleasant music. After singing the committee on permanent organization reported the following named persons as officers of the "Old Settlers' Association of Pike and Calhoun Counties, Ill."

For President, Col. Wm. Ross, Newburg; 1st Vice President, Col. Benj. Barney, Pleasant Vale; 2d Vice President, Daniel B. Bush, Pittsfield; 3d Vice President, Capt. B. F. Westlake, Newburg; 4th Vice President, Capt. Benj. L. Matthews, Perry; 5th Vice

President, Jos. Brown, Chambersburg; 6th Vice President, John Lyster, Detroit; 7th Vice President, Jas. Grimes, Milton; 8th Vice President, Abel Shelley, Griggsville; 9th Vice President, Perry Wells, Atlas; 10th Vice President, Sam'l G. Sitton. Hardin; 11th Vice President, Wm. Grammar, Hadley; 12th Vice President, Montgomery Blair, Barry; 13th Vice President, John Brittain, Martinsburg; 14th Vice President, Thos H. Dimmitt, Griggsville. Secretary, Marcellus Ross, Newburg; 1st Assistant Secretary, Dr. E. M. Seeley, Pittsfield; 2d Assistant Secretary Wm. Turnbull, Flint.

Col. Barney presided at this meeting, Col. Ross being absent on account of sickness. A 'communication was however read from the President. Rev. W. D. Trotter, one of the pioneer preachers of the county, spoke for about an hour, reviewing the early life of the pioneers. Hon. William A. Grimshaw delivered the address of the day. It was an ably prepared historical review of the county's history. Indeed, so replete is it with interesting facts of pioneer times that we give the entire address in this connection:

ADDRESS OF HON. WILLIAM A. GRIMSHAW.

Mr. President, Ladies and Gentlemen :—Selected by your committee of arrangements to bid you welcome here to-day, I do so most cordially, as an old settler myself, of, say, the second period of Pike county, coming here in the year 1833 ; that being after the winter of the deep snow, which was our early noted period in the annals of this then wild, romantic, and beautiful country, sparsely settled and embraced in the bounds of Pike county. That snow with us, once, was the starting point of the date of current events, although our records of the courts of justice do not legally recognize that as a " day in law," yet we even in courts, in the simplicity of our early language, often heard events traced by that snow as the date point.

In the early days we all enjoyed the largest constitutional liberty; we voted for him we liked best, as I, a Whig, did for " honest Joe Duncan," a Democrat, on a deep question in those days, the Illinois and Michigan Canal, " the deep cut ;" we also each worshipped God according to the dictates of our own conscience and under our vine and fig-tree. When Brother Trotter, who is now present, venerable with years and revered for piety, or old Father Woolf, now gathered to his fathers, blessed for his good deeds, came around to his appointment, all, of every religion and no one religion, turned out to meeting in the woods or the log school-house or at a settler's home. We had no fine churches in those days. Mormons puzzled the unwary by their startling pretense at new revelations. Or, if disappointed by the regular minister, old Father Petty would recite, in prayer, Belteshazzar's feast, in trembling tones of piety.

Our worthy and venerable President (elect but absent), Col. Wm. Ross, who has been often honored by the people of Pike Co. by their votes, electing him to high offices of public trust, could tell you much of the first period or earliest years of the settlement of your county, as he arrived in the county in 1820 and settled at Atlas, which was the county-seat in its day, and was laid out by the Ross brothers. Atlas was yet the place at which the county records were kept in 1833, but in the spring of the year Pittsfield was surveyed and laid off into lots and the sale thereof made at different periods, the first sale of lots being in that spring. A court-house was built in the summer of 1833 at Pittsfield ; from that event the greater prosperity of the county and an increase of population began.

The terror infused into the public mind, beyond the settlements of Illinois, by the Black Hawk war, which had retarded emigration to our State, the Indians being removed to the West of the Mississippi, the tide of emigration began to set in, and you witness to-day, in the presence here of this assemblage, the vast change in a little over fifty years since the Yankees (who came before the clock-peddlers) set foot within the limits of Pike county, as it now exists. Clock peddlers were the only gentlemen in those days, as they rode in the only covered carriages.

It is true, when you consider the rise and growth of Chicago in our own State, and of St. Louis in Missouri, rival cities, each of nearly four hundred thousand people, we don't seem to have much to brag of as to our growth. Consider, however, that we are almost strictly an agricultural county, that being our chief and most profitable pursuit, and then the greatest zealot for progress must admit that, from a beginning of a few families in 1821, we are now a county not to be sneezed at, and especially when our vote at the polls is counted. Excluding counties in which cities have arisen, we are most densely populated, more so than many in our beautiful Illinois, and yet we have broad acres of valuable lands in a state of nature.

Once our prairies were the home of the bounding deer in vast herds, of the prarie wolf, the prairie fowl in great flocks, the timber land abounded with the squirrel, the turkey and the pigeon, and in the hollow trees we had the beautiful but noisy paroquet; as well as in their haunts numerous other birds and animals. These have in a great measure disappeared until game is a rarity. The wild fruits once abounding have been superseded by more luscious cultivated fruits. And yet, who of the old settlers does not remember with a twinkle in his eye the old settlers' first substitute for an apple, a big turnip; and also find a good taste in the mouth when he thinks of those nice preserved plums, crab-apples and ground cherries, and the pumpkin pie, and the pork mince meat. We then think of the prairie and woodland each abounding in the season in beautiful flowers, rivaling in their colors the rainbow. These were the holiday delights of dame and maiden, and the husband and lover were alike made glad in their contemplation. The retrospect of nature has its beauties. The reality of the first settler's life in a new country is often full of prose and but little poetry. Compare the simple and even poor furniture of our early homes with the elegant furniture now in use, and what a contrast! But with all the drawbacks of an early settler's life few repine at their lot in this beautiful land. None can who accept with reflection and thankfulness the many mercies which crown our lives.

I am reminded by this retrospection, that yesterday, on returning home, I found a written, kind notification from your Committee, in charge of the convening of this your first Old Settlers' meeting, that I was invited and expected to address you to-day. I then took my pen to endeavor to bridle my thoughts and to bid them serve the request of the Committee, that I should speak as to the "honesty, patience, industry, self-sacrifice and hospitality of the old settlers."

Honesty was the rule, crime the exception, in early days. It would seem as if at the first mention of the honesty of the old settlers it was a sarcasm, on the idea of lawyers settling here, and as if I had some personal experience and revelation to make. Of course I know something and much of the facts, and will relate them.

It was well known that because we had no locks we never locked our houses and out buildings; it was proverbial that the deer skin of the door latch was never pulled in, that is the latch string was out; then we had not much to tempt people to steal; so our things lay about loose; our plows with their wooden mold-boards hung on the fences with impunity; but at Christmas time, the plow or ox skull hung upon a tree by the way side, reminded the passer-by, on the three-year old, riding to see his girl, that a fool's head was too soft to butt either of those pendants in the tree.

At an early day an old ax, worth fifty cents perhaps in these days being stolen, the vile thief was ordered to leave the settlement of Atlas, and did leave for his country's good. It was said that loud porcine cries were heard upon the "Sny Island" at times, because men would kill their neighbor's hogs : that was a trifling affair and cost only the penalty of going halves with the nearest justice; thus dividing the meat—unless the head and ears were found and those bearing some man's recorded mark; then that was a case for the Grand Jury. Hog stealing was said to be caused by drinking Sny water.

We have told only of the style of dishonest tricks in those days. With more facts to bear us out, we can now affirm that the general reputation of our early settlers was remarkably good for honesty in general, but there was a slight propensity to "hook timber" to make rails and to use as house logs, and some fellows in the land, held, in fact it was "common law," that a "bee tree" even in your pasture lot was lawful plunder.

As to the patience of our people, if that means bearing up with the courage of a true man and true woman under the perils to limb and property, the early settlers were exemplary for that; the

trials of an early settler's life were legion. His resources, so far
as supplies for his family, were small; his debts were a great vexation, and some, if not all, had these pests, until the lands were
entered and paid for, the money often being loaned at interest as
high as 75 per centum per annum. Then if you went to mill, you
journeyed a score, aye, three-score miles; to meeting often as far.
No bridges, and but few roads existed; the saddle, or the ox cart,
or truck, wooden-wheeled wagon, and no fine carriages, was the
mode of travel.

Corn dodger, without salt, and pork or side-meat, were great staples;
vegetables and fruits, unless wild fruits, were rarely on the table,
unless when company came to spend the afternoon, or to a quilting, then the best the house or the neighborhood afforded was
forthcoming for the visitor. The quilting parties were generally
the resort of young and old. Marriages were rare in those days,
because bachelors were more plenty than belles.

As to the industry of the old settlers, as a class, industry was to
the extent of present ability, implements, health and condition, and
was not surpassed by the toil of men of the present day. The ma-
tron and the few young ladies had much toil and vexation, and that
was often more excessive on wash-day, because of having to pick up
fuel as it could be gleaned, or carrying the clothes to and from
the wash place, which was a branch or spring. The clothes-line
was a grape vine or a fence, and the hogs and calves trespassed on
that to "chaw the things," and to keep the "creeters" off, old
boss and the old woman (not yet 25 years old) often had a hard
fight lest the baby in the cradle sitting near the out-door fire should
be "up sot."

Self-sacrifice was one of the many and noblest virtues of the
early settler; in times of sickness you were free to call up any
neighbor for help, to sit up with the sick, to ride 25 or even more
miles for the doctor, and that mostly, as our doctors said, in the
dead of night, to the great horror of the doctor, who had to saddle
up and travel, even in the dead of night, to the farthest limits of
his own or to an adjoining county.

Although the county of Pike was naturally healthy, the over
toil, the privation, the imperfect protection from the inclemency of
seasons, the water used from shallow water-holes, all these tended
to multiply disease and death. This county was never, as a general thing, visited so much with sickness and death as other counties in our State.

In the early day no iron horse snorted and raced over our
prairies. The steamer once perhaps in several weeks dragged itself
along. Twelve days was a short time for a trip from New York
here, and that mostly by stage. Our mails arrived once a week,
and a letter cost us our "last quarter." News from Europe a
month old was fresh. No troublesome quotations of daily markets
puzzled or enlightened us. A counterfeit United States bill was
almost legal tender. Hoop-poles, staves and cord wood were equal

at a later day to gold. Store pay was better than any of the fore-going, but often lead to heavy mortgages and secret bills of sale. The laws were quickly enforced. Once a client of a celebrated lawyer was taken out of Court and the penalty of the law put on his back with stripes before the motion for a new trial was over; then the client protested against a new trial lest if convicted he would be a second time whipped.

Now how changed is everything around us! In the early day there was more variety in dress, if less taste. All dressed in their best, and sometimes (if the ladies will pardon such an o'er true tale) a white satin bonnet, the worse for the wear, was seen over a blue "Dolly Varden" ruffled cap. The most distinguished man at shows, for a number of years, was an old, gaunt, straight man, with a bell-crowned hat, in the height of the fashion when he was young, which was nearly twelve inches perpendicular; horses often carried double in those days, if girls were plenty, and about spark-ing and wedding time. Oh how sociable! and yet all was modesty and innocence.

Hospitality—that signifies strictly "practice of entertaining strangers," but in its true early settler's ways much more was meant, intended, and done. On a journey almost every house was a welcome home to the weary traveler; if any charge was made for the entertainment it was very moderate; at times the parting word to you was, " You are welcome to such as we had, and please call again when traveling this way."

Hospitality scarce expresses the fine sensibility, the manly Chris-tian spirit, of many of the olden time. The pioneer feels that each and every settler of his neighborhood (and he does not criticise much as to who is his neighbor) is entitled to such help and good feeling as may be asked or should be extended.

I felt and still feel a large degree of sympathy, and that the most cordial, with the old settlers. It occurs to me that as Pike county once included Calhoun, and as some of the settlers there are co-temporaries with our earliest settlers, we should include the Cal-houn old settlers in our Society—in fact just this week that was named to me in that county.

With great hopefulness as to the prosperity of this new Society, desiring for it many happy re-unions, I offer to you the thanks of myself, an old settler, for your courtesy in inviting me to address this meeting; and may God bless our vast population, spread over our large county, which had when first known to myself about three thousand people, and now contains approaching forty thou-sand, although the hive of people has swarmed many times.

Farewell, my friends, one and all. Let us part with mutual good wishes, as we never more can all meet again in this life.

At the first meeting it was decided to invite the old settlers of Calhoun county to join with the Pike county Old Settlers' Society.

In harmony with this decision Calvin Twichell, Smith Jennings and William Wilkinson were elected Vice-Presidents.

SECOND MEETING.

The second meeting of the Old Settlers' Association was held in September, 1873. The following letter from Judge William Thomas, of Jacksonville, was read:

"JACKSONVILLE, Aug. 30, 1873.

"MR. MARCELLUS ROSS, Secretary:—Dear Sir,—I have received two invitations to attend the Old Settlers' Meeting in Pike county on Wednesday next. I regret that I cannot accept either, for I would be glad to meet the survivors of those with whom I became acquainted forty-five years ago. I attended the Circuit Court in Atlas in June, 1827, which was my first visit to Pike. The Court was held by Judge Lockwood, who now resides at Batavia, in Kane county. The attorneys in attendance were John W. Whitney, N. Hanson, and John Jay Ross, of Pike county, Gen. James Turney and Alfred W. Caverly, of Greene county, now of Ottawa, and J. W. Pugh, of Sangamon county, Mr. Jenkins, of Calhoun county, John Turney and myself, of Morgan county. Capt. Leonard Ross, one of nature's noblemen, was Sheriff. Col. Wm. Ross was Clerk; James M. Seeley was an officer of the Court. Of all these, Judge Lockwood, Mr. Caverly, and myself are the only survivors. The Court was in session three days, and then went to Calhoun county. It was held in a log cabin in the prairie, near which was a log cabin. occupied by the grand jury. The traverse jury had the privilege of the prairies.

"In September afterward, returning from the Winnebago war I left the boat at Quincy, where I purchased a horse, saddle and bridle for $40. From Quincy I came to Atlas, a good day's travel; remained in Atlas one day and two nights, and then set out for home. Passing Col. Seeley's, I found no other house until I reached Blue river, where Van Deusen had a small grist-mill, and I crossed the Illinois river on Van Deusen's ferry. That night I reached Exeter. The weather was pleasant, the roads were dry and smooth.

"Pike county was then a wilderness. I came as directed, the nearest and best route home. I could never then have been made to believe that I should live to see a population of 30,000 within its boundaries.

"Capt. Ross entertained the jury and the lawyers in their double log cabin free of charge, expressing his regret that we could not stay longer. I was at Atlas at the Presidential election in 1824 and voted for John Quincy Adams for President. ·

"Judge Lockwood, Mr. McConnell and myself, in attending Court at Atlas (the year I do not recollect), passed the present site of Griggsville and saw the man, Mr. Scholl, raising the first log cabin on that hill. I suppose the land had been laid out in town lots.

"In the early settlement of the Military Tract traveling cost but little. The old settlers were always glad of the opportunity of entertaining travelers, and especially the judge and lawyers, from whom they could obtain interesting accounts in relation to what was going on in the world around them. Besides, we often had to encamp in the woods and prairies because no house was within reach at dark, and this was called "lodging at Munn's tavern," because of the large number of quarter sections of land owned by him. I have often fared sumptuously in the log cabins on bread made of grated meal, venison, honey, butter and milk and stewed pumpkins, and slept comfortably and soundly on the puncheon floor. *   *   *

"Feb. 14, 1823, Wm. Ross was elected Judge of the Court of Probate. In 1823 Geo. Cadwell, then of Greene county but afterward included in Morgan, was elected to the Senate for Greene and Pike, and Archibald Job, who was still living, for the House. Cadwell's term expired in two years, and in 1824 Thos. Carlin, afterward elected governor in 1836, was elected to the Senate. Cadwell was an educated physician, a man of talent and stern integrity: he died in 1824 or 1825.

"At the meeting of the Legislature in 1824 Nicholas Hanson and John Shaw both produced certificates of election to the House. The question which was entitled to the seat was referred to the Speaker, who decided in favor of Hanson. During the session the question was again brought before the House, and decided by a unanimous vote in favor of Hanson. Near the close of the session the question was reconsidered and Shaw admitted, in consideration of which Shaw voted for the resolution for a call of a convention.

"For several years after I came to the State, deer, wild turkey and wild beasts were plenty, especially on the Illinois and Mississippi rivers. But for this fact many of our early settlers would have suffered for provisions, or have been compelled to retreat for supplies.

"In passing from Rushville to Quincy, the Judge, Mr. Caverly and myself slept on the prairie during the night, and the next morning, which was Sunday, we found a house a few miles distant in the barrens; and we could not make the family believe it was not Saturday. The nearest neighbor lived five miles distant. They lived on wild game, grated corn meal and roasted ears, and lived well. We thought at breakfast we could not wish for better fare.

"In passing from Atlas to Gilead in Calhoun county we always made the house of an old gentleman named Munn our stopping-place. He and his wife were always glad to see us and made sumptuous preparations for our comfort.

"If I were at the stand and questioned I could probably answer many questions in regard to matters of interest to the present inhabitants; but as I do not know the points on which they would question me, and as I have already extended this letter, considering the hot weather, to what may be considered a reasonable length, I close, hoping that you may have a good day and a good time.

"Respectfully your friend,   "WILLIAM THOMAS."

This meeting was addressed by many old settlers, who related very interesting experiences. The exercises were interspersed with music and a grand picnic dinner, etc. Letters were read from Edwin Draper and Levi Pettibone, of Louisiana, Mo., besides the one from Judge Thomas, above given. Wm. A. Grimshaw was elected President, James McWilliams, of Griggsville, Vice President, and Geo. W. Jones Assistant Secretary. The following resolution was adopted: "*Resolved*, That the old settlers of Pike and Calhoun counties be requested to notify the President and Secretary of the Old Settlers' organization, the names of all members of this Association who shall depart this life during the present year, and that the Secretary be instructed to enter the same upon record."

Among those who addressed the assembly were Hon. Wm. A. Grimshaw, John T. Hodgen, of St. Louis, Calvin Twichell, of Calhoun county, J. T. Long, now of Barry, for many years a resident of Adams county, Wm. Turnbull, of Flint, A. P. Sharpe, of Griggsville, Alvin Wheeler, the oldest living settler of Pike county · (came here in 1818), now 75 years of age. Col. D. B. Bush closed the line of history by giving a sketch of Pittsfield. Dr. Worthington claimed Frederick Franklin, of Montezuma, as the oldest living settler of Pike county now living. He was the son of Ebenezer Franklin, the first settler in the county.

In this connection we give the very interesting letter of Mr. Draper:

"LOUISIANA, Mo., Sept. 1, 1873.

"HON. WM. A. GRIMSHAW AND OTHERS: Gentlemen,—Through the politeness of some friend of your county-seat I am indebted for an invitation to attend the meeting of old settlers of your county at Pittsfield, on the 3d inst.; for this invitation I presume I am indebted for the fact of being nearly connected by marriage with Levi Pettibone, Esq., an old settler and perhaps the oldest man in Pike county, Mo., and perhaps with few exceptions the oldest man in Missouri, he being now nearing the completion of his 93d year. But from whatever cause, I esteem it a compliment altogether undeserved to myself, but which nevertheless I should take the greatest pleasure, if circumstances permitted, of meeting with the old settlers of your county, among whom I am proud to recognize, not only the many distinguished public men, but many old and long esteemed personal friends, some of whom have long been settlers of Pike county Ill., and not a few of them old settlers of Pike and Lincoln counties, Mo., who, not content with aiding to break up the wilds of Missouri and bring them into the paths and fields of civilization, have largely colonized Pike county Ill., where they have been long enough to earn the appellation of 'old settlers,' where they are realizing the rich fruits of their industry in land flowing with milk and honey, and as I lament to know, many of them are resting beneath the sods that are no respecters of persons in the final winding up of human affairs. The memory of many of these persons, both living and dead, carry me far back into the history of the past, in the early history of Missouri, of whose soil I have been an occupant since the year 1815, before either your State or Missouri had a State Government. Though then quite young (but eight years old) I was old enough to remember everything I saw, and everybody I knew,—much more so than persons and facts of later years; but to attempt to recount or name any considerable number of them would be to inflict a bore upon you that I dare not presume upon; but as I presume that a part of the exercises of the occasion would be to recur to the early history of the West, including your State and ours, I cannot resist the temptation to jot down a few facts and names, even at the risk of being laid upon the table as a bore.

"The date 1815 shows that the early settlers, among whom was my father, were crowding into Missouri even before the forts were all vacated, whither the old settlers had fled for the purpose of protection from hostile savages, who had but recently had almost undisputed possession of a large part of our State. To get into Missouri, then largely considered as the promised land, we had to cross the Mississippi river, the Father of Waters. I don't know how much of a father he was at that time, but I have been acquainted with him since that time, and I don't know much difference in his size between then and now, except occasionally, as in 1851, he got into a terrible rage and had uncontrolled possession from Louisiana to Atlas, and rolled on, whether vexed or unvexed, in solemn majesty to the Gulf of Mexico.

"But to continue. He had to be 'crossed' to get into Missouri. In 1815, as history shows, no steam-boats were known on our rivers, and the only modes, or rather mode, of crossing the river at St. Louis was by means of a small keel-boat or barge without any deck or covering, propelled by poles; and our wagons were crossed by placing two planks or slabs across the keel, running the wagons by hand upon these slabs across the boats and 'scotching' the wheels with billets of wood, filling in the inner parts of the boat with horses, children, etc. Yet we conquered the old gentleman and rode across in triumph, but not, however, until after waiting two days on the eastern bank for the wind to lie, which had so ruffled the surface and temper of the 'father' that he could not, safely at least, be mounted by an insignificant keel-boat until the cause of his irritation had ceased.

"Safely on the Missouri shore, the first night was passed in the city of St. Louis, then containing about 1,200 inhabitants and very few brick houses : I did not count them, however. No railroads then were even thought of in the West, so far as I remember, but now—well, you can tell the tale yourselves. St. Louis has now

450,000 inhabitants, and would likely have a million but for Chicago and the railroads, which have revolutionized the course of nature and the natural rights of St. Louis, which depended on the navigation of the great rivers to work for her ; and while her great land-owner slept a quarter of a century Chicago and the railroads were surging ahead of her.

"Excuse this digression, which I could not help while reflecting on the immense change all over the West since I first crossed the great river.

"I have alluded to the fact of your county being largely colonized from Pike and Lincoln counties, Mo. It would be impossible for me to enumerate all of them, even if I knew them all ; but among the names I remember well those of the Gibsons, the Sittons, Buchanan, Yokems, Galloway, Uncle Jake Williamson, the Cannons, Collard, Wellses, Kerrs, Noyes, Metz, Johnsons, McConnells, Andersons, etc., etc., all of whom went from Pike or Lincoln. All of them were good citizens, while some of them held high and honorable positions in public office. Your former valued Sheriff, Ephraim Cannon, was for a while a school-mate of mine, larger and older than I, but still a school-mate. The only special recollection I have of our school-boys' life was that the teacher once asked him, when nearly time to close school, 'How high is the sun ?' He replied he had no means of measuring the height, but 'from appearance it was about a rod high.'

"John J. Collard, Esq., a former Clerk of one of your Courts, was the son of an old settler of Lincoln county, dating before the war of 1812, if my memory is not at fault. I have attended your Courts when held at the old county-seat, Atlas, and since its location at your beautiful town Pittsfield. The old settlers at Atlas, as well as of Pittsfield, were the Rosses, most of whom I knew personally, and had a slight acquaintance with the 'Bashaw' of Hamburg, Mr. Shaw. Old Father Burnett and his boys John and Frank belonged to both Pikes, in Illinois and Missouri. The sons wore out their lives in trying to sustain a ferry between the two Pikes.

"But I must forbear, fearing that I have already bored you, a thing I feared at the start. I could write a half quire of recollections of Pike in Missouri, and some of Pike in Illinois, if there were any market for them. But I must close with my best wishes for your people, both old and young.

"EDWIN DRAPER."

THIRD MEETING.

At the Old Settlers' meeting, Sept. 2, 1874, Hon. Wm. A. Grimshaw delivered an address of welcome, and interesting speeches were made by Col. Benj. Barney, Rev. J. P. Dimmitt, Dr. Hodgen, Mr. Turnbull, Judge Grigsby and others. Dr. P. E. Parker was elected Secretary in place of G. W. Jones, resigned. A motion was adopted changing the time of membership from 1840 to 1850; also a motion to establish a portfolio and gallery of likenesses of old settlers; and members and others were invited to send pictures. A social reception of old settlers was given in the evening at Bush's Hall.

FOURTH MEETING.

At the 4th annual meeting of the old settlers at Perry, Aug. 19, 1875, old-time customs were commemorated by the erection of a cabin complete in all its details. It looked as if a family had been living in it for years. Cooking utensils hanging around the wall, suspended on a string were slices of pumpkin and dried apples, corn hung from the posts, suspended by the husks, the rifle hung on the wooden hook over the door, the spinning wheel, the reel and the hand-cards occupied prominent positions; the mammoth gourd for a water bucket and the lesser one as a dipper attracted considerable attention. On the outside walls the skins of different fur-bearing animals were stretched; climbing vines were turned up to the roof, and the sunflower in all its magnificence nodded here and there close to the house, and last, but not least, the latch-string hung on the outside. The cabin was presided over during the early part of the day by Mr. Wm. Grotts, who entertained his visitors with his "fiddle," playing Arkansas traveler, Money Musk, Old Rosin the Bow," etc. Mr. Grotts was born in this State in 1802, in Madison county. His father was killed by Indians in Bond county in 1814.

FIFTH MEETING.

During the Old Settlers' meeting at Griggsville, Aug. 30, 1876, they formed a procession in front of the M. E. Church, headed by an old truck wagon drawn by oxen, containing a band, the people being dressed in the Sunday attire of pioneer times, girls and boys riding double on horseback without saddles, showing how they went to church in olden times. This was one of the most attractive features of the procession, the young ladies especially conducting themselves with becoming grace, and appeared as if they were inspired with the spirit of their grandmothers. An old dilapidated wagon drawn by oxen was loaded with the old-fashioned loom, spinning wheel, flax wheel and reel, and an old plow was followed by most of our modern machinery in the shape of reapers, mowers, harrows, etc. After these a man dressed in Indian costume on his pony, ladies and gentlemen in modern style in buggies and carriages, the fire engine drawn by members of the base-ball clubs in uniform, and a modern child-wagon with children was drawn by a very small donkey.

CHAPTER XIV.

THE REBELLION.

FIRST INDICATIONS OF THE WAR.

When, in 1861, the war was forced upon the country, the people were quietly pursuing the even tenor of their ways, doing whatever their hands found to do,—working the mines, making farms, or cultivating those already made, establishing homes, founding cities and towns, building shops and manufactories; in short, the country was alive with industry and hopes for the future. The people were just recovering from the depression and losses incident to the financial panic of 1857. The future looked bright and promising, and the industrious and patriotic sons and daughters of the North were buoyant with hope, looking forward to the perfecting of new plans for comfort and competence in their declining years. They little heeded the mutterings and threatenings wafted from the South. They never dreamed that there was one so base as to attempt the destruction of the Union their fathers had purchased for them with their life-blood. While thus surrounded with peace and tranquillity they paid but little attention to the rumored plots and plans of those who lived and grew rich from the sweat and toil, blood and flesh, of others.

The war clouds grew darker and still darker, the thunders of treason grew louder and louder until April 12, 1861, when the fearful storm burst upon the country and convulsed a continent with its attendant horrors.

On that day the rebels, who for weeks had been erecting their batteries upon the shore, after demanding of Major Anderson a surrender, opened fire upon Fort Sumter. For hours an incessant cannonading was continued; the fort was being damaged severely; provisions were almost gone, and Major Anderson was compelled to haul down the stars and stripes,—that dear old flag which had seldom been lowered to a foreign foe; by rebel hands it was now trailed in the dust. How the blood of patriotic men of the North boiled when on the following day the news was flashed along the telegraph wires that Major Anderson had been forced to surrender! And nowhere was greater indignation manifested than in Pike county.

B. L. Matthews

THE FIRST CALL FOR TROOPS.

Immediately upon the surrender of Fort Sumter, Abraham Lincoln, America's martyr President—who but a few short weeks before had taken the oath of office as the nation's chief executive—issued a proclamation calling for 75,000 volunteers for three months. The last word of that proclamation had scarcely been taken from the electric wires before the call was filled, and men and money were counted out by hundreds and thousands. The people who loved their whole government could not give enough. Patriotism thrilled and vibrated and pulsated through every heart. The farm, the workshop, the office, the pulpit, the bar, the bench, the college, the school-house,—every calling offered its best men, their lives and fortunes, in defense of the Government's honor and unity. Bitter words spoken in moments of political heat were forgotten and forgiven, and, joining hands in a common cause, they repeated the oath of America's soldier statesman, *"By the Great Eternal, the Union must and shall be preserved."*

> Call the young men in the prime of their life;
> Call them from mother, from sister, from wife;
> Blessed if they live, revered if they fall,—
> They who respond unto Liberty's call.

Seventy-five thousand men were not enough to subdue the Rebellion; nor were ten times the number. The war went on, and call followed call, until it began to look as if there would not be men enough in all the Free States to crush out and subdue the monstrous war traitors had inaugurated. But to every call for either men or money there was a willing and ready response; and it is a boast of the people that, had the supply of men fallen short, there were women brave enough, daring enough, patriotic enough, to offer themselves as a sacrifice on their country's altar. Such were the impulses, motives and actions of the patriotic men of the North, among whom the sons of Pike made a conspicuous and praiseworthy ecord.

VARIOUS MEETINGS HELD IN THE COUNTY.

The tocsin of war was sounded, meetings were held in every township, village and city, at which stirring and spirited addresses were made, and resolutions adopted admitting of but one interpretation,—that of unconditional allegiance and undying devotion to their country and their country's flag; that, at whatever cost of blood or treasure, the stars and stripes, wherever floating, must be honored; and the supremacy of the law of the National Union sustained.

A Union meeting was held in Pittsfield April 20, 1861, the Chairmen of which were David A. Stanton, Wm. R. Wills and D. D. Hicks, and the Secretaries F. C. Brown and A. C. Matthews. The Committee on Resolutions were Wm. A. Grimshaw, C. L. Higbee, J. W. Mackintosh, D. B. Bush, jr., Nathan Kelly and Wm. Steers.

23

L. H. Waters, of Macomb, delivered the principal speech, which was a very eloquent one, and Hon. Scott Wike, Messrs. D. H. Gilmer and S. M. Hayes made short speeches. A series of resolutions were adopted setting forth the inauguration of the war by the firing on Fort Sumter and the necessity of rallying to the support of the Government.

April 22 a meeting was held in the court-house for the purpose of forming a company of home guards. The company organized, electing S. M. Hayes Captain. M. J. Noyes presided at this meeting. About this time the " Pike County Union Guards " were also organized, with John McWilliams for Captain. In July Jas. S. Barnard was elected Captain of the latter company and P. G. Athey Captain of a cavalry company of 130 men, all from Pike county.

During this summer also Wm. W. Taylor, a Breckenridge Democrat of Perry, was suspected of disloyalty and made in an informal manner to take the oath of allegiance by some soldiers of Col. Grant's regiment.

Aug. 5, 1861, a company called the " Henderson Home Guards " was organized in Pittsfield, numbering 130 men, with Daniel D. Hicks as Captain, each member to arm and equip himself; it was also called the " Henderson Union Guards."

BOUNTY.

The subject of bounty for soldiers was one that engaged the undivided attention of the law-making power of this county during these trying times. That the reader may know what was done by the county officials we give a very full account of the proceedings of the Board of Supervisors whenever the bounty subject was being considered by that honorable body.

At a special meeting of the Board of Supervisors held Aug. 4, 1862, for the purpose of considering the feasibility or propriety of offering bounty to soldiers, Supervisor Smith moved that the Chair appoint a committee of five to draft resolutions expressive of the sense of the meeting. Thereupon the Chair appointed Messrs. Smith, Westlake, Wallace, McWilliams and Adams.

Mr. Wallace presented a petition from the citizens of Barry, asking an appropriation by the Board of $16,000.

The Committee on Resolutions submitted the following report the next day:

WHEREAS, Several Southern States of this Union in convention assembled have absolved themselves by resolution from allegiance to the United States of America and formed themselves into a so-called "confederacy," thereby disclaiming any right, benefit or protection from or under the Constitution of the United States; and

WHEREAS, Said confederacy have organized, armed and equipped hostile armies and did fire upon, reduce and take into their possession Fort Sumter with all its defenses, and unlawfully seize and take into possession other forts, arsenals and other property belonging to the United States, thereby bidding defiance to the Constitution and the laws of the same; and

WHEREAS, It still exists and unsubdued, and our present army is insufficient in numbers to put down the rebellion; and

WHEREAS, The President of the United States has recently made a call upon the several States of this Union to raise 300,000 men in addition to the present army;

Therefore we, the representatives of the several townships of the county of Pike and State of Illinois have here assembled for the purpose of considering the propriety of offering encouragememt to the volunteers who will immediately enter into the service of the United States; therefore be it

Resolved, That the sum of $3,000 be paid to the first three companies that are raised or organized in the county of Pike under said call, provided said companies are organized on or before the 20th inst.; and that the Clerk of this Court be authorized to issue orders on the Treasury for the said sums of money whenever said volunteers are accepted and mustered into service;

Resolved, That $1,000 be appropriated to the families of those who have heretofore volunteered in the service of the United States, and we recommend that each township shall through their Supervisor call a meeting to provide for the future wants of all families of volunteers; that the Supervisor of each township shall be a committee to distribute all appropriations made by the county or town;

Resolved, That the Supervisors of each township shall report at the September meeting the number of families of volunteers in their townships, and their names.

By invitation Judge Higbee addressed the Board briefly, after which Cols. Ross and Bush made short addresses.

Mr. Dennis moved to amend the report by striking out " $3,000 " and inserting " $50 to each volunteer private who may enlist under the present call." Mr. Westlake moved to amend the amendment of Mr. Dennis by striking out " $50 " and inserting " $25;" which motion was lost. The amendment offered by Mr. Dennis was also defeated.

Mr. Landrum offered the following resolutions:

Resolved, That the proposition of the appropriation by the county of $6,000 to be submitted to the people for their vote for or against levying a tax to meet said appropriation, at an election to be held at the usual places of holding elections in the several towns, on Tuesday, the 13th inst.; said fund, if so voted, to be appropriated to aid in raising volunteers.

Resolved, That a proposition be also submitted at the same time for or against appropriating $2,000 as a fund for the necessitous families of volunteers as have heretofore or may hereafter be mustered into the service of the United States.

Mr. Wallace moved to strike out that portion of Mr. Landrum's resolution referring to the submission to the people, and that the Board appropriate the amount specified in said resolution; which motion was carried.

The question recurring on Mr. Landrum's resolution as amended it was put and lost.

Mr. Dennis moved to strike out the first resolution and amend the second so that $4,000 be appropriated for the support of destitute families of soldiers in the service.

Mr. Frye moved to lay all on the table without further action until the September meeting; which motion was lost. The question then recurring on the amendment of Mr. Dennis, it was adopted.

The substance of the resolution as passed appropriated $4,000 for the families of destitute soldiers.

At a special meeting of the Board of Supervisors held June 23, 1865, to either offer a bounty for enlistments or to aid persons who may be drafted into the service of the United States, Supervisor Roberts offered the following resolutions:

WHEREAS, The President of the United States has called for 300,000 volunteers, and ordered, in case the same are not made by the 15th of February next, that a draft shall be made to fill the quota; and

WHEREAS, Such draft will fall heavy on many poor persons in this county who have large families to support; and

WHEREAS, The property of the county receives the protection of the Government, as well as persons, and should be made to bear its just proportions of the burdens of war; therefore

Resolved, That our Representatives in the Legislature now in session be respectfully requested to procure the passage of an act as speedily as possible, authorizing the Board of Supervisors of this county to offer a bounty to volunteers and to aid in procuring substitutes for drafted persons, and to provide such funds as will be necessary therefor by issuing bonds payable within 20 years, bearing interest not exceeding ten per cent. per annum.

Resolved, That in case of the passage of such an act, the Board of Supervisors will pay to each volunteer credited to any town in this county subject to the draft a bounty of $500, and in case of a draft, each person so drafted in this county who shall procure a substitute shall receive from the county the sum of $500 to aid him in paying for such substitute.

Mr. Shields moved to postpone the resolution indefinitely. After remarks by Supervisors Shields, Roberts, Kelley, Dunn and others, Mr. Shields withdrew the motion, and in lieu thereof moved that it be postponed to the April meeting of the Board. This he, however, withdrew, and Supervisor Dimmitt moved to refer the resolution offered by Mr. Roberts to a committee; and Mr. Dimmitt, from this committee reported on the following day this resolution:

Resolved, That there be paid to each volunteer or drafted man in this county under the call of Dec. 19, 1864, the sum of $400, such money to be raised by the issue of county bonds (interest not to exceed ten per cent.) payable annually in lawful money of the United States.

Resolved, That when such bonds shall have been issued they shall be divided among the several townships in proportion to the amount of taxable property assessed in each township for the year 1864; and it shall be the duty of each supervisor to receive said bonds and pay over to each drafted man and volunteer the sum of $400 when actually mustered into service.

Mr. Shields moved that said resolution be laid on the table until the April meeting; which motion was lost. Mr. Smitherman then moved that it be submitted to the people of the county on Jan. 28, 1865; and Mr. Vail moved to amend by taking said vote on the 30th; which motion was withdrawn; and Mr. Roberts moved that whatever action this Board may take shall be submitted to the people on Jan. 30, 1865; which motion was adopted. Mr. Roberts then moved to amend the first resolution by inserting "$500" in place of "$400;" which was adopted.

At a meeting of the Board held Jan. 31, the day after the election, they found after a canvass of the returns that 3,416 votes had been cast, of which 2,131 were for the tax and 1,285 against it. It was then resolved by the Board to give a bounty of $500 to each volunteer to fill the quota of Pike county; and in case said quota shall not be filled by volunteers, then a bounty of $500 shall be paid to each person who shall be drafted. For this purpose $127,-000 were raised in the county.

Kinderhook township gave $1,500 bounty, and paid $180 for transportation.

PIKE COUNTY'S SOLDIERS.

A few statistical items will show what was done by Pike county, and whether she was worthy the trust reposed in her. According to the census of 1860 the county had a population of 27,182. The war, however, continued for several years, and the county increased in population; accordingly we will place the population in round numbers at 30,000. There are five persons to every voter, according to the customary basis of reckoning. That would make the number of men in the county 6,000. Pike county put in the field 3,132 men, being over one-half of her voters.

The quota of the county for the calls of 1861 was 762, which were quickly furnished. In 1862 the quota for this county was 521. For the calls of Feb. 1 and March 14, 1864, it was 786, and for the call of 500,000, July 18, 1864, it was 617, making the large number of 2,687 men as the quota for this county up to Dec. 31, 1864. The county not only furnished this number, but sent of her brave sons 2,853, being 166 in excess of her various quotas. Subsequent calls increased the quota of Pike county to 3,221, which the county did not fill by 89.

Pike county was largely represented in the following regiments and companies. Besides those referred to, her sons were in many other regiments, but we give only those which were largely made up from this county.

EIGHTH REGIMENT.

Company G of this Regiment was entirely furnished by Pike county, with James S. Barnard as Captain: afterward Elisha Jones and Charles H. Hurt served the Company in that position. The 1st Lieutenants in succession were Elihu Jones, Wm. P. Sitton, Charles H. Hurt and George Sanderson. The 2d Lieutenants were Wm. P. Sitton, Charles H. Hurt and Wm. A. Saylor.

The 8th Illinois Regiment was organized April 25, 1861, Colonel Oglesby commanding. A contest for rank and seniority arose between the 7th and 8th, both being organized on the same day. The contest was finally ended, giving to Col. Cook the first number 7, as the number of his Regiment, with the second rank of Colonel, and Col. Oglesby the second number for his Regiment, with the first rank as Colonel.

The first enlistment was for three months, during which time the

Regiment was taken to Cairo. July 25, 1861, its term of three months having expired, the 8th reorganized for three years' service. It took part in many of the most important engagements of the war; was in the advance attack on Fort Donelson, where it lost 57 killed, 191 wounded and 10 missing. It was also at Pittsburg landing, where it lost 26 killed, 97 wounded and 11 missing; and it went through the fatigue and dangers of the siege of Corinth. The Regiment re-enlisted in 1863 and was veteranized March 24, 1864; took part in the engagement at Vicksburg, Spanish Fort and many other important engagements.

SEVENTH REGIMENT.

Company D, of the 7th, being a new company of that old Regiment, was from Pike county. It was organized Feb. 14, 1865, under Capt. Samuel N. Hoyt, of Griggsville, with Andrew Moore as 1st Lieutenant and Wm. J. Hanlin as 2d Lieutenant. The Company served until July 9, 1865, when it was mustered out.

SIXTEENTH REGIMENT.

Company K, of the 16th Infantry, was largely, indeed almost altogether, from Pike county. They enlisted May 25, 1861, and served until July 8, 1865. The Company was organized by Geo. D. Stewart, Captain, who served until April 25, 1865, and John Bryant, of Pittsfield, was appointed to fill the position. The 1st Lieutenant was James Hedger, and following came French B. Woodall, John Bryant and Franklin J. Cooper. The 2d Lieutenants were Richard B. Higgins, Joseph E. Haines and Asbury Brown.

The 16th was organized and mustered into service at Quincy, Col. Robert A. Smith commanding. In July, 1861, it was removed to Green river as railroad guard, after which the Regiment was scattered along the line of the road as guard. July 10, Col. Smith's force was attacked at Missionary Station by 1,600 mounted rebels, but he held his position until the arrival of reinforcements, when the enemy fled. It participated in the battle of Bird's Point, Mo., and New Madrid, where it supported the siege guns. They captured 5,000 prisoners and a large amount of artillery, small arms and ammunition at Tiptonville, Tenn. In January, 1862, it participated in the siege of Corinth and Nashville. It was mustered out July 8, 1865.

TWENTY-EIGHTH REGIMENT CONSOLIDATED.

Pike county furnished Company B of this Regiment, and almost all of Companies E and I. Company B was commanded first after consolidation by Capt. John T. Thomson, of New Hartford, who was honorably discharged May 15, 1865, when Geo. W. Chrysup was appointed and served until March 15, 1866. The 1st Lieutenants in succession were Robert Young, Henry L. Hadsell, Geo. W. Chrysup and Job Pringle. The 2d Lieutenants were Geo. W.

Chrysup, Job Pringle and Thomas James. The officers of the Company were James M. Gale, Henry S. Stokes and Joseph A. Hanks.

Companies B, E and I of the original organization were from this county. Company B was first commanded by Capt. Thomas H. Butler, deceased, then by Capt. Geo. W. Stobie, and finally by Capt. John T. Thompson. The 1st Lieutenants were John T. Thompson and Robert Young: 2d Lieutenants, George Stobie, David C. Troutner and Cyrus K. Miller. Lieutenant Troutner soon died and Lieutenant Miller died July 8, 1863. Company E was first commanded by Captain Thomas M. Kilpatrick, who was promoted to Lieutenant Colonel and was killed in battle at Pittsburg Landing. John M. Griffin then commanded the Company. The 1st Lieutenants were John M. Griffin, Fredrick C. Bechdoldt, who was killed July 12, 1863, and Wm. B. Griffin; the 2d Lieutenant was Burrel McPherson. Company I was commanded until consolidation of Regiment by Capt. Elisha Hurt; 1st Lieutenants, Philip S. Likes and David Dixon; 2d Lieutenant, David Dixon and Henry L. Hadsell.

The 28th Infantry was organized at Camp Butler in August, 1861, by Lieut. Col. Lewis H. Waters and Maj. Charles J. Sellon, the latter from Pike county. Aug. 28 it was ordered to Thebes, Ill.; Sept. 9, to Bird's Point, Mo.; Oct. 2, to Fort Holt, Ky., where it remained until Jan. 21, 1862, when it was assigned to Brig. Gen. Lew Wallace's Division. Feb. 6 it took part in the capture of Forts Henry and Heiman; Feb. 13 a detachment of 48 men and 12 officers under Col. Johnson met the enemy 500 strong at Little Bethel Church, five miles from Fort Holt, and immediately attacked and routed them. The Regiment also took part in the battle of Pittsburg Landing; was assigned to the left line in a peach orchard, where it was immediately attacked by the enemy, but who were repulsed. On the morning of the 7th it held a position on the right line and was hotly engaged until the battle closed and the victory won. During these two long, trying, bloody days the Regiment behaved nobly and was never broken or driven back by the enemy, though often most heavily pressed. It sustained a loss of 239 killed and wounded. In May, 1862, it was engaged in the siege of Corinth: Oct. 5 engaged in the battle of Metamora, losing 97 killed and wounded; engaged in the siege of Vicksburg from June 11 to July 4, 1863; on the 12th of July, 1863, near Jackson, Miss., the 41st, 53d and 28th Illinois and 3d Iowa, not exceeding 800 men, were ordered to charge across an open field some 600 yards and carry a strong line of the enemy's works, mounting 12 guns and manned by at least 2,000 men. The Brigade swept gallantly forward under a destructive fire of grape, canister and minie bullets. The enemy appeared upon both flanks as it reached the ditch; it was compelled to fall back with a loss of more than half of their rank and file killed or wounded. The eight Companies of this Regiment, in line, numbering 128 men, lost 73 killed and wounded and 16 taken prisoners.

Jan., 1864, the Regiment re-inlisted as veterans, took part in the advance upon Spanish Fort, and were mustered out March 16, 1866

THIRTY-THIRD REGIMENT.

Company I of the 33rd was made up in Pike county. The original Captain was Wm. H. Lawton, who resigned June 8, 1863, and Wm. T. Lyon received the commission. The 1st Lieutenants were Wm. T. Lyon, Charles T. Kinney and Nathaniel W. Reynolds; the 2nd Lieutenants were Edward A. F. Allen, Charles T. Kinney, Nathaniel W. Reynolds and David F. Jenkins. The Company was wholly from the northern part of the county.

The 33rd was organized at Camp Butler Sept., 1861, by Col. Charles E. Hovey ; Nov. 20, it removed to Ironton, Mo., beyond St. Louis, where it remained during the winter. In March, 1862, it removed to Arkansas, engaging in many expeditions through that State. In 1863 it returned to Pilot Knob; was engaged in the battles of Port Gibson, Champion Hills, Black River Bridge, the assault and siege of Vicksburg, and the siege of Jackson; in August, 1863, moved to New Orleans and engaged in the campaign up the Bayou Teche, and returned to New Orleans in November; thence ordered to Brownsville, Tex., but before landing was ordered to Arkansas Pass. The Regiment re-enlisted Jan. 1, 1864, took part in the engagement at Spanish Fort, Mobile, and April 14, 1865, moved to Vicksburg, and in November ordered to Camp Butler, Ill., for final payment and discharge.

SIXTY-EIGHT REGIMENT.

Company B of this Regiment, which was organized for three months' service in June, 1862, was from this county, mostly from the northern part. Capt. Daniel F. Coffey served the Company as Commander. 1st Lieutenant, Judson J. F. Gillespie; 2nd Lieutenant, Wm. Reynolds.

SEVENTY-THIRD REGIMENT.

Company H of the 73rd Illinois Infantry, commanded by Capt. James I. Davidson, who subsequently was promoted to Lieut. Colonel, was from Pike county. After Capt. Davidson's promotion Joseph L. Morgan was appointed to the Captaincy. The 1st Lieutenants were Samuel Purcell, who resigned April 28, 1863, Joseph L. Morgan and James G. Wolgemath. The 2nd Lieutenants were Clement L. Shinn and De Witt C. Simmons.

This Regiment was organized at Camp Butler, in August, 1862, and immediately became a part of Gen. Buell's army. It participated in every engagement fought by the Army of the Cumberland from Oct., 1862, until the rout of Gen. Hood's army at Nashville and the winding up of the whole matter. The dead of this Regiment are found on the battle-fields of Perryville, Murfreesboro,

Chickamauga, Missionary Ridge, through East Tennessee and the succession of battles from Chattanooga to the fall of Atlanta. It had two Majors and two Adjutants killed, and nearly every officer of the Regiment wounded at some one time : several of them many times. It was mustered out June 10, 1865.

NINETY-NINTH REGIMENT.

The 99th was, strictly speaking, a Pike county Regiment. It was organized in Pike county in August, 1862, by Col. George W. K. Bailey, and was mustered in at Florence, Aug. 23, 1862, by Col. J. H. Rathbone. Upon the same day it removed to St. Louis, going into Benton Barracks, and was the first Regiment out of the State under the call of 1862. Sept. 8, ordered to Rolla; served in that department to the spring of 1863; was assigned to the Brigade of Brig. Gen. Fitz Henry Warren; engaged in the skirmish at Bear creek, losing one killed and four wounded and one taken prisoner, and in the battle of Hartsville, Mo., losing 35 killed and wounded; went into camp at Houston; Jan. 27, moved to West Plains, Mo., reporting to Brig. Gen. Davidson; March 3, removed to Pilot Knob, thence to St. Genevieve, arriving the 12th; and March 15, 1863, embarked for Milliken's Bend, La., arriving the 26th, and was assigned to the 1st Brigade, Brig. Gen. W. P. Benton commanding; 14th Division, Brig. Gen. E. A. Carr commanding ; 13th Army Corps. Moved from Milliken's Bend April 11, arriving at New Carthage the 12th; was at Grand Gulf April 29; crossed the river, and May 1 was engaged in the battle near Port Gibson, called Magnolia Hills, losing 37 men killed and wounded; marched with the army toward Jackson, and returned by Champion Hills and Black River Bridge; May 19, was at the defenses of Vicksburg; on the 22d the Regiment took a prominent part in the assault, losing 103 killed and wounded, out of 300 men. The Colonel and Major were wounded early in the day, leaving Capt. A. C. Matthews in command. Its line during the day was close to the enemy's works, and its colors planted on their breastworks. This position was held until 4 P. M., when it was relieved by another Regiment and moved back 150 yards to where its knapsacks had been left. While calling the roll the line which had relieved the Regiment was driven back in great confusion. The 99th advanced and opened a heavy fire, drove the enemy back into his works and held him there, probably saving the whole Division from stampede. Was engaged during the siege in Gen. Benton's Brigade—8th and 18th Indiana, and 33d and 99th Illinois. The 99th lost during the entire campaign and siege 253 killed, wounded and missing. July 5 the 9th, 13th and 15th Corps, Maj. Gen. Sherman commanding, moved after Johnson's army to Jackson; returned to Vicksburg July 24; Aug. 21 removed to New Orleans, and on the 26th went into camp at Brashear City. Oct. 3, 1863, the campaign of the Teche was commenced. The Regiment was in several skirmishes, and a de-

tachment of the Regiment, Capt. A. C. Matthews commanding,
was engaged in the battle at Grand Coteau; Nov. 9, returned to
Brashear City and moved to New Orleans; Nov. 16, embarked for
Texas, landing on the 25th at Mustang Island; marched up to Matagorda Island and commenced the attack on Fort Esperanza, which
was soon surrendered.

The 99th remained in Texas during the spring of 1864. June
16 of this year it evacuated the island and reported to Gen. Reynolds,
at Algiers, La. The Regiment performed garrison duty on the
Mississippi during the entire summer, in the First Brigade, Brig.
Gen. Slack; 1st Division, Gen. Dennis; 19th Corps, Gen. Reynolds.
The 99th was brigaded with the 21st Iowa, 29th Wisconsin and
47th Indiana.

In November, 1864, removed to Memphis, where the Regiment
was consolidated into a Battalion of five Companies, and Lieut. Col.
A. C. Matthews assigned to the command, Col. Bailey and the other
supernumerary officers being mustered out.

Moved to Germantown and went on duty guarding railroad;
Dec. 25, three men of the Battalion were captured and murdered by
guerrillas; moved to Memphis Dec. 28; Jan. 1, 1865, embarked
for New Orleans, arriving on the 9th. Feb. 1 embarked for Dau-
phine Island, Ala.; was assigned to the 1st Brigade, 1st Div., 13th
Corps, with 21st Iowa, 47th Indiana and 29th Wisconsin, Gen.
Slack commanding Brigade, Brig. Gen. Veatch commanding Division.

March 17, moved to Fort Morgan; on the 26th, arrived at Fish
river; took part in the siege of Spanish Fort until the 30th, when
the Division was sent to General Steele's army, and April 1 went
into position at Fort Blakely. The 99th assisted in the investment
and capture, and on the 12th entered Mobile.

In June, 1865, the Division was ordered to Red river to receive
the surrender of Kirby Smith, and it proceeded to Shreveport, La.;
from this place Col. Matthews was detailed to proceed with a body-
guard of the 6th Missouri Cavalry to the Indian Territory and
receive the surrender of Brig. Gens. Cooper and Standwaite, and to
form temporary treaties of peace with the Indian tribes. The Col.
formed treaties with ten tribes, including the Choctaws, Cherokees,
Chickasaws and Osages, and returned (having traveled a thousand
miles) on the 3d of July.

July 19, ordered to Baton Rouge, and July 31 was mustered out
by Capt. E. S. Howk, A. C. M.

Arrived at Springfield, Ill., Aug. 6, received final payment and
discharge Aug. 9, 1865.

The Regiment was commanded by Col. Bailey until Dec. 16,
1864, when he was mustered out. The Lieut. Colonels were Lem-
uel Parke and Asa C. Matthews; the Majors at various times were
Edwin A. Crandall, Asa C. Matthews and John F. Richards; Adjutants, Marcellus Ross, Harvey D. Johnson and Joseph R. Furrey;
Quartermasters, Isaac G. Hodgen, Joshua K. Sitton and James F.

Greathouse; Surgeons, Joseph H. Ledlie and Edwin May; 1st Asst. Surgeon, Archibald E. McNeal and John F. Curtis; 2d Asst. Surgeon, Abner T. Spencer; Chaplains, Oliver A. Topliff and Wm. M. Evans.

Company A.—Captains—Geo. T. Edwards and Isaac G. Hodgen; 1st Lieutenant—James K. Smith ; 2d Lieutenants—James F. Stobie, Thos. A. Hubbard, John W. Saylor. (Hubbard died Feb. 15, 1863.)

Company B.—Captains—Benj. L. Matthews and James W. Fee; 1st Lieutenants—James W. Fee, James A. Elledge and Harvey Thornbury ; 2d Lieutenants—James A. Elledge, Harvey Thornbury and Milton L. Tiell.

Company C.—Captains—Asa C. Matthews and John A. Ballard ; 1st Lieutenants—Joshua K. Sitton, Lucien W. Shaw, John A. Ballard, Wm. B. Sitton (died July 10, 1864), N. Henry Kinne ; 2d Lieutenants—Lucien W. Shaw and Wm. B. Sitton.

Company D.—Captains—John F. Richards and Wm. B. Clandy; 1st Lieutenants—Francis M. Dabney, Wm. B. Clandy and John Bowsman ; 2d Lieutenants—Wm. T. Mitchell, Wm. B. Clandy and John Bowsman.

Company E.—Captains—John C. Dinsmore, Allen D. Richards ; 1st Lieutenants—Joseph G. Colvin, Allen D. Richards and Robert H. Griffin ; 2d Lieutenant—Allen D. Richards.

Company F.—Captains—Eli R. Smith, Daniel McDonald. Captain Smith was killed in battle May 22, 1863. 1st Lieutenants —Leonard Greaton, Jacob E. Stauffer ; 2d Lieutenants—Daniel McDonald and Jesse Parke.

Company G.—Captains—Henry D. Hull and Henry B. Atkinson ; 1st Lieutenants—James H. Crane and Henry B. Atkinson ; 2d Lieutenant—Lewis Dutton.

Company H.—Captains—Lewis Hull and Melville D. Massie; 1st Lieutenants—Melville D. Massie, Benj. L. Blades and Daniel Riley; 2d Lieutenants—Gottfried Wenzel and Benj. L. Blades.

Company I.—Captain—Joseph G. Johnson; 1st Lieutenants— John G. Sever and George S. Marks; 2d Lieutenant—Robert E. Gilliland.

Company K.—Captains—Isaiah Cooper and John G. Sever; 1st Lieutenants—Wm. Gray (died May 30, 1863, of wounds received in battle May 22, 1863), Augustus Hubbard and Zebulon B. Stoddard; 2d Lieutenants—Thos. J. Kinman (killed in battle May 22, 1863) and John Andrew.

NINETY-NINTH REGIMENT AS CONSOLIDATED.

April 2, 1863, according to orders from the War Department, the 99th was consolidated into a Battalion of five Companies,—A, B, C, D and E, officered as follows:

Colonel, Asa C. Matthews; Adjutant, Joseph R. Furrey; Quartermaster, James F. Greathouse; Surgeon, Edwin May; 1st Asst. Surgeon, John F. Curtis; Chaplain, Wm. M. Evans.

Company A.—Capt., John F. Richards; 1st Lieut., Wm. B. Clandy; 2d Lieut., John Bowsman.

Company B.—Capt., James W. Fee; 1st Lieut., Jacob E. Stauffer; 2d Lieut., Joseph Dugdell.

Company C.—Capt.. Melville D. Massie; 1st Lieut., Henry B. Atkinson; 2d Lieut., Wm. L. Carter.

Company D.—Capt., Isaac G. Hodgen; 1st Lieut., James K. Smith; 2d Lieut., Sylvester Durall.

Company E.—Capt., John A. Ballard, 1st Lieut., N. Henry Kinne; 2d Lieut., Clayton B. Hooper.

ONE HUNDRED AND THIRTY-SEVENTH REGIMENT.

Company F of this Regiment was organized by Robert B. Robinson, of Barry, this county; Company G, by Orville C. Holcomb, of Milton, and Company I, by Levi Barbour, of Pittsfield. These three Companies of this Regiment were made up from Pike county. The 1st Lieutenant of Company F was De Witt C. Simmons, of Griggsville, and the 2d Lieutenant David D. Kidwell, of Barry. The 1st Lieutenant of Company G was John M. Johnson, and the 2d Lieutenant, Joseph S. Latimer. The 1st Lieutenant of Company I was Henson S. VanDeventer and the 2d Lieutenant, Wm. A. Hubbard.

This Regiment was organized at Camp Wood, Quincy, by Col. John Wood, and was mustered in June 5, 1864, for 100 days. June 9, the Regiment left Quincy and proceeded to Memphis, Tenn., where it was assigned to the 4th Brigade, District of Memphis, Col. E. L. Baltwick, of Wisconsin, commanding. On July 9 it was assigned to the 3d Brigade, Col. John Wood commanding, and was stationed on the Hernando road, on picket duty. The Regiment was mustered out of the U. S. service at Springfield, Ill., Sept. 4, 1864.

SECOND CAVALRY.

Of this regiment Company K and parts of other Companies were from Pike county. It was organized July 30, 1861, with Pressly G. Athey as Captain, who resigned Jan. 27, 1862, when Thos. W. Jones, 1st Lieutenant, was promoted Captain. He was subsequently promoted to the position of Major. Daniel B. Bush, jr., was at first Major, and was subsequently promoted to the rank of Lieutenant Colonel and finally Colonel. In 1865 Montgomery Demmons was promoted to the Captaincy. The 1st Lieutenants were Thos. W. Jones, Benj. F. Garrett and Wm. R. Scull, and the 2d Lieutenants, Benj. F. Garrett, Franklin Kinman, L. Mitchell, Montgomery Demmons and David C. Rock.

Besides the Regiments and Companies noticed above, Pike county gave many men to numerous other Companies. Her sons fought upon every battle-field of that great war, and upon the field of every great battle during that long, hard struggle for the supremacy of the Union the life-blood of some of her sons was shed. They were found in the foremost of the fight : indeed, they were found

wherever duty called them. It is an easy matter to be a patriot
" in the piping times of peace, in the sunny hours of prosperity,"
but when war, discord and rebellion present their horrid forms to
strike the liberty of a hundred years, it is then the patriot shines
in his devotion to his country. When the painful duty presented
itself to the patriots of this county to send thousands of her citizens into danger, and many of them to certain death, there was no
hesitation. Men enrolled their names with a steady hand, bade wife
and little ones, fathers, mothers, brothers and sisters farewell, and
went boldly to the front and saved this glorious blood-bought
Union.

LEE'S SURRENDER.—LINCOLN'S ASSASSINATION.

Our armies bravely contended until finally, after four long years
of bloodshed and carnage, the news was flashed over the wires that
Lee had surrendered. This joyful news reached this county Monday, April 10, 1865, being within two days of four years from the
time the batteries were opened on Fort Sumter. On receiving the
news of the fall of Richmond the people were very jubilant over
the success of the Union forces. They assembled in all parts of
the county and had grand jubilees. The streets of the cities were
brilliantly illuminated; bonfires, rockets and music were seen on
every hand; it was indeed a season of rejoicing; and well might it
be, for what had been endured, what had been suffered.

Scarcely had the downfall of the Southern Confederacy been received ere the sad news of the assassination of Abraham Lincoln
was flashed over the wires. On that beautiful April morning, five
days after the announcement of Lee's surrender, the people, joyful
over the near approach of the return of their loved ones from the
South, the sorrowing news of the President's death was announced.
Mr. Lincoln was bound to the people of this county with stronger
cords than simply being a good ruler. He had spent many days
here, had many warm personal friends, and it was like the loss of a
brother. They felt the loss keenly; the tolling bells, the sympathetic dirges, interpreted not merely the grief of the people at the
loss of a President, but the sorrow of a community at the death of
brother, a son, one who was closely akin to all. Meetings were
held and appropriate resolutions passed. Dwellings, stores, churches
and public buildings were draped, and the flags which had been sent
up in moments of rejoicing were taken down, draped, and sent up
at half-mast.

THE CLOSE.

The war ended and peace restored, the Union preserved in its integrity, the sons of Pike, who had volunteered their lives in defense of their Government, and who were spared to see the army of
the Union victorious, returned to their homes to receive grand
ovations and tributes of honor from friends and neighbors who had
eagerly and zealously followed them wherever the fortunes of war

called. Exchanging their soldiers' uniforms for citizens' dress, most
of them fell back to their old vocations,—on the farm, at the forge,
at the bench, in the shop, and at whatever else their hands found to
do.   Brave men are honorable always, and no class of citizens are
entitled to greater respect than the volunteer soldiery of Pike
county, not alone because they were soldiers, but because in their
associations with their fellow-men their walk is upright, and their
honesty and character without reproach.

> Their country first, their glory and their pride,
> Land of their hopes, land where their fathers died;
> When in the right, they'll keep their honor bright;
> When in the wrong, they'll die to set it right.

The soldiers of Pike county met at the court-house Aug. 23,
1866. The meeting was called to order by Maj. T. W. Jones, when Dr.
E. M. Seeley was called to the chair, and James H. Crane was appointed Secretary.   The object of the meeting was to take measures
for raising funds for the erection of a monument.   Elaborate resolutions were adopted with reference to the loyalty and fidelity of the
soldiery, etc., and sympathy with the suffering, the widows and or-
phans etc.; and committees of soldiers, five in each township, were
appointed to solicit donations.   A central committee for the county
was also appointed, and a committee to solicit $10,000 from the
county treasury.   Considerable enthusiasm was manifested in this
work of love, and a wish to honor the heroic dead, the citizen
soldiers who yielded their lives a sacrifice to their country, but
nothing definitely toward the final carrying out of the project was
ever done.   Although no marble pile rises heavenward to commemo-
rate the fallen heroes, yet we know that the memory of their valor
and heroic devotion to our country will never fade in the minds
and hearts of the citizens, and that their love and gratitude are as
strong and undying as though a monument of stones were piled
up as high as Babel's tower.

CHAPTER XV.

PIKE COUNTY BAR.

PIONEER COURTS.

The records of the early Courts found in the Circuit Clerk's office open as follows:

"At a Circuit Court begun and held at Cole's Grove, within and for the county of Pike, on Monday, the first day of October, in the year one thousand eight hundred and twenty-one. Present, Hon. John Reynolds, Judge.

"The Sheriff of the county returned a panel of grand jurors, which being called over, sixteen of them appeared and were sworn agreeably to law, viz: Levi Roberts, foreman; Ebenezer Franklin, Gardner H. Tullus, Joel Bacon, George Tully, Ebenezer Smith, David Dutton, Amos Bancroft, James Nixon, Nathaniel Shaw, Thomas Proctor, Richard Dilley, Stephen Dewey, William Massey, Comfort Shaw, Daniel Phillips; and the following persons were called but made default, to wit: Leonard Ross, Henry J. Ross, Daniel Shinn, James M. Seeley, Abraham Kuntz, Levi Newman, Henry Loup, John Bolter and John Jackson.

"Joseph Jervais and John Shaw, interpreters sworn to give evidence to the grand jury."

The first case called was "Solomon Smith, assignee of Elias K. Kane, *vs.* Wm. Frye, action of debt." The case was continued, as the defendant was reported by the Sheriff not found.

The second case was a "libel for a divorce," by Salley Durham, plaintiff, *vs.* John Durham, defendant. The defendant not appearing, the case went against him.

The fourth case was the indictment of two Indians for murder, an account of which is given in our chapter entitled "Criminal Record."

Pike county was originally in the 1st Judicial Circuit, then in the 5th, and is now in the 11th, comprising the counties of Adams, Hancock, McDonough, Fulton, Schuyler, Brown and Pike. By provision of a recent State law the Circuit elects three Judges, who divide the work between them.

Four Appellate Districts were defined in the State in 1877, for each of which the Supreme Court appoints three Judges, and these

Judges elect one of their own number the presiding Judge. Each District elects its own Clerk, and these officers are all chosen for six years. The sessions of the Court are held the 3d Tuesday of May and November each year. Pike county is in the 3d Appellate District, and the Court is held at Springfield.

CIRCUIT JUDGES.

We now proceed to give a short sketch of all the Judges and attorneys who have been or are now connected with the Bar of Pike county.

Hon. John Reynolds was a native of Pennsylvania, of Irish descent, and was reared amid pioneer associations and imbibed the characteristics, manners and customs of the pioneers. He disliked polish, condemned fashion, and was addicted to inordinate profanity. These, garnished by his varied reading, a native shrewdness and a wonderful faculty of garrulity, make him, considering the high offices he held, one of the public oddities of Illinois. He was one of the Justices of the Supreme Court when he held Court at Atlas.

Hon. John Y. Sawyer.—By the Constitution the terms of office of the Supreme Judges were to expire with the close of the year 1824. The Legislature re-organized the judiciary by creating both Circuit and Supreme Courts. The State was divided into five judicial circuits, providing two terms of Court annually in each county. The salaries of the Circuit Judges were fixed at $600. Judge Sawyer was the first Circuit Judge to hold Court in this county. He was chosen for the First Circuit.

Hon. Richard M. Young was appointed Judge of this Circuit in 1828, and remained in the office till January, 1837, when he resigned to accept a seat in the United States Senate. Judge Young was a native of Kentucky, and was one of the first settlers of Northern Illinois. He ranked high in his profession, and his counsels did much to shape the policy of the State. In his manners he was gentle, courteous and entertaining, which qualities rendered him attractive and popular. He was generous in his feelings and liberal in his views; possessed liberal endowment of intellectual ability and literary and legal acquirements, and these, with his other qualifications, admirably fitted him for the post he was called to fill. He died from insanity.

Hon. James H. Ralston, a native of Kentucky, was elected by the Legislature in 1837, and in August of the same year he resigned on account of his health, with a view of going to Texas, whither he went, but soon returned to Quincy. In 1840 he was elected State Senator. In 1846 President Polk appointed him Assistant Quartermaster of the U. S. army. Having discharged his duties faithfully during the war with Mexico, he returned home and soon after emigrated to California.

Hon. Peter Lott, a native of New York, was elected the successor

GRIGGSVILLE

of James Ralston, and continued in the office until January, 1841. He was subsequently appointed Clerk of the Circuit Court of Adams county, and served until 1852; he then went to California and was appointed Superintendent of the U. S. Mint in San Francisco by President Pierce, and was removed in 1857 by President Buchanan, and afterward moved to Kansas and lived in humble life.

Hon. Stephen A. Douglas was elected Judge by the Legislature in 1841. The life and career of this great man is so well and widely known as to render any extended notice of him useless. It is sufficient to say that the circumstances under which he entered upon the duties of his office were such as to thoroughly try the scope of his ability. The Circuit was large; the previous incumbent of the office had left the "docket" loaded with unfinished "cases," but he was more than equal to the task. He "cleaned out the docket" with that dispatch and ability which distinguished his subsequent course; and so profound was the impression he made upon the people that, in the first Congressional election which occurred after he was established in his character as Judge, he received nomination as a member of Congress, and was elected.

Hon. Jesse B. Thomas was appointed in August, 1843, and continued to hold the position until 1845, when he resigned. Judge Thomas possessed high legal abilities and acquirements, and discharged the duties of his office with honor to himself and to the satisfaction of the people. After his resignation he was appointed to another Circuit, and soon after died. He was a delegate to Congress from Indiana as early as 1808. His district was what are now the States of Indiana, Illinois, Wisconsin and Michigan. He was one of the first U. S. Senators of Illinois.

Hon. Norman H. Purple was the next incumbent of the office. He was elected in 1845 and served till May, 1849, when he resigned. The probable cause for this was the insufficiency of salary. The people of this district were anxious to retain him as Judge, and probably would, but for the cause stated. He was distinguished for high legal abilities and executive talents, and the office was rendered the more honorable for his having occupied it.

Hon. William A. Minshall was elected in May, 1849, and continued to hold the office till his death, in October, 1851, although in 1850 his district was changed. Judge M. was a native of Tennessee, and came early into the State. He was an active and successful lawyer, and attained distinction in his profession. Previous to his election as Judge he had been a member of the Constitutional Convention, and also a member of the State Legislature.

Hon. O. C. Skinner succeeded Judge Minshall and occupied the office from May, 1851, to May, 1853, when he was elected to the Supreme Bench, and remained there till 1858, when he resigned. He was a sound, able lawyer, and popular as a Judge, and gained eminence in his position as a Judge of the Supreme Court.

Hon. Pinkney H. Walker served until his appointment, in 1858,

24

to fill a vacancy on the Supreme Bench. In 1859 he was elected to the Supreme Court for nine years, which position he now holds. Judge Walker is a native of Kentucky, and came into the State with his father among the first settlers, and located in McDonough county. He had only such advantages for obtaining his literary acquirements as a newly settled country afforded, but a strong determination, added to high intellectual abilities and good health, carried him over all of the educational wants of the times, and gave him a fair position as a scholar. The same qualifications rendered him thorough as a student of law, and gave him superiority as a counselor. His present residence is at Rushville.

Hon. John S. Bailey was the succeeding incumbent of the office and served for three years. Previous to his appointment he was State's Attorney for this district. He was considered a sound lawyer, and made an impartial Judge. He now resides at Macomb, and yet follows his chosen profession.

Hon. Chauncey L. Higbee, of Pike county, was first elected in 1861, and was re-elected twice, each time for six years. His reputation as an able lawyer is unquestioned, and fewer appeals were made from his decisions than from any other Judge in the State. He was elected to the Appellate Court in 1877, when the present incumbent, Judge Shope, of Lewistown, was chosen.

Hon. S. P. Shope.—Judge Shope, of Lewistown, was born in Mississippi but reared in Ohio. In the spring of 1839 he came to Illinois, read law with Judges Purple and Powell in Peoria, and was admitted to the Bar June 11, 1856. He first opened an office in Metamora, Ill, but in a short time removed to Lewistown, where he still resides. He has had a large practice as a lawyer, not only in his own Judicial District, but also in Logan, Mason and Cass counties. In August, 1877, he was elected Judge of this District without opposition. His thorough knowledge of law, quick comprehension and well-known impartiality, render him a popular Judge.

PROSECUTING ATTORNEYS.

During the earliest period of the county's history the Attorney General of the State acted as Prosecuting Attorney in Circuit Districts. After the expiration of Attorney-General Forquer's term the Circuit was given a State's Attorney. This mode remained in vogue, although, of course, the districts were often changed and cut down, until 1872, when the county was given a Prosecuting Attorney, who is known both as State's Attorney and County Attorney. This official is not now, as formerly, called out of the county to prosecute for the people.

The Prosecuting Attorneys serving this county are as follows:

Hon. Thomas Ford served for several years previous to 1835. He was possessed of high and noble qualities of manhood, a thorough student, a keen, energetic, untiring lawyer, of strict integrity and laudable aspirations, and was universally esteemed and respected. He afterward became Judge of the northern district, and when he had become known over the State, was chosen Governor by a spontaneous movement of the people. Mr. Ford failed to appear at the Courts of this county very much, and in his place in 1832 Hon. J. H. Ralston served, and in 1833 Gen. John J. Hardin.

Hon. William A. Richardson, who served till 1837. Mr. Richardson's personal merits and characteristics are too well known to require any delineation. His predominating traits were courage, unyielding perseverance and unvarying adherence to the cause to which he was committed. He had command of a regiment of Illinois volunteers during the Mexican war, and in the battle of Buena Vista his cap was carried from his head by a musket ball. He returned home and was elected to Congress, and re-elected five times. He was also appointed Governor of Nebraska by Buchanan.

Hon. Henry L. Bryant, of Lewistown, succeeded Mr. Richardson, and served until 1839. He is characterized as a gentleman of fine qualities and as an able lawyer.

Hon. William Elliott served from January, 1839, till January, 1848. He was esteemed as a worthy man, a warm friend and a good lawyer. He served in the Black Hawk war, and was wounded in a hand-to-hand conflict with a single Indian, whom he killed. He was Quartermaster in the 4th Regiment during the Mexican war, and served through. He returned to Lewistown and continued his practice until about 1856, when he moved upon a farm in Peoria county, near Farmington, where he died in February, 1871.

Hon. Robert S. Blackwell was the successor of Mr. Elliott, and served from 1848 till 1852. Mr. Blackwell was one of the most distinguished lawyers in the State, and is the author of " Blackwell on Tax Titles."

Harmon G. Reynolds.—From 1852 to 1854, Hon. Harmon G. Reynolds, of Knoxville, held the office. Mr. Reynolds was an attorney-at-law of great ability, and an active man in all beneficent enterprises. He came from Rock Island to Knoxville some time about 1851, where he practiced law, was State's Attorney and postmaster, and held prominent positions in the Masonic order. He moved from Knoxville to Springfield, where he served as Grand Secretary of the order. He now resides in Kansas.

William C. Goudy.—Hon. William C. Goudy, of Lewistown, succeeded Mr. Reynolds. Mr. Goudy was a shrewd Democratic politician in earlier days, as well as a faithful servant of the people as a delegate to conventions, as a member of the State Senate, etc. As a lawyer he is accounted one of the ablest that ever practiced at the Bar. He has accumulated large wealth and now resides in Chicago, where he moved in 1859.

Calvin A. Warren followed Mr. Blackwell in the office. Mr. Warren served from May, 1852, until August, 1853. This gentleman was a popular, fluent speaker and successful lawyer.

Hon. John S. Bailey, of McDonough county, filled the office until September, 1858, when he resigned for a seat upon the Bench.

Daniel H. Gilmer served as State's Attorney *pro tem* in 1860, as also did Thomas E. Morgan in 1862, and Wm. R. Archer.

Hon. L. H. Waters was appointed by the Governor to fill the unexpired term of Mr. Bailey. He was from Macomb, and served until the fall of 1860. A year later he entered the army as Lieutenant-Colonel of the 28th Illinois Infantry. Resigning, he was commissioned to raise another regiment, which he succeeded in doing and received the appointment of Colonel. This was the 84th Illinois Infantry and did excellent service under his efficient command. At the close of the war he returned to Macomb and practiced law, and about four years later moved to Missouri. He now resides at Jefferson City that State.

Thomas E. Morgan was the next incumbent. Mr. Morgan was a lawyer of fine ability and ranked at the head of the Bar in this part of the State. He died July 22, 1867.

L. W. James, of Lewistown, was the next incumbent. Mr. James is a lawyer of more than ordinary talent, and was one of the best prosecutors in the district, and is said to be one of the most brilliant young men in the State. He now resides at Peoria.

Jeff Orr.—When each county throughout the Circuit was given a Prosecuting Attorney Jeff Orr was chosen for Pike county, and since has served with marked ability. He is a young member of the Bar, endowed with great energy, and gifted with superior native talent. He has resided in Pittsfield since 1873.

THE BAR.

The Bar of Pike county has ever stood foremost of all in this great State. Some of the best legal minds, and fairest logicians and finest orators of the age have practiced at this Bar.

In reviewing the Bar of the county our readers must bear in mind that as the prosperity and well-being of every community depends upon the wise interpretation, as well as upon the judicious framing, of its laws, it must follow that a record of the members of the Bar, to whom these matters are generally relegated, must form no unimportant chapter in the county's history. Upon a few principles of natural justice is erected the whole superstructure of civil law tending to relieve the wants and meet the desires of all alike. But where so many interests and counter interests are to be protected and adjusted, to the judiciary is presented many interesting and complex problems. But change is everywhere imminent. The laws of yesterday do not compass the wants and necessities of the people of to-day. The old relations do not exist. New and satisfactory ones must be established. The discoveries in the arts and sciences, the invention of new contrivances for labor, the enlargement of industrial pursuits, and the increase and development of commerce are without precedence, and the science of the law must keep pace with them all; nay, it must even forecast events and so frame its laws as will most adequately subserve the wants and provide for the necessities of the new conditions. Hence the lawyer is a man of the day. The exigencies he must meet are those of his own time. His capital is his ability and individuality. He can not bequeath to his successors the characteristics that distinguished him, and at his going the very evidences of his work disappear. And in compiling this short sketch one is astonished at the paucity of material for a memoir of those who have been so intimately connected with, and who exerted such an influence upon, the county's welfare and progress. The peculiarities and the personalities, which form so pleasing and interesting a part of the lives of the members of the Bar, and which indeed constitute the charm of local history, are altogether wanting. Unlike the fair plaintiff in Bardell vs. Pickwick, we have no pains-taking sergeant to relate " the facts and circumstances " of the case. The Court records give us the facts, but the circumstances surrounding and giving an interest to the events are wanting.

The great prominence in history occupied by the Bar of the Military Tract is well known, and ranking with and a part of this is the Pike county Bar. High as stood the local standard of its attainment and repute, whenever its chieftains were called to combat on other arenas, they left no lost laurels there. Here were taught, needed, developed, the stalwart qualities that attach to and betoken the most complete fruition of legal excellence, as attained in the recognition, study, comprehension and application of the abstruse and limitless principles and history of that noblest portion of jurisprudence, land law.

It is no such difficult task to become what the world calls a lawyer, but with hope to tread the higher paths of the profession, easy effort, varnished knowledge, common mind muscle, need not apply. There are grades to which any may attain, but there are also summits to which few can aspire. Education, industry, and persistency may rightly demand and ensure success and even eminence in the settlement of commercial collisions, or in the adjustment of the thousand ordinary interests that constantly appeal to a lawyer's guidance. The babbling charlatan may, equally with the profound jurist, claim a fictitious standing as a criminal advocate; but such will always stumble among the rugged paths of " land law " practice, where rests the settlement of the earth's ownership and where true learning, combined with most grasping mental strength, can only be at home.

On this broad field, years since, inviting and fast filling with adventurous immigration, where existed land titles of every shade, affected by conflicting legislation varying as the years, was gained the rare training and reputation of the legal athletes, an arena such as was found in no other section of the State; and in addition to these advantageous themes of practice, the professional necessities of the Bar vastly aided its members in their advance to self-reliant supremacy. The reasons for this are novel, but conclusive.

Law in those past-off days demanded of its votaries different qualities from now. It exacted the instincts of the smarter men, of genius and nerve and novelty. It was the intellectual over the educated who chiefly led the van. Of books there were few. Authorities and precedents slumbered not in the great handy libraries. The entire resources of the Bounty Tract could hardly fill out the shelves of one ordinary lawyer's library to-day. Hence alike, whether engaged in counsel or in litigation, native resource, remembrance of past reading, but mainly the readiness and aptitude with which legal principles drawn from rudimental reading or educed by intuition could be applied to any interest or exigence in "the infinite vanity of human concerns," were the armories whence were drawn their welded weapons of assured success.

He was a luckless lawyer who had to hunt his books to settle a suddenly controverted point, or answer a bewildered client's query; and he was a licensed champion, who, theorizing from his instored legal lore, or instinctive acumen, knew on the instant where best to point his thrust and was equally ready with every form of parry and defense. The off-hand action and advice of such men, nerved by necessity and skilled by contest, became of course to be regarded almost like leaves of law.

One can thus somewhat realize what keen, pliant, incisive resource was attained by such careers, how inspiring and attractive were their collisions, how refined and subtle and sharpened their intellects must have become.

It should not be supposed that looseness, lack of accuracy or legal formula, marked the rulings of the Bench or Bar. There was friendship and familiarity, it is true, because everybody knew everybody; the court-houses were shambling great log shanties, their furniture, chairs and desks, split-bottomed and unplaned, would have set a modern lawyer's feeling on edge, but the Bench was always filled with character, knowledge and dignity (in fact, the second Judge who held Court in Pike county, John York Sawyer, weighed 386 pounds, and if that Bench was not full of judicial dignity where will the proper amount of avoirdupois be found?), and forensic ruling and requirement was governed by as much judicial precision and professional deference as would mark the records of the most pretentious tribunals in the land.

The Bar in those days was a sort of family to itself. There was a mutual acquaintance. All traveled the Circuit, went to every county on Court week, came from all quarters. Egypt and Galena had their representatives. Some went there because they had business; some because they wanted to get business, and all that they might learn.

In Court, by practice and observation, was acquired much of knowledge that the paucity of books denied the student and young practitioner. Out of Court their association was like that of a debating society or law school. They mingled in common, ate, drank, smoked, joked, disputed together. The Judge had at the tavern the spare room, if such a room there was, and the lawyers bunked cosily, dozens together, in the "omnibus," as the big, many-bedded room was called, and there they had it. Whatever of law point past, pending, or probable could be raised, they "went for," discussed, dissected, worried, fought over it until, whether convinced or not, all knew more than when they commenced; and thus, struggling over these made-up issues of debate, became sharpened, by mutual attrition, the legal faculties that were panting for future and more serious contests.

These lawyers were on exhibition, too, and they knew it. Every man in the county came to town Court week if he could. There were but few people in the country then, and Court week was the natural periodical time for the farmers to meet, swap stories, make trades, learn the news, hear the speeches and form their own opinions as to which of these "tonguey fellers it is safest to give business to or vote for for the Legislater."

A pretty good idea how universal was the gathering of necessity at the county-seats in those primitive days may be gleaned from the fact that often Sheriff, Capt. Ross and Deputy Sheriff "Jimmy" Ross had to go on the jury to make up the number. They could not find enough men in reach to sit as jurors. They had jolly old times, those limbs of the law—jolly, indeed. Most of them were young. All were instinct with the very cream of zeal, enterprise and originality that inheres to a new community, and among them jibe and jest and fun and yarn and repartee and sell were tossed about like meteoric showers.

An amusing incident is told in which figured an eminent surviving member of the Bar, of the Military Tract. He, the Judge, and the Prosecuting Attorney, traveling over the prairie, while lighting their pipes, either thoughtlessly or accidentally set the grass on fire. It spread, swept toward the timber, destroyed a settler's fences and improvements, and some luckless wight was indicted for the offense. The lawyer above was engaged as counsel for the culprit. The Prosecuting Attorney of course had his duty to perform to the furtherance of the ends of justice; the Judge had the outraged interests of law to protect under the solemnity of his position and oath; but it required all the earnest effort of the gifted counsel, all the generous ruling of the Judge, all the blundering action of the Prosecuting Attorney, the united sympathies, in fact, of this secretly sinning legal trinity to prevent the jury from finding a verdict against the innocent accused. Countless are the racy legends of Illinois life and law, unrecorded and fast fading away as the memories that hold them pass from existence, but time and space give now no warrant for their recital.

BAR OF THE PAST.

Of those attorneys who resided in the county at one time, or practiced here, and are now either dead, have quit the practice or moved away, we will speak first :

Gen. E. D. Baker, whose father was an Admiral in the English navy, and whose brother, Dr. Alfred C. Baker, now resides at Barry, was an eminent lawyer, a fine rhetorician and orator, a man of great intellect, and a leader in the halls of legislation. After many years' practice in Illinois he went to California, which State soon sent him to Congress as Senator, but he was finally slain by treachery at Ball's Bluff in Virginia.

Hon. O. H. Browning, of Quincy, too well known to describe here, has practiced at this Bar.

Col. D. B. Bush, of Pittsfield, is the oldest man in the county who has been a member of the Bar at this Court. He was admitted to practice in 1814.

Hon. J. M. Bush, the present editor of the *Democrat*, has practiced law here with commendable success.

Nehemiah Bushnell, a partner of Mr. Browning's at Quincy, has also practiced law in the Pike county Circuit Court. He was an easy, quiet and thorough lawyer, and a superior man in the U. S. Court. He died in 1872.

Alfred W. Cavalry was a smooth, pretty talker. He moved to Ottawa and died there a year or two ago at a very advanced age.

George W. Crow, of Barry, was a young man but not much of a lawyer. He went to Kansas.

Stephen A. Douglas practiced at the Pike county Bar in early days.

Daniel H. Gilmer was a young but able lawyer, thorough-going, learned, careful and popular. For a time he was a partner of Archibald Williams, and was subsequently a Colonel in the army, succeeding Col. Carlin : he was killed at Stone river. His daughter Lizzie is now Postmistress at Pittsfield.

Jackson Grimshaw, younger brother of Hon. Wm. A. Grimshaw, was leader of the Bar in his day. He resided at Pittsfield fourteen years, then went to Quincy, where he died in December, 1875.

The following high eulogy was paid to the memory of Mr. Grimshaw by Hon. I. N. Morris before the Bar of Quincy, at the time of his decease : "I rise to second the motion to place on the records of this Court the resolutions adopted by the members of the Bar of Quincy, as a slight testimonial to the memory of Jackson Grimshaw. It is but little we can do, at best, to keep the defacing march of time from obliterating every sensitive memory of our departed friends, but we can do something toward it and let us do that little in this instance. Jackson Grimshaw deserves a living place in our minds and in our hearts. Yet he was mortal. He, like other men, had his faults and his virtues. His faults belonged to himself. His virtues to all. When the melancholy news came out from his residence, at 11 o'clock yesterday, that he was dead, its echo went over the city like the sound of a funeral bell, and "poor Grimshaw" was the general wail amid the heartfelt sorrow of all. His genius was of no ordinary kind; his energy was tireless, and he was true to his profession, his client and his honor. I challenge any man to say if he ever heard either impeached, even by a suspicion. If there was any thing the deceased hated more than any other, it was an illiberal, tricky, unmanly, dishonorable act, inside or outside of the profession, more especially inside of it. He had no patience with anything low or mean. These words grate on the ear, but I know of none more appropriate or expressive. His impulses flowed from a pure and noble inspiration, and were guided by a cultivated mind. I repeat it with pride, Jackson Grimshaw was an honest man. He bowed to no expediency, nor to sordid motive. He was easily excited, and the blood would mount to his cheeks instantly at a wrong or indignity, and he would rebuke it on the spot. All will concede there was not a particle of deceit or hypocrisy about him. What he was he was, and we all understood him. He did not ask a favor in a smiling, cunning, obsequious way, but he trod the world as a man, and he looked with pity and disdain upon the servile who crawl upon their belly. In short, I say from a long and intimate acquaintance, notwithstanding his quick resentment and hasty words, he was superior in all the better qualities of the head and heart, for he never meant or planned a wrong: never coolly devised an evil, or gave the least countenance to it in another. I do not speak the language of romance or eulogy, but the simple, unadorned language of truth, and by that standard let him be judged. He would not prostitute his profession to plunder the widow or the orphan, or, in other words, he did not study or practice it merely as a means of gain, but for the higher and nobler purpose of establishing justice among men, and not degrading the court-house into a place of tricks, technicalities and legal legerdemain. His sense of right was exalted, and he was not a spawn of nature, but was cast in the best mold. I repeat it, he was in the broadest sense of the term an honest and honorable lawyer and man.

It is no disparagement to others to say that in his profession he was the peer of any of them. He was a close student, but what was better, he was a close thinker. The principles bearing on his case shone through his mind as the face in the mirror, and they were unfolded to the Court and the Jury in language clear, forcible and convincing. His plain law, his impressment of facts, his elucidation, his power of analysis, his clear, forcible language and delivery, placed him justly in the front rank at the Bar.

Zachariah N. Garbutt was born in Wheatland, N. Y., about the year 1813; graduated at the University of Vermont; studied law in Washington city in the office of Matthew St. Clair Clark; he directly emigrated to Jacksonville, Ill., where he finished his legal course; he came to Pike county about the year 1839, returned East for a year, and then came back to Pittsfield, where he established the *Free Press* in 1846, and from which paper he retired in 1849; he also practiced law some, was Justice of the Peace and

Master in Chancery. He was a strong anti-slavery Whig and a temperance advocate, and in the Mormon war, as Mr. Grimshaw says, "He earned laurels by piling up big sweet potatoes for the troops of the anti-Mormons." Earnest and somewhat original in his opinions, very independent in the expression of his thoughts, he was an upright, jovial man, and something of a genius. Finally, while traveling for a firm in St. Louis on commercial business, he was attacked with varioloid in Memphis, Tenn., where he died in 1855. In 1841 he married Phimelia B. Scott, a native of New York State, and who has since married Mr. Purkitt, and still resides in Pittsfield.

Alfred Grubb was first Sheriff, then a member of the Legislature, then County Judge, and then admitted to the Bar, and practiced in the Courts. He had considerable legal knowledge, and was well versed in the rules of practice, but his natural ability was comparatively deficient.

Gen. John J. Hardin, who had descended from a stock of soldiers and lawyers, was a fine attorney. He used to practice considerably at the Bar in this county, and often stop here on his way to Calhoun and return. For a period he was State's Attorney on this Circuit. He was killed at the battle of Buena Vista.

Milton Hay, formerly of the firm of Hay & Baker, now ranks high as a lawyer at Springfield, Ill., being a member of the firm of Hay, Greene & Littler, and has accumulated a fortune. He has been a member of the State Constitutional Convention and of the State Legislature.

Mr. Hewitt practiced here a while, and went to Iowa.

Capt. Joseph Klein, of Barry, was admitted to the Bar, but never practiced in the Circuit; was a partner of J. L. Underwood until 1869. He had considerable ability. He was once a steamboat captain, and came from St. Louis to this county.

Josiah Lamborn, a lame man, once Attorney General of the State, resided at Jacksonville, and afterward at Springfield. He had a great deal of talent, but was a corrupt man.

Abraham Lincoln practiced at the Pike county Bar in early days.

Samuel D. Lockwood, who resided at Jacksonville, was a very superior man as a lawyer and as a gentleman. He was once Attorney General of the State, Judge of the old Fifth Circuit, and was the author of the original criminal code of Illinois. He resigned the office on account of ill health, and went up to or near Aurora, where he died a short time ago. He was also one of the original trustees of the Asylum for the Blind at Jacksonville.

Gen. Maxwell, of Rushville, has appeared before the Bar in this county. His favorite song was, "The big black bull went roaring down the meadow." At one time he was a partner of Wm. A. Minshall, and at another of Wm. A. Richardson.

Isaac N. Morris, of Quincy, but recently deceased, has practiced law in Pike county.

Murray O'Connell, of Jacksonville, practiced here considerably. He was a rough-speaking man, but of great wit. During Buchanan's administration he was 5th Auditor of the Treasury. He was murdered at the age of seventy.

John G. Pettingill, School Superintendent for a number of years, was also a lawyer in this county, but is now living in Missouri.

N. E. Quinby, another Pike county lawyer, is now deceased.

James H. Ralston, formerly of Quincy, used to practice here and was for a time Circuit Judge. He was finally killed and devoured by wolves in California.

Hon. Wm. A. Richardson, State's Attorney for a long time, used to practice here, but of late years he has visited the county more in the role of a politician.

John Jay Ross, son of Capt. Leonard Ross, was a lawyer of Pike county, but his practice was mostly confined to Atlas. He is now dead.

David A. Smith, once of Jacksonville, practiced here a great deal. He was a partner of Gen. Hardin at the time the latter died.

Thomas Stafford, a Barry lawyer, had not much ability. He soon removed from Barry to parts not now remembered.

Mr. Starr practiced at Coles' Grove in very early day : he afterward went to Cincinnati.

John T. Stewart, of the firm of Stewart, Edwards & Brown, Springfield, is a shrewd lawyer of the Scotch kind. He was the first antagonist of Stephen A. Douglas in the Congressional race that the latter made in 1838, and was beaten by eighty-odd votes. The noted "Black Prince" turned the election. This district then extended to Galena and Chicago.

E. G. Tingle, Barry, whose father was a Judge in Maryland, was a well-read lawyer, but he did not stay in Barry long.

Hon. Lyman Trumbull, ex-U. S. Senator and now practicing law in Chicago, has appeared as attorney in the Pike county Court.

James Ward was a native of Ohio, and in this county was Justice of the Peace and Probate Judge. He died, leaving a family at Griggsville and numerous relatives.

Calvin A. Warren, of Quincy, but now dead, has visited here some as a lawyer, and was State's Attorney for a time.

Charles Warren, for a time partner of Milton Hay in Pittsfield, was counsel of the commission appointed to ascertain the damages incurred by the damming of Copperas creek.

Alpheus Wheeler, an eccentric preacher and lawyer, came from old Virginia to Pike county at the close of the Black Hawk war, residing for some time at Highland. In 1838 and 1840 he was elected to the Legislature of Illinois where he made his peculiar speeches and encountered the wit and humor of another remarkable man, but of a more elevated type of manhood and education, namely, Usher F. Linder, who died recently at Chicago. On one occasion Mr. Wheeler addressed the Chair, saying, "Mr. Speaker, I

have a-rose—" " Does the gentleman keep a flower garden?" interrupted the Speaker. Mr. W. practiced law in Pittsfield and obtained considerable business. He took great pride in his oratorical
efforts and made some lofty flights in speeches to the jury. On one
occasion when D. M. Woodson, State's Attorney, submitted a case
without argument for the purpose of preventing Wheeler from
speaking, the latter replied: " Gentlemen, I admire the State's Attorney; he has shown the most sublime eloquence, as from some
men it consists in most profound silence." He used to say of
Woodson, " His eloquence is like the tall thunder amongst the lofty
oaks, coming down for to split things." This remark at one time
excited some one who had a ready hand at a rough pencil sketch to
draw a picture of a man's head with a big nose elevated in a tree-
top, upon the west wall of the court-room at Pittsfield, and it remained there for many years, until the house was whitened up on
the inside. That big nose was a caricature of Wheeler's. In a case
for killing a cow, when O. H. Browning made some points for the
defendant, Mr. Wheeler replied: " The gentleman tells you, gentlemen of the jury, that the plaintiff, my client, cannot recover in this
suit because the cow warn't no cow because she never had a calf,
but that she war a heifer. Gentlemen, that are not the notion of a
sound and legal lawyer but the notion of a musharoon." This almost convulsed the court-house with laughter. Another objection
of Browning's in this case was thus replied to by Mr. Wheeler:
" Gentlemen of the jury, Mr. Browning says that our cow warn't
worth a cent. Now, gentlemen, where were there ever a cow that
warn't worth a cent? That cow were worth something for her meat,
if she warn't worth nothing for a milk cow. She war worth something for her horns; she war worth something for her hide, if not
for her meat or milk; and gentlemen, she war worth something because the tail goes with the hide." The cause of Browning's point
was, that Wheeler had failed to prove by witnesses the worth of the
cow.

A suit brought by Wheeler for one Harpole against his brother
was for damage done to hogs by cutting the toe-nails off the hogs
so as to prevent them from climbing. Wheeler, in describing the
injury done to the hogs, insisted that the hogs had a right to toe-
nails and a right to climb, and that, although they had done damage, yet it was laid down, " root hog or die."

One Zumwalt was indicted for destroying a mill-dam of Dr.
Hezekiah Dodge's. Wheeler in this case assailed the character of
Dr. Dodge, who was a respectable man and whom the jury did be-
lieve. Zumwalt was convicted upon evidence that he had said
at his son-in-law's, on the night of the destruction of the dam of
Dodge's, " Just now the *musrats* are working on old Dodge's dam."
Wheeler said of Dodge on the trial, " Dr. Dodge are a man so de-
void of truth that when he speaks the truth he are griped."

During another of the lofty flights of our hero, a wag, John J.
Ross, a lawyer and a man who made and enjoyed a joke, laughed

so at one of Mr. Wheeler's speeches that he became excited, and, turning upon Ross in a very contemptuous way, with a majestic sweep of his long arm brought down at Ross, said: " I wish I had a tater: I'd throw it down your throat." Wheeler did not close his speech that evening, and the next morning early, when he was again addressing the jury and Ross at the Bar table, by some hand several large potatoes were put down in sight of Wheeler's eye. He fired up and let out a torrent of invective upon Ross, every one, Judge and all, in a loud roar of laughter.

In a fine frenzy at one time, Mr. W. parodied Shakspeare thus:

> "Who steals my purse steals trash;
> Robs me of that which not enriches him but makes me poor,—

all to injure my client."

Wheeler went to Bates county, Mo., since which time he has been lost sight of by people of this county. It is reported that he is not now living.

James W. Whitney was denominated " Lord Coke " on account of his knowledge of law. For a sketch of him see chapter on the early settlement of this county.

Archibald Williams, formerly of Quincy but later of Kansas and U. S. Circuit Judge, has been an eminent practitioner at the Bar of Pike.

John H. Williams, now of Quincy and a Circuit Judge, is a son of Archibald Williams, a man of good sense, and has been an able pleader at the Bar of Pike county. He is one of three Judges of this Circuit, but seldom holds Court in Pike county.

David M. Woodson was a State's Attorney of the old 1st District, which then included Pike county; afterward was Circuit Judge for 18 years, then was member of the Legislature. His partner in the law was Charles D. Hodges, late Circuit Judge of Greene county.

Gov. Richard Yates delivered his "maiden" speech as an attorney here in Pittsfield.

THE PRESENT BAR.

We have endeavored to mention the names and give what facts we could learn of every attorney who has ever practiced in the courts of Pike county. We will now speak of those who compose the Bar at present. No name will intentionally be omitted. The list we give was furnished by some of the leading attorneys of the county, and we believe full and complete.

Hon. Wm. R. Archer is a native of New York city, where he read law and was admitted to the Bar in 1838, and shortly afterward moved to this county, where he has ever since resided, ever active to forward any movement for the progress and prosperity of the county.

R. M. Atkinson was admitted to the Bar in 1868; was elected County Judge in 1865 and served two terms.

Quitman Brown is engaged in the practice of law at Milton.

A. G. Crawford.—Mr. Crawford is a native son of Pike; studied law at Pittsfield, and graduated from the Chicago law school. He received his non-professional education in the schools of this county and at Blackburn University at Carlinville.

Joseph L. Dobbin.—This gentleman, who resides at Pittsfield, has been gaining a foot-hold in this county as an attorney of high rank.

Edward Doocy, Griggsville, is a graduate of Illinois College at Jacksonville, and was admitted to the Bar in 1874. He was born in Griggsville in 1851, and as a lawyer he now has a successful practice.

Isaac J. Dyer, Time, was reared in Jacksonville; had but limited literary education; received his professional education at the law school of Washington University at St. Louis, and was admitted to the Bar in 1873. He served in the late war and was disabled for life by wounds in the left arm.

James F. Greathouse, of Pittsfield, is a son of one of the early pioneers of Pike county. He was reared in Montezuma township and has thus far continued to reside in the county. He served his country during the trying days of the Rebellion.

Delos Grigsby, son of Judge Grigsby, has recently been admitted to the Bar.

Hon. Wm. A. Grimshaw, the oldest practicing attorney of the county, ranks as one of the leading lawyers of the State; was admitted to the Bar in Philadelphia at the age of 19; in 1833 he came to Pike county, since which time he has been actively identified with almost every public interest of the county.

Samuel V. Hayden is engaged in the practice of law at Milton.

Harry Higbee, son of Judge Higbee, and partner of Messrs. Wike & Matthews, attended Columbia Law School, New York city, and the Chicago Law School, and was admitted to the Bar in 1878.

Geo. W. Hinman is engaged in the practice of law at Perry.

James S. Irwin was a college class-mate of the noted John C. Breckinridge, who was once Vice President of the United States and afterward a leader in the Southern Confederacy. Mr. Irwin is one of the leading lawyers of the State.

Henry C. Johnston, of Pittsfield. Mr. Johnston has resided in Pittsfield for some time, engaged in the practice of law.

J. W. Johnson was admitted to the Bar in 1869, came to Pike county the following year, taught school for two years and then located at Pittsfield. He is at the present engaged in the practice of law in company with J. S. Irwin.

W. I. Klein, who graduated at Ann Arbor, is practicing law at Barry at the present time.

A. C. Lang is also practicing at Barry.

Hon. A. C. Matthews is a native of this county, his father being one of the sturdy pioneers. He served in the late war with distinction as Colonel of the 99th, and subsequently was Collector of Internal Revenue for several years in the 9th District, then Supervisor of Internal Revenue.

Jefferson Orr. Mr. Orr is at present the State's Attorney. As a lawyer and as a man of integrity and ability he ranks high.

Peter T. Staats, Griggsville. While engaged in the practice of law Mr. Staats also teaches school occasionally.

J. L. Underwood, of Barry, was born in New York city May 10, 1826, the son of Robert L. and Martha Underwood; emigrated first to Adams county, and in 1837 to Pike county, settling at Eldara; read law here and was admitted to the Bar in 1865, but had been practicing law four years before that time. Although living at Eldara his office for many years was at Barry, to which place he has more recently moved.

Hon. Scott Wike studied law at Harvard University, and was admitted to the Bar in 1858; the following year he located at Pittsfield and began the practice of his chosen profession. He is one of the leading lawyers of the Circuit.

Thos. Worthington, jr., son of Dr. Thos. Worthington, was born in Tennessee while his mother was there on a visit during the holidays. But he is, strictly speaking, an Illinoisan. He read law with Judge Atkinson and in the law school at Chicago, and was admitted to the Bar in 1877. He is now in the office with Judge Atkinson at Pittsfield.

Ed. Yates, a partner of Jeff Orr, the State's Attorney, at Pittsfield, ranks among the leading attorneys at this Bar, and unrivaled in his ability to relate anecdotes.

TOWNSHIP HISTORIES.

CHAMBERSBURG TOWNSHIP.

This township lies in the extreme northeastern part of the county. It is bounded upon the north by Versailles tp., Brown co., on the west by Perry tp., on the south by Flint, and on the east by the Illinois river. Along the river is much bottom land, whole sections of which are entirely useless for agricultural purposes. Both the north and south forks of McGee's creek traverse this township: they join on section 27, and empty into the Illinois river about a mile above Naples, which is on the opposite shore, in Scott county.

The first pioneers who came to this township were James Wells, Samuel Atchison, a Mr. Brewster and a Mr. Van Woy. They came in 1822. The first named located on section 20, and Mr. Atchison erected his cabin on section 17. The first sermon preached in the township was at the house of Rachel Brown, in 1827, by Rev. John Medford, a Methodist preacher. The first church edifice was erected on section 31. The first school was taught in 1830 in an old log house which stood near where Joseph Brown lives, by John Lyster. The first Sunday-school in the township was organized by the Methodists in the town of Chambersburg. The first wedding in the township was in 1826, the contracting parties being James Medford and Eliza Brown. The wedding occurred at the residence of the bride's mother, and the ceremony was performed by Esquire Wells. The first person overtaken by death in the township was Michael Brown, who died in 1826. He came to the township in the fall of the same year.

Joseph Brown is the oldest pioneer living in the township. James Pool is the next oldest. Harvey Dunn was an early settler here. He was a member of the convention which framed the Constitution of 1847. He was an unassuming, intelligent and honest man, and died many years ago.

The privations of the pioneer families in this township were in some respects very great, cut off as they were from almost all social, religious, educational and commercial advantages. Of course they enjoyed these in a limited degree. The first settlers were people who valued greatly such privileges, and though they were for many

Martin Harrington.

PERRY

years without school-houses and churches, easily found the facilities for enjoying themselves, both socially and religiously. The greatest privations arose from the want of the means of communication with the outside world. The absence of railroads, or even good wagon roads, rendered the locality almost inaccessible to postal and commercial facilities, and traveling for other than business purposes was out of the question. Most of the original pioneers are represented here by descendants, but they, with few exceptions, have passed to a country that is always new, where, however, the trials of pioneer life are unknown.

The first settlers were all farmers, after a fashion now unknown. They raised a little corn and a few vegetables, and, like their red neighbors, depended largely upon their rifle for subsistence. Their houses were but little superior to those of the Indians, being merely little cabins erected only with the help of the ax and perhaps an auger. No locks, nails or any other article of iron entered into their construction, but such devices as could be wrought out on the ground by the use of the tools named and of such materials as the locality afforded. The only boards used for any purpose were such as could be hewed out of logs.

CHAMBERSBURG.

The town of Chambersburg is located on the north fork of McGee's creek, on section 8. It was surveyed and laid out May 7, 1833, by Seabourn Gilmore and B. B. Metz. McIntosh and Givens were the first settlers of the town. They owned a distillery and store here before the town was laid out. There are several good stores, churches, a school-house, shops, etc., in the town; and for an inland village it transacts a very good trade.

PERSONAL SKETCHES.

James Barry is a native of Morgan county, O., and was born in 1834; he is a son of Wilson and Rosanna Barry, the former a native of Pennsylvania and the latter of Vermont; he was brought to this county at the age of nine years; Feb. 1, 1855, he married Eleanor E. Kurfman, who was born in Pennsylvania in 1838. Everything was in its native wildness when Mr. B. came to this county, and as his father soon died, he began life for himself at an early age, working for $13 a month; he had many obstacles to overcome, but his enterprising, persevering disposition overcame all of them. He prospered for a time here and removed to Rockport, with the intention of going to Missouri the following spring, but the outbreak of the war prevented him. He bought land again in this county, met with disasters, but has again established himself, now owning 190 acres of land. Mr. B. is a member of the U. Baptist Church. P. O., Chambersburg.

Joab Brooks ; P. O., Chambersburg. Mr B. was born in Pike county in 1832, and is a son of A. H. and Lucy Brooks, natives of Tennessee. In 1863 he married the widow Brooks, whose maiden

25

name, was Elizabeth Hume. She was born in 1833. Six children have blessed this union. Mr. B. is engaged in farming on sec. 9, but formerly followed blacksmithing. Members of M. E. Church.

Joseph Brown, farmer, sec. 17; P. O., Chambersburg; is a native of the Green Mountain State, where he was born in 1816; his father, Michael Brown, is a native of Ireland, who came to this country when 18 years of age; his mother, the daughter of Joseph Greir, was born near Philadelphia, Pa. Mr. B. came with his parents to Illinois in 1820 and located near Shawneetown, Ill., and in the fall of 1824 was brought to this county, and has lived on the same farm since the spring of 1825, and has been engaged in farming and running flat and steam-boats on the river. In 1858 he married Mrs. Catharine Jones, a native of Coshocton Co., O. Three children have been born to them, two of whom are dead. Mr. Brown is an old pioneer, coming here when the wolves were thick as squirrels and could be heard in all directions, and turkey and deer seen in large numbers. He is the oldest pioneer now living in the township. His wife is a member of the Methodist Church.

Nancy Burrows, widow of the late Robert G. Burrows, was born in East Tenn. Dec. 18, 1825, and is a daughter of William Deviney, deceased. She was married to Mr. Burrows June 5, 1850. They had 8 children, of whom 3 are living,—Ada E., wife of David M. Reynolds, of Pike county; Ella F. and Laura A. Mrs. B's brother, Capt. P. Deviney, who spent most of his life on the waters, now resides in St. Louis, where she also has a sister residing, and one sister in California, whom she has not seen for 29 years. Mr. Burrows, her husband, was born in New York city, May 2, 1819; by profession he was a civil engineer, but desiring a more active life he went upon the waters; he was mate of the Calhoun on the Illinois river from the time she was launched until his death, which occurred Jan. 13, 1879. He was a man of culture and education, widely known and highly respected, and a worthy member of the M. E. Church.

James W. Chenoweth was born in 1847 in Pike county, and is a son of Wm. and Sarah Chenoweth; he first married Mary Erving in 1874. One child was born to them. Mrs C. died the same year, and in 1878 Mr. C. married Miss Maggie Erving, who was born in 1857. Mr. C. commenced buying and shipping stock eight years ago, and in this business has succeeded very well.

Miles B. Chenoweth; P. O. Chambersburg; was born in 1827 in Bartholomew Co., Ind. His parents, Abraham and Rachel Chenoweth, were both natives of Kentucky; they moved to Clinton Co., Ind., in the fall of 1832, and in 1836 to Pike county, Ill., where our subject grew to manhood and embarked in farming; in 1848 he was united in marriage to Miss Anna E. Allen, a native of Madison Co., N. Y., born April 7, 1830, and they are the parents of 4 children. They have been members of the Christian Church for 35 years, and in all public enterprises Mr. C. is very liberal.

E. D. Cooper was born in 1812 in Sumner Co., Tenn., and was the son of George and Elizabeth Cooper, the former of N. C., and his mother of Tenn. With his parents our subject moved to Ky., and in 1829 came to Illinois, and worked at the carpenter's trade in Pittsfield. In 1843 he married Miss Veturia Hobbs, who was born in Ky., in 1818. Mr. C. followed farming up to 1857, and then embarked in the grocery business; he went West, and in 1860 came back to Illinois, and again engaged in the grocery business until 1865, then embarked in the milling business, which he continued two years; farmed for a year; engaged in the milling business in Versailles, Ill., for about a year and a half; returned to the farm,, where he lived for 7 years; then sold out and bought the Chambersburg Mills, which he has been running since. In connection with the flouring-mill, which he has put in excellent repair, he has a saw-mill.

J. H. Dennis, Chambersburg, is one of the leading citizens of the township, indeed of the county. Mr. D. has served many terms as a member of the Board of Supervisors, and as Chairman of that body.

Thomas Dorman, farmer, sec. 4; P. O. Chambersburg. Mr. D. is a son of Lewis and Eliza J. Dorman; born in 1851 in Brown Co., Ill.; his father is a native of Ohio and his mother a native of Brown Co., Ill., where Thomas was raised until the age of 15; he then engaged in engineering, and for 3 years followed blacksmithing, at Hersman Station, then went to Jaques' Mills, where he worked two years. He was married to Miss America Berry in 1872; she was born in Ohio in 1850. Of the 3 children born to them one is dead. Mr. and Mrs. D. are members of the Christian Church.

George H. Dunn was born in Morgan Co., Ill., Feb. 28, 1838. His parents, Harvey and Angeline Dunn, were born in N. Y. and Mass., respectively. Mr. D. was brought to this county by his parents in 1839, and up to the year 1850 lived in the town of Chambersburg, and then moved on a farm on sec. 5, where he lived until the death of his father in Dec., 1869. He shortly afterward returned to Chambersburg and has since lived in retired life. In April, 1864, he married Miss Susan M. Dennis. Mr. D. is a brother of Dr. Dunn, of Perry. He is a member of the Blue Lodge, also the Chapter of Knight Templars of the Masonic fraternity.

Thomas Grayham, farmer sec. 17; P. O. Chambersburg. Mr. G. was born in 1833 in Kentucky; at the age of 22 he came to this county and followed carpentering and boat-building. His parents were John and Susan Grayham. Our subject was married to Miss Siretta J. Rushing, who was born in Nashville, Tenn. To them have been born 10 children, 6 of whom are living. Mr. G. has been very successful as a farmer. Mrs. G. is a member of the Methodist Church.

Joel Ham, farmer, sec. 20; P. O. Chambersburg. In Rutherford Co., Tenn., in 1829, there was born to James and Mary Ham the subject of this sketch; they moved to this county when their son was one year old; here he grew to manhood, and May 9, 1850, was married to Miss Sarah A. Wells, who was born in this township

April 29, 1833. James A., Orson, Sarah H., Bennett D. and Charles are the names of the children born to them. Mrs. H. died, and Sept. 8, 1859, Mr. H. married Miss Malvina Lee, who was born May 24, 1836, at Orleans, Ind. Ten children have been born to them,—Benj. F., Angenettia, Lucretia, David L., Enoch, Walter S., Harvey, Anna E., Dollie P., Frederick A. The following of his former children are dead: James A., Orson and Charlie; and of the latter, Benjamin, Lucretia and Dollie. Mr. H. began life very poor, but now owns 400 acres of land. He well remembers about the early settlers pounding corn with an iron wedge in the top of a stump burned out for the purpose, and when it took two days for his father to go to mill with the grist in a sack thrown over the horse's back. All the sugar they used was from the maple trees standing in the forest. Mrs. H. is a member of the Christian Church.

John H. Ham, farmer, sec. 20 ; P. O. Chambersburg ; is the son of Lewis and Julia A. Ham, and was born in this county in 1855 ; his mother died in December, 1878. In 1874 Mr. H. took unto himself a wife in the person of Miss Alice Conner : she was born in Pike county in 1854 : only one of the two children born to them is living. Mrs. H. is a member of the Christian Church.

James L. Ham, one of the largest farmers in this county, was born June 15, 1832, in this township ; his parents came here in 1830 from Rutherford county, Tenn.; their names were James and Mary (Broiles) Ham, one a native of S. C. and the other of Tenn., and of German descent,—both very old families in those States, and took part in the Revolutionary war, their great-grandfather, Gen. Williams, serving under Washington. James Ham, the father of our subject, during his life-time was a very large and successful farmer, owning and working 1,500 acres of land in this township at the time of his death, which occurred in 1868. He began life in 1830 with a team and 35 cents. He raised a large family of eight children, seven of whom lived to be grown,—four now living in this county and one in Stark county. James L. was married Sept. 25, 1853, to Julia A. Wells, daughter of James Wells, the oldest settler in this township. He had a family of four children,—John H., who is married and lives on sec. 20, Henry A., Marshall A. and Reuben L. Mr. Ham has served the township for several years as Supervisor, and was Chairman of that body : he is now acting as Justice of the Peace. He has been a member of the Christian Church for many years. He is also a member of the Masonic and Odd Fellows fraternities, and has been prominently connected with the Pike County Agricultural Society, being President, Vice-President or Director for the last fifteen years, and is now Vice-President.

William Hawk, farmer, sec. 4 ; P. O. Chambersburg; was born Aug. 3, 1842, and is a son of James and Rachel Hawk. He came with his parents to Brown county, Ill., when nine years of age, and in 1854 located in Pike county. Mr. H. served three years in Co.

G, 99th Ill. Vol. Inf.; was in the siege of Vicksburg, then transferred to the Army of the Gulf; was in the battle of Fort Blakely,
then returned to New Orleans, then to Memphis, then to Mobile,—
was there when that place was captured, then to Shreveport and
Baton Rouge. He returned home and engaged in farming.

Henry Hendricks, farmer, sec. 16 ; P. O. Chambersburg. Mr.
H. is a son of Thomas and Elizabeth Hendricks, the former a native
of Kentucky and the latter of Vermont. They were married in
Jennings county, O., where in 1836 the subject of this sketch was
born ; in 1849 Mr. H. came with his parents to Brown county, Ill.,
where he lived until he became of age and married Miss Elmina
Hume, who was born in 1837. To them have been born seven
children. Mr. H. has held some township offices ever since he
came to this county in 1861. Mrs. H. is a member of the Christian
Church.

D. J. Hobbs, of the firm of Smith & Hobbs, was born in 1848
in Pike county, Ill., and is the son of Henson and Jane Hobbs ;
his father was born in Kentucky and his mother in this county ;
in 1857 he moved with his parents to Missouri, and returned to
Pike county in 1861. He worked two years in a woolen mill at
Perry, this county. In 1868 he married Miss Bettie Ann Wilkins,
who was born in Ohio Dec. 22, 1848. Four children have been
born to them. Mr. H. embarked in the wagon business in 1870,
turning out good wagons and buggies and meeting with fair success. Both Mr. and Mrs. H. are members of the Christian Church.

Geo. T. Hume, merchant, Chambersburg, was born in Pike
county in 1855, and is a son of Thos. and Elmina Hume, father a
native of Pike county and mother of Brown county, Illinois. Mr.
H. grew to manhood in this immediate vicinity, receiving a liberal
education, and embarked in the mercantile business; he carries a
large stock of dry goods, hats, caps, boots, shoes, notions, etc., and
transacts a large business. He married Miss Vienna McPherson
in 1877; she was born in DeWitt county, Illinois, in 1858.

W. A. Hume, merchant, Chambersburg, was born in 1837 in this
county, and is a son of W. A. and Margaret Hume, both natives of
Kentucky. They came to this State in 1828 (where both of them
died) when the subject of this sketch was bound out; in 1864 he
married Miss Caroline Pool, who was born in Pike county in 1846.
Two of the four children born to them are living. Mrs. H. died in
1873, and Mr. H. married again in 1874 Miss Mary Winegar. Miss
W. was born in this county in 1850. Of this union two children
have been born. Mr. H. has held the offices of Collector, Treasurer
and Town Clerk. He embarked in the dry-goods business in 1865
and met with good success. He owns a farm of 230 acres.

John G. Irving was born in 1852 in Pike county and is a son of
Christopher and Mary Irving, the former a native of Scotland and
the latter of England; they came to America and were married in
Massachusetts and emigrated to Illinois in early days. In 1878
Mr. I. married Miss Ida M. Newton, who was born in Morgan

county, Illinois, in 1859; they have one child. Mr. I. has been engaged in farming since he was of age. Mrs. I. is a member of the Christian Church.

R. M. Irving, farmer and stock dealer, was born Sept. 25, 1848, in Pike Co., Ill., and is the son of Christopher and Mary Irving; at the age of 15 R. M. commenced doing business for himself, engaging in farming and finally becoming a stock-shipper. When he and his brother commenced in the cattle business they borrowed $200 and bought calves, and from the start kept increasing their number until now he is shipping about 200 head a year. He and his brother own a fine farm of 280 acres.

E. C. Jackson was born in Indiana in 1845; he is the son of Samuel and Harriet (Twichell) Jackson, natives of New York State. He is a farmer and owns 100 acres of land. He was educated in a seminary in Orland Town, Ind. At the present time he is running a "leveeing" machine, throwing up embankments along streams of water, so as to make bottom lands tillable. It has proved a success. This machine will throw a cubic yard of dirt in a minute, and the expense is only 5 cents per yard. It takes 12 horses and 3 men to do the work. Over 100 acres of wheat was raised in 1879 on lands that had been ponds of water before; the machine had been used for grading roads, but Mr. Jackson has improved it till he can do all kinds of work with it. In 1876, he married the daughter of Mr. Gardner, one of the early settlers of this county.

A. W. James, farmer, sec. 32 ; was born in 1818, Rutherford county, Tenn., son of Casey and Martha James, natives of Virginia. In 1838 he married Matilda Clardy, who was born in Bedford county, Tenn., and died in Sept., 1844. March 19, 1848, he married Elizabeth Sartain, who was born in 1827, in Tenn., and they had 6 children. Mr. J. came to Adams county in 1852, and in 1862 to this county, where he has since resided. He has held the offices of Constable, School Director and Road Commissioner.

John M. Kelsey was born in this county in 1852, son of Samuel and Annie E. Kelsey, the former born Nov. 18, 1827, and the latter April 26, 1834. In 1875 he married Matilda Smith, who was born in this county in 1859, and they had 3 children. Mr. K. is a farmer and also follows grain threshing with the Spence machine. He is a member of the Christian Church. His father was in the late war, belonging to Co. B., 99th Reg. Ill. Inft., and died at Memphis, Tenn., while in service.

Andrew Kleinlein was born in Germany in 1820, and is a son of Peter and Martha Kleinlein. At the age of 33 he crossed the ocean and landed in Baltimore, Md., and followed butchering for 10 months, then worked in an engine house 2 years for the Great Western R. R. Co., and in 1858 came to this county and commenced farming. In 1856 he married Miss Caroline Berceka, who was born in 1833 in Hamburg and came across the ocean in 1855. Of their 9 children 7 are living, 2 of whom are married. Mr. and

Mrs. K. have been members of the German Lutheran Church, and he owns 140 acres of good land.

John Leahr, son of Joseph and Anna M. Leahr, was born in Germany in 1840. He came to New York when but 15 years old, thence to Pike county, where he commenced farming, and in 1867 he married Miss Emma Smith, who was born in 1847, in Ohio. They had 7 children, of whom 5 are living. Mr. L. has been School Director and is a member of the Christian Church.

David E. Loer, farmer, sec. 5 ; P. O., Chambersburg; son of Henry and Matilda Loer; was born in Hamilton county, Ohio, in 1832. His father died in 1847 and his mother in 1879. He moved to Indiana with his parents when quite young; in 1852 he married Miss Sarah Leisur, who was born in Rush county, Ind., in 1833, and died in 1867, in Grant county, Ind. They had 3 children, 2 of whom are living. In 1868 he married Mrs. Maria Glassgow, a widow having 3 children, and who was born in Ohio in 1836. Mr. and Mrs. L. have 3 living children and are members of the Christian Church.

John Loer was born Aug. 22, 1814, in Colrain tp., Hamilton Co., Ohio. His father, Thomas Loer, was a native of Virginia, and son of Henry Loer, a native of Germany, who emigrated to America with his parents before the Revolutionary war, being then 8 years of age. He served under Washington during the war, for which he received a pension until his death. After the war he married Sarah Barkus and settled in Virginia; thence they removed to Ohio about 1795; he died in Hamilton in 1841. Thomas Loer, the father of our subject, died in Henry county, Ind., in 1873, aged 86. John's mother, Sarah (*nee* Patterson) was the daughter of George Patterson, a native of Scotland, who came to America before the Revolution, settling in Grant county, Ky., where he resided until his death. John Loer married Martha Hickman in 1835, in Ohio, and moved to this county in 1839, locating in this township. He was a cooper by trade and brought 5 coopers with him, intending to conduct that business here; he built a frame cooper shop 20 x 40, bought timber and opened up business, which he followed 2 years with success; then went into the pork speculation, buying pork at $1.50 per cwt., or $5.00 per barrel, shipping to New Orleans, some of which brought only 75 cents per barrel. Mr. L. lost heavily by this venture, and returned to coopering, which he followed with varying success until 1849. At one time during the wild-cat-money period he took a cargo of barrels to Alton and was obliged to sell them for 50 cents, when they had cost him 62½ cents to have them made, besides the freight, which was 25 cents each. He took Shawneetown money for pay and was advised to hurry home and dispose of it, as it was liable to become worthless any day. Mrs. Loer died in 1847, leaving 5 children. In 1849 Mr. L. married Mary, daughter of John and Hannah Hall Reese, of Ky , and they had 6 children, 2 living. In 1849 he invested in a saw-mill on McGee's creek, which he carried on until 1862, then traded for a farm on sec. 16 and carried on farming until 1877; sold the farm in 1879 and bought a flouring will in Chambersburg which he now operates. Mr. L. has served as Supervisor for several years : also as Road Commissioner, Collector and School Director. The present fine school building was built under the administration of Mr. Loer while he was Director. Mr. and Mrs. L. are members of the Christian Church, and Mr. L. belongs to the Masonic fraternity.

Frank Marden is one of the leading and enterprising citizens of Pike county. Residence, Chambersburg.

Mark McGinnis was born in East Tennessee in 1823. His father, David, was a native of Tennessee, and his mother, Sarah, a native of Virginia. When he was 9 or 10 years of age he moved with his parents to Indiana, living there six years; then came to Morgan county, Ill., and then to Pike in 1844 and located at Chambersburg. He followed coopering 16 years, and in 1842 married Mary Bushfield, who was born in 1828 in Kentucky. They had 7 children, only one of whom is living, Thomas B. Mr. McG. is now farming and has considerable property. Mr. and Mrs. McG. are members of the Christian Church.

Henry Metz was born in this county in 1842; his father, Benj. B., was born in Maryland in 1806, and his mother, Jane Metz, was born in Ohio in 1812. In 1871 Henry married Alvira Morrison, who was born in this county in 1855; of their 4 children 3 are living. Mr. M. is a farmer, his land lying adjoining the town of Chambersburg. Mr. M. served 4 years in the late war, first in Co. L., then transferred to Co. I, 10th Ill. Cav.; was mustered out in 1865 at San Antonio, Texas. In 1864 he was taken prisoner by Joseph Shelby; was held for 14 days and then paroled, and was exchanged in 6 months. Mrs. M. is a Methodist.

James L. Metz, son of Benj. B. Metz, was born in this county Jan. 27, 1834. His father moved from Maryland to Virginia, where he married Miss Jane Lawson. They came to Pike county in 1833, and became one of the first and most influential settlers of Chambersburg township. He died April 9, 1870. James L. married Emily Morris, daughter of John and Emily Morris, of Pike county.

Dr. John W. Murphy, son of John, a native of Vermont, and of Nancy, a native of Ohio, was born in Highland county, O., in 1844. His father died Jan. 10, 1845, in Ohio; in 1850 his mother removed to Indiana and then back to Ohio. During the late war he enlisted in Co. H, 39th O. V. I.; was in the battle of Corinth, was in the siege of Vicksburg, then at Chattanooga and in the Atlanta campaign and through to the sea and around by Washington, and was mustered out at Louisville, Ky.; then came home and learned the cooper's trade and milling business. The Doctor came to Pike county in 1869; commenced the study of medicine in 1871, and attended the American College at St. Louis, Mo.; in 1874 he located in Chambersburg and commenced the practice of medicine; in 1877-'8 attended medical college and returned home, continuing his profession. In 1876 he married Annie Lockerbie Thompson, who was born in 1851 in Cincinnati, O., and who was a teacher. She is a member of the M. E. Church.

Augustus Myers was born in 1819 in Baden, Germany. His parents were Andone and Catherine Myers, both natives of Germany. He emigrated to America in 1846, worked in Cincinnati 8 years by the month, then in this county to 1858, when he married Louise Carterman, who was born in 1829, in Lippe Detmold, Germany, who came to this country in 1857. Of their 8 children 7 are living. Mr. M. has been very successful in farming, now having 300 acres of nice land, sec. 19. He and his wife are members of the Lutheran Church at Perry. P. O., Chambersburg.

Thomas J. Smith, of the firm of Smith & Hobbs, wagon and carriage manufacturers, was born in 1835 in Clarke county, Ind., a son of Nicholas W. and Susan E. Smith, the former born in Kentucky, the latter in Vermont. In 1852 he married Margaret T. Montgomery, who was born in 1837, also in Clarke county, Ind. Of their 10 children only 5 are living. Mr. S. studied and practiced medicine 4 years in Indiana, and since 1871 he has practiced medicine and been connected with the carriage manufactory at Chambersburg. From 1863 to 1865 he served in Co. I, 40th Ind. Vet. Vol. Inf.; fought in the battles of Pulaski, Columbia, Spring Hill, Franklin, Tenn. (where he was wounded), Nashville, and in the whole campaign after Gen. Hood. Mr. and Mrs. S. are Methodists, and he is an Odd Fellow.

Valentine Smith was born in 1819 in Baden, Germany, near the river Rhine; his parents, Vincent and Mary, were also natives of Baden. He crossed the sea in a sail vessel, landing at New Orleans; then went to Cincinnati, and in 1855 he came to this county, where he has lived ever since, a prosperous farmer, owning 373 acres of good bluff land. In 1848 Mr. S. married Martha Thrasher, who was born in 1830 in Hamilton county, Ohio, and of their twelve children nine are living. Mr. and Mrs. S. are members of the Christian Church, reside on sec. 30, and their postoffice is Chambersburg.

George L. Thompson, blacksmith, Chambersburg, was born in Woodford county, Ky., son of William and Elizabeth Thompson, the former a native of Pennsylvania, and the latter of Scotland; in 1833 he emigrated to Indianapolis with his grand-parents, and the next year with his parents, to Perry township, in this county; in the spring of 1835 he left his parents, returning to Indianapolis, where he learned his trade; in the fall of 1855 he settled at Chambersburg, where he has since followed his trade. In 1845 he married Hannah S. O'Harrow, who was born June 20, 1829, in Hamilton county, Ohio, and they have had six children. Being an early comer to this wild West, Mr. T. has often seen large packs of wolves and killed many a deer. One day when well on his way home with a deer on horseback, the wolves attacked him, and he was compelled to abandon his booty and seek safety. The wolves devoured the deer with characteristic greed. Mr.

Thompson used to go to the town of Perry to buy such things as were kept for sale in an old log hut 12 feet square, kept by Joseph King, who was an old bachelor, and cooked, ate and sold goods in the same room. His wife is a Methodist.

Franklin Todd was born in 1825 in Bourbon county, Ky.: his father, John P., was born in Vermont, and his mother, Mary, in Pennsylvania; his father died in 1827, and in 1832 he accompanied his mother to their new home in Chambersburg, when there were but two cabins there, occupied by James and John Fike. In 1843 Mr. Todd married Lucretia Draper, who was born in Scott county, Ill., in 1825, the daughter of Samuel and Huldah Draper, her father a native of Massachusetts, and her mother, of Ohio. Mr. and Mrs. T. have had 11 children, 7 of whom are living. From 1840 to 1855 Mr. T. followed coopering in Chambersburg, part of the time when there were 40 coopers at work. Since that time he has been a successful farmer, and now owns 160 acres of land. Twelve years ago he was $4,000 in debt, but has now paid it all. He has been School Director and Road Commissioner. He and his wife are members of the Christian Church, and are public-spirited, worthy citizens.

Robert Todd was born in Bourbon county, Ky., in 1819, son of John and Mary Todd, natives of Maryland and South Carolina, respectively. His father died in 1828, and in 1832 he came with his mother to this county. In 1843 he married Margaret Edwards, who was born in 1824 in Greenup county, Ky.; they have had 3 children. Mr. T. now owns 120 acres of good land on sec. 5, besides other valuable property; he has been Constable, Tax Collector, School Trustee and Director, and was in the Mormon war. In his early day here Indian trails were sometimes his only guide in traveling over the country, and for two years St. Louis was his trading post. P. O., Chambersburg.

Eli D. Tucker was born in 1857 at Sutton, Worcester Co., Mass., son of Ebenezer and Elizabeth T., the former a native of Rhode Island, and the latter of Massachusetts; both his parents dying while he was very young, he was bound out at the age of 7, but at the age of fourteen, being maltreated, he ran off to West Warren, Mass., where he worked at $10 a month on a farm; commencing in 1871, he worked two years in a rubber manufactory; in 1874 he came to Illinois, worked on a farm and repairing telegraph wires on the O. & M. R. R.; in 1877 he became an employee at the Perry Mineral Springs; Nov. 8. 1878, he began to learn the blacksmith's trade under Frank Marden, of this place, and is doing well.

James T. Varner was born in 1830 in Morgan county, Ill., son of John and Sarah (Wood) Varner, natives of Kentucky, and of German ancestry. He came to this county in 1849 and now owns 90 acres on sec. 6, and is a farmer and cooper. In 1850 he married Nancy Hanks, and they have one son and three daughters living. Mr. V. has been Road Commissioner and is a Democrat P. O., Chambersburg.

Wm. W. Winegar was born in this place (Chambersburg) in 1844, son of John and Freelove Winegar, his father a native of Massachusetts and his mother of Ohio; he served three years in the army, in Co. F, 99th Ill. Inf., being in the siege of Vicksburg, etc.; transferred to the Army of the Gulf; was wounded at Fort Gibson. In 1866 he married Mary E. Breden, and they had one child, which died in infancy; Mrs. W. died in 1867, and in 1874 Mr. W. married Clarinda Jones, who was born in Brown county, Ill., in 1851, and they have had one son. Since 1865 Mr. Winegar has followed blacksmithing, with fair success. He and his wife are members of the Christian Church.

Dr. Henry R. Walling was born March 28, 1836, in Orange county, Ind., son of James and Catherine Walling, the former a native of Tennessee, and the latter of Orange county, Ind. In 1852 the subject of this sketch came with his parents to Coles county, Ill., and in February, 1854, they moved to this county. Sept. 12, 1863, Henry R. was married by T. M. Hess, at Homer Ill., to Miss S. S. Gaston, who was born Aug. 18, 1840, in Lawrence county, Ill. Her migrations were: at the age of three months she was taken to Cinncinnati, in 1850 to Paducah, in 1861 to Douglas county, Ill., and in 1863 to Homer, Campaign Co., Ill. After their marriage Mr. and Mrs. W. first settled at Arcola, Douglas Co., where he followed preaching for a while; but he took to the study of medicine, which he pursued with zeal while working his way at manual labor; in 1866 he attended medical college in Ohio, and then went to Mt. Vernon, Ill., where he clerked in a drug store; he then went to Bridgeport, where he had a driving practice; but health failing, he went to Ætna, Ill., where also he had a large practice, and in 1870 he settled at Perry in this county, where he again preached the gospel as well as practiced medicine. He now has a nice piece of property in Perry.

In 1877 he moved to Louisiana, Mo., where he again followed preaching (for the Christian denomination), and the next year back to this place(Chambersburg), where, Sept. 2, he opened an office and commenced business; he also has a drug store. His wife is an intellectual woman and a good painter of pictures. In this family there have been born 5 children, only 2 of whom are living. The Doctor is a Republican.

FLINT TOWNSHIP.

This is the smallest township in the county and was the first one settled. In 1817 a Canadian Frenchman by the name of Teboe, located on section 33 in this township. He was the first resident of Pike county, as mentioned in the first chapter in this book. Mr. Teboe's residence, which was on the banks of the Illinois river, was the favorite resort of hunters and trappers. He was killed at Milton in the year 1844. Garrett Van Deusen was the next settler. He opened a ferry across the Illinois, which is still carried on at Valley City, near Griggsville Landing, and is known as Phillips'

Ferry. Mr. Van Deusen sold his claim to Mr. Nimrod Phillips, many of whose descendants are still residents of Pike county.

The early settlers were alive to the importance of educating their children and anxiously desired to have the proper facilities, or as good as they could afford, to carry on this great work. Accordingly the citizens met on section 19, near Flint creek, in 1846, for the purpose of inaugurating or organizing for school purposes. There being no houses in the vicinity their deliberations were carried on upon a log in the wild forest. Among those present at this meeting were Josiah Wade, Wm. Thackwray, James Crawford, Richard Sweeting, James L. Thompson, James G. and David Pyle, E. A. F. Allen, Francis Wade, J. Husband and Wm. Turnbull. Peter Kargis presided over the deliberations of this body. The first school in the township was taught in the winter of 1845–'6 by Wm. Turnbull, James G. and David Pyle, and James L. Thompson, who gave their services without any compensation. The school was held in an old log house bought and paid for by a few of the citizens.

The first and only church ever built in the township was erected at Griggsville Landing in 1871 ; it is known as Union Church, but the M. E. society is the only one having an organization at this place. We were unable to obtain its history definitely, as we failed to find the records.

Flint township was named from a stream which runs through it called Flint creek. The name is very appropriate, as the bluffs of Flint township contain a variety of flint rock. In the crevices of the rocks, in the bluffs on Flint, are found a variety of fossils whose formation would puzzle the most skillful geologist. They are mostly of the crinoid family. Mr. Wallace, who has a very fine collection and many relics of the Indian days, gave us much information on the point. Mr. N. A. Woodson, of Griggsville, also showed us a very fine and rare collection of fossils, which he had obtained by many days of hard labor on the bluffs and in the rocks of Flint township.

The township is divided into three school districts, and contains three school-houses, known as North, Middle and South Flint.

To a stranger Flint township presents at first sight, as he approaches from the east, a rugged and desolate appearance ; and one would suppose that an ignorant and rather indolent class of people dwell here ; but such is far from being the case. We were not a little astonished at the intelligence and enterprise of its noble-hearted citizens. Although the surface of Flint township is rough and broken, it is a fine locality for growing and feeding stock.

Flint Magnesia Springs.—In the south-eastern portion of Flint township, on the land, or rather rock, of Wm. Reynolds, there is a living spring of magnesia water flowing from a crevice in the rock, and empties into the Big Blue river. It would require a volume as large as this to describe fully all the wonders of nature found in Flint township.

VALLEY CITY.

This little village, and the only one in Flint township, was founded at Phillips' ferry by Wallace Parker in the year 1877. The postoffice at Griggsville Landing, one-half mile below, and known as Flint, was then discontinued and another established at the new town, taking the name of Valley City. The town contains one store and postoffice.

Valley City Christian Temperance Union.—This society was established in the spring of 1879 on the Murphy plan, and has thus far been very successful. In the fall of the same year the society, by the aid of the citizens of the township, erected a hall 28 by 40 feet in size, with 16-foot story, and finished in first-class style, at a cost of $1,000. The ground upon which the hall was erected, which is valued at $100, was donated by Wallace Parker.

PERSONAL SKETCHES.

Wm. Bright, lumber dealer, Valley City, was born in this county Oct. 13, 1847. His father, Geo. W., was a farmer, a native of West Tennessee, and was a soldier in the Mexican war. He was one of the first pioneers of Pike county, and died in 1855. In 1867 William married Hannah Davis, who died in 1869, and Mr. B. again married in 1872. this time Belle Griffin, and they had 2 children, William, deceased, and Mabel L. Mr. B. is proprietor of the saw-mill at Griggsville Landing, formerly owned by I. S. Freeman, and is doing a good business.

Levi Butler, farmer, sec. 17; P. O., Valley City; was born in Genesee Co., N. Y., Oct. 4, 1831; he came with his parents in 1833 to this county, where he still resides. Oct. 14, 1853, he married Louisa Wilson, and of their 10 children 9 are living: Parvin, Joseph, John, David, Ellen, Emma, Loraine, Ann and Maggie. Parvin married Elizabeth Walker, and resides in this township.

George Carrell, farmer and stock-raiser, sec. 29; P. O., Valley City; was born June 25, 1823, in Morgan Co., O.; his grandfather was a soldier in the war of 1812; his father, Joseph, a farmer, was a native of Pennsylvania, and died Jan. 13, 1867. George has been Constable or Deputy Sheriff 12 years. March 27, 1845, he married Providence Wells in Morgan Co., O., who was born in Guernsey Co., O., March 19, 1829; they have three children—John J., Nancy J. and Sarah E.; the two former are married.

John Carrell, farmer, sec. 29; P. O., Valley City; was born in Morgan, now Noble, Co., O., April 26, 1846, the son of George Carrell, of this township; he was brought by his parents to this county when but 3 years old; has pursued various vocations, but for the past 9 years has been farming. Feb. 7, 1870, he married Sarah Bartlett, daughter of N. Bartlett, near Maysville; their 3 children are Wilbur, Robert and an infant girl.

James L. Cawthon, farmer, sec. 19; P. O., Griggsville; was born March 4, 1836, in Virginia, the son of Christopher Cawthon, deceased, who was a soldier in the war of 1812, and hence a pensioner until his death in 1853. James L. came to this county in 1857, where he has since been farming. At first he worked by the month until he laid by enough to begin for himself. Nov. 14, 1858, he married Louisa Hensell, daughter of the late Daniel Hensell, of Griggsville, and they have had 8 children, of whom 5 are living—Mary, Laura, Eddie, Albert and Frankie.

John Clark, farmer, sec. 7; son of the late John Clark, of Griggsville; was born in Hamilton Co., O., Sept. 14, 1830; was brought by his parents to Ogle Co., Ill., in 1835; was reared on a farm, and came to this county in 1857. June 8, 1852, he married S. Janett Berger, daughter of Samuel Berger, of Polo, Ill., and of their 6 children 5 are living—Henry, Julia E., Libbie, Jennie and Fred A.

Rachel Conover was born in Northampton Co., Penn., Nov. 7, 1807; married, in New Jersey, Abraham Conover, and had 2 children—Catherine, now Mrs. Wallace Parker, of Valley City, and Rachel, deceased. Mr. Conover died Aug. 1, 1827. Mrs. C. kept house for a Mr. and Mrs. Moore in Pennsylvania; the former came to Pike county and erected a house on the present site of Griggsville, which is still standing; he then returned to Pennsylvania, where he died in 1835, Mrs. Moore having previously died. In 1836 Mrs. C. came with the Moore family and her own children, and occupied the house that Mr. Moore had previously built. She now resides with her daughter, Mrs. Parker.

William Glenn, sr., sec. 29; P. O., Valley City; born in March, 1800, in Ireland; in 1830 he landed in Philadelphia; he remained in Pennsylvania 5 years; is a mason by trade; came to Pike county and entered the land whereon he now resides in 1835; then went to St. Louis, Mo., where he followed his trade for five years, and then moved back to this county; has been a prominent farmer and stock-raiser, but being old, has turned the business over to his son William. In 1835 he married Maria Topping, and of their 6 children 5 are living,—James, Thomas, William, Catharine and Maria. Their son Robert was killed in the late war during Gen. Forest's raid through Tennessee.

Elizabeth Husband, sec. 30; P. O., Valley City; was born in Coshocton Co., O., May 1, 1834, the daughter of George McCune, deceased, also a native of Coshocton Co., O., who was the first white child born in that county. He removed with his family to St. Louis Co., Mo., in 1835, where he resided until the fall of 1864, when he came to Pike county, and died Dec. 18 of the same year. He was Sheriff in St. Louis county, Missouri, County Treasurer, Tax Collector and held other offices of trust. Mrs. Husband's grandfather, Joseph Fuller, was a soldier under Gen. Washington. She was married Aug. 20, 1850, to Edward Monnier, in Rock Hill, Mo., and had 3 children,—Henry E., born Oct. 6, 1853; Ida L., Oct. 25, 1860; and James, Feb. 19, 1862. Mr. M. died Feb. 19, 1863; in 1865 she married Jonathan Husband, who was born in Yorkshire, Eng., Sept. 21, 1803, and emigrated to America in 1825; he died Nov. 28, 1870.

Robert Husband, farmer, sec. 20; was born April 11, 1842, in this tp., the son of Jonathan Husband, deceased, an early pioneer of this county, who in company with Mr. Wade and Wm. Turnbull owned the same coffee-mill. March 15, 1871, Robert married Esely Grable, and of their 3 children 2 are living,—Nellie and Eddie. Mr. H. was a prosperous farmer, but worked 2 years in a saw-mill in Wisconsin.

Sylvester McKee, farmer and stock-raiser, sec. 19; P. O., Griggsville. This man was born in Noble county, O., Feb. 22, 1850, and is the only son of Ezra, who now resides with him. The family emigrated in 1864 to this county, where he still resides. Oct. 20, 1869, he married Sarah A., daughter of Wm. Orr, of Derry tp. Of their 4 children 3 are living,—Addie C., Rosie E. and Alma. Little Wilbert W. died Oct. 26, 1879. Sylvester's mother's maiden name was Elizabeth Mummy, and she died Jan. 17, 1870.

Wallace Parker was born in Clinton county, N. Y., Feb. 17, 1825, and is the son of James Parker, of Griggsville; came with his parents to Pike county in 1844, where he followed farming until 21 years of age, when he became a merchant in Valley City; has been very successful except in some grain speculation in Chicago and St. Louis. At present he carries a stock of about $3,000 worth. In Feb., 1849, he married Catharine Conover, and of their 7 children only 4 are living, Rachel C., Hardin W., James H. and Helen F. Mr. P. is also Express Agent, Postmaster and Justice of the Peace, at Valley City. He has given his son James H. an interest in the store. He also has a fine collection of Indian relics, as battle-axes, arrowheads, pipes, frying-pans, a copper needle, the burnt jaw-bone of an Indian and numerous other curiosities. Some of these he has picked up and others he has obtained by opening Indian graves.

David Pyle, farmer, sec. 18; P. O. Griggsville. This gentleman was born in Harrodsburg, Ky., Feb. 4, 1817; his parents, Ralph and Rachel Pyle, deceased, emigrated with him to New Orleans in 1818, where he was reared and educated. In 1834 he came with his mother to Phillips' Ferry on a visit; went to Philadelphia, Pa., then to Cincinnati, O., and then back to this county in the fall of 1835; the next spring he bought a farm on sec. 19, where he lived for 21 years, and which he then sold, removing to Morgan county, Ill.; in 1862 he returned to this township, purchasing a farm on sec. 18, where he still resides. He was married Aug. 2, 1838, to Martha A. Willsey, and they have had 11 children, all living; namely, Ralph W., Joseph H., Christopher W., Rachel E., Isaac N., Martha A., Carrie, David W., Morgan L., James C. and Emma L. All but three of these are married, and living in this county.

E. M. Roberts, farmer, sec. 28, was born in London, Eng., June 23, 1828; in 1836 the family emigrated to America, settling in Pike county. Feb. 19, 1867, he married Susan W. Kempton, while visiting friends in Fairhaven, Mass. They have had 5 children, of whom 4 are living: Sarah M., Even M. Louis F. and George B

Mr. Roberts is a cousin to the popular Roberts Brothers, publishers, Washington street, Boston, Mass.

Joseph A. Rulon is of French ancestry. During the Catholic persecution of the Protestants in France two of the Rulon Brothers, being Protestants, were arrested and placed under a guard in a private house up stairs. They knew it would be certain death if they were brought to trial; hence they attempted to bribe the guardsmen to let them escape, but in vain. They then asked the guards simply to remain just outside the room and they would take care of the rest; the guards then received the offered fees, stepped out of the room and guarded the door. The Rulons then made a rope of the bed-clothes, by which they made their escape through the window; and in the night found their way to the wharf where they boarded a brig bound for America. Some time after landing in America one of these men married, and his descendants are scattered throughout the country. One of these, Jesse, was a soldier in the Revolution, participating in the battle of Monmouth, and he was the father of Joseph C., a sailor, who in 1832 settled on a farm in Indiana; but after a short time he began trafficking and came to Meredosia, Ill., in 1849. He was capsized and drowned in the Mississippi river Jan. 12, 1852, while attempting to board a steamer from a small row-boat. He was the father of Joseph C. Rulon, the subject of this sketch, who was born Sept. 5, 1831, on the Monmouth battle grounds, on the very spot where his grandfather fought in the bloody battle of Monmouth in the Revolutionary war. He was married June 6, 1856, to Mary E. Bonds, and their two children are Albert E. and Flora E. The latter is teaching instrumental music. Mr. R. came to Pike county in 1871, where he still resides, and is foreman of the railroad bridge at Phillips' Ferry.

John C. Scott is a native of Scott Co., where he was born Dec. 22, 1823, being the first white child born in that county; was brought up on a farm; came to this county in 1836, in 1843 returned to Scott Co., where he married, in Jan. 1845, Mary A. Hobson, who died the next year; then Mr. S. returned to this county, where, in 1850, he married Martha Wilson, and of their 11 children the following 9 are living: Charles W., James M., Leonard G., David W., Frank W., Joseph L., Benjamin E., Margaret J. and George E. Mr. Scott is a farmer on sec. 7. His father, John Scott, was the first settler in Scott county, and for him that county was named. Having been a soldier in the war of 1812 he was a pensioner until his death in Jan., 1856. He was a noble-hearted man.

John G. Sleight, sr., was born in Lincolnshire, Eng., Oct. 5, 1805; in 1827 he married Rebecca Walker, and their 8 children are: Betsy G., Sally G., Ann G., Walker G., Eliza G., Mary G., John G. and Rebecca G., deceased. They came to America in 1857, stopping at Griggsville until the following spring, when they settled on sec. 6, where Mr. S. still resides. Mrs. S. died June 19, 1862, and Mr. Sleight's son-in-law, Joseph Wilson, resides with him and conducts the farm. Mr. Wilson was born in 1838 in Griggs-

Thomas Reynolds

PERRY TP.

ville tp., and is the father of 4 children, of whom but one, Elizabeth F., is living.

Walker G. Sleight was born in Lincolnshire, Eng., Aug. 29, 1833; came to Pike county in 1856, where he still resides, a farmer, on sec. 7; P. O., Griggsville.

Samuel Thackwray, farmer, sec. 32; P. O., Griggsville. He was born March 25, 1837, in Pike county, and is a son of Wm. Thackwray, deceased; his mother, Hannah T., is now in her 80th year, residing on the old homestead, sec. 31, with her son James. Mr. T. is a successful farmer and stock-raiser. Nov. 9, 1865, he married Mary A. Lynde, daughter of Henry Lynde, of Griggsville. She was born Nov. 10, 1843, in this county. Of their 4 children, these 3 are living: Annie, Cassie and Melva.

James L. Thompson, farmer, sec. 18; P. O., Griggsville. This early settler of Pike county was born in Charlestown (now part of Boston), Mass., Sept. 11, 1812, and is the son of Dr. Abraham R. Thompson, a native of the same place and a college class-mate of Daniel Webster; they were intimate friends all through life. Dr. T. died in Charlestown in 1870. James L. was educated in Boston in the school of Willard Parker, now a noted physician of New York city. He was commission merchant in the city of Boston, 4 or 5 years, when he suffered a severe loss by the crisis of 1836; in the fall of 1837 he emigrated West and settled on sec. 18, this tp., where he now resides, on a farm of 160 acres of well-improved land. When but 19 years of age Mr. T. went to sea, taking a cargo of ice from Boston to New Orleans, where he loaded his ship with staves, cotton and coffee, which he carried to Tarragona, Spain; there he loaded with a cargo of wine and dried fruits, and shipped for Buenos Ayres, S. A.; at this place he took on a cargo of jerked beef, which he brought to Havana, Cuba, whence he took a load of coffee and sugar to Boston. Fifteen months were consumed in this round trip, which was full of interest and had its frightful scenes. In 1850 Mr. T. went overland to California, suffering untold privations on the way. *En route* he met with Col. Robert Anderson, afterward of Fort Sumter notoriety, and had a conversation with him. In California Mr. T. met with Admiral James Alden, who procured for him a situation as Purser on the U. S. Surveying Steamer "Active." He was on the survey of the northwestern boundary, the report of which was accepted by Emperor William. This report, requiring about a quire of foolscap, was all written by Mr. T. It took two seasons to complete the survey. After being absent about 5 years he returned to his family here in 1856, where he has since resided. He has been married four times, and is the father of seven children,—James L., J. B., Henry, Frederick W., Katie, Charlie and Benj. F.

Austin Wade, farmer, sec. 6; P. O., Griggsville. The birth of this gentleman took place July 23, 1832, in this county; he is the son of Josias Wade, of Griggsville; Sept. 27. 1855, he married Mary A., daughter of Joseph Pyle, of Naples, Ill., and of their 8

26

children 6 are living,—Willard, Elizabeth, Arthur, Luranie, Ferber and Homer.   Mr. Wade resided 7 years in Morgan county, Ill., and two years on the Pacific coast.

Coleman Wade, farmer, sec. 19; P. O., Valley City; a native of Pike county, and was born July 7, 1837, the son of Josias Wade, of Griggsville, and brother of the preceding; was educated in Griggsville; has been very successful in farming and stock-raising.   Jan. 20, 1859, he married Rachel, daughter of Joseph Pyle, of Naples, and they have had 6 children, of whom 5 are living: Lillian, Ernest, Raymond, Clifford and Irene. The four youngest are attending the Middle Flint school, where Lillian is engaged as assistant teacher.

John Wade, farmer, sec. 30; P. O., Griggsville; born Jan. 12, 1822, in Blyth, Nottinghamshire, Eng., and is the son of Francis Wade, deceased.   All the school education he has had he received before he was 8 years old.   The family emigrated to America in 1834, locating in Trenton, N. J., thence to Pennsylvania, and in July, 1838, landed at Phillips' Ferry, in this county; May 18. 1866, he married Ann Stoner.   Their 7 children are: Maria, Mary J., Arthur, Francis. Fred, John and George.   Mr. W. now owns 370 acres of land, and is a successful farmer and stock-raiser.

DETROIT TOWNSHIP.

Detroit township is situated on the Illinois river and consists for the most of broken land. To Lewis Allen belongs the honor of being the first settler in the township. He came in 1823 and erected a cabin on section 31. He was a native of Warren county, Ky., and was born Nov. 11, 1794. Garrett Van Deusen, Wm. Meredith and a Mr. Morgan, also, were very early settlers in this township. The first birth in the township was a daughter of David and Hannah Mize, who died in infancy, which was also the first death to occur. The first marriage was Robert Cooper to Nancy Rice in 1826, at the residence of Wm. Meredith. The first sermon was preached by Rev. Elijah Garrison, a Christian minister, at the house of David Mize in 1826. The early pioneers were industrious people and were not neglectful of the education of their children; for as early as 1827, David Mize, Ezekiel Clemmons, Wm. Meredith, Joseph Neeley and others banded together and erected a school-house on section 16, and employed a teacher, placing their children in their charge for instruction and intellectual improvement. The first teacher was Abraham Jones.

The next great question which occupied the minds of these noble fathers and mothers was the preparations for public worship. They accordingly organized themselves into a body, or rather each person considered himself one of the building committee, and as early as 1834 there was a church · building erected by the Baptists at Blue river graveyard: Previous to this meetings were held in school-houses and private dwellings.

Garrett Van Deusen was the first Justice of the Peace, and Isaac Teniff the first Supervisor. The township received its name from the postoffice which had been established several years previously, and named by Col. Daniel Bush at Pittsfield and Wm. Johnson, the first postmaster at Detroit.

The pioneers had many encounters with wild animals during the early settlement of the county, two or three of which, related by Mrs. Dinsmore, who is still residing in this township, we will place on record in this connection. On one occasion, while she and her husband were passing through the woods, a huge lynx came bounding up behind her and grabbed her dress with his claws. She hastily called the dogs and they quickly came to her side. The wild animal loosened his hold and gazed upon the dogs. They were greatly frightened and did not attempt an attack upon the lynx, but ran to the house. The lynx, too, concluded to leave and took to the forest.

This same lady tells of another time when she was attacked or about to be attacked by one of these fierce creatures. She was engaged in the woods making sugar, with her camp fire near a large log. She heard a noise upon the opposite side, which was made by the lynx just in the act of preparing to make a leap, as she supposed. She set the dog upon it, and as it sprang over the log he alighted upon a large, powerful lynx. The fierce contest that ensued was a short one, for the dog was completely overpowered; and as soon as he could release himself from the clutches of his antagonist he " run home a-howlin' " with his tail between his legs, and run under the house," where he remained for some time.

We will give Mrs. Dinsmore's panther story in her own language as nearly as we can. " One day when I was a-comin' thro' the woods I seen a large painter come out of the brush and begin to drink out of a puddle of water in the path; and I shooed at him, and he paid no attention to me, and I took off my bonnet and shooed and shooed at him; but he wouldn't shoo; he jist staid there and lapped away till he got done and then went off."

Mrs. Dinsmore also relates that she was once standing in the door when she saw her father stab and kill an Indian.

Big Blue Hollow.—This is quite an historical locality. In 1842 it ranked as the second place in the county in the amount of business transacted. There were then three flouring mills, a saw-mill, and a store in this mountainous-looking region; these mills were known by the name of Providence Mills, and were owned by Jonathan Frye. In 1835 he erected there a two-story frame house and sided it with shaved clapboards; this house is still standing there, with the old siding upon it, and is occupied by Mr. Wm. Reynolds and family.

FLORENCE.

This is the oldest town in Detroit township, and was founded in 1836 by the Florence Company; this company was composed principally of Pittsfield business men, among whom were Austin Barber, Robert R. Greene, Wm. Ross, Thos. Worthington and James Davis. The town is located on the Illinois river, and was intended for river transportation for the town of Pittsfield, and a gravel road was constructed from Pittsfield to this place. The land was first settled by John Roberts. Col. Wm. Ross and Stephen Gay kept the first store in the place. A saw-mill was erected here in 1836, by the Florence Company, which was converted into a steam flouring mill in 1842. During the early pioneer days Florence was known by the name of Augusta.

DETROIT.

This lively little business village was founded in 1837 by Peter H. Lucas, and named by him after the postoffice which had been established at this point some years previous. Soon after Henry Neeley added to the town plat what is known as Neeley's addition, and consists of all that part of town north of Main street.

Detroit contains 2 general stores, 1 drug store, 2 blacksmith shops, 1 wagon manufactory, 1 shoemaker's shop, a millinery store, and a broom factory. Three physicians reside in the place. There are in the town 3 church edifices and 4 church organizations. The citizens have erected a fine two-story brick school-house and employ two teachers.

CHURCHES.

Detroit Christian Church.—This church was organized Feb. 25, 1876, by Elders Rufus Moss and J. W. Miller, with a membership of 33. The first deacons were Nathaniel Smith and John Turner. C. L. Hall was appointed Elder and afterward elected to that office, in company with his brother, W. C. Hall. The present Deacons are Albert Field and John Turner. The congregation sustains a large and interesting Sunday-school, which was organized the first Lord's day in 1876, with 25 members. It now has an attendance of about 85, with W. C. Hall as superintendent. The congregation at present worship in the house belonging to the Predestinarian Baptists. The present membership is 140. Elder Thomas Weaver is Pastor.

Detroit M. E. Church, South.—This society was organized in 1861, and consisted of parties who left the Methodist Episcopal Church on account of the political excitement that then pervaded all of the Churches. They erected a meeting-house in 1870, and sustain a Sabbath-school: membership 30. Services are held each alternate Sabbath morning and evening by Rev. J. Metcalf, Pastor.

Detroit M. E. Church.—The Methodists had an organization in this township at an early day. As early as 1828 this people held a camp-meeting on the Meredith farm, sec. 16. The exact date, however, of the first organization of this society is not certainly known. The congregation erected a brick house, 36 by 48 feet in size, in the town of Detroit, in 1857, at a cost of $1,500. The Church now sustains a good Sunday-school, has preaching each Sunday evening and each alternate Sunday morning, by Rev. James A. Wills, Pastor. The number of communicants at present is 75.

Detroit Predestinarian Baptist Church.—In the year 1828 the Baptists began holding services in the Blue River school-house, and in 1834 they erected a church edifice. Soon after this the question of missions divided them, and the Missionary Baptists retained this house, and in 1840 the Predestinarians formed another organization. The former society is now extinct, and the latter, by the help of others, in 1857 erected a house of worship in Detroit. They have no regular services, the society being very weak.

PERSONAL SKETCHES.

Below are personal sketches of many of the old settlers and leading citizens of this township.

Wm. Anthony, a native of this county, was born Dec. 9, 1833. His father, Martin Anthony, came to this county about the year 1831. William was reared on a farm and had limited school advantages. He attended school a mile and a half from home, in an old log cabin with no ceiling, and a fire-place across one end of the house. His books consisted of a testament and spelling-book. July 17, 1867, he married Orle A., daughter of the late Leander Jeffers, of the vicinity of Hannibal, Mo. Mrs. Anthony was born Aug. 22, 1847, in Cincinnati, O. They have had six children, of whom three are living,—Ida, Mattie and Nellie. Mr. A. is engaged in general farming on sec. 6, this township. P. O., Griggsville.

D. J. Aldrich was born in Worcester county, Mass., Oct. 3, 1802, and is the son of Jesse Aldrich, deceased. He was educated in the academy at Uxbridge, and after leaving school engaged in teaching at $8.50 per month in winter, and worked on a farm by the month in summer, receiving $40 per month. For two and a half years he traveled throughout the Middle and Western States, a distance of 13,000 miles, visiting many points of interest. In 1825 he visited Ann Arbor, Mich., and while there entered 160 acres of land eight miles north, in Dexter township. May 8, 1837, he married Eliza A. Taft and they had two children,—Adaline, deceased, and Augusta. Mr. A. came to Pike county in 1838 and settled on sec. 18, this township. Mrs. Aldrich died April 30, 1871. She was a woman of fine education and a worthy member of the M. E. Church.

Sarah Allen was born in Yorkshire, Eng., Jan. 21, 1828, and is the daughter of John Burlend, deceased, who brought his family to America in 1831, and, like all pioneers, endured many hardships. He died April 4, 1871, aged 88 years. Mrs. Allen was married May 4, 1852, to Francis Allen, and they had 4 children,—Charlotte M., John W., deceased, Francis E. and David Franklin. Charlotte is married to Sylvester Thompson, and resides near Pittsfield. Mr. Allen was a farmer on sec. 16 until his death, which occurred July 23, 1874. He belonged to the Episcopal Church, and was a prominent and worthy citizen.

George P. Bechdoldt was born in Germany March 28, 1828, the son of Jacob P., who came to America with his family in 1837, and settled in Little York, Pa., where he remained until 1839, when he removed to Calhoun county, Ill., and died the same year, leaving a widow and 8 children, who had to endure many hardships and privations. Two of the children had married and remained in the East. Geo. P. is the 9th of 11 children; his education was principally in German, before he came to America. April 10, 1851, he married Frances S. Price, daughter of Robert Price, well known in the early settlement of Scott and McDonough counties.

She was born May 29, 1834, in McDonough Co., Ill. They have had 11 children, of whom 9 are living—Julia, Helen, Theodore, Maria, Anna, Esther, Ettie, Edith and Frederick. Mr. B. is a prominent farmer and stock-raiser on the north ½ of S. E. ¼ of sec. 32. P. O., Milton.

Dr. Wm. Cobel was born in Middle Tennessee May 30, 1826, the son of Geo. A. and Mary Cobel, who emigrated with their family to Hendricks county, Ind., in 1833. The doctor is a graduate of both the Keokuk (regular) Medical College and of the Eclectic Medical College, of Cincinnati, O., and began practice in 1859. He has lost but one case out of 300 in the last 12 months, and that was a chronic case of heart-disease. He settled in the town of Detroit, this county, in 1873; in 1878 he met with an accident, dislocating his hip joint, but he still continues to ride day and night. Nov. 21, 1851, he married Elizabeth J. McClure, and of their 5 children only 2 are living, Wm. M. and Fannie A. Mrs. Cobel died Nov. 12, 1878, aftering a lingering illness of 22 years' standing. She was a member of the M. E. Church, and a faithful and respected worker in the moral interests of society. Wm. M. Cobel is now teaching school near Detroit.

John L. Cravens was born Jan. 1, 1844, in Jefferson Co., Ind., the son of John C. Cravens, of the same State; was educated at Hanover College, Ind.; he chose the profession of teaching, entering upon this work in 1866; he taught three terms in Boone county, Mo., when he went to college until 1870, and then to Wapello Co., Iowa, where he raised a crop, and in September he returned to Boone county, Mo.; taught school until 1875, when he came to Pike Co., and now has charge of the Toll-Gate school, district 4, in this township. In the late war he served 4 months in Co. K, 137th Ill. Vol. Inf., and was honorably discharged. In 1873 he married Elizabeth D. Snyder, of Boone county, Mo., and their two children are Lillian B. and W. Guy.

Thomas Dalby, farmer and stock-raiser, sec. 5, was born in England in 1853, the son of David and Sarah Dalby, deceased. His brother James was in the 73d Reg., I. V. I., under Capt. Davidson, of Griggsville; was taken prisoner and confined in the pen at Andersonville, where he died from starvation. He lost another brother, Joseph, who died from a wound received by a saw-log rolling off a wagon and catching him; so that Mr. D. now has no brother in America. Aug. 27, 1849, Mr. D. married Hannah Burland, who was born in Yorkshire, Eng., in 1853. Mr. Dalby is the owner of 400 acres of land.

James W. Dempsey was born in Chillicothe, O., Aug. 20, 1834, the son of Coleman Dempsey, who emigrated to Missouri in 1854. After spending two years in Texas, erecting telegraph wire from Galveston to Houston, and thence to Shreveport on Red river, James W. returned to Missouri. By profession he is a civil engineer, and by trade a gunsmith. He is a "natural genius." He came to Pike county in 1856, where he followed engineering mostly

·for 14 years. In 1870 he began trading in guns, ammunition, etc., in Detroit, and also dealt in sporting goods, cigars, tobacco and confectionery: he now has a full supply of dry goods, groceries, hardware and confectionery, the stock being about $3,000 in value. His trade is increasing. Aug. 22, 1856, he married Minerva, daughter of Jesse Sinff, deceased, of Detroit. They had four children, of whom but one, Harry, is living, who was born Dec. 11, 1868. Mrs. D. died May 20, 1879, mourned by all who knew her.

Miss Virginie Dinsmore, teacher, was born Dec. 26, 1853, in Hardin township. Her father, John C. Dinsmore, deceased, was Captain of Co. E, 99th I. V. I., in the Rebellion, and was also an officer in the Mexican war, participating in the battles of Buena Vista, Cerro Gordo and others, and saw Col. Hardin fall. He died in February, 1874, on the old homestead near Time, this county. Miss Dinsmore has been a teacher for 7 years, and now has charge of the primary department of the Detroit schools. She is well liked as an instructor and disciplinarian.

William Douglas was born March 9, 1817, in New Galloway, Kircudbrightshire, Scotland, where he received a common-school education, and came to America in 1836, stopping in the East for several years. Dec. 19, 1841, he married Permelia, daughter of Edmund Strawn, who came to this county in 1830, just in time to suffer the privations of the severe winter of the deep snow. Mrs. Douglas was born in Guilford Co., N. C., Aug. 25, 1823. Mr. and Mrs. D. have had 12 children, of whom 7 are living,—Andrew, Mary, Edmund, John T., Churchwell, William W. and James S. The 4 eldest are married. Mr. Douglas is a mechanic by trade, in which capacity he wrought during the earlier portion of his life, but is now a prominent farmer and stock-raiser on sec. 33. He spent one year in Canada and 6 years in Missouri. He helped erect the State University in the latter State, and also assisted in the erection of the first mill in Pittsfield in 1849.

John W. Dunniway was born in Gallatin county, Ky., Jan. 17, 1834, the son of David and Annie (Crow) Dunniway. They came to Pike county in 1836, settling on sec. 18, enduring the usual hardships of that day, their houses consisting of little log cabins, etc. They came by boat, having sent their teams through by land, and when the teams arrived the hair was all worn off the horses' legs, so terrible were the roads and swamps through which they passed. Mr. D. died March 5, 1869, at the age of 69 years, and Mrs. D. resides with her son on the old home place, at the age of 77. She was born in Clark county, Ky. John W. was married Nov. 29, 1855, to Julia A., daughter of David Rupart, who came to Pike county in 1840. They have 4 children, viz: Mary E., William A., David F. and Frederick A. Mr. D. is a farmer and stock-raiser.

James W. Ellis, a native of this tp., was born Oct. 10, 1838, and is the son of Thomas Ellis, deceased, and brother of John and T. B. Ellis. He received his education in a log cabin known as "mud college," raised a farmer, and knows all about heavy work in pioneer times.   Dec. 28, 1869, he married Miss C. J. Phillips, daughter of James Phillips, of this tp., and they have had 2 children, Charlie, deceased, and Lillian.   Mr. Ellis is a farmer on sec. 16.

John B Ellis was born Oct. 17, 1834, in Lockport, N. Y., the son of Thomas Ellis, deceased, who brought his family to this county in 1836.   John B's mother, Elizabeth Ellis, still resides on the old homestead, at the age of 74.   Nov. 6, 1862, Mr. E. married Ellen Croft, daughter of George Croft, of Montezuma tp., and their 7 children are, Ellen E., Thomas G., John W., Peter J., David C., Annie S. and Mary E.   Mr. Ellis is a farmer and stock-raiser on sec. 16.

Thomas Ellis, deceased, was born in the village of Milton, Oxfordshire, Eng., Dec. 18, 1808; educated in the village school, and March 16, 1832, married Elizabeth Brooks, and they have had 7 children: Thomas B., John B., Peter, James W., Elizabeth A., Harriott and Ellen J., deceased.   Mrs Ellis was born July 15, 1804, in Shipton, Oxfordshire, Eng.; they came to America in 1832, locating at Lockport, N. Y., where they remained until 1835, when they removed to this county; resided on a rented farm one year; then purchased 80 acres at a sale of school land in Detroit tp., where Mrs. Ellis still resides.   Mr. E. died March 21, 1868.

Thomas B. Ellis was born in Lockport, N. Y., Nov. 8, 1832, son of the preceding; is a farmer on sec. 15.   Oct. 9, 1873, he married Fannie Allen, daughter of J. W. Allen, of Milton.   Their 4 children are Thomas H., John A., Charles I. and Elizabeth.   Mr. Ellis served 3 years in the late war in Co. C, 99th I. V. I., participating in the siege of Vicksburg and in other engagements; he was taken prisoner while on a scouting expedition in Texas near Victoria; he was held in camp in Camp Ford, Texas, for 6 months and then exchanged.   He was discharged in 1865.

Bernard W. Flinn, farmer, sec. 5, and the present County Treasurer, was born in Philadelphia, Pa., March 29, 1814, the son of John Flinn, deceased, who was a native of Ireland; he was brought by his parents to Morgan county, O., in 1819, where they remained until 1826, and then were in Zanesville, O., until 1839; a portion of this time he engaged in wholesale dry goods, and afterward in the mercantile business in Coshocton Co., O.   In 1841 he moved to Cincinnati, O., and became proprietor of the St. Charles House; in 1852 he removed to St. Louis, Mo., and to Pike county in October, 1856, settling on sec. 5, this tp., where he still resides, owning 335 acres of land.   In February, 1841, he married Sarah Brownell, and they have had 8 children, of whom 5 are living, namely: James, who married Charlotte Stephens and resides at Pana, Ill.; Esley, now Mrs. James Dimmitt, of Detroit tp.; Cornelia, Lewis H. and Charles. Mr. Flinn was elected Treasurer at the November election in 1879 by a majority of 323 votes.

Norton Foreman, farmer and stock-raiser, sec. 31; was born Aug. 2, 1843, in Newburg township, this county, and is the son of James Foreman, who came to this county in early day; was educated in Detroit and reared on a farm. Dec. 17, 1863, he married Sarah E., daughter of James Bond, of Piatt county, Ill. Their 5 children are William, James F., Annie, Nellie and Edwin.

Townsend Foreman, farmer, was born July 28, 1845, in New-burg tp., this county, the son of James W. and Jane Foreman; was raised on a farm and received a common-school education; May 15, 1867, he married Mary J. Goldman. He was a merchant in Detroit 4 or 5 years, then a farmer until 1874, when he moved to Lewistown, Fulton county, Ill., where he again engaged in mer-chandising 2 years; he sold out and entered the livery business in that place; he then returned to Detroit, where he is engaged in farming. He is also proprietor of an "Eclipse" thresher, which he operates each season to the entire satisfaction of his many patrons.

James E. French was born Oct. 25, 1832, in Indiana, and is the son of Jacob French, deceased, who came to this county in 1834, settling in Griggsville township; received his education in an old log cabin, in a subscription school at a distance of 4 or 5 miles from home. Nov. 10, 1850, he married Caroline C. Madden, daughter of Bonham A. Madden, an early settler of the Illinois river valley. Mrs. French was born Feb. 10, 1833, in Indiana. Their 4 children are George N., who married Frances Thackston, and resides in Greene county, Ill.; Henry C., who married Mari-etta McEvers, and resides near Montezuma; M. E. and William A. Mr. French is a farmer and stock-raiser on sec. 32.

Paul P. French, P. O., Florence, was born September 20, 1832, in Harrison county, Ind., and was brought to this county by his parents about 1842; was reared on a farm and is now engaged in farming, and also has a half interest in the Florence horse ferry. Dec. 20, 1853, he married Mary E., daughter of Edward Farthing, deceased, and of their 9 children only 4 are living, namely: Wm. P., Nancy J., Edward and Annie. Mr. French traded in live stock and followed general merchandising in Florence for several years, but his health failing, he had to change business.

Elizabeth Goldman, widow of the late Benjamin Goldman, was born in Clark county Ky., Dec. 29, 1830, the daughter of David and Anna Dunniway, who brought their family of 5 children to this county in 1836, settling on sec. 7, this township, where Mrs. Dunniway still resides, at the age of 77. Mr. and Mrs. Goldman were married Nov, 26, 1848, in this township, and of their 4 chil-dren 3 are living, Mary J., Julia C. and Elizabeth D. Julia mar-ried Taylor Foreman, who is managing the farm of his mother-in-law. Mr. Goldman was born Dce. 24, 1824, in Clark county, Ky., and is the son of Abraham and Susannah Goldman, deceased, who brought him to Pike county in early day, where he was brought up on a farm amid all the privations of pioneer times. He was a Class-Leader in the M. E. Church for many years. An eminent Christian and a worthy head of the family. His death occurred October 20, 1874.

Elizabeth A. Goldman was born in this county January 31,

1841, and is the daughter of Thomas Ellis, deceased, and a sister of John and Thomas B. Ellis, of this township, elsewhere noticed. Jan. 2, 1852, she married Josiah Goldman, and 8 of their 9 children are living, viz: John, Millicent, Fannie, Hettie, Thomas, Jane, Ellen and James Monroe. John is superintending the farm.

Wm. C. Hall was born May 29, 1844, in this county, and is the son of T. L. Hall, of early day here, who came in 1828, when he had to go to Atlas, a distance of 26 miles, to mill. He taught the first singing-school in Atlas, said to be the first in the county. In 1840 he built a saw-mill on Little Blue creek. He was brought up a Presbyterian, but during the latter part of his life was a member of the Christian Church. His death occurred January 5, 1872. Wm. C. was reared on a farm in early day, having all the usual experiences of clearing wood land. October 9, 1866, he married Nellie, daughter of John S. Shinn, of Griggsville, and they have one little boy, Willy. Mr. Hall is a farmer and stock-raiser on sec. 16.

James D. Heavner, farmer and stock-raiser, sec. 32; P. O. Milton; was born Jan. 7, 1835, in this county, and is the son of Jacob Heavner, who emigrated with his family to Sangamon county in 1827, and to this county in 1828; he was a soldier in the Black Hawk war, under Abraham Lincoln. He died in 1867. James D. was married Nov. 4, 1858, to Matilda, daughter of Manley Thomas, an early settler. Of their 7 children the following 6 are living: Clara, Lizzie, Maggie, Nannie, Dovie and Mattie.

Samuel Lightle was brought to this county when a boy by his parents in 1835; educated in the old-fashioned subscription school; married, Dec. 31, 1858, Martha, daughter of Coleman Dempsey, of Pike county, Mo. Of their 10 children these 8 are living: Mary A., Isaac S., Clara H., John W., Annettie J., Charlotte M., Nellie E. and James W. Mr. L. is a farmer on sec. 8. P. O., Detroit.

Stewart Lindsey, farmer and stock-raiser, sec. 31, owning 200 acres of land, was born Oct. 1, 1808, in Scott county, Ky., and is the son of Robert Lindsey, who emigrated with his parents from Virginia to Kentucky in 1788. Stewart's grandfather, Aaron Reynolds, was one of Daniel Boone's associates as an early settler of Kentucky. His mother was born in a fort called Craig's Station, in Woodford county, Ky. He was educated in a log cabin with a triangular fire-place across one end of the room, with a window ten feet in length and one light high. The text books consisted of a Webster's speller, Testament and Guthrie's Arithmetic. The seats consisted of split logs with legs fastened in them. Jan. 27, 1835, he married Mary Hays, and they had 10 children, of whom 9 are living,—Falissa A., John W., Newton J., James, Oscar, Mary, Robert, Charles and Frank. The name of the deceased was Samuel. Four of his sons were in the late war; Samuel was a prisoner at Andersonville, where he contracted a disease that caused his death. The others were honorably discharged.

Aaron Loveless was born in Medina county, O., Dec. 7, 1883, and is the son of Wm. Loveless, of Detroit tp., who brought his family to this county in 1839. Oct. 13, 1858, he was married to Rebecca Yelliott, daughter of Luke Yelliott. She is a native of England, and was born in 1840. Mr. Loveless is a farmer and resides on sec. 7; he is also proprietor of a portable saw-mill, which he has successfully operated for two years, and which is now situated on Cicero Scoby's farm, between Pittsfield and Griggsville. Mr. and Mrs. Loveless have had 5 children, of whom 4 are living, —Addie, Albert, Wesley and Clayton.

Wm. Loveless was born in Monmouth county, N. J., Oct. 26, 1816; was brought by his parents to Medina county, O., in 1830, where he remained until he attained his majority, when he married Rebecca Snyder, Feb. 22, 1838. They emigrated to this county in 1839. Mr. Loveless is a mechanic, and worked in various places in this county for several years. About 1848 he purchased a farm on sec. 18, Detroit tp., but has resided in this tp. all the time. They resided in Rockport, this county, for about 3 years, and in Wisconsin for 5½ years, where he pursued his profession. Mr. and Mrs. Loveless have 3 children,—Aaron, Wilson and Emily. Aaron married Rebecca Yelliott, of this tp.; Wilson married Nellie Oleson, and resides in Oak county, Wis.; and Emily married James Shriver, and resides in the house with her parents.

Samuel S. McAtee was born near Baltimore, Md., July 23, 1855, and is the son of Samuel I. McAtee, of Shelby county, Mo. He was educated in the common schools of Missouri, where his parents took him in 1857, and in 1872 came to Pike Co., and to Detroit in 1875, where he engaged in the manufacture of wagons, in which he has been successful. Dec. 24, 1877, he married Ollie Sanderson, daughter of Reuben Sanderson, of Detroit.

Wm. Moore was born in Detroit, Pike Co., Ill., Dec. 29, 1853, and is the son of Wm. Moore, of Detroit tp. He was reared on a farm, and at the age of 21 was apprenticed to A. F. Reinika, a blacksmith of Detroit, and in 1878 he began business for himself, and has a good trade. He also manufactures wagons in company with Mr. McAtee.

George M. Neeley, P. O., Detroit, a native of this county, was born March 1, 1839, where Detroit now stands. His father, Henry Neeley, was a resident of Horse-Shoe Bend, on the Sangamon river, before Illinois was a State. In 1821 he went up in a keel-boat to a French trading post on the Upper Mississippi. He emigrated with his father, Joseph Neeley, from North Carolina to Tennessee, where they remained several years, when Joseph Neeley emigrated to Illinois, and soon after was followed by his son, Henry, who came to Pike Co. in 1831 and settled on sec. 18, Detroit tp. Henry saw the first house erected in Pittsfield, and states that the parties erectting it began at the top of the rafters to lay on the roof. Mr. Neeley died Aug. 1, 1869, at the place where he first settled in Pike Co. Geo. M. was married April 4, 1861, to Lizzie McIver, by whom he had 2 children, Alfred and Emma. He again married Sept. 10,

1874, Lizzie Stephens, daughter of Elijah Stephens, of Jasper county, Mo. They have 2 children,—Lillie and George Arthur. Mr. Neeley is a farmer; also proprietor of the Detroit House in Detroit; he spent about 18 years of his life in Texas, Mexico and the Southern States, and while there served three years in the Confederate army. He is now Justice of the Peace for Detroit tp.

Henry Perry, farmer and stock-raiser, was born in Manchester, Eng., Dec. 10, 1840, and is the son of John Perry, deceased. He came to America in 1856 and settled in Detroit tp., where he still resides. July 14, 1859, he married Sarah H., daughter of Amos Taylor, a pioneer of this Co. They have had 9 children: 8 are living,—Maria, Laura A., John H., Rosa M., Elizabeth H., Wm. M., Mattie M. and Lillie M. The name of the deceased was Robt. H.: he accidentally shot himself with a gun while climbing a fence in the fall of 1878. Mr. Perry served in the late war in Co. I, 99th Reg. I. V. I. and participated in the battle of Hartsville, Mo., where he received a slight wound, and in the campaign of Vicksburg. He was discharged in 1865.

James Phillips was born in Cherry Valley, Otsego county, N. Y., March 12, 1812, and is the son of Barnabas Phillips, dec. He came to this county in the fall of 1837 and settled in the town of Griggsville. His father was a soldier in the war of 1812. He worked in a flouring mill at intervals for about 10 years, then settled on sec. 21, Detroit tp., where he still resides a prominent farmer. Dec. 29, 1842, he married Armina Hughes: they have had 9 children, 8 of whom are living,—Clarissa J., Edward D., Francis M., Martha E., Lucinda C., Mary C., Owen R. and James M. Mr. Phillips is a very worthy citizen.

A. F. Reinika, blacksmith, was born in Germany, Sept. 15, 1848, and is the son of Simon Reinika, of Pittsfield; was reared on a farm until 17 years of age; was then apprenticed to August Sitler, a shoemaker of Detroit, but the trade not being pleasant to him he went back to farming, which he pursued 2 years, when he engaged upon a saw-mill for 9 months; he then apprenticed himself to Conrad Winant, a blacksmith of Pittsfield, with whom he worked 18 months; then went back to the farm again for one season, then went to work for Geo. Carrier, a blacksmith of Pittsfield. In Oct. 1872, he began business for himself in Detroit, where he still remains, doing a large business. Nov. 27, 1871, he married Mary E. Ayers, and their 4 children are Allie M., Harry O., Lurie and Wm. A.

Wm. Reynolds was born in Gallia county, O., Oct., 1825, and came to Pike Co. in 1840; was raised on a farm; served 21 months in the Mexican war, then returned to Ohio and married Susan Fry, by whom he had 12 children, of these 10 are living,— Geo. W., Wm. L., Stephen A., Frances J., Emily, Maud, Henry and Mary. Mr. R. returned to Illinois in 1850, and now resides on sec. 4, Detroit tp., in the Big Blue valley, and is engaged in farming. He was 2d Lieutenant in Co. B. 68th Reg. I. V. I., in the late war. About 1854 or 1855 he engaged in brick-laying and assisted in laying the brick in all the principal buildings in Pittsfield, Griggsville, Perry and New Salem, up to about 1870.

Joseph Rhodes, farmer, sec. 6, was born in Yorkshire, Eng., Jan. 8, 1824; learned the business of a wool-stapler under Mr. Atkinson; then worked as journeyman until 1848, when he came to America and worked with one Greenbanks, of New England, until 1856, and then came to Pike county and settled upon his farm. Although farming was entirely new to him he has by good sense, hard work and economy made for himself a nice farm of 190 acres. He is a prominent farmer in this tp. and makes wheat-raising a speciality. In 1844 he married Martha, daughter of James Whitfield, a hind for Arthur Heywood, a large land-owner in England. Their 9 children are William, Henry, Charles, Albert E., Manuletta, Daniel E., Sarah J. and Mary J. (twins), and Julia A. Mrs. Rhodes also is a native of Yorkshire and was born July 10, 1823.

William Sanderson was born Dec. 28, 1826, in Highland Co., O., and is the son of George Sanderson, dec.; was reared on a farm, received a common-school education, came to Pike county in 1855, where he still resides, on sec. 30, this tp. In Nov., 1848, he married Sarah Faris, and their children are Alva C. and Rufus A. Mrs. Sanderson died in 1852. Sept. 17, 1857, Mr S. married Jane, daughter of John A. Williams, dec., who was a native of North Carolina and settled in this county in the fall of 1830, just in time to help wade through the "deep snow." Mr. and Mrs. Sanderson have 5 children: Gilbert C., Linnie L., Orin R., Willy A. and Clara B. Mr. Sanderson's father was a soldier in the war of 1812. His widow draws a pension and resides among her children.

Joshua K. Sitton; P. O., Detroit; was born Nov. 25, 1824, in Lincoln Co., Mo., the son of Jesse Sitton, who brought his family here in 1828, and died in the fall of 1832, a Baptist minister. He preached all over Pike county and in the counties of Morgan and Sangamon. He was a soldier in the war of 1812, and was in the battle of New Orleans under Gen. Jackson. Oct. 6, 1847, Joshua K. was married to Mary A. Heavner, daughter of Jacob Heavner, dec., an early settler in this State. They have had 6 children, of whom only 3 are living, namely, Jesse, Mary E. and Annettie. Mr. Sitton is a farmer and stock-raiser on sec. 20. In 1849 he went overland to California and returned in 1851. He served 18 months in the late war, in Co. C, 99th I. V. I., and participated in the battles of Magnolia Hill, Black River, Raymond, Wilson Creek, siege of Vicksburg and others. He was wounded at Vicksburg, in consequence of which he was discharged in 1864. He was a commissioned officer all the time he served in the army. He went out as First Lieutenant and was discharged as Quartermaster.

Mary J. Smith was born in Cumberland Co., Ky., Feb. 4, 1828, and is the daughter of Samuel Baker, who brought his family to this county in 1834, settling on sec. 33, on what is now known as the "Douglas farm." He died in March, 1837. Mary J. was married

Sept. 1, 1846, to Richard R. Smith, a native of Clark Co., Ky., who was born July 19, 1821 and was brought to Morgan, now Scott Co., Ill., in 1828, settling in Winchester. He was raised on the farm, and in 1848 came to Pike county, settling on sec 33, Detroit tp., where he resided a farmer and stock-raiser until his death, which occurred Oct. 19, 1862. Mr. and Mrs. Smith had 7 children,— Harriet A., now Mrs. Wm. H. Butler; Sarah J, now the wife of Mr. A. Armstrong; Judith V., now the widow of Mr. A. Landers; Mary H., dec.; Martha C., now Mrs. Henry T. Bagby; Wm. S. and Richard D.

Mrs. Nancy Smith. This lady's father, Samuel Blake, brought his family to this county in 1833; the next year he died, leaving a widow and 7 small children. The subject of this sketch has therefore seen hard times,—times when wolves made the night hideous, when young live-stock had to be kept in pens, when a hewed-log house was considered almost an extravagant luxury, and when milling was almost impossible; she has worked in the field at picking brush, rolling logs, building fence, gathering corn, etc. She built traps and caught turkeys, and her sister Margaret at one time waded into the Little Blue creek, waist deep in the water with an ax and killed a deer, which the dogs were trying to drag down; several times Mrs. Smith went 5 miles to mill taking a sack of corn horseback. The first steam-boat that she saw on the Illinois river she remembers was the "Raccoon." Feb. 9, 1842, she married George V. Stackpole, a native of Thomaston, Maine, who died Sept. 3, 1871. He was Capt. of various boats on the Illinois river; filled every position on boats from deck-hand to proprietor. Our subject was again married Nov. 3, 1878, this time to Nathaniel P. Smith, who was born in Ohio, Oct. 16, 1823; he was raised a farmer's boy; taught school most of the time for about 14 years; came to this county in 1873, and now resides on sec. 28, this tp.

William K. Smith is a native of Scott county, Ky., born April 4, 1804; came to Morgan county, Ill., in 1839, where he followed farming until 1851, when he came and settled on sec. 33, this township, where he has since resided; but he has placed the farm in charge of his son-in-law, John F. Kingman. In July, 1825, Mr. Smith married Lucinda Kendrick, and they have had one child, James W., now living in Montezuma tp. Mrs. Smith died Oct. 13, 1841, a member of the Cumberland Presbyterian Church, and Mr. S., in Oct., 1843, married Elizabeth Kendrick, a sister of his former wife, and they have had 4 children, of whom 2 are living,—Susan J. (now Mrs. J. F. Kinman) and Joanna I. Mrs. Smith died Oct. 3, 1875, a worthy member of the M. E. Church.

James Stoner was born in Yorkshire, Eng., Nov. 21, 1827, the son of Thomas Stoner, who brought his family to America in 1844, settling in this township, where James still resides, a farmer on sec. 17. In 1856 he married Mary A., daughter of George Croft, of Montezuma tp. They have 2 children, Ellen and Frederick. Mrs. S. died in 1865, and in 1866 Mr. S. married Harriet, daughter of Mrs. Elizabeth Ellis, of this township; their 2 children are Fannie and James.

Creed Strawn was born Sept. 9, 1833, in this county, and is the son of Edmund Strawn, deceased, who came to this county in 1830; July 12, 1857, Mr. Creed Strawn married Helen, daughter of Zachariah Ownby. Her grandmother relates this interesting incident: An Indian chief entered the house one day, and, looking at the baby (Mrs. Strawn's uncle) which was lying in the cradle, said: " Pretty pale-face, how swap? Give pony to boot." This baby is now Thomas Ownby, of Eldara. Mr. and Mrs. Strawn have had 2 children, both dead.

L. B. Taylor, farmer, sec 29, was born Feb. 10, 1840, in this county, the son of Amos Taylor, who was born near Hartford, Conn., and who died Oct. 31, 1866. Aug. 15, 1862, L. B. married Hannah, daughter of Jeremiah Walker, deceased, and their children are Alonzo, John H., Edward, Robert, Clara, Emma, Alva O. and Ira. Mr. Taylor served three years in the late war in Co. I, 99th I. V. I., and was in the battles of Magnolia Hill, Black River, siege of Vicksburg, etc., and was discharged July 30, 1865.

William B. Thompson, who has resided in this State since 1817, was born in Borrulee Bottom, Mo., March 13, 1813. His father was James, deceased, a native of Virginia, and a pioneer in Missouri Territory, who settled in Washington county, Ill., in 1817. He was in the Indian war of 1791, and was at St. Clair's defeat, where he was wounded in the right leg, which rendered him a cripple for life. March 17, 1844, Wm. B. married Mary A. Brooks. Their children are Benjamin F., Sylvester W., Susan J., James S., Sarah E. and William D. Mr. T. is a farmer on sec. 32.

Thomas Wade, farmer, sec. 16. A native of this county, was born April 7, 1842, and is the son of Henry B. Wade, who was a pioneer of Pike county, having been brought here by his parents when but 6 years old. There were but 13 families in the county when he settled there. Thomas Wade was raised on a farm three miles south of Griggsville. Sept. 25, 1857, he married Ellen, daughter of Mrs. Elizabeth Ellis, a widow lady of Detroit township. They had 3 children,—Thomas, Albertie and James. In Sept., 1875, Mrs. Wade died, and in April, 1876, he married Frances Lindville, and they have one little boy, Harvey. Mr. Wade owns a half interest in the Florence horse ferry. He served in the late war in Co. H., 73d Regiment, I. V. I., and participated in the battle of Stone river.

Birrel Walk, farmer, sec. 35; P. O., Milton; was born Dec. 14, 1832, near Lexington, N. C.; was brought by his parents to this county in 1836, and settled near Milton. His father, Teter Walk, worked very hard and endured many privations in preparing for future prosperity. He died in the winter of 1839-40. Our subject was raised on a farm and knows all about grubbing, picking bush, rolling logs, driving oxen, etc., etc. Jan. 3, 1861, he married Eliza J. Roland, and their children are Hardin W., Cordelia J.,

James Manton

PITTSFIELD TP.

Hulburt C., Sarah A., Cora B. and Lincoln Teter. In 1852 Mr. Walk went overland to California and returned in 1856.

Jasper Walk, farmer, sec. 36, was born in this township Aug. 17, 1839. His mother, Mahala Walk, came to this county in 1836, and still resides with her son at the age of 70 years. She was born in Davidson county, N. C. Her father owned the Horshoe Neck on the Yadkin river. Our subject lives in a house made of hewed logs 39 years ago, built by Thomas Clemons, the original settler on section 36. March 28, 1860, he married Rachel Anthony, and they have had 7 children, 5 of whom are living, namely, Ella Bell, Alice A., Harvey C., Charlotte A. and Jasper C. Mr. Walk was a soldier in the late war, in Co. I, 99th Reg. I. V. I., and participated in the battles of Port Gibson, siege of Vicksburg, Black River and others. At the siege of Vicksburg he was under fire for 47 days; was wounded at the battle of Black River, and was discharged July 30, 1865, at Baton Rouge.

Augustus F. White, farmer, sec. 35, was born in Cornwall, Connecticut, May 6, 1832, and is the son of Comfort White, deceased. He received a common-school education, and attended the great Barrington Academy, of Berkshire county, Mass.; he also attended the Stockbridge Academy of the same county. He taught school most of the time for 22 years. April 9, 1858, he married Harriet Watts, and they are the parents of 3 children—Charles A., Mary A. and John E., deceased. In 1852 Mr. W. went to California by ship, crossing the isthmus of Panama by way of Lake Nicaragua, and returned by the Panama route the next year. His ancestors came across the ocean in the Mayflower, and he is a descendant of the same family of which Perigrine White was a member, the first white child born in America.

Elijah Williams was born in Clinton county, O., Aug 6, 1844, and is the son of Joseph Williams, deceased, also a native of Ohio. He received a common-school education, and in 1867 came to Illinois and located in Sangamon Co., and in 1872 to Brown Co., where he engaged in various occupations for one year, and then became salesman in a wholesale tin and hardware store for F. H. Hudson, of Versailles, Ill. In December, 1877, he engaged with J. W. Wright & Co., of the same place, in retailing dry goods and notions through various parts of the country; in the spring of 1878, he was elected to the office of Assessor. The June following he opened a restaurant, and in March, 1879, he removed to Florence and went into the mercantile business, where he now has a thriving trade. In December, 1869, he married Ida Campbell. Their 4 children are Charles H., Effie M., Joseph F. and an infant girl. Mr. W. served 3 years in the late war in Co. D, 79th Reg. O. V. I., and was in the battles of Resaca, Peach-Tree Creek, Atlanta, Stone River, Savannah, Charleston and others. He was taken prisoner by a company of Hood's cavalry, while out foraging, and placed in Libby prison, but was released in 21 days.

Harvey D. Williams, Principal of Detroit Schools, was born in
27

Carroll Co., Va., Nov. 10, 1847, and is the son of Nicholas Williams, who came to Hancock county about the year 1852. The Professor was educated in Quincy College, Ill., and began his chosen profession in 1868, in Hancock county, and in 1870 came to Pike county, where he has since taught, and is now teaching his sixth year in Detroit. He gives general satisfaction as an instructor and disciplinarian. Aug. 22, 1872, he was married to Cammie, daughter of David Williams, of this township.

Samuel M. Williams, lawyer, was born in Salisbury, N. C., Feb. 9, 1829, and is the son of John A. Williams, a pioneer of this county, who brought his family here in 1834, and endured all the privations of pioneer life. He was Deacon in the Baptist Church in Detroit 25 years, and died March 26, 1876, in Pettis county, Mo., where he had resided four years. May 1, 1864, Samuel M. married Eunice, daughter of Ede Hatch, deceased, who resided in this township until within two years of his death, which occurred in Newburg township, May 15, 1842. He was a worthy citizen and a member of the Baptist Church. Mr. and Mrs. Williams have three children, viz: Frances, Claiborne and Samuel. Mrs. Williams had previously been married and had three children, Henry, Henrietta and Harlow Hosford, deceased. Mr. Williams has practiced law 25 years.

Bula A. Wilson was born Jan. 13, 1828, and was brought to this county by her parents in 1833, and has seen many hardships and troubles; has done all kinds of heavy farm work, pulled, hackled, spun and wove flax, and hauled many a load of wood. She was unusually kind, benevolent and charitable, and wherever there was sickness and suffering Mrs. Wilson was found; yet when she was left a widow, sick with rheumatism, and a little speechless boy, she was placed in a poor-house. Sept. 26, 1861, she married John Holiday, who was drowned in the Mississippi river at St. Louis, Sept. 16, 1863. They had one son, John H. Jan. 13, 1876, she married Charles Wilson, a native of Sweden.

Luke Yelliott, P. O. Detroit, was born in Doncaster, Yorkshire, Eng., about 1809, and is the son of Luke Yelliott, sr. In 1842 he came to Pike county and settled on the farm he now owns, and where he resides. He was married in Yorkshire, Eng., Feb. 10, 1840 (just one week after the marriage of Queen Victoria), to Mary, daughter of John and Rebecca Burland, who came to this county in 1831, enduring many of the hardships of pioneer life. Mrs. Burland used locust thorns for pins, such was the scarcity of household articles. They both died in the house of Mr. Yelliott, aged 87 and 77 years, respectively. Mr. and Mrs. Yelliott have had nine children, of whom seven are living, Rebecca and Sarah (twins), John and Annette (twins), Luke, Edward B., and Mary A.

MONTEZUMA TOWNSHIP.

This township borders on the Illinois river and lies between Detroit on the north and Pearl on the south. It was one of the first townships in this early settled county to receive the pioneer. A very complete and interesting historical sketch of this township was prepared by Mr. F. M. Grimes, editor of the Milton *Beacon*, in 1876, and we make no apology for quoting much of this sketch. The people of Montezuma and neighboring townships had a grand centennial celebration at Milton, July 4, 1876, and Mr. Grimes was appointed to the pleasant yet arduous and difficult task of preparing an historical sketch of this township as a Centennial History. After his introductory, he begins the sketch of the settlement as follows :

SETTLEMENT.

One hundred years ago the sound of the white man's ax had not been heard in our forests. The ringing of the anvil, the rattle of the reaper, the hum of the thresher, and whistle of the engine would have been strange music to the ear of the wild Indian, whose song and warhoop were the only sounds indicative of human existence. The soul-stirring music of the band, the melodious tones of the organ and the still sweeter voices of the choir, would have been in strange contrast with the howl of the wolf or the scream of the panther as they roamed fearlessly o'er the spot where we now stand. The bark canoe and the majestic steamer; the rude wigwam and the stately mansion; the Indian pony and the iron horse; the slow footman and the lightning telegraph,—but faintly illustrate the vast difference between the savage of then and the civilized of to-day.

But little is known of the history of Montezuma township prior to the year 1819, at which time Ebenezer Franklin settled upon the lands now owned by his son Frederick Franklin, our townsman. Other settlements were afterwards made by Charles Adams, James Daniels, David Daniels, David Hoover, Daniel Hoover, Joel Meacham, Thomas Davis (1826), Elijah Garrison (1826), Solomon Farrington (1827), John F. Long (1828), Fielden Hanks (1829), William Morton, Frederic Franklin (came with his father), E. C. Clemmons, James Cheatham (1834), Josiah Hoover (came with his father in 1826), George Hoover (came with his father), Daniel Hoover (182).6 The last eight are still residents. Z. A. Garrison, John Batter-

446 HISTORY OF PIKE COUNTY.

shell (1832), now a resident of Spring Creek township, Ezekiel Clemmons, Boone Allen, John Morton, George Morton, Peter Dillon, John Garrison, Joseph Garrison, John Loop, Nicholas Jones, John Jones, Wm. McBride, Smith Aimes, Joshua Davis, Josiah Simms, William Kenney (1826), Solomon Seevers, —— Roark, James Grimes (1836), John Bacus, Job Wilkirson, B. Greathouse, John Greathouse, Louis Allen, Elijah Garrison.

Like all settlers of new countries they suffered many hardships and inconveniences. The nearest mill for the first few years was Edwardsville, 80 miles distant. Mr. Franklin informs us that there were then about 200 Indians in the neighborhood. * * * *

In the year 1829 a horse-mill was built by Freeman Tucker on the lot now occupied by Mr. Franklin. The nearest trading points were at Atlas and Bridgeport, opposite Bedford. The first regularly laid out road ran from Montezuma to Atlas, and was among, if not the first, in the county. Houston was the physician. Polly Davis taught the first school in a small cabin on the land now owned by Josiah Hoover. In addition to her labors as teacher she had the care of eight children.

The inhabitants were pre-eminently religious. Shouting was very common and the " jerks " had not ceased to afflict the religious fanatic. Preaching and prayer meetings were held at private houses until better accommodations could be had. The Christian Church prevailed at that time, and an organization was effected prior to 1828. There were five resident ministers; four of the Christian and one of the Baptist faith. The present Christian Church has been perpetuated since the year 1833.

The call for volunteers for the Black Hawk war created no little consternation among the people. A meeting was called at Florence and John Battershell, Joseph Gale, William Kenney, Joshua Davis, Smith Aimes, Josiah Simms and Edward Irons enlisted. The first two are still living. There were others from the adjoining towns or counties who afterwards became residents, as Jesse Lester, then a resident of Detroit, now residing here, James Grimes, resident of Greene county, and others whose names we cannot give.

About the year 1830, by virtue of a law allowing slaveholders the privilege of passing through this State with slaves, slavery existed in the township for a period limited by the law to 30 days. Jacob Rosel brought a negro woman here, and not wishing to remove for the time, kept her until the expiration of the 30 days and took her to Missouri for a few days, and brought her back again, and so continued to do, thus evading the law for nearly a year.

The first marriage so far as we can learn was that of Joseph Gale and Elizabeth Garrison, about the year 1830. John F. Long is now the oldest resident voter in the township, having been a legal voter 47 years, and has not missed to exceed three general elections. The oldest native-born resident is Daniel G. Hoover, son of Daniel and Rebecca Hoover. Calvin Greathouse, son of John and Catherine Greathouse, was the first native-born. He is now a resident of Texas.

Even in the earlier days the settlers regarded the education of their children as their first duty. In many instances the tuition was paid by the father's labor with the maul and wedge, or the mother's work at the wheel and loom. The first board of school trustees now on record was composed of the following names: · Nathan Tucker, R C. Robertson, Jacob Wagner, John F. Long and Solomon Farrington, who met at Milton July 15, 1840, and apportioned the funds then on hand, $83.06, upon the schedules of W. M. Porter and Charles Daniels.

A subsequent meeting is recorded as follows:

June 5th, 1841.

Trustees of schools met at Milton and ordered:

1st. That the debtors to the school fund be required punctually to pay the interest when due, and annually to pay ten per cent. of the principal.

2d. That 65 days be considered one quarter of a year, and that each school teacher teach 8 hours in each day.

3d. That the trustees receive for their services 50 cts. per day, and the treasurer receive $1.00 per day.

MATHEW BAKER,
WALTER W. TUCKER,
JAMES GRIMES,
FIELDEN HANKS,
JOHN S. BACUS,
Trustees.

At a meeting held at Thomas Davis' house in November of the same year, the township was laid off in districts, Nos. 1, 2, 3, and 4. Lots No. 4, 14 and 15 of the 16th section were ordered to be sold on the 24th of December on 1, 2, 3, 4 and 5 years' time. From 1840 to 1850 we find the name of B. Greathouse as Treasurer most of the time. The names of a portion of the teachers are as follows: T. M. Johnson, Louisa Greene, W. W. Tucker, A. Meacham, A. D. Robertson, W. Porter, G. Lester. Joseph M. Jones (now resident of Oregon), N. W. Saxton, J. J. Meacham, A. Jones, H. D. Bennett, C. L. Easley, T. P. Hoit, Noble Shaw, Martha Greathouse, B. F. Turpin, Matthew Morton, Sidney Coffey, James Brook, Nancy L. Reed, John Porter, Sherman Goss, Edwin Woolley, Joseph Colvin (now living in Time), W. F. Anderson, Addison S. Smith, John W. Allen (now residing near Milton), R. R. Clark. James M. Grimes, Adam Acott, Mary A. Clemmons, Caroline E. Davis, Harmon J. Kimball, Wm. B. Grimes, Edwin P. Simmons, John S. Woolley, Emeline Spencer, Robert Owen and Samuel Heaton. From 1850 to the present we can only mention a few of the names: Hampton, Eaglin, Hurley, Roberts, Walden. Underwood, Eakins, Harris, Ewing, N. C. Boren, P. A. Long, J. H. Long, W. M. Landess, N. J. Colvin, Fannie Allen, Jane Allen, A. F. White, W. N. Barney, Sarah B. Stuart, N. D. Mc. Evers, G. W. Manley, J. L. Harris, Lucinda K.

Smith, G. B. Garrison, W. Z. Garrison, Amanda Boren and J. M. Faris. The teachers during the last year were John King, Miss Cromwell, Mrs. A. Binns, L. D. Riggs, Geo. A. Holcomb, C. E. Thurman, J. G. Webster, J. L. Craven, W. F. Colvin, and the writer. Several of the above named persons have devoted the greater portion of their lives to the profession. During the past 20 years Mr. F. M. Grimes taught 19 successive terms in this township.

Montezuma has always been proud of her schools, and according to her population she stands second to none in the county, perhaps in the State. Liberal wages have been paid, and there seems to be a determination on the part of the patrons to spare no pains in giving to their children the greatest of blessings, a liberal education. As evidence that our schools have been all that we claim for them, we point to the business and professional men who received their education in our schools, viz: J. F. Greathouse, who now ranks among the best lawyers of the county, F. M. Greathouse, his brother, now present State's Attorney of Calhoun, and stands at the head of the Bar in that county; W. B. Grimes, ex-County Clerk, and V. A. Grimes, present Deputy; W. H. Thomas, attorney, now in California; J. H. Nicolay, who held a position in the U. S. Treasury at Washington; John G. Nicolay, present Marshal of the Supreme Court of the U. S., held his residence here for several years prior to entering upon his apprenticeship as a printer in Pittsfield, and what education he received in the common schools, was obtained in the schools in this township.

AGRICULTURE.

For many years the tillers of the soil were, of necessity, compelled to use such implements as came within their reach. The plow with wooden mold-board is within the recollection of many who were raised in our midst. The sickle and the scythe were sufficient for the amount of small grain raised, but as the acreage increased, the demand for something more expeditious was supplied by the introduction of the reaper. Mr. R. H. Robertson was the first to lead in this progressive movement, and in about the year 1845, bought and cut his grain with a McCormick reaper. Next year Mr. E. C. Clemmons followed the example. A. Boren and John F. Long soon after introduced one in the south part of the township. Flailing and tramping with horses soon gave way to the "beater," which was run by Wm. Stults. This was quite a relief to the boys who rode the horses from day to day, and bareback at that, on a tramping floor not more than 30 feet in diameter. Our recollections on this point are very vivid indeed. The "beater" soon gave way to the improved thresher and cleaner; the wooden fork was not adequate to the task of taking care of the straw; the wooden plows were laid in the shade and the Stebbins and Modie plows took their places; the wooden harrow was not in keeping with the times, and the material from which it was made served for other purposes. That the soil from which our crops is produced is of the best and most endurable quality, is demonstrated beyond a doubt by the manner in which it has from year to year been tilled. Until late years the clover crop was as rare as the flax crop is at the present. Year after year have our lands yielded bountiful crops, without rest or nourishment in return, and why should we wonder that it should show some signs of diminished productiveness? The improved methods of culture, deep plowing, clovering and pasturing, have made much of our land better than it was when it was first turned by the plow-share.

The introduction of improved and blooded stock was left to a few of our most enterprising farmers, who, in the past 25 years have made rapid strides in this particular, so much so that this for the past two or three years may be called the banner township, so far as the show of fine cattle is concerned. Isaac Brown & Sons, John O. Bolin, E. N. French, Geo. Hoover, R. C. Allen and others, have done a commendable work in the improvement of cattle, hogs and sheep.

The majority of our farmers now have more or less of the improved breeds upon their farms. The original scrub hog is as scarce now as the imported was 20 years ago. In order that the progress of the next century may be readily estimated by the readers who at that time may chance to see this record, we give some of the statistics furnished by Eli Grimes, present Assessor:

Merchandise, value, $27,460; moneys and credits, $66,485; improved lands, 12,257 acres, $327,925; unimproved lands, 8,261 acres, $43,660; wheat, 3,019 acres; corn, 4,148 acres; oats, 509 acres; meadows and pasture, 3,085 acres; town lots, improved, 155; unimproved, 391; total value of town lots, $58,919; total value of personal property, $173,175; total value of real estate, $371,585. Grand total, $607,539.

VILLAGES.

There are three villages in this township, the largest and most important of which is Milton, situated on section 5. At the close of the Black Hawk war in 1832, and when the people of the South and East were assured that the settlers through this section of the State had no more to fear from the Indians, there was a most wonderful influx of settlers here. There has never been a period in the history of the settlement of the Mississippi valley or the Great West, when emigration was greater than it was to Central Illinois during the few years subsequent to the close of the war, say from 1833 to 1837. The people poured in by thousands, and the beautiful groves and "points" of Pike county received their portion. During this period we find unprecedented prosperity on every hand. Then, to add to the almost wild excitement incident to the prosperity and speculation then rife, the State inaugurated the most stupendous system of internal improvements ever attempted by a government. The wildest imagination can scarcely conceive the magnitude of this vast system. Suffice it to say that it proved an incentive to the settlers here to embark in speculations, especially in land. Towns were laid out on every hand, and a majority of the villages of Pike county were platted. christened and started upon their career during this eventful period. In this township the villages of Milton, Montezuma and Bedford were ushered into existence at this time.

The beautiful little village of Milton was platted by Freeman Tucker, March 2, 1835. As early as 1828 Wm. Kenney erected a log cabin here. Some little improvement was made in the neighborhood from that time until they laid off the town. There are several good store buildings, filled with a fine assortment of goods in their various lines, situated around a beautiful little square, which is set with trees, etc., and forms a pleasant summer park. The first store was kept by Tucker & Wethers, and the first school was taught by George Lester. The first church structure was situated on the Public Square. Milton is situated upon a beautiful prairie, and enjoys a fine local trade.

The village of Montezuma, which is located on the Illinois river, on section 12, and four miles from Milton, was laid out by an Alton Company for a river landing. In 1836 Joel Meacham, who ran a ferry across the river at this point for many years, laid out an addition, which comprises about one-half of the town. Montezuma had great promise of making a town of some importance, being an excellent landing for boats at all stages of water, but the introduction of railroads and the springing up of inland towns, have so crippled river transportation that at present it affords profit to scarcely any one. The village contains at present about 100 inhabitants.

Bedford, which is situated on sections 13 and 24, and about one mile and a half below Montezuma on the river, was laid out by David Hoge, April 16, 1836. It has an excellent river landing, and for years a vast amount of grain, pork and various kinds of produce, were annually shipped from here. It no longer, however, claims any great prominence among the towns of the county. Its present population numbers about 100.

PERSONAL SKETCHES.

We refrain from dwelling longer on the history of the township, or any of its villages, choosing rather to devote the space to giving personal sketches of the more prominent citizens of the township, believing such sketches are of equal importance, and afford greater interest.

Austin R. Allen, physician, is the son of John W. and Louisa Allen, who settled in this county in an early day. He was a farmer by occupation but taught school for many years ; was Justice of the Peace in pioneer times, and in 1861 was elected County Judge; in 1865 he completed the canvas for the census, and is now traveling in Virginia. Austin R. began his medical studies with his brother, C. I. Allen, a practitioner in this section since 1866; attended medical lectures at the St. Louis Medical College 1875–8, and March 5 of the latter year he was graduated, and established himself in Milton, where he now has a large practice. He was born in Detroit township in 1857.

John Battershell, sr., of the firm of Battershell & Mitchell, merchants, Milton, was born in Clark county, Ky., March 13, 1811, and is the son of John and Abigail (Rector) Battershell, natives of Maryland and Kentucky. Mr. B. settled in Scott county, Illinois, in 1829, where he engaged in farming; in 1859 he settled in Pike county, on a farm of 305 acres, in this township, valued at $50 per acre. In 1829 he married Miss Betsey Richards, a native of Virginia, who died at Winchester, Ill. They had 8 children, 7 of whom are living,—Martha, Mitchell, Sarah, Hezekiah, Mary, Matilda, and John, jr. He then married Anna Smith, a native of Tennessee, by whom he has 3 children: Charles, Eva and Emma (twins). The present business partnership was formed in 1878, which is the largest and controls the most extensive trade in Milton.

A. W. Bemis, retired farmer and claim agent, was born in Worcester county, Mass., in 1814, and is the son of Aaron and Martha (Frost) Bemis, who settled in Summer Hill, this county, in 1835, where he purchased land and resided until his death, in 1874. The subject of this sketch married Mary P. Ford, a native of Greene county, and they have 2 children, Albert and Laurie. He first settled at Atlas, then on the old homestead at Summer Hill, then in 1851 he engaged in the lumber business in Montezuma, and in 1853 he became extensively engaged in the mercantile trade at Time, where he resided until 1873; he then returned to his present place in Montezuma. He was Township Treasurer 13 years, Justice of the Peace many years, was the first Supervisor of Martinsburg tp., and in 1851–3 he was Postmaster at Montezuma.

John O. Bolin, retired farmer; P. O. Milton; was born in Pickaway county, O., in 1824, and is the eldest son of Charles and Betsey (Griffin) Bolin, natives of Delaware, who came to this county in 1838 and settled in Pleasant Hill township; in 1848 they moved to Martinsburg township, where Mrs. B. died the next year; he then moved to Milton, where he married Miss Minerva Clemmons, and engaged in the mercantile business. In 1851 John O. was admitted to the partnership, and for 10 years this firm carried on a large dry-goods trade. Mr. Charles Bolin then retired, and in 1868 died. He was a minister of the Gospel. John O. then disposed of the stock of goods in 1865, and built his present residence, where he has 60 acres of land, valued at $100 per acre. He also has a farm of 155 acres on sec. 16, valued at $50 an acre. In 1845 he married Rebecca McCoy, a native of Missouri, who died in 1863. His present wife, Mary, is a daughter of Daniel Hoover. Mr. Bolin was Supervisor for a number of terms. He is a Democrat, and a member of the Christian Church.

Absalom Boren, jr., farmer, sec. 32, P. O. Milton ; is the son of Absalom and Catherine (Anderson) Boren, natives of Indiana, where, in Posey county, the subject of this sketch was born in 1819; he came to this county in 1839, and settled in this tp. where he has since made his home. The same year he was married to Miss Lucinda, daughter of James Grimes, an early settler of this county. She was born in White county in 1823. The fruits of this union are 5 children, living,—Nancy K., John W., Uriel E., Angeline Q. E., and Sarah A. • Mr. and Mrs. B. are members of the Christian Church. Mr. Boren has served as School Director, and his name is linked with those who were the founders of Montezuma.

John W. Boren, harness-maker, was born in this county, Aug. 2, 1842, and is the son of Absalom and Lucinda (Grimes) Boren, who settled in Montezuma tp. in 1836, where they still reside. He was married in 1872 to Miss Mary Smith, a native of this county. He first established himself in business on the northwest corner of the Square, and in 1876 settled in his present location. He carries a stock of $1,500, and has a good trade. Is Justice of the Peace, having filled that office 4 years, and is a member of the Christian Church.

John M. Brooking, farmer, sec. 32; P. O. Milton ; born on the Ohio river, in Ohio, in 1822, and is the son of Wm. and Sarah (Rubell) Brooking, natives of Ohio, where they both died. The subject of this sketch was married May 4, 1842, to Miss Elizabeth, daughter of John Colvin, who came to this county in 1852 and settled in this tp., where he has since made his home; moved to his present estate in 1858, consisting of 120 acres, valued at $40 per acre. Their children are Andrew F., Arnold D., John W., Amanda, Sarah J. and Rebecca M. Mr. B. served as School Director one term, and is a self-made man, who, by his energy and perseverance has secured for himself a good home.

James Cheatham, retired farmer, residence Milton, was born in Cumberland Co., Ky., in 1812; is the son of Richardson Cheatham, a native of Kentucky, where he died at an early day. The subject of this sketch came to this county in 1834, and settled in this tp. on sec. 4, where he built a log cabin and cultivated 80 acres of land ; the same year he married Miss Virginia Robertson, a native of South Carolina, who with her mother and brother came to this county the same year. The license for this pioneer couple was the 3d one issued at Pittsfield. Three children have been born to them; Samuel, who married Sarah Lyster, and resides on the homestead; Lucy Ann, wife of F. McFadden, residents of Magnolia ; and Walter, who was drowned when 19 years of age. Mr. C. settled on his present place in 1872, where he lives in retirement and enjoyment of past industry. They number among the living relics of Montezuma.

J. P. Clemmons, farmer, sec. 3; P. O. Milton ; is the son of Ezekiel and Phœbe (Reed) Clemmons, natives of Rouen Co., N. C., where the subject of this sketch was born in 1814. The family emigrated to Illinois in 1823 and settled in Lawrence county. In 1825 they moved to this county and settled in Detroit tp., and 3 years afterward settled in this tp., where his parents both died. Mr. C. moved on his present farm in 1836, consisting of 196 acres, valued at $60 per acre. The same year he was married to Miss Jane, daughter of Wm. Hayden, and they had 3 children, 2 of whom are living, Mary and Phœbe. His present wife, Polly, *nee* Grimes, is a native of White county, Ill., and they have had 2 children,—Henry and Sarah. Mr. C. had no opportunities for an early education, and at the age of 21 years he was enabled to purchase 40 acres of land, which by his energy and perseverance he had accumulated. To him belongs the honor of being the oldest living settler in Montezuma, a record which he may value, and to which his posterity ever look with pride. He built the first school-house erected in Detroit tp., and has experienced all the hardships of pioneer life.

George Croft, farmer, sec. 2; P. O. Milton; is the son of Mathew and Mary (Rumans) Croft, natives of York, England, where the subject of this sketch was born in 1806. He acquired his early education in the colleges of his native place, where he engaged as teacher in the academy. In 1831 he was selected by the Wesleyan Missionary Society, of London, to preach the gospel in the West Indies. He reached the Islands in 1831, and preached throughout the different Islands for 13 years. While there he met and married (in 1834), Miss Ellen Stoner, a native of Leeds, England, where she was born in 1807. Mr. C. has crossed the Atlantic 9 times, and lived under most of the flags of Europe. He spent the summer of 1879 in his native home, but prefers to live under the flag of our common country. His farm of 440 acres is the fruits of his own industry, his first purchase being but 160 acres. It is valued at $50 per acre. Here he settled in 1856, living in a log house until he had erected his present commodious residence. He is the father of 6 children, 5 of whom are living; David S., Helen, George, Hannah L. and Thomas. He is Local Elder in the M. E. Church, and a gentleman well known throughout the county.

S. W. Daniels, of the firm of Merchant & Miller, and who resides at Bedford, was born in this county in 1829, and is the son of James and Olive Daniels, natives of N. Y., and Vt., who emigrated to Madison county, thence to this county in 1826, settling on the section where he entered 120 acres of land, where they both died. He was a soldier in the war of 1812, and an early pioneer of Pike county. The subject of this sketch was married in 1846, to Miss Frances E., daughter of John French. To them have been born 5 children: Wesley P., George, Julia, Thomas, and Rozella. Mr. D. began milling in the early days. He is also engaged in the mercantile trade at Bedford and runs the ferry at that place; is conducting a good business.

Joseph Dugdell, farmer, sec. 22; P. O. Milton; was born in

Yorkshire, England, Dec. 25, 1810; was married Jan. 28, 1832, to Miss Elizabeth Farra, also a native of Yorkshire, Eng., where she was born Oct. 11, 1810. He emigrated to America in 1843 and spent one winter in Morgan county, thènce he went to Scott county, and in 1847 to this county, setling in this tp., where he has since made it his home. He moved to his present place in 1852, upon which was a log cabin, and which has long since given place to his present commodious residence. Mr. D. has a farm of 280 acres, valued at $40 per acre. He is the father of 4 children: Charles, Joseph, jr., Wm. T., and Hanna E., all of whom are married, and grandchildren surround him in his declining years.

Taylor B. Franklin, farmer sec. 11; P. O. Milton; is the grandson of Ebenezer Franklin, the earliest settler of Pike county, and eldest son of Frederick Franklin, who passed a life of usefulness in Montezuma tp., where he died in 1878. The subject of this sketch was married in April, 1869, to Miss Priscilla Stathen, a native of Ohio, and there have been born to them 4 children; Augustus, William, Fred E. and Cora H. Mr. F. resides upon a portion of his father's estate, consisting of 141 acres, valued at $25 per acre. Sixty years have passed since Ebenezer Franklin set foot on the soil of Pike county, and to his posterity belong the honor of his name.

David Foreman, farmer and harness-maker, sec. 31 ; P. O. Milton ; was born in Highland county, O., in 1834, and is the son of Jacob and Margaret Briggs, natives of Kentucky and Ohio, who came to this county in 1850, and settled on sec. 1, Spring Creek township, where he resided until 1863, when he moved to his son's home, where he died Feb. 8, 1871 : she died Nov. 30, 1857. The subject of this sketch purchased his present estate, consisting of 80 acres, valued at $3,000 ; has been engaged at his trade since 1852 at Pittsfield and Milton, and has a good business. Was married Jan. 21, 1855, to Miss Nancy Russell, who a short time afterward was accidentally burned to death. In 1859 he was united to Miss Phœbe N., daughter of Abner Long, a native of McDonough county. To them have been born 7 children, 4 of whom are living : Henry L., Sarah M., Margaret R. and Araminta J.; the deceased are Milton A., Jacob N. and John H. Members of the Christian Church.

Edward N. French, farmer, sec. 8 ; P. O. Milton ; born in Caledonia Co., Vt., in 1829, the fourth son of Isaac and Rebecca (Folly) French, natives of that State, where they both died. The subject of this sketch emigrated to the West in 1849, and settled in Rock Co., Wis. Two years afterward he moved to this county and engaged as clerk with George Underwood in Milton. While in this capacity he purchased 40 acres of land on sec. 4, a portion of which is included in his present estate of 330 acres, valued at $100 per acre. He was married in 1852 to Miss Sarah, second daughter of Daniel Hoover, by whom he has 4 children: Noel E., Mary A., George H., now a student of engineering in the

University at Champaign, Ill., and William O. Mr. F. is a self-made man in every respect. His mother died when he was 7 years of age, and he was bound out until 14 years of age. Without the advantages of education he has accumulated a handsome landed property, secured by his own industry and close application to business. Is a Republican.

Harrison C. French, farmer, sec. 30 ; P. O. Milton ; was the youngest child of Isaac and Rebecca (Folly) French, natives of Vermont, where they both died. The subject of this sketch was born in Caledonia Co., Vt., in 1834 ; emigrated to this county in 1856, where he resided until 1861, when he enlisted as 2d Sergeant in Co. E, I. V. I., and served 9 months; was taken prisoner at the battle of Shiloh and confined in prison at Tuscaloosa, Ala.; thence to Macon, Ga., and in Libby at Richmond, Va., where he was exchanged April 6, and sent to Annapolis as paroled prisoner. He was reduced to a mere skeleton by the effects of prison life. Returning, he was married in 1865 to Miss Emily, daughter of John Long. Their 7 children are all living, Augustus H., Orra J., Lefie A., Herbert, Nellie, Walter and Ruth. He settled on his present estate in 1872, consisting of 160 acres, valued at $40 per acre. His wife is member of the Christian Church, and he is a Republican.

Zachariah A. Garrison, farmer, sec. 36; P. O. Pearl; was born in Posey Co., Ind., March 29, 1815, and is the son of Elijah and Sally (Allen) Garrison, natives of Kentucky, and a lineal descendant of Daniel Boone. The subject of this sketch came to this county with his parents in Oct., 1826. His father entered a large tract of land near Milton, which he lost by unsuccessful speculations. He then moved upon the river bottom, where he died in 1840. His devoted wife lived until 1846, when she too was called to join the settlements of a better home. The subject of this sketch was married in 1834, to Miss Louisiana, daughter of Thomas Davis, who died in 1839, leaving one child, Mary L., who resides in Oregon. He again married in 1842, Miss Cynthia Waters, who died in 1852. Of this marriage one child was born, Hannah J., wife of Orsen Gilbert. His present wife, Lydia Wilson, is a native of Ohio. Mr. G. was engaged in running log rafts down the river as early as 1835, and afterwards followed the river as pilot until 1852, when he built a hotel, where he was engaged for 11 years. In 1861 he enlisted as Captain of Co. E., I. V. I., and two months afterward was appointed recruiting officer. In this capacity he served until 1864, when he moved to Oregon and spent some years. On his return he settled on his present place.

W. V. Grimes, M. D., was born in this township in 1857. His parents were Milton and Mary (McClintock) Grimes, early settlers of Pike county. He began the study of medicine with Dr. A. G. Jones, of Milton, and spent 2 years in the drug business with W. M. Crary. Soon afterward he entered the Missouri Medical College at St. Louis, and was graduated at that institution in 1877. The following year he began the practice of his profession in this village and established himself in the drug business the same year. Mr. G. has been local editor and correspondent of the Milton *Beacon* a greater part of the time since it started, and is deservedly popular with all classes. He is a member of the Masonic fraternity and of the Christian Church.

S. V. Hayden, attorney at law, is the son of Elisha and Virginia (Sweringen) Hayden, natives of Kentucky and Missouri, who came to this county in 1833 and settled in Detroit township. In 1852 they moved to this tp., and in 1867 upon their present farm, where they still reside. To them have been born 5 children, 3 of whom are living,—Gabriella L., Samuel V. and Mary B. His farm of 132 acres is valued at $70 per acre. The subject of this sketch was born in this county in 1856, and entered upon the study of law at Hillsboro, Ill. He then entered the Union Law College at Chicago and was graduated at that institution in 1879, when he began the practice of his profession in this village. The family number among early pioneers and are highly respected members of the Christian Church.

Wm. Hess, farmer and stock-raiser, is the son of David and Ann (Wheeler) Hess, natives of Ohio, who emigrated to this State at an early day and settled in Pearl tp., Pike Co., in 1836, where he still resides. Mrs. H. died in 1877. The subject of this sketch was born in Greene Co., Ill., in 1830. He was married Oct. 18, 1855, to Miss Margaret C. Wagner, who died, leaving him one child, J. D. His present wife, Nancy C., *nee* Smith, is a native of Pike Co. To them have been born 6 children,—Sarah A., L. C., Wm. H., Eva R. B., Ada B., and Ruthy B. He settled on his present place in 1862, the homestead land consisting of 240 acres, valued at $50 per acre. He has also land on secs. 20, 21, 32 and 16, amounting to nearly 800 acres, making him the largest landholder in the tp.

O. C. Holcomb, merchant, dealer in groceries and crockery, succeeded Geo. Underwood in 1857. In 1863 he disposed of his stock and enlisted as Captain of Co. G., 137th I. V. I., 100-day men, and served his time. He again entered upon a mercantile pursuit in the store now occupied as the postoffice, and moved to his present location in 1879. He was born in Portage Co., O., in 1833. His mother, Dafney Holcomb, settled in this township in 1842, where she died in 1879. He was married in 1854 to Miss Sarah E. Kinman, by whom he has 3 children: Lillian, George A. and John H. Mr. H. is one of the oldest living merchants of Milton, and enjoys a good patronage.

David G. Hoover, farmer, sec. 17; P. O. Milton; is the youngest son of Daniel Hoover, jr., who emigrated to Illinois in 1825 and settled in White county, where he remained until 1827, when he moved to this county and settled in this township on sec. 9. Here he pre-empted land and resided until his death, May 24, 1868. The subject of this sketch was born June 23, 1826; was married Oct. 16, 1856, to Miss Eunice A. Stults. Mr. H. left the homestead in 1869 and moved to Vernon Co., Mo., where he remained 2 years. Again in the fall of 1879 to the same county, where he is residing on a farm of 320 acres. His eldest son, Charles, who lives on the homestead, was married Jan. 1, 1880, to Miss Mary E., daughter of Jackson Morton. Upon them and others of his children devolves the care of the farm, consisting of 240 acres, valued at $50 per acre. William L., Ruth A., Frank L., Fred A., Alva B. and Fayette, were the children of this industrious pioneer, and grandchildren of one of the first pilgrims to Pike county.

David J. Hoover, farmer, sec. 8; P. O., Milton; was born in White Co., Ill., in 1829; is the eldest son of John and Cynthia (Patton) Hoover, who settled in White Co. in 1825, and in this township in 1830, where they both died. The subject of this sketch was married in 1859 to Miss Amanda F. Smithers, a native of this State. To them have been born 7 children, all of whom are living: Edgar W., Willie H., Cordelia, Minnie V., Orphy O., Ina E. and Arty E. He settled on his present estate in 1862, consisting of 404½ acres; the eastern section, 200 acres, is valued at $60 per acre: the remainder at $40. Mr. H. has been School Director for the past 6 years, and numbers among the early settlers. Without the opportunities of educational advantages his devotion to his profession has placed him among the independent farmers of this county.

Eli Hoover, farmer, secs. 9 and 10; P. O. Milton; is the fourth son of John and Cynthia (Patton) Hoover, natives of Maryland and Kentucky, who came to this county in 1829 and settled in this township, on sec. 8, where he entered 60 acres of land and resided until his death in 1867. His wife preceded him to the spirit world in 1864. The subject of this sketch was born on the homestead in this township in 1836; was married in 1863 to Miss Mary Stewart, a native of Greene Co., Ill., where she was born in 1841. The fruits of this marriage are 4 children: Della A., Arthur V., Otis C. and Caddie G. The homestead upon which he resides consists of 236 acres, valued at $60 per acre. Mr. and Mrs. H. are members of the Christian Church, and number among the early pioneers.

George Hoover, farmer, sec. 11; P. O. Milton; is the second son of Daniel and America (Greathouse) Hoover, natives of Maryland and Kentucky, who emigrated to Illinois in 1825 and settled in White Co., and in 1827 moved to this county and settled on sec. 9, near Milton, where he made a claim which he afterward pre-empted. Here he lived until his death, May 24, 1868. His respected wife followed him to the better land in September of the same year. The subject of this sketch was born in Posey Co., Ind., Oct. 23, 1821, and came with his parents to this county, where he was married Jan. 24, 1844, to Miss Sophia A. Hatcher, a native of Franklin Co., Va., and daughter of John and Charlotta (Thurman) Hatcher, who settled in this township in April, 1838, where they passed the remainder of their years on earth. Mr. H. settled upon his present estate in 1867, consisting of over 500 acres of land, the valuation of which will range from $30 to $50 per acre. This tract of land includes the same farm he occupied in 1847. He is the father of 5 living children, 3 daughters and 2 sons—Geneva A., Louisa F., Eddie A., Laura and Ulysses G. He is the oldest native-born settler of this township, a life-long supporter of the Whig party, and a strong advocate of the Republican form of government.

John A. Hoover, sec. 18; P. O. Milton; is the son of John Hoover, one of the pioneers of this county who settled in Montezuma tp. in 1829, where the subject of this sketch was born in 1834. In 1859 he engaged as clerk in the mercantile trade at Milton, in which capacity he was engaged until 1871. Since then he has been engaged in farming and speculation, and by tact and energy has secured a good property. Mr. H. is one of this extensive family, unmarried, but his social qualities of mind and heart have won for him a host of friends.

Josiah Hoover, farmer, sec. 9; P. O. Milton; the eldest living son of David and Mahala (Greathouse) Hoover, natives of Maryland and Kentucky, who settled in White Co., Ill., in 1820, and were among the early pilgrims of that county, where the subject of this sketch was born in May, 1823. In 1827 the family came to this county, crossing the Illinois river on a pirogue, a large canoe. He erected his shanty south of Milton on sec. 9, where he died in March, 1876, in the 79th year of his age. She died Aug. 7, 1873. The subject of this sketch was married in 1848 to Miss Caroline, daughter of Thomas Smith, an early settler of White Co. He is the father of 9 children, 7 of whom are living—Smith, Alice, Mary, Mattie F., Sidney J., Ida M. and Lincoln. His opportunities for an early education were limited, and his success in life is due to his indomitable will and perseverance. His homestead near Milton consists of 246 acres, valued at $75 an acre. He is one of Montezuma's early pilgrims, and although in declining health, is made happy by the large circle of children and grandchildren that surround him.

William Hutton, farmer, sec. 3; P. O. Milton; was born in England in 1833, and is the son of John and Betsey, (Watenworth,) natives of England, where they both died. Mr. H. emigrated to America in 1855, settling in this tp., where he has since made it his home. He was married in 1873 to Miss Sarah E. Clemmons, and they have 2 children, John and Mary. Mr. H. settled on his present estate in 1868, consisting of 84 acres, valued at $60 per acre. Mr. H. is a School Director, and one of Montezuma's best citizens.

J. G. Johnson, proprietor of the Johnson House, Milton, is a son of Joseph and Esther (Jolly) Johnson, natives of South Carolina, who emigrated to Indiana in 1800, and settled in Posey Co., being among the pioneers of that State, where they both died. The subject of this sketch was born in Posey Co., Ind., in 1821; was married in 1843 to Miss Mary E. Henderson, who died in Indiana in 1847, leaving one child, Mary A. He then married Elizabeth Travers, a native of Indiana, who bore him one child, D. R., and she

MONTEZUMA TP

too was called to a better home.   His present wife is Judith C., daughter of Samuel Baker, an early settler of Detroit tp., where she was born in 1835.   The fruits of this marriage are 2 children, Johanna H. and J. G. H.   Mr. J. came to this county in 1856 and settled in Milton, where he engaged in merchandising, and in 1862 received appointment as Captain, and raised Co. I, 99th I. V. I., and served 2½ years, participating in the battles of Vicksburg, Port Gibson, Champion Hills and Mobile, and was mustered out in Jan., 1865, by reason of consolidation.   Returning, he formed the partnership of Johnson & Goodin in the dry-goods trade.   Two years afterward he sold out and engaged in farming, until 1875, when he disposed of his farm and opened a private boarding-house. The following year he leased the Eagle, now Johnson House.   Mr. J. has been prominently identified with the interests of the town in several offices.   He is a radical Republican, a good citizen, and an excellent hotel keeper.

Solomon T. Johnston, farmer, sec. 19; P. O. Milton; is the son of Thomas and Catherine (Main) Johnston, natives of Pennsylvania, who emigrated to Pike Co., in 1850, settling in Hardin tp., where he died.   His aged wife still survives.   The subject of this sketch was born in Beaver Co., Pa., in 1832; was married in 1853 to Miss Susan, daughter of John Heavener; settled on his present farm of 240 acres in 1856.   In 1862 he enlisted as Corporal in Co. E, 99th I. V. I., and served 15 months, participating in the battle at Port Gibson, where he was wounded by a minie ball that passed through the lungs and lodged in the back, where it still remains.   He was confined in the hospital 6 months, when he was discharged.   In consequence of this wound Mr. J. is disabled from physical labor.   He served one term as Collector.   Is politically a Democrat.   His children are Melinda, Louisa, Ellen, Thomas, Andrew, Allen, Otis, Eva, Poe and Frank.

Urban B. Kennedy, principal of the high school at Milton, was born in Morgan Co., Ill., in 1854, and is a grandson of John Wright, a native of Tennessee, who settled in that county in 1825, and son of William and Sarah (Wright) Kennedy, natives of Kentucky and Tennessee, living residents of Morgan county.   Mr. Wright died in 1872, and Wright's Precinct still bears the honor of his name.   The subject of this sketch entered upon the studies of his profession in the State Normal University at Bloomington, Ill., where he remained 3 years, and began teaching in 1872 in Scott county, where he remained 3 years, when he returned to his native county and officiated 2 years, where he was married in 1877 to Miss Kate, daughter of John Stewart, of Scott county. They are the parents of 2 children, Walter I. and one not yet christened.   Mr. K. has filled his present position 3 years, and he is highly esteemed by the community.

Wm. M. Landess, merchant, dealer in hardware, stoves and tin-ware at Milton, succeeded Long & Riggs in this business in 1871, the copartnership being Landess & Colvin.   Eighteen months

28

afterward Colvin retired, and the business has since been conducted by Mr. L., who carries a stock of $3,000, and has a lucrative trade. He was born in Highland county, O., March 11, 1839; came to this county in 1863 and engaged in teaching school until he began his business career. He was married Dec. 16, 1866, to Miss Jennie Van Pelt, daughter of William Van Pelt, of Perry. They are members of the Christian Church.

John F. Long, farmer, sec. 32; P. O. Milton; was born in Tennessee in 1805, son of Robert and Betsy (Wasson) Long, natives of North Carolina, both of whom have died. The subject of this sketch came to this county in Oct., 1828, and settled west of Milton. A few years later he entered the land of his present estate, where he has since made it his home. He was married in Vanderburgh county, Ind., Feb. 23, 1826, to Miss Sally A. Patton, a native of that county, where she was born in 1809. To them have been born 8 children, 7 of whom are living, Phœbe J., Robert N., William H., James H., Samuel A., Mary E. and Sarah M. Mary E. married F. Bowman and they reside on the homestead. Their children are William, Robert, John O., Leroy and Henry M. Mr. L was Justice of the Peace at one time, and has been otherwise identified with the interests of the town. His farm consists of 200 acres, valued at $5,500. Himself and wife are members of the Christian Church, and he is one of the few living pioneers of this township. In the 75th year of his age he enjoys good health, and is happily surrounded at his home by his children and grandchildren.

Thomas C. Lytle, farmer, sec. 23; P. O. Bedford; was born on the Potomac, Washington Co., Md., in 1824. Is son of James and Eleanor (Burckhurtt) Lytle, natives of that State, where they died. The subject of this sketch was married in 1846 to Miss Elizabeth Miller, a native of Maryland, who died leaving him 2 children, Josiah and Thomas. His present wife, Eliza Killbren, is a native of Scott county. They have had 4 children,—Elizabeth, William, John and Charles A. Mr. L. came to this county in 1856, from Berkshire Co., Va.; moved on his present farm in 1873, consisting of 80 acres, valued at $30 per acre. Has been Justice of the Peace 2 terms, and Commissioner of Highways. Politically he is a Democrat.

Malinda Mahair, farmer, sec. 34; P. O. Bedford; widow of Michael Mahair, who was born in Ireland in 1829 and emigrated to America in 1849. He engaged in farming until his marriage in 1857, to Miss Malinda, daughter of Benjamin Barringer, an early settler of this county. After marriage he settled on the Little Blue, where he lived until 1865, when he moved on the present estate of 170 acres, valued at $40 per acre. Their living children are William A., James B. and Lydia A.; they lost 3: Edward, John, and one in infancy. Mr. Mahair died in 1875. He was School Director many years.

N. D. McEvers, merchant, Montezuma, was born in this township in 1846; is the only living child of T. L. and Sarah (Aiken) McEvers, natives of Ohio, who emigrated to this county in 1829, traveling the entire distance in keel-boats. He settled on his present place at Montezuma and was for years engaged in boating. He is still a living relict of early times. The subject of this sketch received his early education at the Jacksonville Business College, at which institution he was graduated in 1868. Returning home, his time was divided between teaching and advancing his education at the Normal School at Bloomington. In 1874 he purchased the building and stock of goods of S. B. Clemmons, to which he has built an addition and increased the stock, now amounting to about $4,000, with an increasing trade. He is also extensively engaged in the grain and commission business. He has been Township Treasurer many years and Township Collector one year; is Supervisor at the present time, being the first Greenback Supervisor in the county; has also been Postmaster most of the time during his business career. In 1873 he was married to Miss Adelia, daughter of Franklin Morton, a native of this county. Theodore F. is their only living child.

John C. Mitchell, firm of Mitchell & Battershell, merchants. The subject of this sketch was born in Monroe Co., O., in 1835. He was married in 1859 to Miss Abby McCurdy, a native of Pennsylvania, who died in Ohio. In 1865 he enlisted in the 194th O. V. I., Co. I, as private, and was promoted to 2d and 1st Lieutenant, which he filled at the close of the war. Same year he moved to this State and settled in Lawrence Co., where he engaged as clerk; subsequently he removed to Clay Co. and followed the same calling for 7 years, when he cast his lot in a large commercial house in St. Louis in the capacity of book-keeping. In 1875 he came to this county and engaged as clerk with Butler & Adams, until the formation of the present partnership in 1878. His present wife, Maggie, *nee* Goshern, is a native of this State, by whom he has 2 children, James M. and Jennie. Mr. M. is a Democrat, a Notary Public, and a member of the Christian Church.

Robert O. Morris, proprietor Grange Company Warehouse, Montezuma, is a native of Adair Co., Ky., where he was born Dec. 8, 1850; came to this county in Sept., 1874, and for a time engaged in farming. Subsequently he purchased an interest in the store of W. H. Hall at Milton. Nine months afterward he sold out and took possession of the warehouse in Jan., 1880, where he is doing a large trade in lumber, grain, lime and cement, and is an active, energetic, thorough business man.

Jackson Morton, farmer, sec. 19; P. O. Milton; son of William Morton, who settled in this township in 1830, where he is still a living representative of the pioneers. The subject of this sketch was born in Hawkins Co., Tenn., in 1827; was married in 1856 to Miss Ann Main, a native of England; the same year he settled upon his present estate, consisting of 120 acres, valued at $40 per acre. He is a lineal descendant of the pioneer family, and well known throughout the town and county. Rosan A., Mary, Emma, and Carrie are his living children: 2 deceased, William, jr., and Ida.

William Morton, farmer, sec. 19; P. O. Milton; was born in Cheatham Co., N. Carolina, in 1800, and is a son of John and Annie (Poe) Morton, natives of N. C., who emigrated at an early day to Tennessee, thence to this county, and settled on sec. 14, in 1830. Both died in this township. The subject of this sketch left home when 16 years of age and went to Tennessee, where he remained until 1830, when he came to this township and settled upon his present farm, consisting of 120 acres of valuable land, at that time but a wilderness and resort for roving Indians. He was married in 1824 in Tennessee, to Miss Cecil George, a native of that State. To them were born 11 children, 6 of whom are living,—Eliza, Jackson, Wilburn, Jeremiah, Wm. C., and Celia. His present wife, Lucinda, *nee* Castile, is a native of Tennessee. Mr. M. is one of the oldest living settlers of this township. He lived 6 weeks in a small brush hut that stood on the site of his present home. He is now almost totally blind, and though 80 years of age, his mind and memory are clear. He served 5 or 6 years as Constable, and is one of Pike's oldest pioneers. He is the father of 2 children by his last marriage, Joseph C. and George F.

Charles H. Renoud, farmer, sec. 32; P. O. Pearl; was born in Fairfield, Conn., in 1820. His parents were Stephen P. and Lydia (Donaldson) Renoud, natives of that State, who came to this county in 1837, purchased land and returned. Their final settlement was made in 1843, in Detroit township, where he lived until '55, when he sold out and went to Ohio. The following year he settled in in Henry Co., Ill., and on the homestead in this county in 1864, where he died in 1866. She is still living in the 86th year of her age. The subject of this sketch was married in 1844 to Mary Wickam, a native of Kent, England, who died March 5, 1865, and 9 children have been born to them: George F., Caroline, Mary, Eliza, Marsha, Robert E., Richard G., Charles H. and Stephen. His present wife, Kary, daughter of Hiram Duff, is a native of Kentucky, who settled near Milton in 1825. The family can be numbered among the early pilgrims of Montezuma tp.

David Roberts, farmer, sec. 33; P. O. Bedford; was born in Delaware Co., Aug. 8, 1833, and is the son of David and Lovina (Pool) Roberts, natives of Vermont and New York, who came to this county in 1837, and entered land on secs. 29 and 36, and went to Ohio; returned in 1838 and settled on sec. 36; subsequently he moved to Hardin township and Spring Creek, thence to Pleasant Hill, and in 1850 he moved the family to Pittsfield and crossed the plains to California, returning in 1851. He died at his home in 1856. He was a minister of the Christian denomination, to which he gave much of his time. His estimable wife died in 1872. The subject of this sketch was married in 1862 to Miss Susan, daughter of Asa Cooper, a native of this county. Lavinia E., Lizzie, John

J., David, jr., and George, are their living children.   Mr. and Mrs. R. are members of the Christian Church.

William Roberts, farmer, ;sec. 27; P. O. Milton; was born in England in 1853, and emigrated to America in 1857, stopping in Peoria county one year, when he came to this county, where he has since made it his home.   He was married in 1875 to Miss Ellen Crane, a native of England.   To them have been born 3 children, Frederick, Caroline and Mary Ellen.   He settled on his present farm in 1865, consisting of 65 acres, valued at $2,000.   He is a Deacon of the Christian Church, of which his family are members.

William P. Sargent, proprietor of hotel, Bedford, was born in Worcester Co., Mass., in 1825, and is the son of William and Polly (Frost) Sargent, who emigrated from that State in 1839 and settled in Summer Hill.   Some .years later they moved to this township and settled south of Bedford, where they both died.   The subject of [this sketch was married in 1853 to Miss Harriet E., daughter of Silas A. Chandler, a native of this county.   In 1838 he moved to Bedford and engaged at milling some years, and opened public house in 1871.   He owns the hotel and 37 acres of land, valued at $3,000.   Mr. S. is the father of 3 children, Wm. O., Hattie E. and Martha.   Is School Director, and one of the oldest and most worthy citizens.

Noble Shaw, farmer, sec. 6; P. O. Milton; is the son of Aaron and Phœbe (Nardike) Shaw, natives of North Carolina, where she died at an early day.   The subject of this sketch was born in Guilford Co., N. C., in 1819, and emigrated with his father to this county in the fall of 1829, stopping through the winter at Montezuma, and the following spring settling on Franklin Prairie, where he died in 1830.   Bereft of parents while yet a youth, and left alone in the wilderness, he sought employment among the scattered settlers of Pike.   By strict economy he was in a few years enabled to purchase 60 acres of his present estate, which he has since increased to 120.   He was married in 1845 to Miss Julia A. Frane, a native of Kentucky, where she was born in 1826.   To them have been born 9 children, all of whom are living: Mary, William T., Ada A., James A., John, Louella, Frank M., Daniel B. and Virgil.   Mr. S. has served as Road Commissioner, School Trustee and Director several years, and numbers among those of the early settlers, an honored and respected citizen.

W. S. Smith, of the firm of Butler & Smith, grocers, Milton, was born in Detroit tp., this county, in 1859, the son of Richard Smith, an early settler of this county, where he died in 1863.   This firm succeeded John T. Hall in this trade in 1879, and although young men, their energies and abilities call out a large and increasing trade.

L. J. Smitherman, retired farmer, was born in Rutherford Co., Tenn., Jan. 7, 1819; was married to Miss Miriel Brown, a native of Lawrence Co., Ala., where she was born March 22, 1821.   Of this marriage 6 children have been born, one of whom is living, William, who married Louisa Lester in 1863, and they have 3 children,

Otis, Mayo and Inez. Mr. S. settled in Morgan Co., near Jacksonville, in 1827. Jesse and Jincy Brown, parents of Mrs S., were early pioneers in that county. Three years afterward he moved to McDonough county, thence to Geneva county, and back to his native State; returning, he settled in Detroit tp., where he still owns 200 acres, the original homestead. Mr. S. has been prominent in the county, having served as Assessor a number of years. Supervisor a number of terms and elected County Treasurer in 1867; was re-elected in 1869, and is Village Trustee at the present time. Democrat.

Elisha Sowers, farmer, sec. 26; P. O. Bedford; was born in Hamilton Co., N. J., in 1813; he is the son of Henry and Ann (Potter) Sowers, natives of that State, who emigrated to Ohio, where they both died. The subject of this sketch was married in 1836 to Miss Caroline Scoggin, a native of Hamilton county, O., where she was born in 1816. Their children are Melissa, Henry, Mary, Thomas A., Oliver, William W., Benton, Edward and Amanda. Mr. Sowers came to this county in 1856 and settled on his present estate, consisting of 730 acres. Mr. S. is the largest land-holder in the township, and is a well-known citizen.

Oliver Sowers, farmer, sec. 34; P. O. Milton; was born in Hamilton Co., O., in 1849, and is the son of Elisha and Caroline (Scoggin) Sowers, and came to this county with his parents in 1856; was married in 1869 to Miss Mary Nicolay, a native of this county; has a farm of 120 acres of well cultivated land. He is a School Director, and numbers among Montezuma's enterprising farmers. Gusty, Francis, John H. and Archey are their children.

Jane Stewart, sec. 20; P. O. Milton; is the widow of Benjamin Stewart, who was born in Rock Castle Co., Ky., April 26, 1809. He came to this county at an early day and settled in this township, where he resided until his death, which occurred at Eldorado, Kan., July 22, 1874. He was married Dec. 6, 1838, to Miss Jane, daughter of Thompson and Sarah A. (Smith) Williams, the subject of this sketch, who was born in Scott Co., Ky., April 8, 1820, a descendant of the Rains family, of Virginian origin. Mr. S. made his first settlement on the present farm of Josiah Hoover, and was among the early pioneers. He was a citizen highly esteemed, and left a large circle of friends. Of their several children 6 are living: Thompson W., Sarah B., Philadelphia G., William L., Julia A. and Emma B. Wm. L. resides on the homestead, upon which his parents settled in 1851. Mr. and Mrs. S. were members of the Christian Church.

Henry Tankersley, farmer, sec. 1, P. O. Montezuma; was born in Scott county in 1854, and is the son of Edward and Phœbe (Sweet) Tankersley, natives of Kentucky, who settled in Morgan county in 1821, then in Scott county in 1849. He surveyed both counties for early settlements, and was County Judge in both Morgan and Scott counties. In 1864 he came to this county, and settled on the farm now occupied by his son and widow, where he died in 1866. His life was marked with a degree of prominence throughout. He was Magistrate many years, and an early pioneer of Morgan county. He left 3 children, all of whom are living: Lyman T., Thomas and Sarah. Mr. T. has a farm of 140 acres, valued at $40 per acre.

David L. Thurman, farmer, sec. 21; P. O. Milton; was born in Cumberland Co., Ky., in 1834, and is the son of James and Polly (Robinson) Thurman, natives of Kentucky and So. Carolina, who emigrated to this county in 1837, and settled on the present homestead, consisting of 140 acres, 100 of which is now under cultivation, valued at $40 per acre. He died Feb. 2, 1871, and she followed him Feb. 2, 1877. The subject of this sketch was married August, 1858, to Miss Martha A., daughter of William Smith, the first settler of Winchester, Scott county, where she was born in 1833. Priscilla and Amarilla are their living children. Mrs. T. has been a life-long invalid, but tenderly cared for by a fond husband and children. Mr. T. had no opportunities for education, but through his energy and indomitable will has accumulated considerable property. The family are members of the Christian Church, and number among the early settlers and highly respected citizens.

Thomas L. Thurman, farmer, sec. 21; P. O. Milton; was born in Franklin Co., Va., in 1799, son of David and Susanna (Leftwich), natives of that State, where they died. The subject of this sketch emigrated to Cumberland Co., Ky., where he was married to Miss Millie Black, who was born in Bedford Co., Va., in 1801; she died in this county in 1871. To them were born 9 children, 5 of whom are living: Sarah A., William H., James L., John T. (who married Mary Boren. By this marriage 3 grandchildren surround him), Lolu, Unie, and Howard. Henrietta, the youngest daughter, resides on the homestead. Mr. T. came to this county in 1842, and settled on his present estate of 120 acres, valued at $40 per acre; he is a member of the Baptist denomination, and politically belongs to the old-line Whigs.

Benjamin F. Wheeler, retired farmer; residence, Milton; was born in Clermont Co., O., in 1818, the son of Benjamin and Mary (McCarty) Wheeler, natives of Kentucky and Pennsylvania, respectively, who emigrated to Illinois in 1834, and settled in Pearl township, where they both died. The subject of this sketch was married in Pearl in 1844 to Miss Almira, daughter of Peter Clemmons, who settled in this county in 1829. Of their several children, but one is living: John A., who married Amanta Morton. Two children have been born to them, Cora B. and Anna R. Mr. W. settled in this township in 1863, and on his present estate in 1875, consisting of 80¼ acres, valued at $100 per acre. The homestead occupied by his son has 173 acres, besides 12 acres of timber. Mr. W. is a self-made man; his opportunities for education were limited, and his success has been effected only through his untiring industry. Is one of the "City Fathers," and is a member of the Christian Church.

Printed in the United States
55660LVS00005B/67-93